The Emergence of Novelty in Organizations

Perspectives on Process Organization Studies
Series Editors: Ann Langley and Haridimos Tsoukas

Perspectives on Process Organization Studies is an annual series, linked to the International Symposium on Process Organization Studies, and is dedicated to the development of an understanding of organizations and organizing at large as processes in the making. This series brings together contributions from leading scholars, which focus on seeing dynamically evolving activities, interactions, and events as important aspects of organized action, rather than static structures and fixed templates.

Volume 1: Process, Sensemaking, and Organizing
Editors: Tor Hernes and Sally Maitlis

Volume 2: Constructing Identity in and around Organizations
Editors: Majken Schultz, Steve Maguire, Ann Langley, and Haridimos Tsoukas

Volume 3: How Matter Matters: Objects, Artifacts, and Materiality in Organization Studies
Editors: Paul R. Carlile, Davide Nicolini, Ann Langley, and Haridimos Tsoukas

Volume 4: Language and Communication at Work: Discourse, Narrativity, and Organizing
Editors: François Cooren, Eero Vaara, Ann Langley, and Haridimos Tsoukas

The Emergence of Novelty in Organizations

Edited by
Raghu Garud, Barbara Simpson,
Ann Langley, Haridimos Tsoukas

OXFORD
UNIVERSITY PRESS

OXFORD
UNIVERSITY PRESS

Great Clarendon Street, Oxford, OX2 6DP,
United Kingdom

Oxford University Press is a department of the University of Oxford.
It furthers the University's objective of excellence in research, scholarship,
and education by publishing worldwide. Oxford is a registered trade mark of
Oxford University Press in the UK and in certain other countries

First published 2015
First published in paperback 2016

Published in the United States of America by Oxford University Press
198 Madison Avenue, New York, NY 10016, United States of America

British Library Cataloguing in Publication Data
Data available

Library of Congress Cataloging in Publication Data
Data available

ISBN 978–0–19–872831–3 (Hbk.)
ISBN 978–0–19–877889–9 (Pbk.)

Cover image: © Shutterstock.com/Sukpaiboonwat

Contents

Acknowledgments

We would like to express our great appreciation to the following colleagues who have generously offered their time to act as reviewers for the chapters published in this volume edited by Raghu Garud, Barbara Simpson, Ann Langley, and Haridimos Tsoukas.

Reviewers Listed Alphabetically

Mats Alvesson, Lund University; Isabelle Bouty, University of Toulon; Arne Carlsen, BI Norwegian Business School; Liliana Doganova, Centre de Sociologie de l'Innovation; Sue Dopson, Saïd Business School—University of Oxford; Joel Gehman, Alberta School of Business; Tor Hernes, Copehnagen Business School; Robin Holt, University of Liverpool; Dian Marie Hosking, Utrecht University; Peter Karnøe, Aalborg University; Kyriakos Kyriakopoulos, ALBA Graduate Business School; Philippe Lorino, ESSEC Business School; Babis Mainemelis, ALBA Graduate Business School; Sally Maitlis, Sauder School of Business; Nick Marshall, University of Brighton; Chris Mowles, Hertfordshire Business School; Frank Mueller, Newcastle University; Tim Newton, Independent Academic; Miguel Pina Cunha, NOVA School of Business and Economics; Caroline Ramsey, University of Liverpool; John Shotter, University of New Hampshire, Durham; Chris Steyaert, University of St. Gallen; Jaan Valsiner, Clark University; Tim Vogus, Vanderbilt Owen Graduate School of Management; Alia Weston, Strathclyde Business School.

List of Figures

List of Tables

List of Contributors

Mats Alvesson is Professor of Business Administration at the University of Lund, Sweden and part-time Professor in the School of Business at the University of Queensland, Australia in Cass Business School, London. Research interests include critical theory, gender, power, management of professional service (knowledge intensive) organizations, leadership, identity, organizational image, organizational culture and symbolism, qualitative methods and philosophy of science. Recent books include *The Triumph of Emptiness* (Oxford University Press, 2013), *Constructing Research Questions* (Sage, 2013, with J. Sandberg), and *Qualitative Research and Theory Development* (Sage, 2011, with Dan Kärreman).

Isabelle Bouty is Professor of Strategic Management at the University of Toulon, France. She earned her PhD in strategy from the University of Western Paris at Nanterre and ESSEC Business School. Her current research explores the links between the individual and collective levels in strategic management and organizations within a processual approach, in such organizations as haute cuisine restaurants, sailing crews, and air display squadrons.

Deborah Dougherty received her PhD in Management from MIT, and taught at Wharton and McGill University before joining Rutgers. Her scholarship concerns organizing for sustained product and service innovation in complex organizations; managing exploratory and science-based innovation; rethinking organization of work, knowledge, and relations to support innovation; comprehension of unfamiliar markets and technologies. Current work focuses on innovation in bio-pharmaceuticals, and on reformulating established innovation management understandings to encompass this science-based innovation process. She teaches innovation management and organizing at the BS, MBA, and PhD levels, was elected chair of the Technology and Innovation Management Division at Academy of Management, served for more than six years as a senior editor for *Organization Science*, and has served on five other journal editorial boards. She has published 50 articles in journals and book chapters on innovation and its management, and 12 essays.

Marianna Fotaki is Professor of Business Ethics at Warwick Business School, and holds a visiting professorship at the University of Manchester. Before joining academia Marianna has worked as EU resident advisor to the governments in transition and as a medical doctor for Médecins Sans Frontières and Médecins

Du Monde for ten years in total. She is a graduate of medicine, public health, and has obtained a PhD in public policy from the London School of Economics and Political Science. Her research is on the marketization of public services, health inequalities, gender and otherness in organizations and business in society. She has published over 30 papers on those subjects and has four books forthcoming: a monograph, on fantasy and reality of patient choice (Edward Elgar), *Gender and the Organization* (with Nancy Harding, Routledge), *Affect in Organizations* (co-edited with Kate Kenny, Palgrave Macmillan), and *Global Challenges to Business in Society* (with Kate Kenny and Juliane Reinecke, Sage). Marianna is also a founding executive member of a think tank Centre for Health and the Public Interest <http://chpi.org.uk> which she co-directs on a part-time basis pro bono.

Raghu Garud is Alvin H. Clemens Professor of Management & Organization and the Research Director of the Farrell Center for Corporate Innovation and Entrepreneurship, Pennsylvania State University. Raghu's research explores novelty emergence. Specifically, he explores how new ideas emerge, are valued, and become commercialized, offering concepts such as path creation, technology entrepreneurship, and bricolage as a collective process. One of his recent articles explores how interlaced knowledge across scientists at ATLAS, CERN made it possible for a distributed collective to identify the Higgs boson particle. Another, that also appears in *Organization Science*, examines a paradox that entrepreneurial storytelling generates—how the very expectations set through projective stories to gain venture legitimacy can also serve as the source of future disappointments and a loss of legitimacy.

Marie-Léandre Gomez is Associate Professor in Management Control at ESSEC Business School, France. She earned her PhD in management from the University of Western Paris at Nanterre. Her current research interests focus on knowledge dynamics, strategizing, and the role of instruments in activity in professional organizations (haute cuisine restaurants and hospitals).

Suzanne Guerlac is Professor of French Studies at UC Berkeley. She is the author of *The Impersonal Sublime: Hugo, Baudelaire, Lautréamont and the Esthetics of the Sublime* (Stanford, 1990), *Literary Polemics: Bataille, Sartre, Valéry, Breton* (Stanford, 1997) for which she was named co-winner of the Scaglione Prize, and *Thinking in Time: An Introduction to Henri Bergson* (Cornell, 2006). She is co-editor, with Pheng Cheah, of *Derrida and the Time of the Political* (Duke, 2009) and the author of numerous articles, including "Humanities 2.0—E-Learning in the Digital World" which appeared in a special issue of *Representations* on The Humanities and the Crisis of Public Education (Fall 2001) and "Bergson, the Void and the Politics of Life," in *Bergson's Political and Social Thought*, ed. Alexandre Lefebvre and Melanie White (Duke, 2012).

Aris Komporozos-Athanasiou is a postdoctoral research associate in Social Science and Health at King's College London. He has an undergraduate degree in Economics and Master's degrees in Organization Studies from the Universities of Warwick and Cambridge. He completed his PhD in public policy at the University of Cambridge, where he also held a postdoctoral post at the Institute of Public Health in 2012–2013. Aris' work is eclectic and draws on the sociology of organizations, social theory as applied to public policy, and health services research. His PhD research was a two-year ethnographic study of citizen engagement in the UK National Health Service, focusing on the political constitution of patienthood and the development of subversive spaces in the periphery of public organization. In addition to a stream of work introducing the philosophy of Cornelius Castoriadis to organization studies, Aris' current research projects include a study of (ir)rationality in the performance of financial institutions, and a comparative analysis of deliberative democracy across public health systems in Europe.

Ann Langley is Professor of Strategic Management at HEC Montréal, Canada and holder of the Canada research chair in Strategic Management in pluralistic settings. Her research focuses on strategic change, inter-professional collaboration, and the practice of strategy in complex organizations. She is particularly interested in process-oriented research and methodology and has published a number of papers on that topic. In 2013, she was co-guest editor with Clive Smallman, Haridimos Tsoukas, and Andrew Van de Ven of a Special Research Forum of *Academy of Management Journal* on Process Studies of Change in Organizations and Management. She is also co-editor of the journal *Strategic Organization.*

Bernadette Loacker works as a post-doctoral researcher and lecturer at the Department of Business Administration at the University of Lund (Sweden). Bernadette's research interests include contemporary forms of work organization, organizational power and control, subjectivities and identities at work, and post-structuralist organization theories. Her work has been published in journals such as *Culture & Organization, Journal of Business Ethics,* and *Business and Professional Ethics Journal.* She is a member of the editorial collective of the journal *ephemera: theory and politics in organization.*

Chris Mowles is Professor of Complexity and Management at the University of Hertfordshire, UK and is director of the innovative Doctor of Management program there. The program was one the first in the world to encourage doctoral students, who are practicing managers and leaders and study part time, to draw on the complexity sciences and processual theories of the social in their research. In doing so they are obliged to come to terms with, and describe, the emergence of their research question as they wrestle with the paradox of theory and practice. The program has produced more than 60 graduates in the last 12 years.

Trevor Pinch is the Goldwyn Smith Professor of Science and Technology Studies and Professor of Sociology at Cornell University. He holds degrees in physics and sociology. He has authored many books and numerous articles on aspects of the sociology of science, the sociology of technology, the sociology of economics, and sound studies. His books include *Analog Days: The Invention and Impact of the Moog Synthesizer* (Harvard, 2004). He is co-editor of *The Oxford Handbook of Sound Studies* (2012). He is also a performing musician with the Electric Golem.

Jörgen Sandberg is Professor in the School of Business at the University of Queensland, Australia. His research interests include competence and learning in organizations, leadership, practice-based research, qualitative research methods, and philosophy of science. His work has appeared in several journals, including *Academy of Management Review, Academy of Management Journal, Journal of Organization Behavior, Harvard Business Review*, and *Review of Educational Research*. His most recent book (co-authored with Mats Alvesson) is *Constructing Research Questions: Doing Interesting Research* (Sage, 2013). He is currently carrying out research on professional practice and its development, frameworks and methodologies for developing more influential and relevant theories, and sense-making in organizations.

R. Keith Sawyer studies creativity, innovation, and learning, with a focus on collaborating groups and teams. He has written over 80 scientific articles, and is the author or editor of 14 books, including *Social Emergence: Societies as Complex Systems* (Cambridge, 2005). Dr. Sawyer uses qualitative and quantitative methods to examine the conversational dynamics of groups in real-world contexts. His theoretical work on emergence was inspired by his early empirical studies of the interactional processes in jazz ensembles, improvisational theater groups, and children at play. To better explain these improvisational situated phenomena, he developed a theoretical framework, in the tradition of sociocultural psychology and distributed cognition, that he calls "collaborative emergence." He has studied collaborative learning groups in classrooms and other settings, and collaborative creativity in teacher teams and in business organizations.

John Shotter is Emeritus Professor of Communication in the Department of Communication, University of New Hampshire, and a tutor on the Professional Doctorate in System Practice in KCCF, London. He is the author of *Social Accountability and Selfhood* (Blackwell, 1984), *Cultural Politics of Everyday Life: Social Constructionism, Rhetoric, and Knowing of the Third Kind* (Open University, 1993), *Conversational Realities: The Construction of Life through Language* (Sage, 1993), *Conversational Realities Revisisted: Life, Language, Body, and World* (Taos Publications, 2009), and *Getting It: Withness-Thinking and the Dialogical . . . in Practice* (Hampton Press, 2010).

Barbara Simpson is Professor of Leadership and Organisational Dynamics at Strathclyde Business School in Glasgow. Her PhD in Management, which was awarded by the University of Auckland in 1998, marked a sea change from her earlier career as a physics-trained geothermal scientist. Nevertheless, traces of this past experience remain evident in her work today, which brings the principles of action, flow, and movement to bear on the processes of creativity, innovation, leadership, and change. She has pursued these interests in diverse organizational settings including hi-tech businesses, professional firms, public utilities, arts companies, SMEs, and micro-enterprises involved in the manufacture of plastics and food products. Her current research is deeply informed by the philosophies of the American Pragmatists, especially George Herbert Mead's thinking on process and temporality. She has published her work in journals including *Organization Studies, Human Relations, Organization, R&D Management*, and *Journal of Management Inquiry*.

Haridimos Tsoukas (www.htsoukas.com) holds the Columbia Ship Management Chair in Strategic Management at the Department of Business and Public Administration, University of Cyprus, Cyprus and is a Distinguished Research Environment Professor of Organization Studies at Warwick Business School, University of Warwick, UK. He obtained his PhD at the Manchester Business School (MBS), University of Manchester, and has worked at MBS, the University of Essex, the University of Strathclyde, and at the ALBA Graduate Business School, Greece. He is the co-founder and co-organizer of the International Symposium on Process Organization Studies (with Ann Langley). His research is informed by process philosophy, phenomenology, and neo-Aristotelian perspectives on reason and the social. His interests include: knowledge-based perspectives on organizations and management; organizational becoming; practical reason in management and policy studies; and meta-theoretical issues in organizational and management research.

Jaan Valsiner is the Niels Bohr Professor of Cultural Psychology at Aalborg University in Denmark, and Professor of Psychology and English at Clark University, USA. He is the founding editor (1995) of the Sage journal, *Culture & Psychology* and Editor-in-Chief of *Integrative Psychological and Behavioral Sciences* (Springer, from 2007). In 1995 he was awarded the Alexander von Humboldt Prize for his interdisciplinary work on human development.

Dvora Yanow is a policy/political and organizational ethnographer and interpretive methodologist whose research and teaching are shaped by an overall interest in the generation and communication of knowing and meaning in organizational and policy settings. Guest Professor in Wageningen University's Department of Social Sciences, Communication, Philosophy, and Technology Sub-Department, and Professor of Organizational Studies, Keele University, her current research includes state-created categories for race-ethnic identity, immigrant integration policies and citizen-making practices, research regulation (ethics board) policies, practice studies, science/technology museums and the idea of science, and built space/place analysis. Her most recent book, *Interpretive Research Design: Concepts and Processes* (Routledge, 2012), with Peregrine Schwartz-Shea, is the first volume in their co-edited Routledge Series on Interpretive Methods; and their co-edited *Interpretation and Method: Empirical Research Methods and the Interpretive Turn* has appeared in a second edition (M. E. Sharpe, 2014).

Series Editorial Structure

Editors-in-Chief

Ann Langley, HEC Montréal, Canada, ann.langley@hec.ca
Haridimos Tsoukas, University of Cyprus, Cyprus and University of Warwick, UK, process.symposium@gmail.com

Advisory Board

Editorial Officer & Process Organization Studies Symposium Administrator

Sophia Tzagaraki, process.symposium@gmail.com

Endorsements

As we become more willing to convert reified entities into differentiated streams, the resulting images of process have become more viable and more elusive. Organization becomes organizing, being becomes becoming, construction becomes constructing. But as we see ourselves saying more words that end in 'ing,' what must we be thinking? That is not always clear. But now, under the experienced guidance of editors Langley and Tsoukas, there is an annual forum that moves us toward continuity and consolidation in process studies. This book series promises to be a vigorous, thoughtful forum dedicated to improvements in the substance and craft of process articulation.

(*Karl E. Weick*, Rensis Likert Distinguished University Professor of Organizational Behavior and Psychology, University of Michigan, USA)

In recent years process and practice approaches to organizational topics have increased significantly. These approaches have made significant contributions to already existing fields of study, such as strategy, routines, knowledge management, and technology adoption, and these contributions have brought increasing attention to the approaches. Yet because the contributions are embedded in a variety of different fields of study, discussions about the similarities and differences in the application of the approaches, the research challenges they present, and the potential they pose for examining taken for granted ontological assumptions are limited. This series will provide an opportunity for bringing together contributions across different areas so that comparisons can be made and can also provide a space for discussions across fields. Professors Langley and Tsoukas are leaders in the development and use of process approaches. Under their editorship, the series will attract the work and attention of a wide array of distinguished organizational scholars.

(*Martha S. Feldman*, Johnson Chair for Civic Governance and Public Management, Professor of Social Ecology, Political Science, Business and Sociology, University of California, Irvine, USA)

Perspectives on Process Organization Studies will be the definitive annual volume of theories and research that advance our understanding of process questions dealing with how things emerge, grow, develop, and terminate over time. I applaud Professors Ann Langley and Haridimos Tsoukas for launching this important book series, and encourage colleagues to submit their process research and subscribe to *PROS*.

(*Andrew H. Van de Ven*, Vernon H. Heath Professor of Organizational Innovation and Change, University of Minnesota, USA)

The new series—*Perspectives on Process Organization Studies*—is a timely and valuable addition to the organization studies literature. The ascendancy of process perspectives in recent years has signified an important departure from traditional perspectives on organizations that have tended to privilege either self-standing events or discrete entities. In contrast, by emphasizing emergent activities and recursive relations, process perspectives take seriously the ongoing production of organizational realities. Such a performative view of organizations is particularly salient today, given the increasingly complex, dispersed, dynamic, entangled, and mobile nature of current organizational phenomena. Such phenomena are not easily accounted for in traditional approaches that are premised on stability, separation, and substances. Process perspectives on organizations thus promise to offer powerful and critical analytical insights into the unprecedented and novel experiences of contemporary organizing.

(*Wanda J. Orlikowski*, Alfred P. Sloan Professor of Information Technologies and Organization Studies, Massachusetts Institute of Technology, USA)

The recent decades witnessed conspicuous changes in organization theory: a slow but inexorable shift from the focus on structures to the focus on processes. The whirlwinds of the global economy made it clear that everything flows, even if change itself can become stable. While the interest in processes of organizing is not new, it is now acquiring a distinct presence, as more and more voices join in. A forum is therefore needed where such voices can speak to one another, and to the interested readers. The series *Perspectives on Process Organization Studies* will provide an excellent forum of that kind, both for those for whom a processual perspective is a matter of ontology, and those who see it as an epistemological choice.

(*Barbara Czarniawska*, Professor of Management Studies, School of Business, Economics and Law at the University of Gothenburg, Sweden)

We are living in an era of unprecedented change; one that is characterized by instability, volatility, and dramatic transformations. It is a world in which the seemingly improbable, the unanticipated, and the downright catastrophic appear to occur with alarming regularity. Such a world calls for a new kind of thinking: thinking that issues from the chaotic, fluxing immediacy of lived experiences; thinking that resists or overflows our familiar categories of thought; and thinking that accepts and embraces messiness, contradictions, and change as the *sine qua non* of the human condition. Thinking in these genuinely processual terms means that the starting point of our inquiry is not so much about the *being* of entities such as 'organization,' but their constant and perpetual *becoming*. I very much welcome this long overdue scholarly effort at exploring and examining the fundamental issue of *process* and its implications for organization studies. Hari Tsoukas and Ann Langley are to be congratulated on taking this very important initiative in bringing the process agenda into the systematic study of the phenomenon of organization. It promises to be a path-breaking contribution to our analysis of organization.

(*Robert Chia*, Professor of Management, University of Strathclyde, UK)

This new series fits the need for a good annual text devoted to process studies. Organization theory has long required a volume specifically devoted to process research that can address process ontology, methodology, research design, and analysis. While many authors collect longitudinal data, there are still insufficient methodological tools and techniques to deal with the nature of that data. Essentially, there is still a lack of frameworks and methods to deal with good processual data or to develop process-based insights. This series will provide an important resource for all branches of organization, management, and strategy theory. The editors of the series, Professors Ann Langley and Hari Tsoukas are excellent and very credible scholars within the process field. They will attract top authors to the series and ensure that each paper presents a high quality and insightful resource for process scholars. I expect that this series will become a staple in libraries, PhD studies, and journal editors' and process scholars' bookshelves.

(*Paula Jarzabkowski*, Professor of Strategic Management, Aston Business School, UK)

1

Introduction

How Does Novelty Emerge?

Raghu Garud, Barbara Simpson, Ann Langley, and Haridimos Tsoukas

Spence Silver, a Senior Chemist working in 3M's Central Research Labs, stumbled upon a novel substance back in 1970 that eventually led to Post-it® Notes. "I was doing some experiments with an interesting new polymer system. When I looked at it under the microscope, it was beautiful! Little crystalline-like spheres. The first time I saw it, I said, 'This has got to be something.' Then I started telling people about it. If your ideas are never exposed to public view, then it's kind of a moot point. I mean, who would care? You say you're creative and have all these creative ideas, but the process is not creative until it becomes something that people can use, something that becomes part of the culture, so to speak. One of the things I've had trouble illustrating and convincing people of is the process that occurred from the discovery of the microsphere adhesive to the production of the actual Post-it® Notes. The whole process took about 12 years. The discovery sort of starts the ball rolling. Things build up and you begin to see the options that this discovery creates. It really takes a bunch of individuals to carry it through the process."

(Excerpted from an interview of Spence Silver conducted by Lindhal, 1988)

> Wayne McGregor is a multi-award-winning choreographer who has established a reputation for creating dance that can touch audiences in novel and unexpected ways. His ground-breaking work draws inspiration from sources as diverse as the visual arts and neuroscience, and appears to be improvised in the moment although it is, in fact, fully choreographed. McGregor achieves this sense of free-flowing movement by drawing on what he describes as the "kinaesthetic intelligence" of his dancers. In a recent TED talk, he described the three techniques he uses to develop and extend "the technicities of creativity" that constitute kinaesthetic thinking in his troupe. Firstly, he uses a "body to body transfer" technique where aspects of his embodied expression of some "mental architecture" are grasped by other dancers, who then generate their own expressions of the movement. Secondly, he uses the dancers "as architectural objects to think with." As they enact his instructions, they reveal new thinking. And finally, he uses a "task-based method where dancers have the autonomy to make all the decisions themselves," so it is their shared thinking that shapes the dance. For him, novel ideas emerge neither through intuition nor divine inspiration, but rather through fast-paced participatory activity.
>
> (Excerpted from McGregor's demonstrative TED talk <http://on.ted.com/McGregor>)

These two vignettes describe very different situations: one concerns product innovation in the context of scientific breakthroughs, while the other describes the development of improvisational dance forms in choreographed performance. Both, however, revolve around the emergence of novelty. For both, it is through interactions that previously unanticipated ideas are generated and developed. Neither breakthrough nor inspiration is enough; something, some tangible artifact such as a new type of glue or a world premiere performance, must be produced; some "thing" is emergent.

The notion of emergence is well established in organization studies (Langley et al., 2013). For instance, Mintzberg and Waters (1985) suggested (somewhat provocatively at the time) that strategy might be more usefully understood as emergent, an idea that has continued to ripple through the strategy literature as interests have turned increasingly towards the practices and processes of strategizing (Chia and Holt, 2009). More recently, scholars have examined emergence in a variety of contexts including new organizational forms (Chiles et al., 2004; Fiol and Romanelli,

2012), improvised actions in organizational crises (Roux-Dufort and Vidaillet, 2003), the institutionalization of values practices in organizations (Gehman et al., 2013), discursive identities (Ellis and Ybema, 2010; Ibarra et al., 2005), and roles in the processes of identity construction (Simpson and Carroll, 2008). In the innovation literature in particular, the notion of emergence is key to understandings of sustained product innovation (Dougherty, 2008; Garud et al., 2011), knowledge-based innovation (Anand et al., 2007), new knowledge creation (Stacey, 2000; Tsoukas, 2009), regional development (Powell et al., 2012), and National Innovation Systems (Sharif, 2006).

Emergence, and by implication novelty, is clearly a useful term for organizational scholars, but what exactly does it mean? In this introduction, we explore the various ways in which this rather slippery term has been used. Our analysis identifies three distinct lenses for studying emergence, which we call *spatial emergence, relational emergence*, and *temporal emergence*. Each lens builds on a unique combination of ontological and epistemological commitments to space and time, and has particular implications for both research and practice. In this, we have been guided by Harvey (1991, p. 205) who suggests that "[h]ow we represent space and time in theory matters, because it affects how we and others interpret and then act with respect to the world." We begin with a brief look at the history of emergence as a theoretical concept, showing how contemporary understandings have been shaped by earlier scientific and philosophical debates. We then go on to elaborate the three lenses and what they imply for research and practice, before introducing the chapters of this volume.

1.1 What Does Emergence Mean?

This word first entered the scientific vocabulary in the mid-nineteenth century as a necessary adjunct to evolution theory. Although valued for its explanation of the continuity of species, evolution theory also needed a way of engaging with discontinuities that introduce novelty and change into evolutionary processes (Morgan, 1923). Early advocates of emergence, both in the physical sciences and in matters of human experience, included John Stuart Mill, George Henry Lewes, Wilhelm Wundt, Henri Bergson, Alfred North Whitehead, and George Herbert Mead. They eschewed "vitalist" explanations of emergence, where unexplained events were attributed to an extra-natural, extra-scientific force, some invisible spirit that mysteriously animates life. But equally, they distanced themselves from the excessively reductionist and mechanistic thinking dominant in science at that time. In arguing for a theory of emergent evolution for example, Morgan sought to go beyond these two opposing logics by elaborating a "constructive philosophy [that] is more than science," but which is "founded on philosophic considerations only" (1923, p. 2). In so doing, he explicitly rejected both vitalist and mechanistic perspectives:

> that [emergence] can only be explained by some chemical force, some vital élan, some entelechy . . . seems to us to be questionable metaphysics. (1923, pp. 8–9)

> the whole doctrine of emergence is a continued protest against mechanical interpretation, and the very antithesis to one that is mechanistic. It does not interpret life in terms of physics and chemistry. It does not interpret mind in terms of receptor-patterns and neurone-routes. Those who suppose that it does so, wholly misapprehend its purport. (1923, pp. 7–8)

The classic definition of emergence is usually attributed to Lewes (1875) who distinguished between "resultant" and "emergent" compounds produced in chemical reactions. Whereas the properties of a "resultant" may be predicted from its chemical components, those of an "emergent" are irreducible to these component parts. So, for instance, the properties of water (H_2O) cannot be deduced from the properties of hydrogen (H) and oxygen (O) as discrete elements. From this perspective then, emergence is understood as "properties at a certain level of organization which cannot be predicted from the properties found at lower levels" (Emmeche et al., 1997, p. 83).

This irreducibility of properties seems to imply that it is possible to get "something" out of "nothing," which is problematic because it violates the logic of nested levels that underpins classical systems thinking (El-Hani and Pihlström, 2002). Various philosophical arguments made in attempts to remedy this problem have ultimately proven unsatisfactory. Furthermore, as scientific discovery has progressed, many previously unpredictable phenomena have come to be well understood. This has led some to suggest that emergence is merely a temporary explanation, a black box, that will eventually be unraveled by better science (Emmeche et al., 1997; Osberg et al., 2008). By the end of the 1920s then, emergence had almost disappeared from scientific writing. It was not until the 1980s that complexity science brought emergence back as a topic worthy of further exploration (Holland, 1998), and scholars began to think about the instruments (theories, assumptions) they use to extract meaning from empirical experience as themselves continuously emergent within our tangled relational complexes (Barad, 2007).

1.2 Three Contemporary Perspectives on Emergence

Throughout the twentieth century, the rigidity of positivistic assumptions in research slowly eased, opening up possibilities for alternative philosophical framings of emergence. However, the co-existence of multiple frames has increased the potential for confusion due to the various different meanings now attributed to this term. We endeavor here to reduce this confusion by articulating three different lenses that, we argue, are evident in contemporary scholarship on emergence. Each lens is identified in terms of its underlying assumptions about space and time, and whether these aspects of context are externalized or endogenous to the perspective it offers on emergence.[1] Inevitably, in making our argument, we have had to simplify the various contributing theoretical positions, deliberately providing only an indicative rather than an exhaustive overview of the rich literature streams we introduce. We readily acknowledge that the boundaries we draw are necessarily permeable and should not be taken as sharp demarcations, but nevertheless, the three lenses do offer a useful way of framing contemporary writing on emergence.

1.2.1 Lens 1: Spatial Emergence

This perspective is best exemplified by the work of Complex Adaptive Systems theorists whose thinking has become increasingly evident in organization studies over the past several decades (e.g. Boisot and McKelvey, 2010; Brown and Eisenhardt, 1998; Marion, 1999; Wheatley, 2006). Drawing on the work of theoretical biologists such as Stuart Kauffman and Brian Goodwin, emergence is conceived as "the arising of novel and coherent structure, patterns and properties during the process of self-organization in complex systems" (Goldstein, 1999, p. 49). Consistent with Lewes' classic definition, complexity theorists have generally taken a structural view that focuses on the emergence of phenomena at macro-levels of a system, but these phenomena are now accounted for at the micro-level in terms of the interactions of autonomous agents over time.

Such complex interactions exhibit nonlinear dynamics that invite stochastic agent-based modeling, where atomistic agents are visualized as distinct from, and operating within, fitness landscapes (Levinthal, 1997). Agents do not derive agency from the networks they are a part of, nor do they possess any capacity to directly influence their fitness landscapes (Anderson, 1999). Whereas the classical formulation of emergence tends to be static in its focus on macro- and micro-level properties, complexity science recognizes the dynamical qualities of movements and interactions at micro-levels of the system as they unfold over time. It is these movements that are the source of emergent novelty (Goldstein, 1999).

We call this lens *spatial emergence* because both space and time are treated as aspects of context that are independent of, and exogenous to, actors' knowledge of them. Emergence occurs within, rather than with, this externalized container, and is evidenced by the appearance of novel properties at macro-levels of the container/system, which could not have been anticipated from preceding events. The processual nature of emergence in this view is represented as changes that occur between one period of observation and the next. These changes are located within the passage of time, which proceeds independently of the unfolding actions. This perspective is thus informed by a realist ontology and a representationalist epistemology that considers knowledge to be "out there" independent of the actors who are involved. Representations of objects and concepts, although acknowledged by complexity theorists to be imperfect (Cilliers, 1998), help us understand how the world really is, and to bring our knowledge of the world into some correspondence with the truth of reality. The assumptions of this lens may be summarized as shown in Table 1.1.

Table 1.1 Summary of assumptions for Lens 1

	Space	Time
Lens 1 Spatial emergence	An exogenous structure within which emergence is contained • Formulated in terms of the properties of higher and lower system levels • Emergent properties are irreducible to the properties of other levels • Properties are spatial representations that are taken to be objectively given • Focus on "what" is emergent • Actors are separate from context	An exogenous variable against which emergence can be tracked • Spatialized (clock) time ticks inexorably and independently of the system • Emergence is defined as changes between t_n and t_{n+m} • Focus on "when" • Emergence is evidenced by properties that cannot be predicted from preceding conditions

1.2.2 Lens 2: Relational Emergence

Another way to understand emergence is to adopt a flat (i.e. non-hierarchical) ontology that collapses the multiple, discrete levels characteristic of systems thinking into a pervasive and intricate network. Actor-network theory is one such perspective (Callon, 1986; Latour, 2005). Here, actors are not atomistic agents working within contexts; rather agency is distributed across social and material arrangements, or "agencements" in Callon's (2005) words. As Callon explained (1986, pp. 8–9), "[t]he agent is neither immersed in the network nor framed by it; in other words, the network does not serve as context. Both agent and network are, in a sense, two sides of the same coin."

From this perspective, "entities take their form and acquire their attributes as a result of their relations with other entities" (Law, 1999, p. 3). This implies that the meanings ascribed to entities, which may be either human or non-human actants, emerge semiotically out of their relationality. Highlighting translation (Callon, 1986; Czarniawska and Sevon, 1996) as a core mechanism underlying emergence, Law observed, "[t]o translate is to make two words equivalent. But since no two words are equivalent, translation also implies betrayal: 'traduction, trahison'. So translation is both about making equivalent, and about shifting. It is about moving terms around, about linking and changing them" (Law, 1999, p. 3).

Callon (1986, p. 196) underscored that "translation is a process, never a completed accomplishment." Here, unanticipated emergents arise performatively. There are unintended consequences of any framing (i.e. misfires or overflows) as felicitous conditions are not met (Callon, 2010). With each misfire, subsequent accommodations and adjustments have to be made. Consequently, performativity is discernible as an unfolding process in which actors and their environments emerge simultaneously (see also Tsoukas and Dooley, 2011).

Based on this relational dynamic, emergence is perceived through Lens 2 as a process that unfolds across a network of relationships. The unfolding translations create entanglements (Callon and Latour, 1981, p. 283) between social and material elements that afford a distributed collective the ability to act. Any apparent sense of closure, however, is illusory, as there are always forces for change brewing under the surface, setting the stage for further translations. In this way, emergence is an ongoing relational process. Actors gain knowledge not through passive observation,

Space

organisation

but rather through their active engagement with a process that unfolds over chronological time, which continues ticking independently of the underlying translations involved. The assumptions of this lens may be summarized as shown in Table 1.2.[2]

Table 1.2 Summary of assumptions for Lens 2

	Space	Time
Lens 2 Relational emergence	An endogenous network that is co-emergent with, and inseparable from, actants • Relational space that transcends the actant/context dualism • Focus on "how" emergence happens through translation • Focus on interactions between actants and semiotically mediated meaning-making	An exogenous variable against which emergence can be tracked • Spatialized (clock) time ticks inexorably and independently of the network • Emergence is defined as changes between t_n and t_{n+m} • Focus on "when"

1.2.3 Lens 3: Temporal Emergence

So far, we have considered two perspectives on emergence—one where complex interactions at a lower level generate new properties at a higher level, and the second where novelty unfolds laterally across tangled networks of relations. A third perspective on emergence is based on process philosophies that endogenize not only relationality but also *durée* (Bergson, 1911/1998), or temporal experience, which we take as pertaining to the human sphere of living. Drawing on Bergson's view of concrete duration, Guerlac (this volume) notes that we know concrete time "from the inside, *as it happens*. It is not a container separate from its contents. We experience it when we attend to the qualities of things, to *how* things happen, in their brightness, their tone, their grace or awkwardness." Barad similarly rejects the "container" metaphor, preferring to understand matter-in-motion in terms of the dynamic and changing topology of spacetime. For her it is the "dynamic intra-play of indeterminacy and determinacy [that] reconfigures the possibilities and impossibilities of the world's becoming" (2007, p. 225).

The temporal approach of this lens focuses on different ways in which the past, present, and future are entwined and mutually reconfigured, as explicated by philosophers such as Bergson, Whitehead,

Mead, Heidegger, and Ricoeur. For Ricoeur (1984), the configured present is forged by prefigured memories and imagined refigurations. Consequently, different imaginaries and memories will generate different experiences of the present. Similarly for Mead (1932), the present is itself emergent in the interplay (or "intra-play" in Barad's words) between pasts and futures that are continuously constructed and reconstructed in the activities of everyday living (Simpson, 2014). For him, the present is a turning point in the unfolding of action. In this, Mead's ideas resonate with Morgan who explained "the emergent step . . . is best regarded as a qualitative change of direction, or crucial turning point, in the course of events" (1923, p. 5). Without such turning points to punctuate the flow of action, the present, as conceived by Mead, cannot be experienced.

Philosophically, this lens is concerned more with different ways of participating in an ongoing, unfinished world than with discovering the realities of an already complete and stable world.

> [W]e cannot have knowledge *of* our environment, once and for all—it is not something we can see, something to look at. Rather, it is something we have to actively feel our way around and through, unendingly. Why unendingly? Because in acting, we create knowledge, and in creating knowledge, we learn to act in different ways and in acting in different ways we bring about new knowledge which changes our world, which causes us to act differently, and so on, unendingly. There is no final truth of the matter, only increasingly diverse ways of interacting. (Osberg et al., 2008, p. 223)

El-Hani and Pihlström (2002) suggest that for this perspective, the strong ontological realism of Lens 1 is inadequate. They propose "pragmatic realism" as an alternative that is deeply rooted in the pluralistic, anti-reductionist and context-sensitive thinking of the American pragmatists, especially James, Dewey, and Mead. The pragmatists understood the apprehensible world as already formed and continuously *becoming* through human practices of inquiry (see also Mesle, 2008; Tsoukas and Chia, 2002), where it is the practical consequences of actions rather than any sense of an absolute "Truth" that matters. Ontological and epistemological commitments are thus inseparable in spacetime, and are necessarily tied to the human purposes and interests that they serve.

For Lens 3 then, space and time are mutually constituting entanglements in the unfolding topology of spacetime. Emergence is understood as an open-ended and continuous process that is sensitive to the ongoing interplay between actions and situations in spacetime. Representations of objects play an important role in this process, but more as temporary placeholders, "things" that exist as "doings" (Shotter, 2013, p. 33) in the ongoing flow of practice. As such, they may be understood as semiotic tools that help us abductively imagine what may emerge in various futures (Peirce, 1965, 5.358–387)[3] by inviting alternative and fluid interpretations of objects and their histories. The assumptions of this lens may be summarized as shown in Table 1.3.

Table 1.3 Summary of assumptions for Lens 3

	Spacetime
Lens 3 Temporal emergence	A dynamic topology of tangled spacetime threads that emerges through and with lived experience • A "becoming" ontology; pragmatic realism • Temporal weaving of past and future together to construct present experiences • Selves and situations are continuously and mutually emergent • Focus on human inquiry and the "how" of emergence • The present is an always emergent movement towards abductively anticipated futures; without emergence, there can be no experience of the present • Semiotically mediated meaning-making

1.3 Implications for Research and Practice

We have explicated three different lenses that embrace the notion of emergence in distinctive ways. In all three, emergence is understood as a "process," but precisely what "process" means is different in each case. In this section, we highlight some implications for researchers and practitioners who are informed by one or other of these lenses.

1.3.1 Implications of Spatial Emergence

For the first lens, process implies an unfolding over chronological time, and within a systemic structure of embedded levels. It is through the complex interactions between agents operating at micro-levels that novelty emerges at macro-levels. From this perspective, Wayne McGregor's studio provides a contextual container, an "interactional frame" in Sawyer's terms (2005, p. 210), within which the members of his troupe can create and explore novel forms of dance. Similarly, the Central Research Labs at 3M represents a container that made it possible for Spence Silver to experiment with new polymers to produce a new substance with unexpected properties.

Researchers who conduct studies through this lens depart from variance theorizing, which tries to establish necessary and sufficient causation between independent and dependent variables (Langley, 1999; Mohr, 1982). Instead, they are likely to be concerned with identifying structures, and tracing the patterns of micro-level movements that produce unanticipated, and unanticipatable, macro-level phenomena. Reflexivity is not prioritized, and agents are assumed to be discrete entities that interact with each other in somewhat mechanical rather than relational ways.

This perspective suggests that novelty may be cultivated by facilitating interactions between parts of a system. For instance, Dooley and Van de Ven (1999) noted that a causal system can be characterized by a "dimensionality space" that represents the degree of freedom available to actors for strategic choice. If the dimensionality space is small (i.e. there are many constraining rules), there is little freedom to maneuver. Such systems are governed by an equilibrating tendency—any perturbation to the system sets in motion counter-reactions that bring the system back into equilibrium. In contrast, if the dimensionality space is large (i.e. few rules), fragmentation may occur. Research has suggested that the dimensional space may be so designed that a system operates at the "edge of chaos" (Brown and Eisenhardt, 1998; Stacey, 1995).

1.3.2 Implications of Relational Emergence

The second lens moves away from methodological individualism, suggesting instead a distributed view on agency. It is not sufficient to look at the attributes and behaviors of individual actors in isolation from the arrangements that afford them the capacity to think and act. At any point in time, it is the performative effects of these arrangements that drive the emergence of novelty.

Rather than shifting from one state of equilibrium to another, process from a relational perspective implies a series of ongoing translations as heterogeneous elements become entangled with one another. People may be purposive, but given the distributed nature of agency, serendipity and disruption are part and parcel of any unfolding process. Artifacts enable, constrain, and perform in their own ways, and consequently are constitutive of agency. At the same time, it is in the interaction between the material and the social that translation occurs and liminal spaces emerge.

Such translations are fraught with tension and controversy. Novel ideas do not just diffuse effortlessly across networks, but instead are more likely to be met with inertia and even resistance. Following this line of reasoning, the more "disruptive" an invention (Christensen, 1997), the more difficult it is to produce a valuable result (Garud and Munir, 2008). Besides having to overcome resistance and inertia, innovators will have to enroll the support of collaborators to develop a whole new infrastructure for the value of the novel idea to emerge in use.

Translation was evident in the case of the novel substance that Silver stumbled upon. Speaking about the series of translations that unfolded before the novel substance eventually became Post-it® Notes, Silver noted, "There are so many hoops that a product idea has to jump through" (Lindhal, 1988). Similarly, translation lies at the heart of Wayne McGregor's approach to improvisation. Dancers translate each other's actions in the context of performance as McGregor sets the pace for the dancers to engage with each other. He is also renowned for the ways in which he translates materials such as computer simulations of bodies in motion as resources to inspire his improvisations.

Research through this lens is driven by the notion of symmetry (Callon, 1986). Symmetry implies that researchers ought to consider not just the social but also the material as exemplified in our two vignettes. Symmetry also requires event neutrality—the same event can hold different implications for different actors depending upon the relational networks that events emerge from. Consequently, symmetry also implies that researchers should avoid attachment to the truth or falsity of any beliefs held by actors, and that success and failure both deserve explanation (Bloor, 1973).

1.3.3 Implications of Temporal Emergence

The third lens folds relational and temporal experiences together in spacetime such that the relational landscape both forms, and is formed by, temporal processes (Ingold, 1993). Actors are not just relational agents operating within contexts; they are constantly engaged in the co-emergence of their selves and their situations. The meaning that Spence Silver and

Wayne McGregor make of their activities is based on the spacetime frames they invoke. For instance, it is Silver's ongoing quest to identify value from the glue he stumbled upon that kept him motivated despite his frustration at the indifference and resistance he encountered from his colleagues. In McGregor's case, temporal experiences are manifest in the visible sense of excitement at the moment of co-creation.

Conducting research from the vantage point of Lens 3 is challenging, as it calls for non-representational methods that go beyond discursive considerations to recognize the ephemeral and dynamic becomingness of human experience as a continuous flow of creative action (Lorino et al., 2011; Nayak, 2008). Shadowing is one research method that holds promise for inquiries that seek to understand the emergence of meanings in real-time (Czarniawska, 2008; McDonald and Simpson, 2014; Vásquez et al., 2012). Not only does this method allow researchers direct access to aesthetic and emotional dimensions of human experiences (Hareli and Rafaeli, 2008; Liu and Maitlis, 2014; Simpson and Marshall, 2010), but in addition, it allows them to follow the temporal unfolding of agentic action. Czarniawska's (2004) "action net" approach also holds potential to more fully engage with the temporal dimensions of experience. She draws attention to the different actions that periodically come together, forming rather than being formed by the temporary connections, or knots, that constitute actors. In this way, she seeks to capture the fluidity and dynamism of organizing in full flight.

In their study of innovation at 3M, Garud et al. (2011) show agents linking different temporalities in practice. Their study documents how "temporal complexity" (p. 757) enabled the organization to "leverage serendipitous moments—moments that cannot be scheduled by the clock or the calendar—whenever they occurred." The authors write of the importance of "endogenizing time" (p. 758) in order to understand how novel ideas can be created and rendered valuable. Similarly, Tsoukas and Hatch (2001) build on Weick's (1979) call for practitioners and scholars to "complicate themselves," noting,

> [o]nly that to which we attend can make the journey from expectation to memory, and in this regard, narrative may be an important attention-giving device. If this is the case, then narrative helps us experience time by offering a means of passing expectation into memory. Furthermore, memory and expectation, once engaged, enlarge our consciousness in (and of) the present. Such enlargement increases our complexity. (Tsoukas and Hatch, 2001, p. 1005)

However, any text that emerges (and by which we mean not just written or spoken words, but also objects and artifacts), is open to reconfiguration, thereby further complexifying situations. As Ricoeur (1984) observed, reading reveals an "unwritten aspect of the text," and "it is the prerogative of reading to strive to provide a figure for this unwritten side of the text." According to Eco (1981, p. 45), "[t]he principal feature of a text is precisely its ability to elicit abductions." Going even further, and resonating with the improvisational dynamics of Wayne McGregor's dance studio, Eco suggested that in musical performance "considerable autonomy [is] left to the individual performer in the way he chooses to play the work" (Eco, 1984, p. 47).

Temporal experiences are based not just on the pattern of spoken words, but also on "the unfolding temporal contours of *words in their speaking*" (Shotter and Tsoukas, 2011, p. 339). Exploring how the extraverbal situation shapes the utterances exchanged, and how particular uses of language enable people to make new distinctions and connections, are important ways through which novelty (be it a new perspective or a fresh distinction) emerges. Narratives and stories are an important part of this process, not merely as objects of retrospective analysis, but also "openings to interlocutors' worlds that point—gesture—towards different relational possibilities in real time" (Shotter, 2011; Shotter and Tsoukas, 2011, p. 344). Indeed, narratives are dynamic entities that take on new forms through their telling, enactment, and retelling (Bartel and Garud, 2003). In this conceptualization, the present is perpetually "in-the-making" through the interplay of remembered pasts and abductive anticipations of imagined futures (Emirbayer and Mische, 1998; Garud et al., 2010; Simpson, 2009, 2014). Neither pasts nor futures can fully determine what unfolds, thereby admitting the possibility of alternative emergent presents.

1.4 Overview of the Chapters in this Volume

The chapters in this volume span a wide range of philosophical, theoretical, and empirical orientations. The eight chapters in Part I touch upon many of the issues that we raised in our explication of the three lenses. While individually each chapter offers something new to our understanding of novelty emergence, collectively they generate a mosaic of ideas that open up new avenues for research. The three chapters in Part II do not address novelty emergence directly, yet contribute to the broader agenda for process organization studies. Below we provide a brief summary of the key arguments of each chapter in the hope that this will entice readers to dig into the richness that this collection offers.

1.4.1 Part I: The Emergence of Novelty

Suzanne Guerlac (Chapter 2) continues her exploration of Bergson's thinking (Guerlac, 2006) by challenging mechanistic ways of understanding. In addressing the question whether mechanism is left behind when we attend to emergence, she draws on Bergson to explore the radical differences between the living and the artificial, the animate and the inanimate. What is "life" in a heavily technological world, dominated by artificial entities? Seeking to recover a Bergsonian view of the living, Guerlac notes the important differences between "abstract" and "concrete" time and their relevance for better understanding living beings. She critiques the functionalist and computational use of "emergence" in contemporary science (especially biology) noting, however, that more recent developments, such as biosemiotics, are promising insofar as they attend to experience. Furthermore, Guerlac notes that the old debates between mechanism and vitalism are far from being outdated, challenging us to think afresh the ethical and political problems that arise.

John Shotter (Chapter 3) turns his attention to the ways in which we participate in our perpetually indeterminate and fluid worlds. He argues that before we can begin to think about emergence, we must first sensitize ourselves, our bodies, to the fragile and ambiguous meanings of what he calls "relational things." These, he describes as having no visible, spatial form, and yet they can be named and they do exert influence upon us as we move about in our worlds. Relational things sit within the temporal flux of experience, mediating between past and future meanings. The puzzle that Shotter raises then, is how are we to conduct research on these intangible, semiotic "relational things" as both we and they flow along in our everyday lives? His response is to set out a new form of inquiry that obliges us to develop new ways of seeing and experiencing the myriad possibilities that come with being "participant parts" in ever-changing situations.

Aris Komporozos-Athanasiou and Marianna Fotaki (Chapter 4) bring the work of the Greek-French philosopher Cornelius Castoriadis, which is very rarely cited in the organization studies literature, to bear on the problem of imagination in the inherently creative processes of organizing. In this, the focus of the authors is very much on the relational and dialogical dimensions of creativity rather than the production of creative outputs per se. They note that the latter perspective dominates the contemporary literature, but at the expense of an adequate theorization of affect, imagination, and "social imaginaries" in creativity. Following Castoriadis' notion of a "radical ontology of creation," they propose an alternative approach that accounts for the emergence of new forms in terms of non-representationalist theories and indeterminate, ever-unfolding significations. Here, creativity is understood as an ongoing process that emerges at the intersection between the individual psyche and the social imaginary. More particularly, they show how intrinsic motivations, passions, and unconscious drives may be integrated into a comprehensive theory explaining the production of creativity in organizations. Their theory of imagination shows organizational creativity to be a process that is both affective and fundamentally political.

Jaan Valsiner (Chapter 5), one of the founders of cultural psychology, approaches the emergence of novelty through semiotics, namely the use of signs in irreversible time. Sign use, he notes, guides actions, and actions feed forward to new construction and further use of signs. This dynamic feed-forward loop involves the building and demolishing of sign hierarchies that control both continuity and innovation. From a semiotic dynamics perspective, using several examples, Valsiner urges organizational researchers to focus on the architecture of sign assemblies that are used to regulate the organizing processes. The regulation of organizational dynamics includes the erection of hierarchies of signs that can demolish themselves when necessary. The functioning of sign hierarchies, argues Valsiner, is on the border of the past and the future. The sign hierarchies construct the relationship with the future, while reconstructing some of the past. Novelty emerges through a process of sign rearrangement in meaning construction.

Trevor Pinch (Chapter 6) explores the processes underlying the emergence of the Moog electronic music synthesizer, a major musical innovation of the twentieth century. His study offers three important insights that add to an understanding of novelty. First, he illustrates how the act of creation is distributed across a number of actors, devices, and tools. Second, he establishes how creative acts involve not only producing new artifacts, but also new ways of socially and materially organizing production, distribution, and consumption. This observation resonates well with the notion of translation that we introduced in Lens 2, and with the social construction of technological systems (SCOT), a research tradition to which Pinch has contributed and from which his current chapter draws.

Third, he shows how creative acts emerge in liminal spaces. These are spaces in between social worlds, with each social world itself an agglomeration of practices and ways of knowing and doing. What is of interest here is that such liminal spaces emerge during play, an under-theorized area of work in organizational studies. Pinch sets the stage for us to go deeper into these issues by focusing on the spaces where play is more likely to unfold. Ultimately, by taking a distributed ontology, and by considering the multiplicity of translations that have to take place in and through play for creative acts to become valuable, he is able to show how emergence of "useful novelty" is such a remarkable accomplishment.

Deborah Dougherty (Chapter 7) acknowledges the importance of emergence in the context of drug discovery, and asks how firms might take advantage of emergence. Her response is to focus on abductive learning routines. These are routines in organizations that help surface configurations of interactions, anticipate emergent perturbations, and reframe emerging models to create new performance objectives. She then applies these three abductive learning routines within projects, processes, strategic initiatives, and ecological sub-systems that together form an overall innovation system. In turn, each sub-system adapts as other sub-systems emerge. In sum, Dougherty's work shows how there are multiple emergent entities informing one another, and at the same time nested within a larger system.

R. Keith Sawyer (Chapter 8) draws on his extensive experience of improvisational theatre to explore the dynamics of emergence in the context of organizational innovation. In his view, innovation is always the product of improvisational encounters in groups, networks, and organizations, but focusing on these encounters alone is not sufficient to account for the emergence of collective group properties. Basing his argument on a combination of complex systems theory and symbolic interactionism, Sawyer proposes a hybrid model that he calls "collaborative emergence." Here, even though an improvising system may have only a small number of active agents (performers), emergence is nevertheless possible because these actors are themselves complex entities, and they interact with each other by means of a highly complex symbolic language. Their conversational encounters are characterized in terms of "denotational" and "metapragmatic" levels of meaning, where the latter provides a vehicle for actors to negotiate their intersubjectivities. Sawyer demonstrates that where metapragmatics remain implicit in conversation, collaborative emergence is more likely to occur.

Isabelle Bouty and Marie-Léandre Gomez (Chapter 9) approach emergence by taking a refreshingly empirical view of creativity as it arises in organizational processes. They seek to go beyond existing literatures, which tend to cast creativity in terms of new and useful ideas, by taking an explicitly processual orientation to understanding how creative work actually comes about in organizations. Specifically, they examine the flow of activities and events, and the material, spatial, and temporal entanglements that contribute to the creativity of Michelin-starred restaurants, for which gastronomic inventiveness is a hallmark. Through their careful analysis of the practices of three elite chefs, Bouty and Gomez find that, at least in the context of haute cuisine kitchens, creativity may be understood as a multi-strand process in which "working on ideas," "creative teamworking," and the "naming" of new dishes are continuously woven together within personal, social, and institutional dynamics of influence. They conclude that creativity work is both highly organized in terms of who, when, and where, and highly improvisational.

1.4.2 Part II: Process Studies

Chris Mowles (Chapter 10) introduces readers to the thinking of Norbert Elias, arguing that he deserves greater recognition in the canon of process-oriented scholarship, and that his ideas have important implications for process organization studies. At the heart of Elias' work is a focus on human interdependence and its ever-fluctuating ramifications in particular types of situations (or "figurations") that cumulate and stratify over the course of history into emergent patterns that recursively enable and constrain further ongoing interactions. Mowles draws attention to the centrality of paradox to Elias' thinking, showing how tensions between continuity and change, inclusion and exclusion, co-operation and competition, involvement and detachment are produced and sustained over time. Mowles shows how Elias offers a perspective that reaches beyond both weak and strong versions of process thinking, Moreover, in line with the theme of this volume, Elias' thinking on emergence is shown to be a precursor and inspiration for later theoretical developments including those on complexity theory discussed earlier in this chapter.

Dvora Yanow (Chapter 11), drawing on "thick" ethnographic accounts, provides an overview of the learning processes involved in achieving mastery, namely in turning novice-ry to mastery. Addressing the question of how practices are learned, Yanow distinguishes seven characteristics of practice-learning processes, highlighting among other things, the role of tools, the body, and tacit knowledge. At the same time, she draws attention to pre-novice learning, a topic that has been relatively unexplored in the practice-learning literature. Furthermore, Yanow explores the learning that goes on after mastery has been achieved, another rarely explored issue. Post-mastery learning, she notes, is achieved when masters, confronted with particular problems, are prepared to reclaim focal awareness. The paradox Yanow discusses is that, while for a novice to become a master, the knowledge involved needs to pushed into subsidiary awareness (otherwise skilled performance cannot be competently carried out), for a master to carry on learning, the subsidiary awareness needs to become focal when the circumstances demand. She ends with a plea for comparative studies to explore the learning that takes place across the life-cycles of practicing and practitioners. Moreover, her overview of the learning processes involved on the way to, and after, mastery suggests new directions for research by exploring pre-novice and post-master learning, focusing in particular on the body, the use of tools and artifacts, and emotions.

Jorgen Sandberg, Bernadette Loacker, and Mats Alvesson (Chapter 12) explore the different uses of "process" in process organizational research. They do so by taking as a case study organizational identity research and reviewing relevant papers in eight leading journals. Unhappy with the hitherto suggested distinction between "weak" and "strong" process, the authors develop a typology of how process has been viewed in identity research, suggesting that there are five different conceptions of process, ranging from process as a state transition to process as a flux. Their chapter explores several constitutive features of process, namely ontology, time, space, and agency. Their typology offers a more nuanced understanding of process, thus helping scholars better understand what view of process they subscribe to, as well as sharpening our understanding of the differences between the different conceptions of process. Operating at the meta-level (namely in discussing the different views of process), the chapter's relevance is far broader than identity research, inviting organizational scholars at large to reflect more systematically on conceptions of process.

1.5 Conclusion

So, after all this, how does novelty really emerge? As we have argued in this introduction, and as the chapters collected together here demonstrate, there are many ways of answering this question. But there are also thematic threads that draw these manifold perspectives together, providing the basis for a more critical and reflexive engagement with the important topic of novelty emergence. Each of the three lenses that we have proposed draws on a unique set of philosophical assumptions about space (spatiality) and time (temporality), each invites its own form of theorization, and each offers a different vantage point for acting (and researching) in an unfinished and indeterminate world. Emergence can no longer be dismissed as a residual category that has to resort to mystical forces as a means of explanation. In contemporary scholarship, it is accepted as part and parcel of our daily lives, especially as they become more interconnected and fast-paced. In such a world, it is imperative to grapple with the notion of emergence all the way from its philosophical underpinnings to its practical consequences. This book challenges readers to examine their own assumptions and views on process, and in particular, how they understand space and time. In doing so, we hope that our fellow travelers in process organization studies will find an abundance of ideas in the chapters in this book to resource and complexify their own further explorations of emergence.

Notes

1. Garud and Gehman (2012) have considered similar lenses to explicate different kinds of sustainability journeys.
2. We have deliberately used a small letter case for "space" to highlight that it is not exogenous to actors.
3. The citation refers to the *Collected Papers*, volume number.paragraph number(s).

References

Anand, N., Gardner, H. K., and Morris, T. (2007). Knowledge-based innovation: Emergence and embedding of new practice areas in management consulting firms. *Academy of Management Journal*, 50(2): 406–428.

Anderson, P. (1999). Complexity theory and organization science. *Organization Science*, 10(3): 216–232.

Barad, K. (2007). *Meeting the Universe Halfway: Quantum Physics and the Entanglement of Matter and Meaning*. Durham, NC and London: Duke University Press.

Bartel, C., and Garud, R. (2003). Adaptive abduction as a mechanism for generalizing from narratives. In M. Easterby-Smith and M. Lyles (eds.), *The Blackwell Handbook of Organizational Learning and Knowledge* (pp. 324–342). Oxford: Blackwell.

Bergson, H. (1911/1998). *Creative Evolution* (trans. A. Mitchell). Mineola, NY: Dover Publications.

Bloor, D. (1973). Wittgenstein and Mannheim on the sociology of mathematics. *Studies in History and Philosophy of Science, Part A*, 4(2): 173–191.

Boisot, M., and McKelvey, B. (2010). Integrating modernist and postmodernist perspectives on organizations: A complexity science bridge. *Academy of Management Review*, 35(3): 415–433.
Brown, S. L., and Eisenhardt, K. M. (1998). *Competing on the Edge: Strategy as Structured Chaos*. Boston, MA: Harvard Business School Press.
Callon, M. (1986). Some elements of a sociology of translation: Domestication of the scallops and the fishermen of St. Brieuc Bay. In J. Law (ed.), *Power, Action and Belief* (pp. 196–233). London: Routledge.
Callon, M. (2005). Why virtualism paves the way to political impotence. *Economic Sociology*, 6(2): 3–20.
Callon, M. (2010). Performativity, misfires and politics. *Journal of Cultural Economy*, 3(2): 163–169.
Callon, M., and Latour, B. (1981). Unscrewing the big leviathan: How actors macro-structure reality and how sociologists help them to do so. In K. Knorr-Cetina and A. V. Cicourel (eds.), *Advances in Social Theory and Methodology* (pp. 277–303). London: Routledge.
Chia, R., and Holt, R. (2009). *Strategy Without Design: The Silent Efficacy of Indirect Action*. Cambridge: Cambridge University Press.
Chiles, T. H., Meyer, A. D., and Hench, T. J. (2004). Organizational emergence: The origin and transformation of Branson, Missouri's Musical Theaters. *Organization Science*, 15(5): 499–519.
Christensen, C. M. (1997). *The Innovator's Dilemma*. Boston, MA: Harvard Business School Press.
Cilliers, P. (1998). *Complexity and Postmodernism: Understanding Complex Systems*. London: Routledge.
Czarniawska, B. (2004). On time, space, and action nets. *Organization*, 11(6): 773–791.
Czarniawska, B. (2008). *Shadowing: And Other Techniques for Doing Fieldwork in Modern Societies*. Copenhagen: Copenhagen Business School Press.
Czarniawska, B., and Sevon, G. (eds.) (1996). *Translating Organizational Change*. Berlin: Walter de Gruyter.
Dooley, K. J., and Van de Ven, A. H. (1999). Explaining complex organizational dynamics. *Organization Science*, 10(3): 358–372.
Dougherty, D. (2008). Bridging social constraint and social action to design organizations for innovation. *Organization Studies*, 29(3): 415–434.
Eco, U. (1981). The theory of signs and the role of the reader. *The Bulletin of the Midwest Modern Language Association*, 14(1): 35–45.
Eco, U. (1984). *The Role of the Reader: Explorations in the Semiotics of Texts*. Bloomington: Indiana University Press.
El-Hani, C. N., and Pihlström, S. (2002). Emergence theories and pragmatic realism. *Essays in Philosophy*, 3(2): Article 3.
Ellis, N., and Ybema, S. (2010). Marketing identities: Shifting circles of identification in inter-organizational relationships. *Organization Studies*, 31(3): 279–305.

Emirbayer, M., and Mische, A. (1998). What is agency? *American Journal of Sociology*, 103(4): 962–1023.

Emmeche, C., Køppe, S., and Stjernfelt, F. (1997). Explaining emergence: Towards an ontology of levels. *Journal for General Philosophy of Science*, 28(1): 83–119.

Fiol, C. M., and Romanelli, E. (2012). Before identity: The emergence of new organizational forms. *Organization Science*, 23(3): 597–611.

Garud, R., and Gehman, J. (2012). Metatheoretical perspectives on sustainability journeys: Evolutionary, relational and durational. *Research Policy*, 41(6): 980–995.

Garud, R., Gehman, J., and Kumaraswamy, A. (2011). Complexity arrangements for sustained innovation: Lessons from 3M Corporation. *Organization Studies*, 32(6): 737–767.

Garud, R., Kumaraswamy, A., and Karnoe, P. (2010). Path dependence or path creation? *Journal of Management Studies*, 47(4): 760–774.

Garud, R., and Munir, K. (2008). From transactions to transformation costs: The case of Polaroid's SX-70 Camera. *Research Policy*, 37(4): 690–705.

Gehman, J., Treviño, L. K., and Garud, R. (2013). Values work: A process study of the emergence and performance of organizational values practices. *Academy of Management Journal*, 56(1): 84–112.

Goldstein, J. (1999). Emergence as a construct: History and issues. *Emergence*, 1(1): 49–72.

Guerlac, S. (2006). *Thinking in Time*. Ithaca, NY: Cornell University Press.

Hareli, S., and Rafaeli, A. (2008). Emotion cycles: On the social influence of emotion in organizations. *Research in Organizational Behavior*, 28: 35–59.

Harvey, D. (1991). *The Condition of Postmodernity*. Malden, MA: Wiley-Blackwell.

Holland, J. H. (1998). *Emergence*. Oxford: Oxford University Press.

Ibarra, H., Kilduff, M., and Tsai, W. (2005). Zooming in and out: Connecting individuals and collectivities at the frontiers of organizational network research. *Organization Science*, 16(4): 359–371.

Ingold, T. (1993). The temporality of the landscape. *World Archaeology*, 25(2): 152–174.

Langley, A. (1999). Strategies for theorizing from process data. *Academy of Management Review*, 24(4): 691–710.

Langley, A., Smallman, C., Tsoukas, H., and Van de Ven, A. H. (2013). Process studies of change in organization and management: Unveiling temporality, activity, and flow. *Academy of Management Journal*, 56(1): 1–13.

Latour, B. (2005). *Reassembling the Social: An Introduction to Actor-Network-Theory*. Oxford: Oxford University Press.

Law, J. (1999). After ANT: Complexity, naming and topology. In J. Law and J. Hassard (eds.), *Actor Network Theory and After* (pp. 1–14). Oxford: Blackwell Publishers.

Levinthal, D. A. (1997). Adaptation on rugged landscapes. *Management Science*, 43(7): 934–950.

Lewes, G. H. (1875). *Problems of Life and Mind* (vol. 2). London: Kegan, Paul, Trench, Trubner.

Lindhal, L. (1988). Spence Silver: A scholar and a gentleman. *3M Today*, 15: 12–17.
Liu, F., and Maitlis, S. (2014). Emotional dynamics and strategizing processes: A study of strategic conversations in top team meetings. *Journal of Management Studies*, 51(2): 202–234.
Lorino, P., Tricard, B., and Clot, Y. (2011). Research methods for non-representational approaches to organizational complexity: The dialogical mediated inquiry. *Organization Studies*, 32(6): 769–801.
McDonald, S., and Simpson, B. (2014). Shadowing research in organizations: The methodological debates. *Qualitative Research in Organizations and Management*, 9(1): 3–20.
Marion, R. (1999). *The Edge of Organization: Chaos and Complexity Theories of Formal Social Systems*. Thousand Oaks, CA: Sage.
Mead, G. H. (1932). *The Philosophy of the Present*. La Salle, IL: Open Court.
Mesle, R. C. (2008). *Process-Relational Philosophy*. West Conshohocken, PA: Templeton Press.
Mintzberg, H., and Waters, J. A. (1985). Of strategies, deliberate and emergent. *Strategic Management Journal*, 6(3): 257–272.
Mohr, L. B. (1982). *Explaining Organizational Behavior*. San Francisco, CA: Jossey-Bass.
Morgan, C. L. (1923). *Emergent Evolution*. New York: Henry Holt.
Nayak, A. (2008). On the way to theory: A processual approach. *Organization Studies*, 29(2): 173–190.
Osberg, D., Biesta, G., and Cilliers, P. (2008). From representation to emergence: Complexity's challenge to the epistemology of schooling. *Educational Philosophy and Theory*, 40(1): 213–227.
Peirce, C. S. (1965). *Collected Papers of Charles Sanders Peirce* (6 vols.). Cambridge, MA: Belknap Press of Harvard University Press.
Powell, W. W., Packalen, K., and Whittington, K. (2012). Organizational and institutional genesis: The emergence of high-tech clusters in the life sciences. In J. F. Padgett and W. W. Powell (eds.), *The Emergence of Organizations and Markets* (pp. 434–465). Princeton, NJ: Princeton University Press.
Ricoeur, P. (1984). *Time and Narrative* (trans. K. McLaughlin and D. Pellauer). Chicago: University of Chicago Press.
Roux-Dufort, C., and Vidaillet, B. (2003). The difficulties of improvising in a crisis situation: A case study. *International Studies of Management and Organization*, 33(1): 86–115.
Sawyer, K. (2005). *Social Emergence*. Cambridge: Cambridge University Press.
Sharif, N. (2006). Emergence and development of the National Innovation Systems concept. *Research Policy*, 35(5): 745–766.
Shotter, J. (2011). *Getting It: Withness-Thinking and the Dialogical . . . in Practice*. New York: Hampton Press.
Shotter, J. (2013). Reflections on sociomateriality and dialogicality in organization studies: From "inter-" to "intra-thinking" . . . in performing practices. In P. R. Carlile,

D. Nicolini, A. Langley, and H. Tsoukas (eds.), *How Matter Matters* (pp. 32–57). Oxford: Oxford University Press.

Shotter, J., and Tsoukas, H. (2011). Complex thought, simple talk: An ecological approach to language-based change in organizations. In B. McKelvey, P. Allen and S. Maguire (eds.), *The Sage Handbook of Complexity and Management* (pp. 333–348). London: Sage.

Simpson, B. (2009). Pragmatism, Mead, and the practice turn. *Organization Studies*, 30(12): 1329–1347.

Simpson, B. (2014). George Herbert Mead. In J. Helin, T. Hernes, D. Hjorth, and R. Holt (eds.), *The Oxford Handbook of Process Philosophy & Organization Studies* (pp. 272–286). Oxford: Oxford University Press.

Simpson, B., and Carroll, B. (2008). Re-viewing "role" in processes of identity construction. *Organization*, 15(1): 29–50.

Simpson, B., and Marshall, N. (2010). The mutuality of emotions and learning in organizations. *Journal of Management Inquiry*, 19(4): 351–365.

Stacey, R. (1995). The science of complexity: An alternative perspective for strategic change processes. *Strategic Management Journal*, 16(6): 477–495.

Stacey, R. (2000). The emergence of knowledge in organizations. *Emergence*, 2(4): 23–39.

Tsoukas, H. (2009). A dialogical approach to the creation of new knowledge in organizations. *Organization Science*, 20(6): 941–957.

Tsoukas, H., and Chia, R. (2002). On organizational becoming: Rethinking organizational change. *Organization Science*, 13(5): 567–582.

Tsoukas, H., and Dooley, K. J. (2011). Introduction to the special issue: Towards the ecological style—embracing complexity in organizational research. *Organization Studies*, 32(6): 729–735.

Tsoukas, H., and Hatch, M. J. (2001). Complex thinking, complex practice: The case for a narrative approach to organizational complexity. *Human Relations*, 54(8): 979–1013.

Vásquez, C., Brummans, B. H. J. M., and Groleau, C. (2012). Notes from the field on organizational shadowing as framing. *Qualitative Research in Organizations and Management*, 7(2): 144–165.

Weick, K. E. (1979). *Social Psychology of Organizing* (2nd edition). Reading, MA: Addison-Wesley.

Wheatley, M. J. (2006). *Leadership and the New Science: Discovering Order in a Chaotic World* (3rd edition). San Francisco, CA: Berrett-Koehler.

Part I

The Emergence of Novelty

2

Time of Emergence/Emergence of Time

Life in the Age of Mechanical (re)Production

Suzanne Guerlac

Abstract: The reach and variety of contemporary studies in the field of emergence suggests a general problematic that challenges the mechanistic theories and methods of the past. But is this really the case? Do we leave mechanism behind when we attend to emergence? To consider this question this chapter takes a detour through Bergson's philosophy of emergence as a way of gaining critical purchase on contemporary developments. Bergson maintained a radical difference in kind between the living and the artificial, the animate and the inanimate. Is this distinction still pertinent in today's technological world? How do we talk about "life" today? Are the old debates between mechanism and vitalism perhaps still quietly at work in discussions of emergence, and of life, today? And what might be the political implications of such debates?

2.1 Detour

Henri Bergson wrote his major works from the 1890s to the 1930s, a time that in many ways resembles our own. The poet Paul Valéry characterized it as a period "completely formed by the sciences, in perpetual technological transformation, where nothing escapes the will to innovation" (cited in Guerlac, 2006, p. 14). It was also a time when the traditional mechanistic model of science was still dominant, even as modern physics was beginning to move beyond it toward uncertainty, ambiguity (as between energy and matter), and dynamic processes—paths opened up by discoveries in thermodynamics, electron theory, and quantum physics. As a philosopher, Bergson was best able to reinforce the perspective of the new physics by turning to evolutionary biology: his popularity soared with the publication of *Creative Evolution* in 1907.

Today, we seem to have arrived at a comparable moment with respect to biology. A mechanistic molecular biology is ostensibly being displaced by a "new biology" that examines dynamic systems and processes, networks, complexity, and the emergence of new forms and patterns. (For various accounts of the new biology see Woese, 2004; Rose and Oakley, 2007; Rubin and Schadt, 2011.) Evolutionary biology led the way into the trans-disciplinary field of complexity studies and the various scientific inquiries that concern emergence.

Complexity theory, which involves the analysis of self-organizing systems, crosses traditional disciplinary boundaries, finding similar patterns of emergence (or critical phase transitions) in completely different domains of investigation and on vastly different scales, from bacteria in the ocean to the network activity of the World Wide Web, from ant colonies to the stock market, including traffic patterns, weather dynamics, neural networks, and the formation of stars. Its astounding reach suggests a general problematic that challenges the mechanistic theories and methods of the past. But is this really the case? Do we leave mechanism behind when we attend to emergence? To consider this question we will take a detour through Bergson's philosophy of emergence as a way of gaining critical purchase on contemporary developments.

Bergson was concerned that the mechanistic, scientific methods (pervasive in the field of classical physics) that had underwritten so much material progress in the modern world were being adopted by the newly emerging social sciences, sociology, anthropology, and above all psychology—and applied to the study of people. He felt the philosophical containment of mechanism to be an urgent matter, necessary to prevent human beings from being reduced to the status of things in a deterministic world. For him, the very possibility of human freedom was at stake. We rarely speak in such terms now. Today the model human subject is the consumer and we speak readily of voluntary choice; social networking platforms, enmeshed with marketing strategies, format our subjectivity in terms of preferences and likes. Questions such as "is this ad relevant to you?" pop up uninvited on our computer screens.

Bergson, who wrote a celebrated essay on laughter, defined the comic as an overlay of the mechanical on the living (Bergson, 1937). Today this is no laughing matter: huge sums of money are being invested to achieve just this kind of hybridization of the living with man-made machines. Scientists are studying how to manufacture avatars of human brains, robotic substitutes for human minds.[1] Embodiment, in this context, is a felt impediment, a distinct disadvantage. Some even whisper the word "immortality" (Itskov, n.d.; Seung, 2013).

If, thanks to digital technologies, our engineering capacity now vastly exceeds what was even imaginable at the turn of the twentieth century (indeed, each decade rapidly outstrips the preceding one, in accelerating fashion), it may also have outrun our ability—or perhaps our will—to think. Since the 1990s, definitions of thinking and of knowledge tilt toward computer processing operations (Guerlac, 2011). It is not just that education is moving online; in doing so, it changes in nature: it is formatted in bits, packets, and chunks; it is quantified, sequenced, and rendered rule-bound (Guerlac, 2011). Thinking is altered when meaning is given to information by data-mining algorithms that arrange data according to classes, clusters, associations, and sequential patterns. The New Biology was born in this context, and with it the research fields of complexity studies and emergence. We are now well within this current. To get some imaginative distance on it, I would like to take a step back and consider what emergence meant in the philosophy of Henri Bergson. I turn to Bergson to retrieve a lost notion of livingness that might give us some perspective on our present epistemic ideologies and invite us to think differently.

2.2 Matter Soaked in Time

Life is a matter of time for Bergson. This is the core of the philosopher's thought: life is matter soaked in time, and openness to time is the distinguishing feature of the living. "Everywhere where something lives, there is, open somewhere, an inscription of time."[2] When it comes to inert things, Bergson says, time doesn't matter. Inert matter does not exist in time or at least does not hold any trace of past time. "The living organism," on the other hand, is "something that exists in time [*chose qui dure*]" (507).[3]

Life is—just—a matter of time. Today we can hear this phrase as a threat or a promise. For Bergson, too, it was both. For much of his career it was a promise of spontaneity, deep feeling, and autonomous action, a promise of vitality and creativity, of an open society and of the emergence of new forms in creative evolution. It implied an escape from determinism and its attendant alienations.

In the bleak months leading up to the Second World War, however, and near the end of his life, Bergson's tone shifts. He concludes his final work, *The Two Sources of Morality and Religion*, with a warning that barely conceals a threat. Depicting humanity as "half crushed under the weight of its own progress," he declares: "it is up to humanity to decide if it wants to continue to live" (1245).[4]

2.3 The Promise of Time

Over the course of several books (*Time and Free Will, Matter and Memory*, and *Creative Evolution*) Bergson argues that the difference between the living and the non-living corresponds to a difference between two regimes of time that he calls "abstract time" and "concrete time" (512).[5] He emphasizes a discrepancy between the ways in which we experience time and the ways in which we think and talk about it. We experience it as dynamic (time passes) and irreversible (we grow older, not younger). Yet the "strange timelessness" of the Newtonian mechanistic view of the world does not seem to take this experience into account (Griffin, 1986, p. 11). When time is related to motion in the tradition of Descartes and Newton, this motion is immobilized by being mapped onto space and viewed as reversible, like a mathematical equation. This is abstract time, and from Bergson's point of view, it is an imposture. It is not really time at all, but just another form of spatialization. It implies either a mapping in graphs or flowcharts of something that has already happened (and so all movement has ceased) or a statistical projection into the future of patterns detected in past events, to which we give predictive weight. In this case the future is reduced to being simply a projected extension of past patterns; it holds nothing new. Scientific reasoning cannot grasp the concrete time of lived experience because it can deal with things only in repetition (519).[6] Because of its fundamentally retrospective logic, this regime of time is both abstract and static (1267).[7] It is rendered oddly timeless. When we try to live according to this regime of abstract space/time, Bergson tells us, we become only a shadow of ourselves. We have all had this experience of imagining time as a container that we try to fill to the brim. Conceived of in this way, there is never enough time.

But, Bergson insists, "Free action occurs *in the time that passes*, not in the time already past" (145).[8] The second regime of time, then—and the only one Bergson deems worthy of the name—is lived time, or concrete duration. This is time that passes; the time of the *happening* of what happens, or of the passing of what passes. We know it from the inside, *as it happens*. It is not a container separate from its contents. We experience it when we attend to the qualities of things, to *how* things happen, in their brightness, their tone, their grace or awkwardness. As Bergson argues in *Time and Free Will*, the time of concrete duration is heterogeneous, continuous, and qualitative. It can't be measured.

In a striking formulation Bergson defines duration as what "prevents everything from being given at once" (1333).[9] He associates it with a kind of slowing down, a *retardement* (1333).[10] This is a bit shocking to us, for in almost all aspects of our lives, from the economy to the changing state of our biosphere, time seems to go faster and faster.

To say that time is what prevents everything from being given at once directly challenges mechanism, which, in a static manner, reduces a whole to relations between the sum of its given parts and in this sense gives everything at once. And it challenges teleology, which also implies that all is given, in that the movement toward an end, and the end itself, would be inscribed in what already is. To think time (or evolution) with Bergson is to reject both these views. It is also to reject the idea that time can be represented abstractly at all, because symbolic representations (including both mathematics and language, as well as flowcharts and algorithms that tie output to input) precisely give everything at once within a homogeneous framework of a delimited space. This is the function of spatialization. To think the time of duration we would have to imagine something quite different—a time of touch, perhaps, or of song.

So what might it mean to imagine time as a kind of slowing down that pushes back against the possibility of everything being given at once? "Our duration," Bergson writes,

> is not merely one instant replacing another. If it were, there would never be anything but the present—no prolonging of the past into the actual, no evolution, no concrete duration. Duration is the continuous progress of the past which gnaws into the future and which swells as it advances. (498)[11]

Here Bergson emphasizes both the reality of the past in this regime of time (the past is real because it survives in us in the memory of our bodies as well as our minds) and its dynamic force, its continual progress. The slowing down that characterizes duration has to do with this impact of the past on how the present becomes present for us, and how it passes, "gnawing into" the future (498).[12]

Time, in Bergson's strong sense of concrete duration, is not a container precisely because it is inseparable from the happening of what happens. So much so that, as Bergson writes, "the same feeling, by the very fact of being repeated, is a new feeling" (131).[13] We never experience the same feeling twice, even if we have to call certain events by the same name. Take for example, getting married. When I say, "I do!" a second time it feels quite different from the first time, simply because I carry with me the sense of having said it before. In fact, "the same concrete reality never repeats itself" (533).[14] Repetition "is only possible in the realm of abstraction [*dans l'abstrait*]" (533).[15] In this concrete, everyday, way, "to exist consists in change [*exister consiste à changer*]" (500):[16] "I am . . . constantly changing [*je change donc sans cesse*]" (495).[17] As Bergson puts it in *Matter and Memory*, "nothing *is* less present than the present" (291, original emphasis).[18] Indeed, he argues there, "all perception is already memory. *Practically, we only perceive the past*" (291, original emphasis).[19] Precisely because duration means constant change, it cannot be known through rational intelligence which must immobilize things, events, or moments of time, as if they were repeatable, in order to grasp them, and which counts things, and graphs them spatially.

In his first books (*Time and Free Will* and *Matter and Memory*) Bergson appeals to consciousness in a (Cartesian) gesture of introspection, to derive this conception of duration as lived time, time that escapes rational intelligence. He ties it to another regime of knowing, one that operates not by rational intelligence but by intuition.

In *Creative Evolution*, duration becomes, as Gilles Deleuze has put it, ontological.[20] Bergson no longer presents duration as a phenomenon of consciousness; it is not an individual, or subjective, experience, as distinct from an ostensibly objective one. In *Creative Evolution*, the whole universe exists in and through the dynamic time of concrete duration as a "continual elaboration of the absolutely new" (503).[21] Bergson argues that there "is *more* in a movement than the successive positions attributed to the moving thing, more in becoming than the forms traversed one at a time, more in the evolution of form than the forms realized one after the other" (762, original emphasis).[22] He calls this "more" *élan vital* (569, 710; 1055–1056),[23] explaining that it is simply a metaphor (a place holder) for a notion of time as energy of being (or life), that is, as multiple rhythms of being or time energy that must be felt because they cannot be captured by abstract concepts or quantitative analysis and so escape the notice of rational intelligence.

Elan vital, then, is not a manifestation of consciousness, not a substance in the usual sense; it is more like a flow of energy, a time-energy. In this strict sense Bergson never was a vitalist. Yet there is a parallelism, for Bergson, between consciousness and living organisms in evolutionary becoming. Both enjoy what Bergson calls an opening in which dynamic time inscribes itself as an active force of growth and of aging, "a perpetual changing of form" (510).[24] Once Bergson begins to speak on the large scale of evolutionary becoming, he extends duration to the cosmological level, that is, to "the totality of the material universe" (507).[25] This materialist formulation is the best way to understand *élan vital*, which was misunderstood for so long by those who relegated Bergson to the realm of spiritualism. It is the force of time that actively relates past and future in the invention of the new, on the level of the individual, the species, and the life of the biosphere.

Bergson construes evolution, then, neither as a pull from the future in a teleology, nor as the unfolding of a logic of static component parts (or mechanical causes) given in the past. Instead, he suggests, it involves a continual persistence—or survival—of the past, which seeps into the present and alters it. From Bergson's perspective, this is the crucial difference between "an artificial system and a natural system, between the dead and the living" (511–512).[26] For Bergson, the promise of construing life as a matter of time is that it yields a sturdy difference in kind between living beings and non-living, or artificial, ones.

2.4 Knowing and Feeling

For Bergson the two regimes of time just sketched out—concrete duration on the one hand and abstract, or spatialized, time on the other—imply two ways of knowing the real. Intuition (or instinct) puts us in contact with lived time and yields knowledge about living beings and about creative evolution. Intelligence (or reason) gives us useful knowledge about inert things. This difference is so fundamental for Bergson that he opens *Creative Evolution* on just this point; he begins with a critique of epistemology, that is, of the claims of rational knowledge to know living beings, or life. Because the real exists as perpetual change, most notably when it comes to living beings in evolutionary becoming, it exceeds what rational knowledge can know of it.

Reason has long been considered to transcend the ever-changing forms of nature, to provide a way of ordering its transitory evidence. Science inherits this status from theology and philosophy. As Bruno Latour, the anthropologist of science, has recently said, it is as if the scientific mind were not part of this world but hovered over it in a disembodied and eternal fashion, considering it from the outside (Latour, 2013). For Bergson, the faculty of intelligence (or reasoned thought) is not a transcendental given, as it was in Kantian epistemology, and as we continue to assume it to be every time we grant it privileged access to the truth, or dismiss other modes of understanding as being non-scientific. Bergson argues in *Creative Evolution* that reason is constructed; human intelligence has itself emerged from, or been constituted along with, other life forms over the long time span of human evolution. It has evolved as a faculty, or instrument, for thinking about matter, a correlate to our need to act on matter in order to survive. Bergson's theory of evolution both requires and implies a critique of epistemology. Performing his own version of a "critique of reason" (but this time against Kant) he affirms limits to reason. Reason, he holds, is perfectly suited to the study of inert matter. But it is constitutionally unable to yield knowledge of life, that is, of living beings *as living*, which is also to say, about "the deep meaning of evolutionary movement [*du mouvement evolutif*]" (489).[27] How could intelligence comprehend (that is to say, completely grasp) life, Bergson asks, given that it has evolved within life, in particular circumstances, and in view of specific adaptive pressures? Moreover, Bergson insists, the line of evolution that led to intelligent human beings, enabling their technological mastery of the world is not, *pace* Herbert Spencer, the only line of development within evolution, or its final end. There have been many others.

Life is (just) a matter of time, of time passing through matter such that the past alters the future as the present moves into it. The promise of this conception of time is to open the concrete world of livingness beyond the limits of a closed or finite system into an indeterminate openness of becoming, which nevertheless remains singular, concrete, and sentient up to, and including, the biosphere.

2.5 The Threat

Bergson's last book, *The Two Sources of Morality and Religion*, theorizes the question of closed and open systems in the social world. It ends, as

I indicated earlier, on a threatening note. Bergson no longer presents life—or the time of life—as an open (and infinite) *élan vital.* Human life on Earth now appears to have limits: humanity will have to choose whether it will go on living:

> Humanity suffers [*gémit*], half crushed under the weight of the progress it has made. It does not fully realize [*ne sait pas assez*] that it holds its future in its hands [*que son avenir depend d'elle*]. It is up to humanity [*à elle de voir*], first of all [*d'abord*], to decide [*voir*] if it wants to continue to live. (1245)[28]

Whereas in his earlier books Bergson treated mechanism as a philosophical problem associated with reductionism and determinism, in *The Two Sources of Morality and Religion,* his analysis of the situation of Western culture—and of the fragility of human life on Earth—concerns mechanization in a very concrete sense. The mechanization of killing during the First World War had brought home the full extent of the human potential for destruction. With the problem of human violence uppermost in his mind, Bergson addresses mechanization as an economic and political reality in this study which brings us back to the question of time, but in a more earthbound, and more menacing, way.

In an image that haunts him in the interwar years, and that appears in many contexts, Bergson figures Western civilization as a grotesquely swollen, and artificially extended, body that holds within itself a disproportionately shriveled soul.[29] Whereas in his earlier work, *Matter and Memory,* he had resolved the philosophical problem of mind/body dualism in an analysis that emphasized interactive and harmonious, dynamic, relations between these two terms, in this passage of *The Two Sources of Morality and Religion,* the two terms are disconnected and the relation between them is pathologically out of balance:

> Machines that run on oil, on coal, on "white coal," and that convert potential energies accumulated over millions of years into movement, have endowed our organism with an extension so vast and a power so formidable, so disproportional to its dimension and its force, that surely nothing like this was foreseen in the structural plan of our species . . . in this inordinately swollen body, the soul remains what it was, too small now to fill it, too weak to guide it. Whence the void between the two [*entre lui et elle*]. Whence the formidable [*redoutables*] social, political and international problems that are so many definitions of this void, and which provoke so many muddles and ineffectual efforts to fill it [*le combler*]. (1238–1239)[30]

What we find here is not a body open to time and informed by it in a process of growth and aging but an artificially augmented body, alienated from its own openness to time; it requires outside energy to operate. The energy sources that are consumed to artificially extend the body's mastery over the material world, the coal, oil, and natural gas, have accumulated over millions of years. These energy reserves are, in a sense, material deposits of time. Bergson's image suggests that this industrial social body consumes time itself in order to achieve "the greatest material success of man on the planet" (1239).[31] This produces a void, Bergson argues, within which social and political conflicts fester. His conclusion is this: "what we need is new reserves of potential energy—this time of moral energy" (1239).[32] This is what is at stake in the choice before us: humanity will have to decide "if it wants to continue to live" (1245).[33]

On the one hand Bergson is alluding to political conflicts over energy resources that contributed to the onset of the First World War and create pressures leading to future war. But his critique goes beyond the specific geopolitical contexts of the two world wars, one just past and the other on its way. To his general philosophical reflection on the limits of mechanism he adds a strong dose of social critique. The problem is a spirit of innovation (Bergson calls it a "spirit of invention [*esprit d'invention*]" (1237))[34] supported by science; it "has created a multitude of new needs; it has not bothered to satisfy the old needs of the greatest number of people . . . it has given too much thought to the superfluous" (1235),[35] and "manufactures with no other thought than to sell" (1236).[36] Bergson points directly to the issue of sustainability. Technology was fine, he suggests, as long as we used energy sources that were actual and visible, renewable energy sources like wind and water. However, "the machine only gave its full productivity when potential energies stored for millions of years were put at its disposal, borrowed from the sun, turned into coal and petrol" (1234–1235).[37] The spirit of innovation, enhanced by an intoxication with reason and intelligence (with scientific thought) has taken us down the wrong path: "humanity needs to simplify its existence with the same frenetic impulse that served to complicate it" (1237).[38]

Until recently, this point of view has been labeled "asceticism" and considered eccentric.[39] Today, however, given the urgency of concerns over the long-term viability of life on our planet, we might hear a desperate appeal for sustainability in these remarks, a statement of the precariousness of life, tied to a critique of an overheated world economy guided only by the desire for profit. "We must look towards a return to simplicity," Bergson affirmed (1230).[40] Global capitalism has moved, frenetically, in just the opposite direction.

2.6 Our Swollen Body

Today our swollen body, to borrow Bergson's image, has an even vaster reach. We appear to have scrambled the difference in kind that Bergson was determined to affirm philosophically: not only the difference between the living and the non-living (or the artificial) but also that between the living and the dead. Once absolute, the limit of death has become a subject of controversy at the intersection between life-sustaining technologies and organ transplant practices.[41] It is also becoming far from clear just what "life" might mean.

Not only are there biotechnical interventions in natural organisms and synthetic biology, which generate new species of life, there is also a new field, Artificial Life (or A-life) that produces "fully digital life form[s]" through manipulations of strings of digital information that operate like DNA. The Open Worm Project has undertaken to make a virtual C. elegans nematode in a computer.[42] The website for Synthetic Biology (a group of scientists from various labs across the country) defines its task as: "A) the design and construction of new biological parts, devices and systems, and B) the re-design of existing natural biological systems for useful purposes" (OpenWetWare, n.d.). The wiki for Harvard's Silver Lab affirms: "Our overarching goal is the rapid and predictable reprogramming of cells of all types. We seek to implement design strategies used by Nature as well as to go where evolution may not readily go" (Silver, n.d.). Evolution stands poised to be supplemented, or even replaced, by human engineering and design: "synthetic biology seeks to assemble the biological tools necessary to redesign the living world" (Specter, 2009). But just what do we see when we look, for example, at the virtual C. elegans? "Imagine downloading the worm and running it in a virtual Petri dish on your computer. What exactly will you be looking at? Will you consider it to be alive?"[43] The very concept of life has become problematic:

> Perhaps creations like the digital C. elegans will break down our binary conception of the matter in the world as either living or not living. We'll discover that we can create systems that exist *in-between* these two spheres, or that certain aspects of life as we know it are not required to meet our definition of being alive.[44]

Indeed, scientists now designate three "material substrates" for life: software (materialized through computer imaging), hardware (or robotics), and wet (or biochemical) substrates; they parse nuanced categories of "living technology" including "primary living technology," "secondary living technology," and "lifelike technolog[ies]," followed only by the "*hypothetical* living proto-cell that self-assembles entirely from nonliving materials and self-reproduces" (Bedau et al., 2013, pp. 292–293, original emphasis). Indeed it seems we are well on our way to moving "beyond a black and white notion of what it means to be 'alive,'" as Stephen Larson, the organizer of the Open Worm Project, suggests, toward "a more functional perspective—living systems are those that self sustain" (cited in Madrigal, 2013).

2.6.1 But Isn't This Just the Problem?

The International Commission on Stratigraphy has not yet made it official, but the designation of a new geological age, the Anthropocene, is under discussion by a designated working group of the commission. The notion already has a lot of traction: many believe we have entered a new epoch of geological time, the Anthropocene, characterized by human impact on fundamental Earth systems and cycles on a scale comparable to that of natural forces. Changes have occurred in areas such as ozone depletion, climate change, biodiversity loss, and nutrient pollution that far exceed the range of such changes for the previous, Holocene, period. We are "remaking the Earth system itself," living on a "planet transformed by humanity," such that "basic goods and services supplied by the planetary life support system, such as food, water, clear air and an environment conducive to human health, are being affected increasingly by global change."[45] The last geological age (the Holocene) began thousands of years ago, after the end of the ice age, which is also to say, well after the extinction of the dinosaurs. Entry into the Anthropocene is also marked by extinctions: the "current human driven wave of extinctions looks set to become Earth's 6th great extinction event," declares one scientist (Zalasiewicz et al., 2010). The Anthropocene may mean "a geological age of our own making," but it has not been made by design (International Commission on Stratigraphy, n.d.). It designates an accumulation of unintended consequences of frenetic global economic development and technological innovation. The effects are concrete: they concern our atmosphere, our climate, our water supply, the acidity of our oceans, and accelerating losses of biodiversity. There is nothing abstract about this. We have apparently already flat-out transgressed four out of nine boundaries for the sustainability of life on the planet: ozone depletion, climate change, biodiversity loss, and nutrient pollution (International Commission on Stratigraphy, n.d.). Life itself has become fragile. We can no longer be sure that the biosphere will be able to sustain life—or life as we know it—on Earth.

2.7 Livingness

Life is (just) a matter of time. Indeed, never has time been more of the essence. We are measuring various indices like crazy, haunted by tipping points, or irreversible changes in relation to the conditions that sustain life on Earth. In spite of our ideology of infinite economic growth and perpetually accelerating innovation—or perhaps because of it—a strange limit now haunts us, a totality closes in. With our entry into the Anthropocene age there has been a seepage of finitude from the concrete level of experience into what we had always taken to be an infinite reach, one suggested by the abstract time of mathematics. Chronos, become vulnerable, has fallen into a kind of virtual finitude. Chronology might not go on forever, at least not on this planet—at least not for us. As the biosphere presents itself to us now as a closed system, a system of limits and boundary conditions required to support life, it might no longer be possible to separate chronological, or abstract, time from the concrete, or lived, time of duration. The two regimes of time that Bergson so adamantly distinguished may have begun to collapse into one another. The economic culture of globalization has introduced an uninvited guest into our picture of the biosphere, a planetary "we" that we hardly know how to think. It is not the familiar "we" of the discourse of human rights. Or the "we" of liberal democracy. It is a "we" that goes beyond the limits of our species. We might call it a "we the living."[46] Life is (just) a matter of time. But for how long will the biosphere continue to enjoy that opening to time, to borrow Bergson's phrase, that marked for him the fundamental difference in kind between the living and the artificial, the living and the inert, the living and the dead?

The Anthropocene epoch, "geological age of our own making," implies an unprecedented entangling of human and natural forces (Working Group on "Anthropocene"). Just as some thought we had begun to wrest ourselves free from the grip of nature by extraordinary feats of science and technological engineering that promised to free us from the contingencies of evolution, we find our fate inextricably tied up with that of natural forces, even if, or precisely because, these are mediated as indirect and unwanted consequences of human agency. We are caught up in the structure Jacques Derrida called "autoimmunity"—"that strange behavior where a living being, in quasi-*suicidal* fashion, 'itself' works to destroy its own protection, to immunize itself *against* its own immunity" (Borradori and Derrida, 2003, p. 94, original emphasis). The adventures of synthetic and executive biology (of bioengineering and biotechnology) that appeal to the possibility of saving lives through medical application belong to a larger structure of technological and economic overextension that is rendering life (as we know it) precarious on a planetary scale.[47] "We have got to a point in human history where we simply do not have to accept what nature has given us," says one synthetic biologist (Jay Keasling, bioengineering professor at UC Berkeley, cited in Specter, 2009). Perhaps, but it seems that nature doesn't have to accept what we have given it, or done to it, either. If the Anthropocene means that the fate of the forces we once called "nature" and those of mankind are intertwined, then just when we thought we were done with nature it has come back to haunt us, putting life very concretely into question and so raising for us, quite urgently, the question of livingness. In our "post-natural" world (where "nature" is understood as something outside us that nevertheless holds us) we might say that it is not nature, or even life (more and more conceived of by contemporary scientists in terms of codes, bio bricks, genetic toolkits, or computational simulations) but rather livingness that is more than ever at stake (see Latour, 2004). We can invest in sublime feats of geo-engineering (Bill Gates has recently made a $125 million gift to Harvard for research in bio-engineering).[48] We can financialize life, but the more we leave nature behind the more we face the urgency of questions of life, without any adequate way of thinking beings in their livingness.[49] Life has become an abstract concept, one that can be instantiated in marketable commodities both organic and artificial. Livingness, on the other hand, is concrete; it takes place in time across systems (transversally, as Deleuze might say) and across agents and environments. Livingness occurs on the level of the smallest organism all the way up to the biosphere. "Like the whole universe [*l'univers dans son ensemble*]," Bergson writes, ". . . the living organism exists in concrete time [*est chose qui dure*]. Its past prolongs itself completely in the present, remaining alive and active there" (507).[50]

2.8 Emergence(s)

Carl Woese, the celebrated microbiologist, saw emergence as a new direction for biology, an opportunity to shift away from the mechanistic approaches of molecular biology that turned more and more to engineering protocols (Woese, 2004). But molecular biology introduced information terminology into the language of biology, transforming it conceptually (Emmeche, 1994a). Digital technologies have introduced a computational notion of emergence. Today emergence pertains to complexity—the "science of the 21st century"—and implies the self-organizing features of complex adaptive systems (Stephen Hawkins cited in Sanders, 2003). Today, however, the ultimate complex adaptive system (CAS) is the cyber system. The cyber network, in other words, has displaced evolution as the paradigm of emergence.

Bergson challenged mechanism and its determinism from the perspective of emergence at the turn of the last century. He was interested in evolution, reproduction, growth, and aging as emergent phenomena, which for him meant phenomena marked by the inscription of active time, time that operates from within. Today, many of these questions have been reconfigured within a new, timeless, discourse of emergence. The origin of life has been rephrased as a problem of production, of producing life. Evolution has been rephrased as a question of design, that is, of interventions in natural evolution for discrete purposes of functional improvement, of creating new species and altering existing ones. Reproduction has been rephrased as self-replication—"an organism 'lives' when its code is executed," we read and "there are usually various methods allowing self-replication" (Wikipedia, n.d.). Craig Venter, biologist and entrepreneur (and one of the first to sequence the human genome) has succeeded in reproducing the DNA of a bacterium, altering it, and inserting this product into an empty cell; the synthesizing procedures of natural processes then play out until, after a few generations, a population of bacteria comes into being with the DNA signature of the altered genetic code. He claims to have created "a very real, self replicating cell" that "most biologists would be unable to readily distinguish from the naturally occurring counterpart" (Venter and Gibson, 2010). He claims to have produced "life."[51] Is it possible that computer calculation, upon which the science of emergence depends, has not only devitalized older, animistic theories of emergence, but devitalized, functionalized, and financialized our very concept of life, leaving us with a lifeless conception of life comparable to the timeless notion of evolution Bergson critiqued in *Creative Evolution*, his challenge to Spenser—life in the age of mechanical (re)production? (Emmeche et al., 1997; Benjamin, 2008). When we call artificial creatures "alive" is it really just a matter of definition, and can we really speak of emergence in this context?[52]

Although popular journalistic accounts of emergence, and YouTube videos about the "new biology," suggest one unified notion of Emergence that has moved beyond the old arguments between mechanists and vitalists, more scholarly literature reveals that there are various levels and kinds of emergence, as well as conflicting interpretations of emergence and conflicting definitions of life. Synthetic biologists consider their science emergent not only because it concerns life and novelty (the production of new species of organisms) but also because of its methods. It requires big data processing and involves complexity because of the scale of computation that it requires. Synthetic biologists seek functional results with commercial, and sometimes humanitarian, promise. Craig Venter wants to problem-solve on a large scale. He dreams of creating organisms that will produce clean energy, feed the hungry all over the world, and decontaminate polluted areas of the natural world. The interventions he envisions in his redesign of the natural world, and of evolution, are targeted, discrete, and instrumental.

But not everyone agrees that we can speak of emergence in this context. Some critics maintain that, precisely because of the targeted, functional, nature of the properties that are manipulated (or created) by the procedures of synthetic biology, this science cannot claim to be truly emergent. According to the philosopher Jaegwon Kim (in an oft-cited article), "to reduce the gene to a DNA molecule we must first prime the target properly, by giving it a *functional* interpretation—that is by construing it in terms of the causal work it is to perform" (Kim, 1999, p. 10, original emphasis). For Kim, emergent properties must display non-functionability. "Will the system exhibit *E* [an emergent property] at time *t*?" he asks; "Can we predict this from knowledge of what goes on in the base domain? Yes, because given the functional definition of *E* we can in principle identify the realizer of *E* from the system solely on the basis of knowledge of the causal/nomic relation in the base domain" (Kim, 1999, p. 14). Kim makes a distinction between inductive and theoretical predictability and claims that "even emergent properties are inductively predictable" (Kim, 1999, p. 8). He adds that "we may have a well-confirmed 'emergence law' to the effect that whenever a system instantiates basal condition *M* it instantiates an emergent, *E*" (Kim, 1999, p. 8). He concludes that "emergentism may yet be an empty doctrine. For there may not be any emergent properties, all properties being physical properties or else functionalizable and therefore reducible to physical properties" (Kim, 1999, p. 18). Truly emergent properties, according to Kim, would be intrinsic, that is properties "that cannot be functionalized," such as *qualia* or phenomenal properties of consciousness (Kim, 1999, p. 18).

Like Synthetic biology, Artificial life (or A-life)—which either produces digital simulations of living systems (weak A-life, as in the Open Worm Project already mentioned), creates "living organisms" with the help of computers in mechanical (robotic) or wet, chemical, material (strong A-life), or creates "living" things simply by manipulating information (computer-generated life)—is considered to be emergent not only because it produces novelty, but because of its complexity (for these distinctions see Olson, 1997; Emmeche, 1993). It lays claim to computational emergence, as do fields such as artificial intelligence and cognitive science that depend on a cybernetic idea of self-organizing systems (Emmeche, 1997a). The theoretical biologist Claus Emmeche suggests that the vastly enhanced computational powers of computer modeling have led to a "final 'devitalisation' of the concept of emergent wholes because the emergent phenomenon is usually considered merely a 'collective effect' . . . of a very large number of local, mechanical or computational interactions on the lower levels of the system that generates coherent behavior when the system is described by macroscopic parameters" (Emmeche, 1997a).

As the claims of A-life researchers get stronger (especially when it comes to what is known as "computational life") the challenges to the notion of computational emergence intensify. Peter Cariani, for example, points to false claims to emergence which he characterizes as simply being developments that exhibit a deviation, in a system, from the observer's model of it. Artificial life simulations (weak A-life) will "always be non-emergent" because "by starting the simulation again on the same machine, with the same program and input values, one gets exactly the same state transitions during the simulation where the same patterns will evolve."[53]

Although scientific researchers might prefer to steer clear of philosophical discussion, seeking practical results, Luciano Floridi, a philosopher of information, argues convincingly that one cannot fully separate certain kinds of scientific claims (claims that concern life, for example) from metaphysical and epistemological concerns.

Synthetic biology, which considers DNA sequences as blueprints for living organisms, and Artificial life, which argues that simulations are equivalent to living organisms (or, even more strongly, that digital information can realize new forms of life) both presuppose a digital ontology, that is, an ontology of discrete elements, or bits, that maintains that information is real and that the real is fundamentally informational. From this perspective, simulations would be considered the equivalents of real life systems—realizations of life—because ontologically the two would be considered the same. To hold that artificial life is equivalent to organic life implies a digital, binary logic and a classical ontology of discrete units.[54]

In addition to these metaphysical issues there are epistemological concerns when it comes to computational emergence, concerns that turn on the crucial role of the observer in computer simulations. Whereas, as we have seen, Claus Emmeche (citing Cariani) addresses the question of the role of the observer in computational emergence, Floridi emphasizes the importance of "levels of abstraction" (LOA, a concept derived from computer science) with respect to claims made on the basis of computational emergence or through computer modeling. The LOA takes into account the position of the observer and, partly on this basis, determines relations between a data set and the information that data set can be said to yield.[55] "Knowing at which Level of Abstraction the system is being analyzed," Floridi argues, "is indispensable for it means knowing the scope and limits of the model being developed."[56] In a Kantian move, Floridi suggests that "our knowledge of the world" is "inescapably mediated by some level of abstraction," and depending on this level, the world can manifest itself as digital or analogue, just as, in quantum physics, light can manifest itself as wave or particle.[57] Similarly, Claus Emmeche argues that although defining life in A-life terms as the "natural selection of replications" (where natural selection is simulated by a programmed randomness) "seems to imply life as an emergent phenomenon," in fact "simulated self replication is not complete," as it would be in an organic cell, because it "needs the information in the embedded program and the computers that run it" (Emmeche, 1997b). It depends, in other words, on material causal conditions. According to Emmeche, "A-life sees their computational or man-made representations of life processes not just as simulations but as 'realizations' . . . realizing enough properties to be considered alive." However, he argues, digital replication is not the same thing as reproduction, and simulation is not the same as a realization of life. Emmeche reminds us that "human ascription of symbolic terms and categories to the natural systems we observe" implies "mediation by human language" and does not coincide with "the real processes in these systems as real entities" (Emmeche, 1994a). We recall that it was precisely this kind of distinction between the abstract (the symbolic or representational) and the concrete that was the point of departure for Bergson's elaboration of duration, upon which his distinction between living beings (which display an openness to time) and non-living, or artificial, ones, depends. On closer inspection then, the distinctions Bergson insisted upon remain pertinent to philosophers of science and of information who seek alternatives to a genocentric, or computational, perspective and to a digital ontology. To accept artificial life as life, then, is to accept "another concept of life"—life as an abstract, immaterial phenomenon (Emmeche, 1994a). It is, Emmeche writes, "not even life as an abstract phenomenon, it is the life of abstract concepts ascribed to a specific interpretation of formal computational structures" (Emmeche, 1994a). It is one that restricts the notion of life to "self propagating patterns of information"—a shadow of life, we could say, adapting Bergson's phrase.[58]

To computationalism and digital ontology Claus Emmeche opposes the perspective of biosemiotics, which emerged in the 1990s as a field in the philosophy of biology that sought to counter reductionist, or genocentric, biological perspectives with an alternative understanding of information, or at least of relations between information processing and life. There are other distinctive features of living systems that A-life neglects (or could only simulate abstractly): metabolism, homeostasis, evolution, and interactions with the environment, including biological time; biosemiotics, which studies life processes as sign processes, takes these into account.[59] Against a digital, or computationalist, perspective, biosemiotics holds that "a sign must materially incarnate its meaning," and proposes a "qualitative organicist account of embodiment."[60] From this perspective the informational activities of living organisms (and their emergent properties) are not programmed, but intrinsic. They are material and interactive with respect to the organism's surroundings.

Biological time, which involves a material, or biochemical, sign system that both operates internally and regulates the organism's relations to its external surroundings, is now generally accepted as a universal feature of life (see Pihlajamaa-Glimmerveen, 2005). The time regulators are not mechanical, or abstractly informational signs; they operate in relation to various concrete rhythms such as passages from day to night (discerned through qualities of light) and the regular activities of other creatures that belong to the same ecosystem. Time, in this sense, implies a co-ordination of multiple rhythms in a way that interconnects all living beings. "Everywhere something lives," Bergson wrote, "there is open somewhere an inscription of time" (508).[61] Internal and adaptive, biological time, which could be said to operate biosemiologically, suggests Bergson's notion of concrete duration rather than abstract, chronological, time. What is more, biosemiotics treats the "organism's own experience of . . . light" (which often serves as a time signal) as something ontological (Emmeche, 2007, p. 464).[62] As a biosemiotic phenomenon, biological time would be an aspect of livingness, then, understood as an ongoing dynamic interrelatedness of beings of varied levels of complexity, inscribed in interconnected ecosystems.

2.9 Virtual Life

The detour through Bergson's insistence on the distinction between the living and the non-living, or the artificial—one based on an openness to time—suggests that Emergence is not a new scientific turn that leaves the old disputes between vitalism and mechanism behind. On the contrary, the tensions and stakes of that argument appear to remain very much in play. Different concepts of emergence carry different ontological and epistemological implications, which in turn produce different social effects. Functionalist and computational versions of emergence tend to isolate specific properties, or forms, from environments, in view of targeted results. Indeed, one might wonder what "environment" might mean in a computer, or computational, context, or in a worldview that holds that a simulation is equivalent to life. Digital ontology fits well with social philosophies that are themselves computationally based and largely abstract. From this perspective beings can appear substitutable one for another and processes can be conveniently privatized. The embodied, qualitative perspective enhances our sense of concrete singularity, on the one hand, and of the dynamic interconnections between beings on the other. Floridi's philosophy of information places epistemological constraints on our quest for mastery which today seems to be heating up dramatically, even as we—the living—become more vulnerable in our livingness.

Luciano Floridi suggests that "the best way of tackling the new ethical challenges posed by ICTs may be from an environmental approach, one which does not privilege the natural or untouched, but treats as authentic and genuine all forms of existence and behavior, even those based on artificial, synthetic or engineered artefacts."[63] I take this to mean that it is essential to include the artificial, the synthetic, or the engineered in our considerations (what Emmeche refers to as the societal embodiment of the cybody) (Emmeche, 2007, p. 468), but not that we should conceptually collapse the difference between "natural" and "artificial." Just as we make a distinction between virtual reality and what we call "reality," and, as the recent marketing strategies of Google glasses demonstrate, seek a balance between the two in our everyday lives, so we can make a distinction between the virtual, the simulated, or the synthetic and the organic when it comes to life. One might wonder what the interests are that encourage us to collapse this distinction (instead of thinking hybridity) all the while appealing to the scientific brand of Emergence, which appears to naturalize this conceptual shift toward the artificial.[64]

In Bergson's figure of the swollen cyborg body, political and social problems fester in the void between the living and the artificial, indeed they constitute that void. So political and social problems fester in our own scattered cyborg culture. When scientific research is primarily subsidized by private companies and biologists, along with computer scientists, become entrepreneurs, targeted efforts at problem-solving become more and more ambitious. They also become more and more entangled with new practices of privatization—the financialization of life—and with issues of politics, power, and capital. Who will pay for the much-vaunted medical treatments of the future and who will have access to them? Who will control the decontamination efforts that require big computing? Who will control the effects of computing itself, which directly contaminates the environment?[65] ICTs can collect vast supplies of data concerning our increasingly frail environmental conditions, but who will receive the warnings based on this digital monitoring? And just what will the largely poor communities who live in regions most vulnerable to the effects of climate change do in response to these warnings? What about transnational effects, and unintended consequences? The same YouTube that flaunts the powers of synthetic biology in medical research anticipates more frequent and more virulent pandemics, inviting an ever-increasing dependency on pharmaceutical interventions. Living systems, of course, are always in flux and will respond to pharmaceutical interventions as well as to other features of our global culture.[66] Biopower, in such circumstances, is no longer an issue of state control over the lives and bodies of citizens, as Michel Foucault theorized; it operates on a global scale, that is, on the scale of our biosphere, in the absence of political institutions that might legislate interventions in life as we know it with respect to the needs of humans and non-humans.

To bring Bergson's perspective of emergence to bear, critically, on contemporary biology (and scientific culture more broadly) is not to suggest that one should turn one's back on the informational or technological dimensions of our contemporary world. Clearly, this would be neither possible nor desirable. Nor, however, can we accept to have our concept of life completely absorbed into a register of the abstract, the artificial, or the computational. We will need to think clearly about the kinds of ethical, political, and environmental problems that our increasingly technological world engenders in the era of global capital. What concept of life will we presuppose as we do so? “Attention to life,” Bergson wrote, is required to keep humans from falling into dreamland (312).[67] But to what will we attend? And in what time? What is livingness—human and non-human—becoming?

Notes

1. Dmitry Itskov is funding the 2045 Initiative, whose goal is to upload human brains into robotic avatars. *The New York Times* reports that he has been funding research labs at MIT, Harvard, and UC Berkeley. See Segal (2013).
2. Bergson (1963), p. 508. Subsequent references to Bergson’s *Œuvres* will be given in parentheses in the text and will refer to this edition. All translations from Bergson are mine. References to corresponding English editions will be given in the subsequent notes. For this citation, see Bergson (2007), p. 11.
3. Bergson (2007), p. 10.
4. Bergson (1935), p. 306.
5. Bergson (2007), p. 14.
6. Bergson (2007), p. 19.
7. Bergson (1968), p. 27.
8. Bergson (1921), p. 221.
9. Bergson (1968), p. 110.
10. Bergson (1968), p. 110.
11. Bergson (2007), p. 3.
12. Bergson (2007), p. 3.
13. Bergson (1921), p. 200.
14. Bergson (2007), p. 29.
15. Bergson (2007), pp. 29–30.
16. Bergson (2007), p. 5.
17. Bergson (2007), p. 1.
18. Bergson (1991), p. 150.
19. Bergson (1991), p. 150.
20. Deleuze speaks of a “leap into ontology” on Bergson’s part in *Creative Evolution*, in Deleuze (1991), p. 57. See Guerlac (2006), ch. 5 for a discussion of Deleuze’s reading of Bergson.
21. Bergson (2007), p. 7.
22. Bergson (2007), p. 202.
23. Bergson (2007), pp. 57, 163; Bergson (1935), pp. 85–86.
24. Bergson (2007), p. 12.
25. Bergson (2007), p. 10.
26. Bergson (2007), pp. 13–14.
27. Bergson (2007), p. xxxv.

28. Bergson (1935), p. 306.
29. Concerning Bergson's previous uses of this figure, see Guerlac (2012). I recapitulate here part of the argument made at greater length in that essay.
30. Bergson (1935), pp. 298–299.
31. Bergson (1935), p. 298.
32. Bergson (1935), p. 299.
33. Bergson (1935), p. 306.
34. Bergson (1935), pp. 296–297.
35. Bergson (1935), p. 294.
36. Bergson (1935), p. 295.
37. Bergson (1935), pp. 293–294.
38. Bergson (1935), p. 296.
39. This was probably because Bergson invokes a notion of mysticism and appeals to the Christian sentiment of Charity, which he glosses as a love that passes through all living beings.
40. Bergson (1935), p. 288. For a contemporary version of this perspective, with an emphasis on sustainability in the face of climate change, see Rifkin (2013).
41. See Potts et al. (2001). Byrne et al. (2001) write that "[m]edical advances have rendered our earlier notions (or criteria or tests or definitions) of death obsolete [. . .]. Through the power of our technological means, the dead may now appear as alive" (p. 24).
42. For more on this project, see OpenWorm (2011–13).
43. Madrigal (2013). Madrigal cites the organizer of the Open Worm Project, Stephen Larson.
44. Madrigal (2013), my emphasis. Larson does not propose a new logic of the in-between. He proposes functionalism as a convenient way of bracketing philosophical questions (both metaphysical and epistemological) through a targeted, pragmatic approach that remains true to the binary logic of an implied digital ontology and a classical ontology of things. By contrast, biosemiotics, which we shall discuss further on, does propose a ternary logic, that of Charles Sanders Peirce.
45. For an overview of the Anthropocene epoch, see Anthropocene (n.d.). Citing from Moore et al. (2001).
46. I would distinguish this from Chakrabarty's notion of a "universal new subject" in a "new universal history of humans" and emphasize the importance of envisaging a notion of livingness that is not dominated by the human, and that, more as Bergson suggests in *The Two Sources of Morality and Religion*, passes through all living things. See Chakrabarty (2009), and a discussion of it in Dibley (2012).
47. In Enriquez (2003), the author emphasizes the wealth production (and redistribution) associated with knowledge of genetic code.
48. Gate's gift was intended to "uncover the engineering principles that govern living things and use this knowledge to develop technological solutions for

the most pressing healthcare and environmental issues facing humanity." See Harvard Magazine (2008).

49. In Cooper (2008), the author speaks of "the expansion of commercial processes into the sphere of 'life itself' " (p. 3). See also Sunder Rajan (2006); Sunder Rajan (2012); Peters (2012).
50. Bergson (2007), p. 10.
51. "Can we create new life out of our digital universe?" he asks in his Ted Talk, and responds affirmatively. Venter (2008).
52. For a notion of "ontodefinitions," of which the definition of life is a special case, see Emmeche (1997b).
53. Emmeche (1997a) suggests that there are truly emergent features in cellular automata, although this is contested by some. He mentions Cariani's critique here and in Emmeche (1994b), p. 151. See Cariani (1992). For another critical challenge see Baas (1991).
54. For a critique of digital ontology from an informational perspective see chapter 14 in Floridi (2011). A version of the chapter—the version cited here—is available online: http://www.philosophyofinformation.net/publications/pdf/ado.pdf.
55. Floridi (n.d.) ("Against digital ontology"): "Reality is experienced, conceptualized and known as digital or analogue depending on the level of abstraction (LOA) assumed by the epistemic agent when interacting with it" (p. 13).
56. Floridi (n.d.) ("Against digital ontology"), p. 22.
57. Floridi (n.d.) ("Against digital ontology"), p. 24.
58. Bergson (1921), pp. 132–133. Emmeche (1997b) associates this view with Dawkins, who, he writes, "embedded his view of gene selection in a reductionist metaphysics of which only the replicating structures were the real entities in evolution, while organisms were like ephemeral, transient epiphenomena."
59. See Emmeche (1999): "Biosemiotics is distinctive, both in relation to the dominating theoretical paradigms in biology and in relation to other kinds of semiotics. In biosemiotics, the focus of attention is neither the natural selection of replicating molecules or genotypes (as it is in the traditional and still dominating paradigm of neodarwinism), nor the operational closure of an autopoietic system (as it is in the alternative paradigm of autonomous systems), but the sign-links and interpretants of various semiotic agents on all biological scales; from molecular recognition to cellular self/non-self-distinction; from the molecular semantics of gene expression and regulation to the semantics of inter-organism communication from *E. coli* to elephants; from individual cognition to the swarm intelligence of ants and humans" (pp. 97–98).
60. Emmeche rehearses the principles of Charles Sanders Peirce's general semiotics in Emmeche (2007). He adds that "meaning always has to be embodied in signs but need not be confined to organic bodies" (p. 467). He maintains an emergent hierarchy of embodiments that passes from the cellular level

to anthropological and societal levels where cyborg embodiment comes into play through the human dependence on smart machines.

61. Bergson (2007), p. 11.
62. An example of this kind of inner experience of life forms without brains might be the phenomenon of chemotaxis exhibited by bacteria. See Vladimirov and Sourjik (2009). The authors write: "Chemotaxis allows swimming bacterial cells to follow chemical gradients in the environment by performing temporal comparisons of ligand concentrations" (p. 1097).
63. Floridi (n.d.) ("The Information Society and Its Philosophy"), p. 10.
64. I am using the term "naturalize" here in the sense of Roland Barthes, in *Mythologies*, where it means to take something as given, instead of considering it ideologically, that is, as historical or constructed.
65. See International Telecommunication Union (2008).
66. See Pacific Biosciences (2011).
67. Bergson (1991), p. 173. On "attention to life" in Bergson, and the related notion of "attachment to life," see Lapoujade (2005).

References

Anthropocene (n.d.). Welcome to the Anthropocene: A planet transformed by humanity. Retrieved from <http://www.anthropocene.info/en/earth-system>.

Baas, N. A. (1991). Emergence, hierarchies, and hyperstructures. In C. G. Langton (ed.), *Artificial Life III, Santa Fe Institute Studies in the Science of Complexity, Proceedings XVII* (pp. 515–537). Redwood City, CA: Addison-Wesley.

Bedau, M. A., McCaskill, J. S., Packard, N. H., Parke, E. C., and Rasmussen S. R. (2013). Introduction to recent developments in living technologies. *Artificial Life*, 19(3–4): 291–298.

Benjamin, W. (2008). *The Work of Art in the Age of its Technological Reproducibility and Other Writings on Media* (ed. M. Jennings, B. Doherty, and T. Y. Levin). Cambridge, MA: Harvard University Press.

Bergson, H. (1921). *Time and Free Will: An Essay on the Immediate Data of Consciousness* (trans. F. L. Pogson). New York: Macmillan.

Bergson (1935). *The Two Sources of Morality and Religion* (trans. R. A. Audra and C. Brereton). New York: Henry Holt.

Bergson, H. (1937). *Laughter: An Essay on the Meaning of the Comic.* (trans. C. Brereton & F. Rothwell). New York, NY: The Macmillan Company.

Bergson, H. (1963). *Œuvres.* Paris: Presses Universitaires de France.

Bergson, H. (1968). *The Creative Mind* (trans. M. L. Andison). New York: Greenwood Press.

Bergson, H. (1991). *Matter and Memory* (trans. N. M. Paul and W. S. Palmer). New York: Zone Books.

Bergson, H. (2007). *Creative Evolution* (ed. K. A. Pearson, M. Kolkman, and M. Vaughan; trans. A. Mitchell). New York: Palgrave Macmillan.

Borradori, G. (Interviewer) and Derrida, J. (Interviewee) (2003). Autoimmunity: Real and symbolic suicides. A dialogue with Jacques Derrida. In G. Borradori, *Philosophy in a Time of Terror: Dialogues with Jürgen Habermas and Jacques Derrida* (pp. 85–136). Chicago, IL: University of Chicago Press.

Byrne, P. A., O'Reilly, S., Quay, P. M., and Salsich, P. W. Jr. (2001). Brain death: The patient, the physician, and society. In M. Potts, P. A. Byrne, and R. G. Nilges (eds.), *Beyond Brain Death: The Case Against Brain Based Criteria for Human Death* (pp. 21–89). Dordrecht: Kluwer Academic Publishers.

Cariani, P. (1992). Emergence and artificial life. In C. G. Langton, C. Taylor, J. D. Farmer, and S. Rasmussen (eds.), *Artificial Life II, Santa Fe Institute Studies in the Science of Complexity, Proceedings X* (pp. 775–796). Redwood City, CA: Addison-Wesley.

Chakrabarty, D. (2009). The climate of history: Four theses. *Critical Inquiry*, 35: 197–222.

Cooper, M. (2008). *Life as Surplus: Biotechnology and Capitalism in the Neoliberal Era*. Seattle, WA: University of Washington Press.

Deleuze, G. (1991). *Bergsonism* (trans. H. Tomlinson and B. Habberian). New York: Zone Books.

Dibley, B. (2012). "Nature is us": The Anthropocene and species-being. *Transformations*, 21. Retrieved from <http://www.transformationsjournal.org/journal/issue_21/article_07.shtml>.

Emmeche, C. (1993). Is life a multiverse phenomenon?" In C. G. Langton (ed.), *Artificial Life III, Santa Fe Institute Studies in the Science of Complexity, Proceedings XVII* (pp. 553–567). Redwood City, CA: Addison-Wesley.

Emmeche, C. (1994a). The computational notion of life. *Theoria—Segunda Epoca*, 9(21): 1–30. Retrieved from <http://www.nbi.dk/~Emmeche/cePubl/compnolife.html>.

Emmeche, C. (1994b). *The Garden in the Machine: The Emerging Science of Artificial Life* (trans. S. Sampson). Princeton, NJ: Princeton University Press.

Emmeche, C. (1997a). Appendix to Explaining emergence—toward an ontology of levels. Retrieved from <http://www.nbi.dk/~emmeche/coPubl/97e.EKS/emerg.cutout.html>.

Emmeche, C. (1997b). Defining life, explaining emergence. Retrieved from <http://www.nbi.dk/~Emmeche/cePubl/97e.defLife.v3f.html>.

Emmeche, C. (1999). The biosemiotics of emergent properties in a pluralist ontology. In E. Taborsky (ed.), *Semiosis. Evolution. Energy: Towards a Reconceptualization of the Sign* (pp. 89–108). Aachen: Shaker Verlag.

Emmeche, C. (2007). A biosemiotic note on organisms, animals, machines, cyborgs, and the quasi-autonomy of robots. *Pragmatics & Cognition*, 15(3): 455–483.

Emmeche, C., Køppe, S., and Stjernfelt, F. (1997). Explaining emergence: Towards an ontology of levels. *Journal for General Philosophy of Science*, 28: 83–119.

Enriquez, J. (2003). The life codes that will reshape the future [Video file, February]. Retrieved from <http://www.ted.com/talks/juan_enriquez_on_genomics_and_our_future.html>.

Floridi, L. (n.d.). Against digital ontology. Retrieved from <http://www.philosophyofinformation.net/publications/pdf/ado.pdf>.

Floridi, L. (n.d.). The information society and its philosophy: Introduction to the Special Issue on "The philosophy of information, its nature and future developments." Retrieved from <http://www.philosophyofinformation.net/publications/pdf/tisip.pdf>.

Floridi, L. (2011). Against digital ontology. In *The Philosophy of Information* (pp. 316–338). Oxford: Oxford University Press.

Griffin, D. R. (1986). *Physics and the Ultimate Significance of Time: Bohm, Prigogine, and Process Philosophy*. Albany, NY: State University of New York Press.

Guerlac, S. (2006). *Thinking in Time*. Ithaca, NY: Cornell University Press.

Guerlac, S. (2011). Humanities 2.0: E-learning in the digital world. *Representations*, 116(1): 102–127.

Guerlac, S. (2012). Bergson, the void, and the politics of life. In A. Lefebvre and M. White (eds.), *Bergson, Politics, and Religion* (pp. 40–60). Durham, NC: Duke University Press.

Harvard Magazine (2008). $125-million gift for bioengineering. *Harvard Magazine*, October 7. Retrieved from <http://harvardmagazine.com/breaking-news/125-million-gift-for-bioengineering>.

International Commission on Stratigraphy (n.d.). Working Group on the "Anthropocene." Submissions on Quaternary Stratigraphy. Retrieved from <http://quaternary.stratigraphy.org/workinggroups/anthropocene/>.

International Telecommunication Union (2008). ICTs for e-environment: Guidelines for developing countries with a focus on climate change. Retrieved from <http://www.itu.int/ITU-D/cyb/app/docs/itu-icts-for-e-environment.pdf>.

Itskov, D. (n.d.). 2045 Strategic Social Initiative. Retrieved from <http://www.2045.com>.

Kim, J. (1999). Making sense of emergence. *Philosophical Studies: An International Journal for Philosophy in the Analytic Tradition*, 95(1–2): 3–36.

Lapoujade, D. (2005). The normal and the pathological in Bergson. *Modern Language Notes*, 120(5): 1146–1155.

Latour, B. (2004). *Politics of Nature: How to Bring the Sciences into Democracy* (trans. C. Porter). Cambridge, MA: Harvard University Press.

Latour, B. (2013). Facing Gaia: A new inquiry into natural religion. *Gifford Lectures* [Video files]. Retrieved from <http://www.ed.ac.uk/schools-departments/humanities-soc-sci/news-events/lectures/gifford-lectures/archive/series-2012-2013/bruno-latour>.

Madrigal, A. C. (2013). Is this virtual work the first sign of the singularity? *The Atlantic*, May 17. Retrieved from <http://www.theatlantic.com/technology/archive/2013/05/is-this-virtual-worm-the-first-sign-of-the-singularity/275715/>.

Moore, B. III, Underdal, A., Lemke, P., and Loreau, M. (2001). 2001 Amsterdam Declaration on Earth System Science. Challenges of a Changing Earth: Global Change Open Science Conference. Amsterdam, The Netherlands, July 13.

Retrieved from <http://www.igbp.net/about/history/2001amsterdamdeclarationonearthsystemscience.4.1b8ae20512db692f2a680001312.html>.

Olson, E. T. (1997). The ontological basis of strong artificial life. *Artificial Life*, 3(1): 29–39.

OpenWetWare (n.d.). Retrieved from <http://syntheticbiology.org/>.

OpenWorm (2011–13). Retrieved from <http://www.openworm.org>.

Pacific Biosciences (2011). New biology. Part II: Cancer [Video file]. Retrieved from <http://www.youtube.com/watch?v=nV6E5i8YrPY>.

Peters, M. A. (2012). Bio-informational capitalism. *Thesis Eleven*, 110(1): 98–111.

Pihlajamaa-Glimmerveen, L. E. (2005). Biological clocks: Cells know the time. Retrieved from <http://www.glimmerveen.nl/le/biological_clock.html>.

Potts, M., Byrne, P. A., and Nilges, R. G. (eds.) (2001). *Beyond Brain Death: The Case Against Brain Based Criteria for Human Death*. Dordrecht: Kluwer Academic Publishers.

Rifkin, J. (2013). *The Third Industrial Revolution: How Lateral Power is Transforming Energy, The Economy and the World*. New York: Palgrave Macmillan.

Rose, M. R. and Oakley, T. H. (2007). The new biology: Beyond the modern synthesis. *Biology Direct*, 2(30).

Rubin, J. and Schadt, E. (Producers), and Farrell, G. and Schadt, E. (Creative Directors) (2011). *The New Biology* [Motion picture]. United States: John Rubin Productions Inc. Retrieved from <https://www.youtube.com/watch?v=sjTQD6E3lH4>.

Sanders, T. I. (2003). What is complexity? Washington Center for Complexity & Public Policy. Retrieved from <http://www.complexsys.org/downloads/whatiscomplexity.pdf>.

Segal, D. (2013). This man is not a cyborg. Yet. *The New York Times*, June 1.

Seung S. (2013). *Connectome: How the Brain's Wiring Makes Us Who We Are*. Boston, MA: Mariner's Books, Houghton Mifflin Harcourt.

Silver, P. (n.d.). Silver Lab in OpenWetWare. Retrieved from <http://openwetware.org/wiki/Silver_Lab>.

Specter, M. (2009). A life of its own: Where will synthetic biology lead us?. *The New Yorker*, September 28. Retrieved from <http://www.newyorker.com/reporting/2009/09/28/090928fa_fact_specter>.

Sunder Rajan, K. (2006). *Biocapital: The Constitution of Postgenomic Life*. Durham, NC: Duke University Press.

Sunder Rajan, K. (ed.) (2012). *Lively Capital: Biotechnology, Ethics, and Governance in Global Markets*. Durham, NC: Duke University Press.

Venter, J. C. (2008). Craig Venter: On the verge of creating synthetic life. Ted Conferences, LLC. Retrieved from <http://www.ted.com/talks/craig_venter_is_on_the_verge_of_creating_synthetic_life.html>.

Venter, J. C. and Gibson, D. (2010). How we created the first synthetic cell. *The Wall Street Journal*, May 26.

Vladimirov, N. and Sourjik, V. (2009). Chemotaxis: How bacteria use memory. *Biological Chemistry*, 390(11): 1097–1104.

Wikipedia (n.d.). Artificial life. Retrieved from <http://en.wikipedia.org/wiki/Artificial_life>.

Woese, C. R. (2004). A new biology for a new century. *Microbiology and Molecular Biology Reviews*, 68(2): 173–186.

Zalasiewicz, J., Williams, M., Steffen, W., and Cutzen, P. (2010). The new world of the Anthropocene. *Environmental Science and Technology*, 44(7): 2228–2231.

3

On "Relational Things": A New Realm of Inquiry

Pre-Understandings and Performative Understandings of People's Meanings

John Shotter

Abstract: It is still far too easy in organization studies research to assume (1) that words stand for things; (2) that we put our thoughts into words; and (3) that when we enter into a new situation, we can begin straightaway to act within it to achieve our own ends. But we cannot immediately embark upon studying emergent processes for we first need to relate our outgoing anticipatory activities in an intelligible way with their incoming results. We need to understand what is around us, not as objects, but in terms of their *meanings*. A new ontological realm of inquiry would seem to be required, concerned not with acquiring new *knowledge* as such, but with developing our *embodied sensitivities* to previously unnoticed aspects of circumstances troubling us. This chapter outlines the nature of this new realm of inquiry, and what we need, initially, to focus on in our studies instead.

We must recognize the indeterminate as a positive phenomenon

(Merleau-Ponty, 1962, p. 6)

Nothing is more difficult than to know precisely *what* we see

(Merleau-Ponty, 1962, p. 58)

In recent years, there has been in the West a radical change in our modes of investigation, a movement of thought unprecedented since our adoption of Greek modes of argumentative inquiry, focused on the "shapes" or "forms" of things, more than 2,000 years ago. Under the influence of such thinkers and writers as Wittgenstein, Bakhtin, and Voloshinov, Mead and Dewey, and Merleau-Ponty (among many others), not only have some of us moved away from a concern with the supposedly fixed (i.e. eternal) but hidden properties of *objects* in the world "out there," as well as away from a concern with events supposedly occurring privately inside the heads of individuals, but we have also ceased our search for "*ideal* realities hidden behind appearances." Instead, we have turned to a direct focus on the unique concrete details of our living, dynamic, bodily involvements—or *participations*—in and with the world around us.

In so doing, we have become concerned both with what goes on *inside* the different "worlds of meaning" we *create* within our *meetings* with the others and othernesses around us, and with noticing the ever-present *background* flow of spontaneously unfolding, reciprocally responsive *intra*-activity[1] between us and our surroundings, against which our expressions have their meaning. It is as "participant parts" within this flow, considered as a dynamically developing, complicated whole, that we have our being as members of a common culture, as members of a social group with a shared history of development between us. It is the recent recognition of this previous unnoticed background of spontaneously responsive, living bodily activity, and its role in "setting the scene," so to speak, within which we grasp the *specific meaning* of people's actions, that I want to explore below.

It is this turn to living *worlds of meaning*, to worlds in which people come to share distinctive anticipations as to each other's future actions in otherwise indeterminate, fluid, not-yet-finalized circumstances, thus to coordinate their activities with each other, that has been difficult to implement and sustain in social theory and organization studies. But the fact is, if we are unable to anticipate, at least partially, how the others around us *will* respond to our actions in each of the *unique* situations within which we happen to find ourselves, organized social life would become impossible. We would have no sense of what, sequentially, *should follow* from what—no sense that a particular expression should be answered in a particular way; an offer by an acceptance or rejection; a question by an answer; and so on—and thus, no capacity as members of a social group to coordinate our activities with those of others.

However, in a Cartesian world of already determinate mechanisms merely awaiting our discovery of them, the effort to place meaning as such at the centre of social theory has had a checkered career. In the classical Cartesian/Newtonian world of separate particles of matter in motion according to pre-established laws, we have assumed the task of science to be that of discovering the *formal* nature of these basic constituents along with their causal relations, and that we should pursue this task by seeking to *prove* our proposed theoretical *representations* of their causal relations *true*. Crucial to this endeavor, of course, was the assumption that once a theory was proved *true*, everyone would both understand and agree with it and find it a fitting basis for their future actions.

As Heinrich Hertz (1894/1956) put it in his *Principles of Mechanics*: "The most direct, and in a sense the most important, problem which our conscious knowledge of nature should enable us to solve is the anticipation of future events, so that we may arrange our present affairs in accordance with such anticipation" (p. 1); and he can be credited with providing the following succinct account of this theory-based, formal approach to how best to conduct our inquiries:

> In endeavouring . . . to draw inferences as to the future from the past, we always adopt the following process. We form for ourselves images or symbols of external objects; and the form that we give them is such that the necessary consequents of the images in thought are always the images of the necessary consequents in nature of the things pictured. In order that this requirement may be satisfied, there must be a certain conformity between nature and our thought. (p. 1)

Yet, strangely, this "instrumental" criterion of truth, if we can call it so, allows for a considerable degree of loose-jointedness in the relations between our theories and the actual character of our surroundings. Indeed, as Hertz went on to comment:

> we do not know, nor have we any means of knowing, whether our conceptions of things are in conformity with them in any other than this *one* fundamental respect. The images we may form of things *are not determined without ambiguity* by the requirement that the consequents of the images be the images of the consequents. (p. 2, my emphasis)

In other words, as Hertz recognized, there is always a great deal of indeterminacy at work even in our most precise formulations of our claims to truth.

3.1 Words, Meanings, and Anticipations: People Coordinating Their Actions With Each Other

I begin with these remarks from Hertz for a number of reasons. One is to do with his influence on Wittgenstein (1953), in orienting him towards his view of philosophy as entailing a critical description of *actual language use* (of which more later), and his claim that there is a kind of philosophical investigation to do with revealing "what is possible *before* all new discoveries and inventions" (no. 126)—that is, a realm of inquiry, not usually considered as crucial in our inquiries into *human, social* phenomena, to do with making clear *what*, in an intrinsically indeterminate circumstance, is in fact available for empirical study *within* it. While in the classical Cartesian/Newtonian world, we can study the world as it is, i.e. seek to discover the facts of the matter, in a still developing, indeterminate, fluid world, our task is to discover available *possibilities* for taking steps that have not ever been taken before. In short, our concern is with *novelties* not *regularities*. Another reason is to do with Hertz's emphasis on the role of our anticipations of the future in shaping our current actions—an issue that I want to relate both to Dewey's (1929/1958, 1938/2008) and to Bakhtin's (1981) account of their importance in the effectiveness of our communications, but also, again, to emphasize the importance of Wittgenstein's focus on language *use*—for the different ways in which we *word* our sense of a circumstance, i.e. give verbal expression to it, will arouse different *anticipations* in our listeners, and can easily (mis)lead them into taking an inappropriate next step.

To turn first to Hertz's influence on Wittgenstein (1953): Immediately after having set out the centrality of the theory-testing approach to the nature of physical reality, Hertz went on to outline a very special set of problems occurring in science, problems arising not out of our lack of empirical knowledge, but out of "painful contradictions" in our ways of *representing* such knowledge to ourselves. Examples for Hertz at the time of his writing arose out of people's talk of "force" and of "electricity"—sometimes "force" was the *cause* of motion, but at other times, with centrifugal force, it was the *effect* of motion; similarly, sometimes "electricity" seemed to be something *static* (a charge created by friction) and at other times *fluid* (as a current conducted through copper wires).

He wondered: "Can we by our conceptions, by our words, completely represent the nature of any thing? Certainly not," he said (1894/1956, p. 7), but the fact is, such painful ambiguities do not plague us with *all* our talk of things as such. For instance, he notes, "why is it that people never in this way ask what is the nature of gold, or what is the nature of velocity?" (p. 7). "I fancy," he says,

> that the difference must lie in this. With the terms "velocity" and "gold" we connect a large number of relations to other terms; and between all these relations we find no contradictions which offend us. We are therefore satisfied and ask no further questions. But we have accumulated around the terms "force" and "electricity" more relations than can be completely reconciled amongst themselves. We have an obscure feeling of this and want to have things cleared up . . . When these painful contradictions are removed, the question as to the nature of force will not have been answered; but our minds, no longer vexed, will cease to ask illegitimate questions. (pp. 7–8)

This lack of a *direct* "hook-up" between theory and reality may not worry most natural scientists, but it should, I think, worry those of us concerned with human affairs. For in studying people, one should be concerned, not just with truth in an "effective" or "instrumental" sense, but with the "ontological adequacy" of our expressions as to whether they do justice to *the whole being* of persons and their relationships.

But to be able to judge that, we must first know what human beings "are," and what their relationships are like. And that problem, as Hertz makes perfectly clear, cannot be solved (without undecidable ambiguities to do with "appropriateness") by formulating models and looking for "conformities" between their products and human products. The discovery of *what* something "is" for us—a "situation," say—can only be discovered from a study, not of how we talk *about* it in *reflecting* upon it, but of how "it" as a whole necessarily "shapes" those of our everyday communicative activities in which it is involved, *in practice*—"its" influence is revealed to us in the "grammar" of such activities.

Thus, as Wittgenstein (1953) realized, arriving at a comprehensive sense of *what* a situation *is* for us, is not a matter of collecting evidence as a scientist, but a matter of our "moving around" within it (in actuality or in imagination) to gather a fragment here and another there in such a way as to gain a grasp of it as a hermeneutical whole, even though we lack a vantage point from "on high," so to speak, to "look down" on it as a whole—it is a "view from the inside," much as we get to know our way around within a city by living in it, rather than from being able to see it all at once from an external standpoint. As Wittgenstein (1953) put it, it is a grasp that "compels us to travel over a wide field of thought criss-cross in every direction," so that the philosophical remarks he provided as a result of his investigations, "are, as it were . . . sketches of landscapes which were made in the course of these long and involved journeyings" (p. ix)—and as such, portray *features* of those landscapes worthy of our attention, features whose *meaning* is of possible importance to us, features that arouse in us *anticipations* as to what next might be connected to them.

As I intimated above, the assumption that a theory proved to be *true* would provide everyone with a solid basis for their future actions, is simply wrong. Conversationally, a theory has the character of a "report" on past events, while what is needed, if we are to help those around us coordinate their activities with ours, is a "telling"—a statement such as "I think we need to take the employees' point of view here seriously," is not a report on the speaker's knowledge of certain facts, but an indicator to listeners as to what next the speaker might go on to do. As Dewey (1929/1958) puts it:

> The heart of language is not "expression" of something antecedent, much less expression of antecedent thought. It is communication; the establishment of cooperation in an activity in which there are partners, and in which the activity of each is modified and regulated by partnership. To fail to understand is to fail to come into agreement in action; to misunderstand is to set up action at cross purposes. (p. 179)

Thus, "To understand is to anticipate together, it is to make a cross-reference which, when acted upon, brings about a partaking in a common, inclusive, undertaking" (pp. 178–179).

Similarly, Bakhtin (1981) also notes the orientation towards the future of much of our talk:

> The word in living conversation is directly, blatantly, oriented toward a future answer-word; it provokes an answer, anticipates it and structures itself in the answer's direction. Forming itself in an atmosphere of the already spoken, the word is at the same time determined by *that which has not yet been said but which is needed and in fact anticipated by the answering word*. Such is the situation of any living dialogue. (p. 280, my emphasis)

This all means—although it may be somewhat awkward to say it—that we cannot regard the goal of our inquiries as a simple search for "the truth." No matter how well supported by evidence, inquiries that do not result in people being able to act *in the future* in concert with each other in a way that was impossible for them in the *past*, must be accounted as giving rise to words "empty" of shared meanings.

My concern below, then, is with what is involved in our coming, first, to a *shared sense* of a shared circumstance, to which we can then give—in our efforts to partake in a common, inclusive, undertaking (Dewey)—*shared linguistic expression,* thus to arouse shared anticipations of a precise kind in each other making coordinated action possible.

Thus central to the new realm of inquiry that I want to introduce is the fact that, as living beings, instead of the classical Cartesian/Newtonian world of separate particles in motion, we live immersed within an oceanic world of ceaseless, intra-mingling currents of activity—many quite invisible—currents of activity which in fact influence us much more than we can influence them. We are not like machines with already well-defined inputs, leading to equally well-defined outputs, unresponsive to the larger contexts in which we must operate. We are much more like plants growing from seeds, existing within a special confluence, rooted within the chiasmic intra-acting (Barad, 2007, 2013) of many different flowing streams of energy and materials that our bodies are continually working to *organize* in sustaining us as viable human beings. Buffeted by the wind and waves of the social weather around us we inhabit circumstances in which almost everything seems to merge into everything else; we do not and cannot observe this flow of activity *as if* from the outside. Indeed, it is too intimately interwoven with all that we are and can do from within it for it to be lifted out and examined scientifically as an object—for after all, wherever we move, we will still find ourselves within one or another region of it. We are too immersed in it to be aware of its every aspect. We are thus continually uncertain as to *what* the situation *is* that faces us, and *how* we might act within it for the best.

Yet we are not often taken totally by surprise. We are aware that certain situations are more conducive to actions we desire than others; we know in some vague general sense that different surroundings "call out from us" different kinds of activities. Thus, for the writing of this chapter, for instance, rather choosing to sit elsewhere, I come first to sit at my desk, with my books and other reading matter close to hand.[2] Yet even here, within a chosen circumstance, I am still radically uncertain as to how, precisely, to "journey" towards a final, satisfactory outcome to my efforts, for after all, I am seeking to say something novel, something new, something that *will* "answer to" my initial sense of a lack of "something-or-other" (Dewey, 1938/2008; Todes, 2001). I make a number of false starts; thankfully, however, my *tryings* seem to be an important aspect of the process—a part of me clarifying to myself exactly *what* it is that I am trying to do. As Todes (2001) points out:

> Whenever there is a distinction in active felt experience between what I try to do and what I do do, it is because I fail to do what I am trying to do, and

> because I thereby, to some extent, and at least momentarily, lose my poise—becoming disoriented in my circumstances, losing track of, and thereby losing, both myself and my circumstances, and dimming the entire world of my experience. (p. 70)

3.2 Relational Things Exist Only *In* Our Dynamical Relations To Our Surroundings

What is special about relational things, is that they only become *rationally visible* to us (Garfinkel, 1967)[3] from within the dynamic *relations* occurring between our outgoing *anticipatory* activities towards our surroundings and their incoming results. So although they can exert very real influences on and in our actions, they are in fact invisible and non-locatable, as well as initially being indeterminate. Their influence in our actions only becomes more specific in terms of the "names" we give to them, the words in terms of which we try to describe their nature—words which clearly do not "stand for them" as things. Indeed, as both Bateson (1979) and Ryle (1949) comment, "relational things" are of a different "logical type" from the seemingly *Bounded, Self-Contained, Separate, Visible* (BS-CSV) objects that we can manually grasp and physically move around in reconfiguring our surroundings in our daily affairs.

Ryle (1949) introduces such relational entities via the following example:

> A foreigner visiting Oxford or Cambridge for the first time is shown a number of colleges, libraries, playing fields, museums, scientific departments and administrative offices. He then asks "But where is the University?" It has then to be explained to her or him that "the University is not another collateral institution . . . the University is just the way in which all that he has already seen is organized." (pp. 17–18)

In other words, the foreigner has failed to recognize that the notion of a university—as an *organized* collection of observable but disparate entities—is of a different logical type or category from the separate, visible entities in which it consists.

The most notable sphere in which we continually make such mistakes is in our attempts to *describe* our own everyday human, social activities. For continually, as Ryle (1949) points out, we use "achievement-verbs" when we should provide an "orchestrated" sequence of "task-verbs," along with their criteria of satisfaction. In other words, we continually talk of "arrivals" and/or "achievements" when we really should speak, not only of the "journeyings" and/or the "tryings" (as well as of the satisfactions we achieve or not, as the case may be, by each step we take along the way), but also of the overall *guiding tension* initially aroused within us by each new bewildering situation that motivates our efforts at "bringing it into focus," so to speak. We far too easily act as if the situation is of an already determinate kind of which we are merely ignorant, rather than it in fact being indeterminate and open to our efforts to determine it in one way or another.

Thus to assume, as many investigators do, that *ideally* we should proceed to inquire into our everyday affairs as professional scientists do in their experiments is, to my mind at least, to confuse hermeneutical, perceptual, and ontological issues, with rational, cognitive, and epistemological ones. It is to (mis)describe a co-emergent, back-and-forth, essentially hermeneutical process—in which "I" as a *Subject* experiencing a certain kind of "thing" in the world, and an *Object* experienced *as* that "thing," arise together in the act of experience—as a cognitive and epistemological process, concerned merely with our thinking "about" our bewilderment in a linear, rational manner. But, to repeat, the reference of the words we use in our talk of such "objects," of such "things," can be identified only within the instance of discourse within which they are contained and being used; their reference in other instances, more likely than not, will be different.

Our task, then, to repeat, is that of finding our "way about" (Wittgenstein) within the different realms of language use within which we participate in our inquiries. As Ryle (1949) somewhat sarcastically puts it: "Theorists have been so preoccupied with the task of investigating the nature, the source, and the credentials of the theories that we adopt that they have for the most part ignored the question what it is for someone to know how to perform tasks" (p. 28). Indeed, theorizing itself is a practice, and as such, may be intelligently or stupidly conducted, and clearly, we need to know what we are *doing* in our doing of it, i.e. how our practices of inquiry influence *what* it is we take ourselves to be inquiring into. What, then, are we trying to deal with here? Why are we always so uncertain, always so anxious as to whether our intended *best* actions are in fact for the best?

3.3 Don't Ask for the "Content" of an Action or Utterance, But What It Is "Contained In"

> An expectation is embedded in a situation from which it takes its rise
>
> (Wittgenstein, 1981, no. 67)

The answer seems to be that, although we easily tend to assume in our everyday talk that we are dealing with clearly nameable, well-defined things, the fact is that we are not; we are continually having to deal with "relational things." And relational things are not at all like the seemingly BS-CSV objects to which we readily give names in our everyday affairs. They are "things" like "language," "meaning," "speech," "trust," "power," "respect," "care," "person," "worrying," "hurrying," the simple act of uttering a "question" and gaining an "answer" to it, and countless other supposed "things" we give names to in our everyday affairs. In a sense, in their lack of a spatial form, they are not thing-like at all; they cannot be "pictured"; yet we continually give names to them as if they can be. In the field of organization studies, they are things like: "organization," "management," "leadership," "strategy," "innovation," "values," "culture," "bureaucracy," and so on, and so on. And as we talk amongst ourselves about such things, we assume we are all talking about the *same thing* when we are not. The fact is, the reference of these terms can be identified only within the instance of discourse within which they are contained. This is why a new realm of inquiry—that is clearly oriented towards inquiring into the strange, invisible nature of relational things—is required.

Immersed, then, in an already ongoing flow of intermingling influences, unaware of its *orienting* effects upon us, we simply find ourselves, conscious of *seeing* and *hearing* (and *smelling* and *touching*) various already familiar and nameable "things" in our surroundings. We also find occurring within ourselves, unconsciously, various distinctive, dynamical *feeling shapes*, so that amongst some of our very first important experiences, are feelings of love and comfort, of rejection and anger, of friendliness, of helplessness and unfairness, and so on—which, as infants (*in-fans*—without speech), we express performatively (in our actions), but later, learn to express in words. For, in growing into a culture of, literally, "like-minded" and "like-speaking" others, we must learn to *use* words as the others around us use them. But to do this, as Wittgenstein (1953) makes clear, "if language is to be a means of communication there must be agreement not only in definitions but also (queer as this may sound) in judgments" (no. 242).

This is so because, if it really is the case that each new, never before encountered, initially indeterminate situation needs to be distinguished and responded to uniquely *"as itself"*—as a "singularity" in physicists' terms, or as a "relational thing" in our terms here—then we cannot be told *about* it in linguistic terms *representative* of objective "things" already well known to us; that would only be to say what it was *like*, while ignoring its unique *differences* from what is already familiar to us. We need first to "introduce" ourselves, or be "introduced" by others to it, so to speak, to become acquainted with it as an *organized* unity (à la Ryle), and to acquire some expectations as to how it will, as such, respond to a range of our actions. For example: "How do I know that someone is in doubt?" asks Wittgenstein (1969). "How do I know that he uses the words 'I doubt it' as I do? From a child up I learnt to judge like this. *This is* judging" (nos. 127, 128). This is why, when we need to talk of relational things—things which can only be seen and heard in the unfolding temporal organization of a person's actions in relation to their circumstances—we must learn to make *judgments* as the others around us do. We must learn to *relate ourselves* to "somethings" in our surroundings linguistically in a certain manner, to distinguish them and then to describe them *being like* Xs rather than *like* Ys, while still being different from them, and thus still amenable to other *likenings* as well.[4]

The acquisition of this awareness of certain very general characteristics of human life and experiences in the (always still developing) course of our first language learning, is crucial to all our activities as members of a particular social group, as members of a culture. Yet, strangely, although we cannot get outside of it to determine its nature objectively, just because it determines for us our most basic ways of making sense of events occurring around us, what we *find* ourselves feeling at any one moment—what we find is familiar to us and what is bewildering, what is real and matters to us and what is illusory, and so on—we can come to know its nature indirectly, by comparing and contrasting its nature *here* with its nature *there*, at different times in different places.

We can get to know of its nature *from the inside*, differentially, just as we can come to know our way around within a new city, by exploring it increasingly, in all its detail. We think we can get from A to S via F, only to find the way blocked by a river; we then search for a bridge and an alternative route (for we take it for granted that, as in other cities[5] (look at note), people build bridges over rivers). And this is the case for us all, not just as leaders, but as ordinary persons acting in the everyday world around us: we continually have to act into an uncertain, "fluid" future, while at the same time assuming that if one way forward proves impossible, another can quite readily be found.

In adopting this *insider's* approach, we must give up Descartes' (1968) vision of an already pre-established world of "particles of matter in motion according to already existing laws"—a world in which he had hoped, with the appropriate methods of rational thought, that we could become "masters and possessors of nature" (p. 78)—and embrace instead the very strange new world of our everyday social lives together in which there are no such pre-existing "some-things" which are *separate* from anything else. For it is a world in which every "thing" is always *in* movement, in both senses of the word, i.e. as always moving along within a larger movement, as well as moving within itself.

Thus the conceptual shift required is a profound one; everything changes; many basic assumptions will need to be reversed. Indeed, we would like to switch, if we could, to a verb-based language away from our noun-based way of talking; to a language in which many "things" would be *known* to us in terms of their *dynamical appearances* within our surroundings instead of in terms of their *static forms*. Rather than merely in terms of our finalized *experience* of them, we need to know them in terms of our *experiencing* of them; for it is in their still open, unfinished unfolding that they arouse a felt tension within us, a uniquely particular feeling, that can both motivate our next step as well as guide us in our execution of it in relation to our surroundings. It is our ignoring of the *unique particularity* of these motivating and guiding feelings that is our crucial mistake, a mistake that cannot be rectified by the provision of objective descriptions, no matter how detailed or complex they may be.[6]

But we cannot easily "verb" our noun-based terms: our language—as a paradigmatic "relational thing"—is one of those all-encompassing "things" within which we are so immersed that we cannot get outside of it. We owe our very existence as autonomous, self-responsible *persons* to our embedding within its ongoing flow. And even if we could, it would not in itself overcome the difficulties we face in coming to an overall, orienting sense of *what* it *is*, in particular, that we are trying to inquire into, for "it" is known to us as more that simply an image. As Ryle (1949) pointed out above, the University of Oxford, as such, becomes known to us as an *organization* of a whole collection of bits and pieces of the University, gathered at different times in different places into a hermeneutical whole. In other words, it consists in a *uniquely* organized sense of a set of *unmerged* particulars, a unity within which a collection of particulars are inter-linked with each other without losing their particularity—as such, it constitutes a unique structure of expectant feelings to which we can refer in guiding our talk in relation to the University of Oxford.

This capacity—to organize fragments of experience, gathered at different times in different places into a hermeneutical unity—seems to be a very basic human capacity, recognized as such, long ago. Indeed, both Weick (2010) and I (Shotter, 2012) refer to Theseus' line in Shakespeare's

Midsummer Night's Dream, in which he describes how "imagination bodies forth the form of things unknown," and how the poet's pen can then go on to give "airy nothing / A local habitation and a name." But what if we draw back from trying to *name* such airy "no-things," and instead, by imaginatively moving about within them—and by *feeling* or *sensing* similarities and differences in their nature *here* compared with their nature *there*—begin to acquaint ourselves with their overall distinctive nature? In other words, in Wittgenstein's (1953) terms, instead of *naming* them, we set ourselves the task of coming to know our "way about" (no. 123) within them.

But as Wittgenstein (1953) realizes, although we are not searching for something hidden behind appearances, but for something "that already lies open to view," it only becomes what he calls "surveyable (übersichtlich)," i.e. sensed as an interconnected whole, "by a rearrangement" (no. 92), by the fragments being presented to us in such a manner we can easily grasp their interconnections—we need a "perspicuous representation (übersichtlich Darstellung)," for it only will produce "that understanding which consists in 'seeing connections'" (no. 122). Gadamer (2000) expresses the hermeneutical task entailed here in a similar manner:

> The subject matter appears truly significant only when it is properly portrayed for us. Thus we are certainly interested in the subject matter, but it acquires its life only from the light in which it is presented to us. We accept the fact that the subject presents different aspects of itself at different times or from different standpoints. We accept the fact that these aspects do not simply cancel one another out as research proceeds, but are like mutually exclusive conditions that exist by themselves and *combine only in us*. (p. 284, my emphasis)

And it is in this sense that I am claiming that we need to orient ourselves towards *a new realm of inquiry*, a form of inquiry in which we are not so much concerned "to hunt out new facts" or "to learn anything *new* by it," as "to *understand* something that is already in plain view. For *this* is what we seem in some sense not to understand" (Wittgenstein, 1953, no. 89). Even though nothing is hidden from us and it is all before our eyes, we are bewildered because we are *looking at* it, or *looking over* it, i.e. surveying it, with an inappropriate set of expectations as to *what* we can see as possibly of importance to us within it. What is needed, suggests Wittgenstein (1980), is "a working on oneself . . . On one's way of seeing things. (And what one expects of them)" (p. 16). Our task, then, as agents of inquiry, is to look over the circumstances before us in relation to our end in view, and to organize what we see *here* and what we see *there* in relation to it, thus to gain a sense of the field of possibilities available to us in making our way towards it.

3.4 Inquiring Into Understandings-Exhibited-In-Our-Actions: Pre-Understandings and Performative Understandings

> The meaning of a question is the method of answering it . . . . Tell me *how* you are searching, and I will tell you what you are searching for
>
> (Wittgenstein, 1991, pp. 66–67)

So, to state the issue facing us in a somewhat convoluted fashion: What *is* involved in our conducting inquiries into how best we might conduct inquiries into our practices? As a first step in answering this question, we must, I think, accept that we face *two* very different kinds of difficulties in our everyday, practical lives, not just one. In the past, we seem to have thought of *all* our difficulties as *problems* that, with the fashioning of an appropriate intellectual (theoretical) framework, can be *solved* by the application of systematic, i.e. rational, thought. There is, however, another more primary difficulty that we need first to overcome *before* problem-solving as such becomes a possibility for us: we need to get oriented, to arrive at a *sense* of *what* the situation *is* within which we must act; we need to know the nature of the opportunities for, and barriers against, as well as the resources for our acting within it; the influence of our surroundings on our actions. Lacking orientation, we find ourselves as if in a thick fog, not knowing where our first step will land. There is thus a realm of "pre-understandings" (Heidegger) that we *show* or *exhibit* in our particular "performative understandings" (Austin) when acting in a given situation. It is these understandings-exhibited-in-our-actions that we need to investigate. But how?

Some time ago, William James (1890, vol. 1) described the *sensings*, the *feelings* guiding us in our acting, as being not like bounded entities with a clear beginning and a clear end, but as being "*feelings of tendency*, often so vague that we are unable to name them at all" (p. 254), but which, nonetheless, crucially function as "*signs of direction* in thought, of which we have an acutely discriminative sense, though no definite sensorial image plays any part in it whatsoever" (p. 253).

It is James' "acutely discriminative sense" that can be the basis of our inquiries. The meaning of a question for us is revealed, for example, as Wittgenstein (1991) points out, in the ways we move about, both out in the world and in our inner mental activities, in our attempts to answer it—the focal unit of study here, being the unfolding sequence of events occurring between our initial sensing of a tension being created within us by its asking and the subsequent exploratory movements we execute in our attempts at satisfying that tension.

But the execution of this back-and-forth, hermeneutical-like process is not a simple matter. As we know from those cases in which people have had their sight restored after having been blind since early childhood, even the sustaining of a stable visual field is a skilled, bodily achievement. Practice at it is required in learning it. In being ignorant of our body's work in achieving a stable world around us, we fail to appreciate the role of "being oriented," of being "in a distinct context" that arouses in us distinct anticipations as to what next to expect (Todes, 2001). As I indicated above, if we are to relate ourselves to "things" which can only be seen and heard and felt within the unfolding temporal organization of people's actions in relation to their circumstances, we must learn to make *judgments* about them as the others around us do—an intricate process of negotiation with the others and othernesses around us, with a *developmental trajectory* to it, is involved. It is not a mere process of pattern recognition, as is often assumed—for once the tension provided by the open incompleteness of a process comes to an end, is satisfied, its role in motivating and guiding the process also comes to an end; nor is it a simple matter of decision-making (Shotter and Tsoukas, 2014). To repeat yet again: It is only by *sensing* and *feeling* similarities and differences as we move about with a situation that we can come to a grasp of its nature.

In other words, in coming to know how to bring words to a new situation in a way in which we can be sure that the others around us *will judge* as meaning what we intend them to mean, we must hermeneutically "place" the situation within a whole web of relationships amongst the rest of what is already known to us. Involvement in doing this, as Kuhn (2000) has recently pointed out, is not a matter of translation—of now saying that something already well known to us in everyday terms is *really* best specified in the terms of a theory, as in learning a *second* language—but is, in fact, a continuation of our *first* language learning:

> When the exhibit of examples is part of the process of learning terms like 'motion', 'cell', or 'energy element', what is acquired is knowledge of language

> and of the world together [i.e. *in relation to* each other]. On the one hand, the student learns what these terms mean, what features are relevant to attaching them to nature, what things cannot be said of them on pain of self-contradiction, and so on. On the other hand, the student learns what categories of things populate the world, what their salient features are, and something about the behavior that is and is not permitted to them. In much of language learning these two sorts of knowledge—knowledge of words and knowledge of nature—are acquired together, not really two sorts of knowledge at all, but two faces of the single coinage that a language provides. (Kuhn, 2000, p. 31)

Thus, rather than treating ourselves as already having a complete mastery of our first language, we must even as adults, it seems, sometimes still treat ourselves as still having to learn, to distinguish, and to respond to the unique *what-ness* of previously unencountered "things"—that is, while still learning to make judgments as to what, linguistically, we should talk of them as *being* in ways similar to how those around us will judge them.

Exhibiting examples is of crucial importance, for as Wittgenstein (1969) remarks: "Not only rules, but also examples are needed for establishing a practice. Our rules leave loop-holes open, and the practice has to speak for itself" (no. 139). Speak? Well yes. For, in showing a student an example, we do not simply statically display a static object and leave students to their own devices; we present it this way and that, draw their attention to different aspects of it, and so on. As Merleau-Ponty (1964) says, in remarking on the cave paintings of Lascaux: "I would be at great pains to *say where* is the painting I am looking at. For I do not look at it as I do at a thing; I do not fix it in its place. My gaze wanders in it as in the halos of Being. It is more accurate to say that I see according to it, or with it, than that I see it" (p. 164). Each new "thing" we encounter—whether a relational thing or not—has its own unique *way of being what it is*, and our first learning to see *it* as a nameable something involves us in *letting it* "tell us," so to speak, as a partner in a communicative activity, how to relate ourselves to it (Shotter, 2006), and this is not a simple matter. Indeed, as I remarked earlier, what an event *is* cannot be found within the event itself; it can only become known to us in terms of *its relations* to the larger context within which it is "contained" (Bateson, 1972/2000).

Clearly, others have noted this fact. For instance, Robichaud, Giroux, and Taylor (2004), in arguing that in the literature to do with exploring the use of language in organizing our activities, the role of recursivity in our talk has been largely overlooked, have introduced the concept of *the metaconversation*. In studying citizens' complaints to a city's mayor about "potholes" in the roads and sidewalks, what they noted first was the use of talk relating to disturbances or breakdowns in a normal order of things, talk to which all involved could relate to, whilst also, in being preoccupied with topics and persons in common, and thus linked to each other, they made similar distinctions to each other. In other words, these aspects of their talk—that they call the metaconversation—set the scene, so to speak, within which each of the specific complaints made by the citizens can be more precisely understood. Indeed, as Robichaud et al. (2004) put it: "The outcome is coorientation, in the sense of a commonality of attention: both citizens' and city administration's attention focussed on the same *object of value*—the state of the streets and sidewalks—although in different ways" (p. 626). Boje (2001) also, with his concept of "antenarrative"—which he defines as a "bet" that a "pre-story" will become a full-fledged narrative—similarly draws our attention to the importance of those context-determining activities without which our talk is, literally, senseless. In short, without the effort to outline what our actions and/or utterances are "contained in," we can have no idea of their "content," of their precise meaning.

What Robichaud et al. (2004) and Boje (2001) draw to our attention here is an important aspect of our everyday activities. But what about our more deliberately conducted research inquiries? As Dewey (1938/2008) makes clear, instead of beginning them by trying to form theories or conceptual frameworks—which, as Dewey sees it, are often so "fixed in advance that the very things which are genuinely decisive in the problem in hand and its solution, are completely overlooked" (p. 76)—we should begin our inquiries by being prepared to go "into" our perplexities and uncertainties, "into" the feelings of disquiet aroused by the circumstances confronting us, for strangely, it is precisely within these feelings, if we take trouble to explore them further, that we can begin to find the guidance we need in overcoming our disquiets. For, says Dewey (1938/2008), "the peculiar quality of what pervades the given materials, constituting them [as] a situation, is not just uncertainty at large; it is a unique doubtfulness which makes that situation to be just and only the situation it is. It is this unique quality that not only evokes the particular inquiry engaged in but that exercises control over its special procedures" (p. 109). Indeed, as Dewey sees it, the *qualitative character* of the situation we inhabit is pervasive both in space and in time, it not only

> binds all constituents into a whole but is also unique; it constitutes in each situation an *individual* situation, indivisible and unduplicable. Distinctions

> and relations are instituted *within* a situation . . . A universe of experience is the precondition of a universe of discourse . . . The universe of experience surrounds and regulates the universe of discourse but never appears in the latter. (p. 74)

Thus for Dewey, it is only as a result of our "sensitivity to the quality of a situation as a whole" (p. 76) that we can come to a precise grasp of a problem as the problem it is—in short, "a problem must be felt before it can be stated" (p. 76).

Such feelings, however, while providing us with motivation and a degree of guidance in our exploratory efforts to find an appropriate way forward, although crucial in that they are quite specific to the particular circumstance within which we find ourselves, can never bring us certainty. Indeed, we are, after all, always facing an indeterminate circumstance whose nature is intrinsically uncertain, never mind whether what we tell ourselves and others we *want* within it truly captures what we in fact *need*.[7] Our real needs often only become clear to us retrospectively, in the course of our attempts at achieving our desires. As Todes (2001) puts it, "the meeting of a need . . . always involves a confirmatory recognition of the need met, a recognition that retroactively determines the true nature of the need that prompted the activity culminating in its filling" (p. 177). For example, we continually feel the prior possession of a causal explanation, expressed in the *general* terms of a theoretical framework, *will* be a help in our deciding how to act in each new, *particular* circumstance we encounter. Whereas, our real need is for an articulated sense of its "inner landscape," the unique "field of possibilities" it actually offers us for a pathway through it—a need that is only slowly becoming clear to us in the face of our continual failure to arrive at such an overall, explanatory scheme.

In suggesting above, then, that we face *two* very different kinds of difficulties in our everyday, practical lives, not just one, i.e. problems that need solving, but difficulties of orientation, to do with arriving at a *sense* of *what* the situation *is* within which we must act, I am suggesting both, that the pre-understanding in terms of which we embark on our inquiries "set the scene," so to speak, for *what* we will focus on and think of ourselves as inquiring into—the relational things that we will give names to—and that the performative understandings that become available to us within our *doings* along the way, will guide us in our journeyings, as we seek to "know how to go on" (Wittgenstein, 1953, no. 154) together with the others around us.

3.5 Conclusions

> The notion of *intra-action* (in contrast to the usual 'interaction', which presumes the prior existence of independent entities/relata) represents a profound conceptual shift. It is through specific agential intra-actions that the boundaries and properties of the components of phenomena become determinate and that particular concepts (that is, particular material articulations of the world) become meaningful. (Barad, 2007, p. 139)

While in the physical sciences we can be concerned just with the truth of our theories, in our activities in the still developing, fluid world of human, living activities, things are very, very different. Instead of seeking truth in a merely effective or instrumental sense, of getting "the facts" right, we face the task of not only doing ethical justice to *the whole being* of persons and their relationships, but also of being sensitive—in outlining the *possibilities* for future developments in present circumstances to which we draw attention—to the political character of our proposals. Thus what I have suggested above, then, is that it is in the very nature of all the bewildering, confusing, or questionable situations that we face in life, i.e. situations provoking inquiry, to be in some degree indeterminate, to be in their very nature, unsettled, and as such, still open to further specification. In short, to *be* now and forever fluid. Consequently, the emergence of novelty as such is a more pervasive phenomenon than we might initially assume. As Garfinkel (1967) so nicely puts it, each time that we make sense of an essentially indeterminate circumstance, and account for the events occurring within it, *as* familiar, commonplace happenings, we do so always "for 'another first time'" (p. 9).

But here we must be careful. For our capacity to do this can easily mislead us into thinking that the fluidity within which we are immersed is of a *general* kind, whereas, what I have also tried to suggest above, is that it is always a *quite specific* fluidity; and that the specific currents flowing in whatever circumstance within which we happen to find ourselves, influence very greatly *what* we can experience as happening within it. Indeed, these unique currents are present and pervasive in the flow of the situation from start to finish, making it to be just and only the situation it is. And it is the unique quality of these currents that not only provoke the particular inquiries we engage in, but which also exercise control over the forms of investigation we try to adopt. In other words, novelty is pervasive.

If Karen Barad's (2007, 2013) account of *intra-action* is correct, as opposed to our more usual assumption of inter-action, then this entails that the organizational "things" that we *name* as topics of importance in organization studies—such things as "organizations," "leadership," "communication," "innovation," "management," etc., and think of as existing out in the world, along with what we take to be important in our inquiries, such things as "language," "ideas," "theories," "knowledge," "meanings," or "observations," and study as the products of processes hidden within the heads of individuals—are *all* better talked of as emerging within material *intra*-actions occurring within the flow of activities occurring out in the world at large. For, in enacting what Barad (2007) calls *"agential cuts"* (p. 140), i.e. taking some aspects of our situation as subjective and others as objective in different ways at different times as we are acting within it, "we do not uncover pre-existing facts about independently existing things" (p. 91); instead, we "enact *agential-separability*—the condition of *exteriority-within-phenomena*" (p. 140), a functional separation appropriate to the purposes at hand.

This is what is entailed if we are to act in the moment. But all too often in our inquiries, we come on the scene too late (after we have already situated ourselves as confronting a specifically formulated "problem"), and look in the wrong direction (towards its possible "causes"), with the wrong attitude in mind (in a search for "objective facts"). In so doing, we fail to appreciate *the body's role in "focussing" us on, and keeping us "in touch with" those aspects of our surroundings of importance to us.* We fail to appreciate that it is *only* within the unfolding dynamics of our living relations with our circumstances that we can find the "action guiding calls" we need to provide us with an anticipatory sureness, thus to be able "to-follow-what-is-still-to-come." If we stop moving in an effort to try to "think" what will happen next, our "felt sense" of "where" we are will disappear. It is this realm of *sensings*, of *action guiding feelings*, that is crying out for investigation—and which cannot be conceptualized as propositional knowledge—as Argyris (2003) suggests[8]—as it provides the shared basis by which those within an intellectual community recognize only certain statements as being "propositional statements."

If, instead, we accept that we ourselves bring such *relational things* into existence as "facts" in relation to our purposes in the moment of our activities, then, although we might talk in our studies of the causal influences at work in various organizational activities—such as leading, managing, collaboration, risk-taking, decision-taking, team-building, knowledge management and transmission, innovation, etc.—all such influences can *only* be seen as *having been at work* in people's performances *after* they have been achieved; and this is the case with many other such topics of study in organizational research. Something else altogether is guiding us in the performance of our actions in relation to our surroundings than the "named things" we claim to have discovered in our research. It is the nature of this "something else," and how it can be publicly studied, that I have been trying to bring attention to here.

If we cannot work at seeking patterns, orders, or regularities, etc., amongst pre-existing objective entities, and must work with ephemeral *relational things*, what can we focus on, with what can we begin our inquiries? We can make use of James' (1890) "acutely discriminative sense" in picking out what Garfinkel (2002, p. 68) calls (awkwardly) *witnessable recognizabilities*, or what I have elsewhere called "real presences" (Shotter, 2003); that is, on the basis of our abilities to sense similarities and differences, we can point out to each other the *happening* of quite *specific* "thisnesses" or "thatnesses"—events which, even when they cannot be specifically named, nonetheless possess distinctive qualities which can, at least, be alluded to linguistically, as being *like* what is already well known amongst us. And it is in terms of such "pointings out"—"do it like *this* not like *that*"—that we can begin to teach practices well known to us to others.

As Wittgenstein (1953) remarks, with respect to our learning to judge the genuineness of other people's expressions of feeling—are they *really* being friendly to us, or just feigning it in order to get something from us?: "Can someone else be a man's teacher in this? Certainly. From time to time he gives him the right *tip*[9]—This is what 'learning' and 'teaching' are like here.—What one acquires here is not a technique; one learns correct judgments" (p. 227). In the new realm of inquiry I have introduced here, it is a "working on oneself" (Wittgenstein) that is required; that is, one needs to learn how *to be* a certain kind of person (Cunliffe, 2004), an ontological rather than an epistemological task.

Notes

1. The distinction between *intra-* and *inter-*action is due to Karen Barad (2007, 2013), and will be elucidated later.
2. While later, once the "inner landscape" of the topic (*topos*—place) of my concern has begun to take on some structure within me, I can meditate on it, i.e. imaginatively "move around" within it, while doing other things.
3. "Ethnomethodological studies analyze everyday activities as members' methods for making those same activities visibly-rational-and-reportable-for-all-practical-purposes, i.e., 'accountable,' as organizations of commonplace everyday activities" (Garfinkel, 1967, p. vii).

4. Working in terms of *likenesses* and *similarities* (and *differences*) rather than *correspondences*, i.e. identities, is central, as we will see, to the approach I am taking here.
5. There are in fact *very many general facts about cities*—that there are shopping areas, entertainment areas, banks, parks, modes of transport, apartments, etc.—which, once we have experienced a few cities, we come to expect to find in each new city we visit; without these characteristics, we would not want to call them cities. Similarly, from our unremitting immersion in the weather worlds of social life, we come to embody a whole realm of mostly unarticulated expectations that both guide us and constrain us in our efforts at *doing* some thing, expectations that we reveal to ourselves only in our performances. As Wittgenstein (1953) remarks, "such facts are hardly ever mentioned because of their great generality" (p. 56), but they are, nonetheless, of very great importance, in that they provide the "feels" guiding us within the invisible currents of activity within which we are trying to act.
6. Both Hosking (2005) and Weick (2010), for instance, have drawn our attention to the role of noun-forms and how *entitative thinking* disables our capacity to think imaginatively *into* the unfolding processes at work in our practices, and consequently become "disconnected" from the *particular* circumstances initially motivating our inquiries—see also Billig (2013) for an extensive account of how such talk *erases* agency.
7. Todes (2001) distinguishes between a need and a desire as follows: "A need, unlike a desire, is originally given as a pure restlessness; as the consciousness of one's undirected activity. It begins with the sense of a lack in oneself, *without* any sense of what would remove that lack" (pp. 176–177)—hence the fact that we are not always as clear as we might be as to what our real needs are.
8. "Actionable knowledge requires propositions that make explicit the causal processes required to produce action" (Argyris, 2003, p. 444).
9. That is, the teacher *enacts* or *illustrates* how these judgments are made in different particular circumstances in such a way, i.e. by contrasts and comparisons, that the pupil can experience what the doing of it actually looks like, sounds like, and feels like.

References

Argyris, C. (2003). Actionable knowledge. In H. Tsoukas and K. Christian (eds.), *The Oxford Handbook of Organization Theory* (pp. 423–452). New York: Oxford University Press.

Bakhtin, M. M. (1981). *The Dialogical Imagination* (ed. M. Holquist, trans. C. Emerson and M. Holquist). Austin, TX: University of Texas Press.

Barad, K. (2007). *Meeting the Universe Halfway: Quantum Physics and the Entanglement of Matter and Meaning*. Durham, NC and London: Duke University Press.

Barad, K. (2013). Mar(r)king time: Material entanglements and re-memberings: Cutting together-apart. In P. R. Carlile, D. Nicoline, A. Langley, and H. Tsoukas (eds.), *How Matter Matters: Objects, Artifacts, and Materiality in Organization Studies* (pp. 16–31). Oxford: Oxford University Press.

Bateson, G. (1972/2000). *Steps to an Ecology of Mind*. Chicago and London: University of Chicago Press.

Bateson, G. (1979). *Mind and Nature: A Necessary Unity*. London: Fontana/Collins.

Billig, M. (2013). *Learn to Write Badly: How to Succeed in the Social Sciences*. Cambridge: Cambridge University Press.

Boje, D. M. (2001). *Narrative Methods for Organizational and Communication Research*. London: Sage.

Cunliffe, A. L. (2004). On becoming a critically reflexive practitioner. *Journal of Management Education*, 28(4): 407–426.

Descartes, R. (1968). *Discourse on Method and Other Writings* (trans. and introd. F. E. Sutcliffe). Harmondsworth: Penguin Books.

Dewey, J. (1929/1958). *Experience and Nature*. New York: Dover.

Dewey, J. (1938/2008). *Logic: The Theory of Inquiry*. Vol. 12 of *The Later Works, 1925–1953* (ed. J. A. Boyston). Carbondale, IL: Southern Illinois University Press.

Gadamer, H.-G. (2000). *Truth and Method* (2nd revised edition, trans. J. Weinsheimer and D. G. Marshall). New York: Continuum.

Garfinkel, H. (1967). *Studies in Ethnomethodology*. Englewood Cliffs, NJ: Prentice-Hall.

Garfinkel, H. (2002). *Ethnomethodology's Program: Working out Durkheim's Aphorism* (ed. and introd. A. W. Rawls). New York & Oxford: Rowman & Littlefield.

Hertz, H. H. (1894/1956). *The Principles of Mechanics*. New York: Dover.

Hosking, D. M. (2005). Bounded entities, constructivist revisions, and radical re-constructions. Special issue on Social Cognition: *Cognitie, Creier, Comportament/Cognition, Brain, Behavior*, 9(4): 609–622.

James, W. (1890). *Principles of Psychology*, 2 vols. London: Macmillan.

Kuhn, T. S. (2000). *The Road Since Structure: Philosophical Essays, 1970–1993* (ed. J. Conant and J. Haugeland). Chicago and London: University of Chicago Press.

Merleau-Ponty, M. (1962). *Phenomenology of Perception* (trans. C. Smith). London: Routledge & Kegan Paul.

Merleau-Ponty, M. (1964). *The Primacy of Perception and Other Essays* (ed. and introd. J. M. Edie). Evanston, IL: Northwestern University Press.

Robichaud, D., Giroux, H., and Taylor, J. R. (2004). The metaconversation: The recursive property of language as a key to organizing. *Academy of Management Review*, 29(4): 617–634.

Ryle, G. (1949). *The Concept of Mind*. London: Methuen.

Shotter, J. (2003). Real presences: Meaning as living movement in a participatory world. *Theory & Psychology*, 13(4): 435–468.

Shotter, J. (2006). Understanding process from within: An argument for "withness"-thinking. *Organization Studies*, 27(4): 585–604.

Shotter, J. (2012). More than cool reason: "Withness-thinking" or "systemic thinking" and "thinking *about* systems." *International Journal of Collaborative Practices*, 3(1): 1–13.

Shotter, J. and Tsoukas, H. (2014). In search of *phronesis*: Leadership and the art of coming to judgment. *Academy of Management Learning & Education*, 13(1): 224–243.

Todes, S. (2001). *Body and World* (introd. Hubert L. Dreyfus and Piortr Hoffman). Cambridge, MA: MIT Press.

Weick, K. E. (2010). The poetics of process: Theorizing the ineffable in organization studies. In T. Hernes and S. Matlis (eds.), *Process, Sensemaking, and Organizing* (pp. 102–111). Oxford: Oxford University Press.

Wittgenstein, L. (1953). *Philosophical Investigations* (trans. G. E. M. Anscombe). Oxford: Blackwell.

Wittgenstein, L. (1969). *On Certainty* (ed. G. E. M. Anscombe and G. H. von Wright, trans. D. Paul and G. E. M Anscombe). Oxford: Blackwell.

Wittgenstein, L. (1980). *Culture and Value* (introd. G. Von Wright, trans. P. Winch). Oxford: Blackwell.

Wittgenstein, L. (1981). *Zettel* (2nd edition, ed. G. E. M. Anscombe and G. H. von Wright). Oxford: Blackwell.

Wittgenstein, L. (1991). *Philosophical Remarks* (ed. R. Rees, trans. R. Hargreaves and R. White). Oxford: Blackwell.

4

Imagination in Organizational Creativity

Insights from the Radical Ontology of Cornelius Castoriadis

Aris Komporozos-Athanasiou and Marianna Fotaki

Abstract: This chapter draws on the works of Cornelius Castoriadis (1922–1997) to explore the relatively under-researched role of imagination in organizational creativity. In doing so it proposes an alternative theorizing of organizational creativity that accounts for both its individual and collective dimensions. The chapter uses the idea of imagination developed by Castoriadis to open up new ways of engaging with the relationship between the unconscious and the social/political milieu in order to further organizational theorizing. It applies Castoriadis' unique ontological framework together with strands of process-oriented literature to unpick the inherently creative nature of organizing. The authors demonstrate how such insights can afford a more complete theorization of organizational creativity as a process of meaning- and form-giving that places human imagination at its core, an alternative theoretical frame which contributes to contemporary debates around representations of emergent forms of organization and organizing.

4.1 Why Imagination?

The relationship between imagination and creativity has until recently rarely been a subject of study in organization and management scholarship (for notable exceptions see Cornelissen, 2006; Zhang, 2007; Shukaitis, 2008; Rehn and De Cock, 2008; De Cock, Rehn, and Berry, 2013). However, organizing can itself be seen as a *process* of re-imagining to reframe old issues and explore new ideas (Wheatley, Anthony, and Maddox, 1991); Clegg (2006, p. 849) defines imagination as "the capacity to be able to conceive a difference" in organizations, and to "undercut the security" of organizational rules through offering other possibilities. Weick (1989) has suggested that the very task of representing and expressing the complexity of organizational phenomena relies on researchers' and theorists' enacted imagination. Yet there is a stark lack of organizational research that recognizes, or attempts to theorize consistently, the role of imagination in creative activity (Shukaitis, 2008; Müller, 2012). Overall, there is little attention given to the links between creativity and individual imaginative life and creativity as related to institutionalization in society—questions that Cornelius Castoriadis' work is fundamentally concerned with (Joas and Meyer, 1989; also see Komporozos-Athanasiou, 2011). In this chapter we draw upon Castoriadis' theory in order to explore creativity in the context of the philosophy of organization (De Cock, 2013).

While the process of creativity remains elusive (George, 2007) and continues to puzzle organizational scholars (Lampel, Honig, and Drori, 2011), its complexity tends to be overshadowed in organizational research by a marked insistence on (creative) outputs. These are often thought to be generated by more or less controllable, individual-level characteristics (Drazin, Glynn, and Kazanjian, 1999; Unsworth, 2001; Driver, 2008), as a "creative behavior" or "the products" of such behavior within an organizational context (Woodman, Sawyer, and Griffin, 1993, p. 293). Organizational creativity is also typically examined through a normalizing and neutral concept of novelty (Amabile, 1996; Osborne, 2003). However, such a focus leaves out affective and unconscious dimensions of human imagination (Vygotsky, 2004) in relation to organizational creativity (Mainemelis, 2001, 2010; George, 2007; also see Nicholson, 2000). Furthermore, the relationality and dialogicality that underpin the ambiguity and surprisingness of organizational creativity (e.g. Morson and Emerson, 1990; Voloshinov and Bakhtin, 1929/1986) have scarcely been considered in extant literature. We seem to miss to date a theory of creativity that accounts for the ways in which individual imagination makes possible the engagement of psychic mechanisms with organizational and social structures in the process of continuous re-creation of "social imaginaries"—a concept deployed by philosopher Charles Taylor (2002, p. 92) to denote the role of imagination in producing new realities.

This chapter argues that such a theorization of organizational creativity necessitates a more nuanced understanding of imagination, of which the autonomous and often deviant nature has traditionally made it difficult to pin down (e.g. March, 1995). Drawing on the body of theory developed by Cornelius Castoriadis, we take imagination to stand in for the *process* as well as the *outcome* of creation and invention in organizations. As such, imagination involves the continuous—and never fully determined—production of new images in the most general sense of the term, encompassing both figurative (visual representations, visible structures) and affective (personal identifications, desires, biographical histories) meanings that serve as central references for the organizing of our collective lives. Such rich theorization of imagination that is explicitly linked to processes of institutionalization and organization (De Cock, 2013) means that its potential extends beyond merely re-theorizing organizational creativity, as is explained in the final section of the chapter.

Through unpacking this unique theory of imagination our chapter contributes to existing debates of organizational creativity within process research, in two key ways: First, it argues that a focus on imagination can offer important insights into the meaning- and form-giving processes characterizing creativity, through its unique treatment of indeterminacy in representation and signification stemming from the pre-cognitive realm of creative endeavors. Second, it demonstrates how imagination can be a vehicle for bringing organizational researchers closer to the political side of organizational creativity through a notion of affect that links the psychical with the social domain, demonstrating the ability of human imagination to posit new legitimacies.

4.2 Castoriadis' Radical Ontology of Creation

Castoriadis developed a highly original ontology wherein Being is conceptualized as an imaginary creation originating in the crossroads of psyche and society (Castoriadis, 1987/2005). His theoretical innovation is to demonstrate how creativity is "proper" to all action (Joas and Meyer, 1989, p. 1189). Hence while Castoriadian creativity, conceived as a driving force behind organizing and a stimulus for social action more generally, is useful for re-theorizing organizational creativity, we should not confuse it with the much narrower scope of the latter. Fundamental to this conception is human imagination,[1] which entails two inseparable dimensions, a creative instituting *process* and an imagined, instituted *outcome*—both of which are equally important. Imagination is a property of the "psychical monad" (individual psyche), while social imaginary is defined not as an "image *of* something" but as "the unceasing and essentially *undetermined* (social-historical and psychical) creation of figures/forms/images on the basis of which alone there can ever be a question *of* 'something'" (Castoriadis, 1987/2005, p. 3; italics in the original). More specifically, imagination is seen as the underlying generator of central representations (which Castoriadis calls social imaginary significations) that serve as frameworks structuring and giving meaning to actions and behaviors within social collectivities, such as organizations and societies. These representations are at the same time affective expressions of an inter-subjective desire for being autonomous and being something else, embodying powerful forms of creation; it is through this process of imagination that the transition from the "old" to the "new" is instituted in a given organization or society (Rosanis, 2011). As we will aim to show in what follows, Castoriadis uses this radical foregrounding of imagination in the psyche to address philosophical and anthropological aspects of subjectivity and to connect it with social-historical developments (Adams, 2011).

Castoriadis' political philosophy has been criticized for being utopian, particularly, when his notion of autonomy is employed to theorize political action and envision the future model of social organization. As Joas and Meyer (1989, pp. 1117–1118) argue:

> Politically, the act of revolution seen as the autonomous self-institutionalization of a better society assumes ever stronger voluntaristic features in Castoriadis's writings. In bitter analyses of present-day Western societies, which are admittedly essayistic and lack empirical grounding for their conclusions, he sees an absence of creativity and of visions of the future and pervasive tendencies toward anomie.

However, the strength of his ontology lies in its ability to offer novel ways of thinking about creative imagination as a driver of human action, without aiming to provide a blueprint for political activism. Castoriadis' notion of creativity in relation to realizing autonomy was developed with an acute awareness of the profound struggles societies are faced with in the institutionalization process. To illustrate this awareness we offer an example that he discusses to counteract the structuralist critique of voluntarism in his theory (Castoriadis, 1987/2005, p. 244). Considering the ability of a group of exploited factory workers to realize autonomy through knowingly and willingly challenging the existing order, Castoriadis ponders on the relationship between autonomy and heteronomy as it appears in the positioning of individuals towards (oppressive) social institutions:

> If it is essential to recall that heteronomy must . . . find its conditions in each exploited individual, it has to find them to the same extent in social structures, which make the individuals' 'chances' (in Max Weber's sense) of knowing and willing practically inexistent. Knowing and willing are not purely a matter of knowing and willing, we are not dealing with subjects which would be pure will to autonomy and entirely responsible, for if this were the case there would be no problem in any domain whatsoever. It is not simply that the social structure is 'designed for' instilling passivity, respect for authority, etc. even before an individual's birth. It is that institutions are there, in the long struggle of each person's life, to place blocks and obstacles in the way at every instant, to push the waters in a certain direction, and finally to rage against whatever might be manifested as autonomy. This is why the person who says he wants autonomy while refusing the revolution in institutions knows neither what he is saying nor what he wants. The individual imaginary . . . finds a correspondence in a social imaginary embodied in institutions, but this embodiment exists as such and it is also as such that it must be attacked. (Castoriadis, 1987/2005, pp. 385–386, n. 46)

Thus returning to Castoriadis' theory of creativity, in which the anonymous collective is the ground of social-historical constellations of meaning for Castoriadis: collective creativity is irreducible to individual psychic creativity; however, nor is psyche ever subsumed by the social-historical domain. In other words, the meaning-giving process occurs when the psychic monad and the social imaginary intersect. In a related argument he posits that while the psyche and creativity pre-exist already in the social, there has been a systematic obscuring of this creative process throughout history. Castoriadis traces this systematic overshadowing of human imagination in inherited philosophy; he posits that imagination in many of those accounts has been "interpreted and explained in terms of [psychology's] products, using flagrantly superficial ideas such as [that of] 'compensation' for some unsatisfied need or desire" (Castoriadis, 1993, p. 2). Hence individuals and societies often fail to recognize their institutions and laws as their own creations and as the products of their own instituting imaginaries but focus instead on what has been already socially instituted. He describes this process of obfuscation as follows:

> The institution is a socially sanctioned, symbolic network in which a functional component and an imaginary component are combined in variable proportions and relations. Alienation occurs when the imaginary moment in the institution becomes autonomous and predominates, which leads to

> the institution's becoming autonomous and predominating with respect to society. This becoming autonomous, or autonomization, of the institution is expressed and embodied in the material nature of social life, but it always presupposes at the same time that society lives its relations with its institutions in the mode of the imaginary, in other words, that it does not recognize in the imaginary of institutions something that is its own product. (Castoriadis, 1987/2005, p. 84)

In order to address this overshadowing, Castoriadis theorizes creativity both as a source *and* as a means of organizing society, moving a step further than Kant, Freud, and the phenomenological tradition, by radicalizing the role of imagination as "the cornerstone of subjectivity" (Adams, 2011, p. 83). This centrality of imagination for defining subjectivity and for instituting various forms of organization in society moves away from a mere critique of such limitations to a productive ontology of Being, thus contributing to the conceptualization of organizational creativity in two substantial ways:

(i) It theorizes creativity as an undetermined process of giving *form* and *meaning* to social institutions that occurs both at the level of unconscious psyche and that of social institutions.
(ii) It elaborates a processual concept of affect that is carefully linked with the ability of human imagination to posit new legitimacies, thus affording a more politically aware conceptualization of organizational creativity.

Importantly, as we will argue, such ontology has significant resonances with some promising approaches to organizational creativity articulated recently within process, and more specifically non-representational (NR) studies of organization (e.g. Dey and Steyaert, 2007; Gino et al., 2010; Argote and Miron-Spektor, 2011; Beyes and Steyaert, 2012), through grounding the important question of representation firmly onto the operation of desires and affects that are generated by human imagination. In what follows we will draw theoretical inspiration from these theories in order to develop a framework that integrates insights from Castoriadian imagination and enables us to re-theorize organizational creativity. Finally, in focusing on the role of social imaginaries intersecting with and emerging from the desire of the individual psyche for creation, we stress the general relevance of Castoriadis' ontology for theorizing organizations and organizing through the prism of imagination while sketching some potential avenues for future research.

4.3 Organizational Conceptions of Creativity from a Process Perspective

The theme of creativity has attracted some interest in process studies, although it lacks the consistent theorizing afforded in other fields of organization research such as organizational psychology and behavioral studies, which have developed dedicated streams of work to understanding the antecedents and outputs of creativity. A useful attempt to introduce a process approach to organizational creativity is offered by Chia (2002), who draws on the works of anthropologist Tim Ingold to develop a nuanced critique of static notions of creativity characterizing mainstream organizational thinking. Ingold (2010) criticizes the passivity of creativity assumed in the "hylomorphic" model of creation that has dominated philosophical thinking since Aristotle; using the example of painter Paul Klee, Ingold argues for an ontology that assigns primacy to the processes of formation as against their final products, and to the flows and transformations of materials as against states of matter. Such prioritizing of process over product is captured powerfully by Klee's own words, "form is death; form-giving is life" (Klee, 1973, p. 269). The question of representability is hence a key from a process perspective for understanding how creativity functions.

More recently, process research drawing explicitly on non-representational theory (e.g. Beyes and Steyaert, 2012) has combined embodied, relational, and affective understandings of everyday organizational practice, to account for creativity in performative and multiply-layered representations of organizing (e.g. Perry-Smith, 2006; Nayak, 2008a). Researchers in this strand of work understand creativity as the ability to "make do" (Nayak, 2008a, p. 421), to be sensitive to the opportune moment; organizational creativity is in that sense inherent to "the everyday struggles and pleasures" (Nayak, 2008a, p. 421) that are lived out in organizations. Similarly, Slutskaya and De Cock (2008, p. 853) draw on embodiment theories to challenge the "intellectualist and discursive view of organizations" and to bring attention to the "body's potential for generating creative and innovative practices." Non-representational approaches are concerned with the dynamic and creative flow of organizational experiences through challenging representationalist depictions of organizations and organizational knowledge (Tsoukas, 1996; Chia, 2002; Fineman, 2008; Shotter, 2008), which are based on the assumption that the human mind can reproduce reality in a way that corresponds to the real world (Goldman, 1986, cited in Lorino, Tricard, and Clot, 2011). By contrast, non-representational approaches foreground becomingness and emergence (e.g. Cooper, 2007; Shotter, 2008; Tsoukas, 2009) and follow the Bergsonian idea of a continuous stream of creativity, intuition, and human imagination (Weick, 1979, 1989). In summary, non-representational approaches offer two important tools for redefining organizational creativity: one is a more nuanced and multi-dimensional notion of representability, that is people's ability of form-giving; the other is a notion of signification, which unpicks the inherent indeterminacy of meaning-giving processes in practical everyday experiences of organizing.

Table 4.1 summarizes the contributions of non-representational organizational theory to the study of creativity. First, non-representational approaches offer an understanding of *representability* as becomingness, through challenging conventional (linear and Euclidean) notions of time and space in organizations, and thus addressing the unprocessual nature of much of social and cultural theory (Thrift, 2008). To do so they focus on the excess of organizational space, which includes embodied and affective encounters, movements, and precognitive triggers (Lorimer, 2005), all of which are unrepresentable in a mimetic sense (Massey, 2005). Theorizing of affect as evoking the states of being and experiences that escape discursive capture on the one hand, and naming that can destabilize and unsettle us into potentially new states of becoming and being on the other hand, speaks to the work of both Deleuze (1997) and Massumi (1996). Both authors, whose work has influenced non-representational and process theories alike, see affects as pre-cognitive and pre-verbal: autonomous from the subject, somewhat automatic, and necessarily reflexive. These two aforementioned processes cannot possibly work sequentially because as Nayak (2008b, p. 186) puts it: "process is pure creativity, always moving beyond itself. It *is not* but it acts; it is not an atemporal and abstract representation of reality, but the active or the useful or, more precisely, the creative." This problematic

Table 4.1 Theoretical implications of non-representational theory to the study of creativity

Concept	Proposal	Implications for creativity
Representation	Organizing is seen a process of becoming wherein discursive, affective, and embodied experiences can never be representable in a mimetic sense and thus always encompass the possibility of new representations.	Creativity is a property of the becomingness and multiplicity of unrepresentable experience.
Signification	Organizational semantics is irreducible to syntax, insofar as the meaning-making process involves continuous re-imagining of organizational practice.	Creativity takes the form of new meanings arising from the indeterminacy of everyday practice.

allows us to consider creativity as a key component of the spatial multiplicity in organizations. Understanding the multiplicity of space through such everyday articulations of experience, importantly points to the possibility of alternative representations, and thus of organizational imaginations (Beyes and Steyaert, 2012; also see Thrift, 2008) that aim to create new representations.

Second, non-representational theories afford a notion of *signification* in organizing that is never fully confined by a predetermined set of organizational rules or syntax. They demonstrate in particular how meaning-giving in organizations cannot be reduced to a mere identification with "pre-established and ready-made concepts, in which the singularity of the living experience has no part" (Lorino, Tricard, and Clot 2011, p. 776). Lorino et al. call this process a syntactic reduction of organizational semantics, whereby formal logical relationships between signs (syntax) unproblematically mirror the symbolic representations of real objects (Varela, Thompson, and Rosch, 1991). They highlight, moreover, that simply paying attention to what people *do* is not sufficient to understand this semantic complexity of organizations, which also involves people's ongoing inquiries to *imagine* their own practice and *redefine* it (also see Clot, 1999). Echoing these concerns, Tsoukas (2013), one of the very few theorists to draw explicitly on Castoriadis, shows how the syntax of abstract representations embodied in organizational rules and structures can only be applied *after* their semantics has been specified. He argues importantly that such semantics "must be established *within a practice*" insofar as it "has a bearing on experience" (Tsoukas, 2013, p. 64; italics in the original), noting that:

> [w]hile for a long time organization has been approached from the spectator's view and, as a result, only the representational (i.e. formal) dimension of organization has been most visible, if organization is approached from a process-based ontology that takes human agency seriously, we are able to appreciate the complexity of organization. The latter is not just representation (although this is important). It is also self-constituting meaning-making and patterned action-taking in the face of inherently incomplete knowledge. (Tsoukas, 2013, p. 64)

Put another way, the signification process is never complete in organizational life; it always entails a degree of indeterminacy. For non-representational theory, this indeterminacy is inexorably linked to the presence of creativity, which continuously negates "the ultimate fixation of meaning" (Müller, 2012, p. 331).

4.4 Limitations and Opportunities

These are important insights for our theorization of creativity via imagination. We propose how to achieve this by bringing together selected insights from the work of Castoriadis and non-representational theories discussed above. Non-representational theories call specifically for a reassessment of the connections between the emotional experiences of those inhabiting organizations (affect), and their ability to constitute and represent them in a meaningful way (representation or more exactly their representability). However such a promising endeavor to reassess practices that stretch beyond representational boundaries in order to capture the creative potential of everyday life is not without its own problems. Most notably, for Harvey (2006), Tolia-Kelly (2006), and other prominent human geographers, non-representational theories take a rather soft approach to the power asymmetries that condition the critical potentiality of organizational practices (also see Beyes and Steyaert, 2012).

Another important offshoot of these limitations is non-representational theories' sparse contemplation of the role of the unconscious in the re-imagining of organizational practice. The psychical domain has indeed been an unsettling experience for most researchers in the field (Philo and Parr, 2003; Lorimer, 2005); there is a surprising lack of dialogue between the notion of "individual psychosocial experience" (Lorimer, 2005, p. 90) specifically of psychoanalytic ontologies, and the practice-centered "experiential exercises" (Lorimer, 2005, p. 90) that are the center of non-representational research. The psychoanalytic focus on the intra- and inter-psychic dimensions of affect, which is also present in the work of Castoriadis, addresses the discursive reductionism that dominates organization studies by introducing the aspect of passionate embodiment (Fotaki, Long, and Schwartz, 2012, p. 1109).

There is, moreover, an issue of obfuscation of agency in the categorization of representational and non-representational domains of experience, with the latter being considered to be the properties of practices themselves, rather than of actors that enact such practices (Thrift, 2008). This pre-individual notion of practice "assumes practices to not be tied to human subjects but stabilized, through material-relational bundles of all manners of resources" (Beyes and Steyaert, 2012, p. 51), offering limiting explanations of how individuals give meaning to, and, crucially, *take ownership of* their representations.

Having discussed the important insights and limitations for organizational creativity of non-representational theories, we are still left with some questions regarding where from and how creativity actually emerges. In the remainder of this chapter we will show how these questions can only be addressed through a more consistent integration of the psychical and affective with the social in creative practices. To this end, it seems particularly important to encompass an analysis of the unconscious layer of subjectivity and of organizational life, while maintaining non-representational theories' focus on the practices of everyday creativity. The insights from Castoriadian theory incorporated in this chapter furnish such a perspective. This integration can moreover offer insights into exactly how rationalities, intrinsic motivations, passions, or unconscious drives *actually* contribute to the production of creative outcomes in organizations, and address some of the *dualisms* appearing in relevant organizational creativity debates, such as those of process/event, conscious/unconscious, and individual/social/political. In what follows, we show how this endeavor is made possible through Castoriadis' unique, integrated theory of imagination, which links together the key concepts of representation, signification, and affect to elucidate the overlooked social and political dimensions of organizational creativity. Table 4.2 summarizes this process, which is detailed in the next section.

Table 4.2 Contributions of Castoriadis' concept of imagination to organizational creativity

Key concept	Castoriadian imagination	Contribution to organizational creativity
Representation	Human imagination puts continuously at work an "afunctional representational capacity" that moves beyond reproduction and repetition of existing structures, being a condition for reality as we understand it.	Creativity should be understood as not simply a potential of creating new representations, but as the process of elucidating the imaginary within the rational.
Signification	Language and syntax are products of human imagination, and as such are neither fixed nor simply empirically inferred; they are reflective of the radical contingencies of human psyche.	The creative potential of "indeterminacy" involved in organizational meaning-making, is not synonymous with "lapsing into chaos," insofar as organizations are the authors/owners of their own indeterminations.
Affect	Imagination operates in the interplay of individual emotions and social affect creating the individual-social self.	Affect unites the psychic and social aspects of creativity in organizations. Creative imagination makes possible the elucidation of those interdependencies and connections; realizing organization as an autonomous, self-instituting entity.

4.5 Discussion: Castoriadian Imagination as an "Integrated Approach" to Organizational Creativity

4.5.1 Elucidating the Links between Representation and Signification

A first important contribution to organizational creativity found in the Castoriadian ontology concerns its unique treatment of the unconscious (desire) as central to the creative meaning-making process—seen as a continuous process of producing representations and significations. It is the unconscious that triggers representation, which is born out of imagination and is not merely confined to linguistic/symbolic/discursive devices. Hence imagination encompasses the embodied and affective practices that sustain it and give rise to creativity. Imagination is different from fantasy and represents a force of surging forth making (social) life possible: by transcending the Cartesian dualism of subject and object and thus leading to a higher level of awareness, it denotes a psychic ability for leaping towards creation *ex nihilo* (Castoriadis, 1987/2005).

This also means that imagination is not enslaved in the merely instrumental process of self-conservation, reproduction, and repetition of pre-existing structures, concepts, and ways of being. Through this non-functional type of representation that is not merely reproductive or re-combinatory, by which we mean a representation that exceeds its utilitarian purpose, we are able to understand imagination not as a mirror or reflection of reality, but as the "logical and ontological condition of the real" (Castoriadis, 1987/2005, p. 336, quoted in Rorty, 1988). Or as Castoriadis puts it elsewhere: "it is because radical imagination exists that reality exists for us" (Castoriadis, 1997b, p. 321) and *represents* [reason] insofar as it makes "figures become figurable" (Castoriadis, 1997b, p. 321).

Crucially, such a notion of representation extends non-representational theory's view of the (un)representability of human experience from the realm of affective subjectivity to that of reason. It shows how even something as structured as mathematical logic relies on imagination—what Castoriadis calls mathematical imagination—in order to give "an incredible accumulation of nonintuitable figures" that are just as "unrepresentable" as any other imaginary signification (Castoriadis, 1997a, p. 267). Like any imaginary signification, such rational figures are not fixed, but neither are they empirically inferred—they constitute conditions for the organization of empirical knowledge. Hence the Castoriadian approach takes a further step from non-representational theories' recognition of the irreducibility of organizational semantics, to propose that syntax itself *is* the product of human imagination.

Central to establishing this creative nature of organizational representations is the Castoriadian theorizing of signification. Castoriadis refers to a "primordial indivisible polysemy" (Castoriadis, 2007, p. 43) that is characteristic of the irreducibility of language to universal meaning. As he puts it, new significations represented through language "do not refer back to any shared matrix of meaning"—a syntax—"from which a spectrum of signifiers and signifieds would burst forth" (Castoriadis, 2007, p. 43). This position resonates with the assumption that many non-representational theories share, namely about the syntactic irreducibility of meaning-giving practices (Thrift, 2008), which is foregrounded in the richness of language itself. Castoriadis' explanation for this irreducibility, however, is to be found in the concept of imagination, which, as it were, precedes language. Put another way, the semantics of language *already* entails the possibility of creativity through meaning something else, insofar as language is not monodic, i.e. producing one singular sound, but is characterized by a harmonic richness that produces a melody of meaning. In Castoriadis' own words: "what makes a word what it is, meaning-wise, is its overtones, its resonances and consonances" (Castoriadis, 2007, p. 43).

The novelty of Castoriadis' notion of signification is that it encompasses the very act of breaking with the "closure of meaning" (Castoriadis, 1992, p. 20)—a closure imposed by heteronomous modes of being in society, which become crystallized in a given symbolic order. Heteronomy and autonomy are central concepts for Castoriadis' political project. The former describes social norms that are imposed by others or self-imposed by evoking a higher instance such as religion or tradition. This is also what sets it apart from the latter and from an autonomous society, which recognizes itself as a self-instituting entity. The act of breaking with closure of meaning thus entails a leap towards more autonomous states of being, which in Castoriadis' view should not be seen as utopian projects, inasmuch as the nature of closure is imperfect and tenuous.

Importantly, organizations as social institutions are able to provide the space wherein individual psyches become attached to and integrated in the collective, by means of socialization. This, in Castoriadis' words, appears when social representations endow "the egocentric, self-centered being" with meaning—through the act of socialization—without which the psyche would be absorbed in the pure pleasure of functional representation (Castoriadis, 2007). These social representations give primacy to the *instituting* over the *instituted imagination*, through their own engagement in the process of collective meaning-giving which is emergent, malleable, and in flux. In dispensing with the primacy of language in favor of a broader concept of imagination, Castoriadis foregrounds the post-humanist concerns with materiality articulated by feminists not as ubiquitous puns on matter but as rethinking of the key concepts (materiality and signification) and the relationship between them (Barad, 2003, p. 801). New materialisms take this point further; Coole and Frost (2010), for instance, call for a reconsideration of the most fundamental questions about the nature of matter and the place of embodied humans within a material world. In the context of current economic and technological shifts, such reconsideration alerts us to the normative and political significance of these relations.

4.5.2 Integration of the Psychical and Collective through Affect in Organizational Creativity

The second major contribution of Castoriadis' theory to organizational creativity is its treatment of the creative potentiality of the meaning- and form-giving processes through *affect*, which addresses the lack of proper integration of the psychical and the collective in organizational creativity research. Castoriadis discusses at length the importance of affect in the "creation of an individual-social self" (Castoriadis, 1997c, p. 87). Every society, he argues, creates its own world as a flow of social imaginary significations, which establish certain types of affect that are, in turn, characteristic of *this* (and no other) society. He provides the example of different affects created—and social-historically instituted—by different societies, such as the Jewish, the Christian, and the modern capitalist society:

> But there really are affects that are characteristic of capitalist society too. Without entering into a description that would risk taking a merely literary turn, allow me to recall that Marx described these capitalist affects very well when he spoke of a perpetual restlessness, constant change, a thirst for the new for the sake of the new and for more the sake of the more—in short, a set of *socially instituted affects*. (Castoriadis, 1997c, p. 88)

Affect is central to the process of instituting and meaning-giving in society through which a specific anthropological type of individual is socially constituted as a "function of all that (s)he is, thinks, wants, loves or hates" (Castoriadis, 1997c, p. 88). Signification and affect are thus closely interconnected although they are irreducible to each other. Put differently, the affective constitution of society and its institutions is inextricably linked to the ways in which it is represented through meaning-making activities, or as Castoriadis points out, every known society has had a representation of itself as *something*; a representation that is:

> [I]ndissociably tied to a society's *wanting itself* as society and as *this* society and to its *loving itself* as society and as *this* society—that is to say, there is a cathexis both of the concrete collectivity and of the laws by means of which this collectivity is what it is. (Castoriadis, 1997c, pp. 88–89, italics in the original)

This nuanced understanding of affect furthers the distinction between emotions and affect made by NR theorists, showing how affective experience runs deeper than its emotive manifestations that are bounded by a social-linguistic fixing (see Simpson and Marshall, 2010). Affect is thus pre- or extra-linguistic, but is also, crucially, produced and transmitted relationally (Navaro-Yashin, 2009). In that sense, affect signifies the potentiality that is inherent in human beings (Navaro-Yashin, 2009, p. 149) and which "far from being simply about pleasure and pain . . . is a way for the instantiated being to locate itself according to a vaster becoming—an index of becoming" (Simondon, 2005, p. 260). Moreover, the links made between the (pre-) individual and collective levels are understood to be engendered through the very interplay of emotions and affect (where the former is defined as individual and the latter as social—see also Ahmed, 2004 for a discussion), by way of action carried out as an expression of individual participation in a wider social space (Venn, 2010). It also furthers the distinction between emotions and affect, which occurs when bodies encounter each other, and before the resulting intensities have been categorized and named as emotions (Deleuze, 1997). For Deleuze this also means that movements *between* bodily states and the intensities that they evoke have to be considered as rhythms of life, which can become meaningful in their repetition.

4.6 Implications for Understanding Rationality and Politics in Organizational Creativity

These contributions have important practical implications for understanding organizational creativity. As we have seen, much of the potentiality of Castoriadian imagination lies in the fact that, although it operates at the unconscious level of subjectivity, it also inhabits conscious practice, effectively opening up to "forms of consciousness and body-to-body interaction that cognitivist approaches of the body–mind coupling, fixated on overt and intentional behaviour, simply cannot comprehend" (Venn, 2010, p. 130). Thus the proposed focus on imagination entails a unique notion of practice, offering significant insights into the self's investment in direct experience, and the ways in which its "affective, cognitive, and physical resources are totally invested in the present-moment activity" (Mainemelis, 2001, p. 553). This also implies *emergence* (Tassis, 2007), a surging forth, in the sense of the content of the practice that unfolds therein, and captures the limits of representation; as Charles Taylor (2002, p. 107) suggests:

> It is in fact that largely unstructured and inarticulate understanding of our whole situation, within which particular features of our world become evident. It can never be adequately expressed in the form of explicit doctrines because of its very unlimited and indefinite nature. That is another reason for speaking here of an imaginary, not a theory.

Though Castoriadis does not refute the crucial role of reason in this "practical" constitution of reality, he considers the "category of rationalism" as being itself a historical creation of the social imaginary "that emerged at a particular moment" (Tassis, 2007, p. 284, our translation). He recognizes the value of so-called reality and rationality as works of the social imaginary, by considering them as processes of continuous creation in the sense of *poiesis*: as an ontological genesis (Fotaki, 2009). This important point of linking imagination and reason entails a key insight for organizational creativity, which is no longer seen as a mere reservoir of the unexpected, the embodied, or indeed the unconscious, *but as extendable to the realm of rationality*. In further advancing this thesis, we observe how Castoriadis picks up the thread from its other end, in order to show how *reflection* is itself inexorably linked with imagination, which in turn activates, as it were, its creative capacity:

> Reflection is definable as the effort to break closure wherever we are each time necessarily caught up as subjects, whether it comes from our personal history or from the social-historical institution that has formed and raised us. In this effort imagination plays a central role: since the putting into question established truths *does not occur within a void* but is always paired with the positing of new forms/figures of the thinkable, created by the radical imagination, which are also subject to the control of reflection. (Castoriadis, 1997a, p. 271, emphasis ours)

From the foregoing insights stems the final key contribution this chapter makes to understanding creativity as *a political process*. Unlike the notion of creativity proposed by NR approaches, which affords autonomy to affective practice/process, our proposed theory of imagination suggests that such autonomy lies not merely in a practice/process but firmly in the hands of individuals within organizations. The type of praxis that Castoriadis calls "active activity" (Castoriadis, 1992, p. 28), suggests "the capacity to place in suspension the ultimate axioms, criteria and rules which are thought of simply as a conscious activity, with the supposition that others, not yet certain, perhaps not yet known, might replace them" (Castoriadis, 1997a, p. 268). This is an important point for Castoriadis, who considers this type of activity as the act of taking ownership of radical (in)determinacy that characterizes the unconscious. In this view, organizations are constituted, as has been emphasized so far, in the generative interaction of psyche and society, but they encompass a creative potentiality, which is undetermined and in the making through practice, and which need not be in contrast to socially created values typically associated with representationalist forms, traditions, and structures. Organizational creativity in that sense exists in the radical acknowledgment of ownership of such values as the works of imagination, and is a first step to the creation of new ones.

4.7 Conclusion and Future Directions for Research

The arguments explored in this chapter propose the necessity to consider imagination as an intrinsic aspect of organizational creativity and use the idea of imagination developed by Castoriadis to open up new ways of engaging with the relationship between the unconscious and the social/political milieu to further organizational theorizing. Castoriadis' work can offer important insights that resonate with and further develop on process and non-representational theories, especially regarding their treatment of affect in representational and semantic multiplicity. While there is a growing interest in the application of some of those theories to explore organizational creativity from this perspective, these discussions are somewhat superficial in spite of the evident key role of imagination in theories of alternative spacing, politics of affect, or politics of the here and now (see Thrift, 2004; Lorimer, 2005). For instance, although such studies acknowledge the importance of understanding sentiments, passions, and personal morality (Nayak, 2008b) they have little to say about the space in which these are generated: the human psyche. The Castoriadian theorization of affect as a psychic property ineluctably intertwined with the social addresses this paucity, and also offers a potentially important contribution through positioning those issues of affect in relation to power and the social embeddedness of the subject.

In summary, Castoriadis' ideas on human imagination enable us to rethink the relationship between the unconscious and the social/political, and between representation/signification and creativity, thus affording a way forward on how to proceed with this task. In response to historical treatment of imagination as being of lesser relevance for understanding creativity, various subtle interconnections between signification and representation were identified in this chapter as an intrinsic aspect of organizational practice. The proposed re-theorization is a far cry from imagination's anchoring in the passions of an individualistic model that emphasizes creative genius, taking the form of brainstorming and strategic planning (Peters, 2009), which is closely associated with the figure of the innovator and hero-entrepreneur (Peters and Besley, 2006) that is common in management discourses. It also leads to a different understanding of organization and to the opening up of some fruitful directions for research agendas in organizational theory more widely.

Castoriadis' theoretical edifice does not solely restore the psychic aspect of human creation through his analysis of the role of imagination, but moreover considers it as a fundamentally political project. Being creative is part of being, indissociably related with the ceaseless quest for individual and collective autonomy, or in other words, the realization that we are co-authors of our histories. The concept of social imaginaries developed by Castoriadis as produced collectively thorough individuals' desires for creative endeavors can not only serve as a resource for understanding our organizational and social practices but also as means for changing them. This thesis resonates with Taylor's (2002) philosophy where: "the social imaginary is not a set of ideas; rather it is what enables through making sense of, the practices of a society" (p. 91), and extends beyond merely providing a means of understanding practice because: "If the understanding makes the practice possible, it is also true that the practice largely carries the understanding" (p. 107).

Lastly, as an example of these important contributions we considered how explanations of "failed" or "bounded" rationality, which are increasingly at play in organizations today, can be enriched by the Castoriadian view of rationality as a product and not a constraint of organizational imagination. These can be used to examine empirical organizational issues such as power and identity; or topics of wider significance such as the current global financial crisis. Citing Castoriadis, Michel (2012), for example, explains how self-destructive behaviors of investment bankers cannot be explained by rationality but rather because "they cannot conceive otherwise (Castoriadis, 1992) and even when it does not make sense to do so" (Michel, 2012, p. 329). Critical research could explore these failures through illuminating the imaginary *within* the rational, rather than simply exposing the instances where organizational members' fantasies become rationalized (cf. Gabriel and Carr, 2002). Such a critical albeit productive outlook is conspicuously absent in existing accounts of predicaments faced by the organizations of today, and in our view, is more important than ever in our attempts not only to understand these predicaments, but also to look for ways of moving forward.

Note

1. Although we are aware that much French scholarship on Castoriadis has made use of the term "l'imaginaire" to speak of "the imaginary," as a more accurate English translation, in our chapter we speak of "imagination," for a number of reasons. Imagination is closer to the Greek term "fantasia" (translated as "imagination"), which corresponds to the Aristotelian term identified by Castoriadis as being used in the first philosophical treatise on the subject. Moreover, in Castoriadis' own talks and writings in his native Greek, we often see references to "fantasia" (as opposed to "fantasiako" which would be the Greek translation of "imaginary") in his philosophical positioning of the concept from Kant to Fichte to Merleau-Ponty. Lastly, we find the term imagination useful because it symbolizes a departure from the Lacanian psychoanalytic theory's use of "the imaginary" as a delusionary reflection that the subject takes for reality (a question to which we return at several points in this chapter).

References

Adams, S. (2011). *Castoriadis's Ontology*. New York: Fordham University Press.

Ahmed, S. (2004). Affective economies. *Social Text* 79, 22(2): 117–139.

Amabile, T. M. (1996). *Creativity in Context: Update to The Social Psychology of Creativity*. Boulder, CO and Oxford: Westview Press.

Argote, L. and Miron-Spektor, E. (2011). Organizational learning: From experience to knowledge. *Organization Science*, 22(5): 1123–1137.

Barad, K. (2003). Posthumanist performativity: Toward an understanding of how matter comes to matter. *Signs: Journal of Women in Culture and Society*, 28(3): 801–831.

Beyes, T. and Steyaert, C. (2012). Spacing organization: Non-representational theory and performing organizational space. *Organization*, 19(1): 45–61.

Castoriadis, C. (1987/2005). *The Imaginary Institution of Society.* Cambridge: Polity Press.

Castoriadis, C. (1992). Logic, imagination, reflection. *American Imago,* 49: 3–33.

Castoriadis, C. (1993). Merleau-Ponty and the weight of the ontological tradition. *Thesis Eleven,* 36(1): 1–36.

Castoriadis, C. (1997a). *World in Fragments: Writings on Politics, Society, Psychoanalysis, and the Imagination.* Stanford, CA: Stanford University Press.

Castoriadis, C. (1997b). *The Castoriadis Reader.* Oxford: Blackwell.

Castoriadis, C. (1997c). The crisis of the identification process. *Thesis Eleven,* 49(1): 85–98.

Castoriadis, C. (2007). *Figures of the Thinkable.* Stanford, CA: Stanford University Press.

Chia, R. (2002). Essai: Time, duration and simultaneity—rethinking process and change in organizational analysis. *Organization Studies,* 23(6): 863–868.

Clegg, S. (2006). The bounds of rationality: Power/history/imagination. *Critical Perspectives on Accounting,* 17(7): 847–863.

Clot, Y. (1999). *La fonction psychologique du travail.* Paris: Presses Universitaires de France.

Coole, D. and Frost, S. (2010). Introducing new materialisms. In D. Coole and S. Frost (eds.), *New Materialisms: Ontology, Agency, and Politics* (pp. 1–43). Durham, NC: Duke University Press.

Cooper, R. (2007). Organs of process: Rethinking human organization. *Organization Studies,* 28(10): 1547–1573.

Cornelissen, J. P. (2006). Making sense of theory construction: Metaphor and disciplined imagination. *Organization Studies,* 27(11): 1579–1597.

De Cock, C. (2013). Imagination and organization: A review of *The Imaginary Institution of Society,* C. Castoriadis. *Scandinavian Journal of Management,* 29(4): 406–408

De Cock, C., Rehn, A., and Berry, D. (2013). For a critical creativity: The radical imagination of Cornelius Castoriadis. In K. Thomas and J. Chan (eds.), *Handbook of Research on Creativity* (pp. 150–161). Cheltenham: Edward Elgar.

Deleuze, G. (1997). *Essays Critical and Clinical* (trans. D. W. Smith and M. A. Greco). Minneapolis: University of Minnesota Press.

Dey, P. and Steyaert, C. (2007). The troubadours of knowledge: Passion and invention in management education. *Organization,* 14(3): 437–461.

Drazin, R., Glynn, M. A., and Kazanjian, R. K. (1999). Multilevel theorizing about creativity in organizations: A sensemaking perspective. *Academy of Management Review,* 24(2): 286–307.

Driver, M. (2008). New and useless. *Journal of Management Inquiry,* 17(3): 187–197.

Fineman, S. (2008). *The Emotional Organization: Passions and Power.* Oxford: Blackwell.

Fotaki, M. (2009). The ghosts of the past, the dreamlands of the future or why fantasies are bound to fail in socialism and the market: The case of public health policy development in the Soviet Union and post-Soviet Russia. *Communist and Post-Communist Studies,* 42: 217–232.

Fotaki, M., Long, S., and Schwartz, H. S. (2012). What can psychoanalysis offer organization studies today? Taking stock of current developments and thinking about future directions. *Organization Studies*, 33(9): 1104–1120.

Gabriel, Y. and Carr, A. (2002). Organizations, management and psychoanalysis: An overview. *Journal of Managerial Psychology*, 17(5): 348–365.

George, J. M. (2007). Creativity in organizations. *Academy of Management Annals*, 1(1): 439–477.

Gino, F., Argote, L., Miron-Spektor, E., and Todorova, G. (2010). First, get your feet wet: The effects of learning from direct and indirect experience on team creativity. *Organizational Behavior and Human Decision Processes*, 111(2): 102–115.

Harvey, D. (2006). Editorial: The geographies of critical geography. *Transactions of the Institute of British Geographers*, 31(4): 409–412.

Ingold, T. (2010). The textility of making. *Cambridge Journal of Economics*, 34(1): 91–102.

Joas, H. and Meyer, R. (1989). Institutionalization as a creative process: The sociological importance of Cornelius Castoriadis's political philosophy. *American Journal of Sociology*, 94(5): 1184–1199.

Klee, P. (1973). *Notebooks, Volume 2: The Nature of Nature* (trans. H. Norden, ed. J. Spiller). London: Lund Humphries.

Komporozos-Athanasiou, A. (2011). Book review: Cornelius Castoriadis, figures of the thinkable (trans. Helen Arnold). *Organization Studies*, 32(5): 708–711.

Lampel, J., Honig, B., and Drori, I. (2011). Discovering creativity in necessity: Organizational ingenuity under institutional constraints. *Organization Studies*, 32(4): 584–586.

Lorimer, H. (2005). Cultural geography: The busyness of being "more-than-representational." *Progress in Human Geography*, 29(1): 83–94.

Lorino, P., Tricard, B., and Clot, Y. (2011). Research methods for non-representational approaches to organizational complexity: The dialogical mediated inquiry. *Organization Studies*, 32(6): 769–801.

Mainemelis, C. (2001). When the muse takes it all: A model for the experience of timelessness in organizations. *Academy of Management Review*, 26(4): 548–565.

Mainemelis, C. (2010). Stealing fire: Creative deviance in the evolution of new ideas. *Academy of Management Review*, 35(4): 558–578.

March, J. G. (1995). The future, disposable organizations and the rigidities of imagination. *Organization*, 2(3–4): 427–440.

Massey, D. B. (2005). *For Space*. London: Sage.

Massumi, B. (1996). The autonomy of affect. In P. Patton (ed.), *Deleuze: A Critical Reader* (pp. 217–239). Oxford: Blackwell.

Michel, A. (2012). Transcending socialization: A nine-year ethnography of the body's role in organizational control and knowledge workers' transformation. *Administrative Science Quarterly*, 56(3): 325–368.

Morson, G. S. and Emerson, C. (1990). *Mikhail Bakhtin: Creation of a Prosaics*. Palo Alto: Stanford University Press.

Müller, B. (2012). Organizational creativity revisited: An audio-visual ethnography of the production of contemporary movement and dance theater as "making events work." Paper submitted to the workshop "Performing ANT: Social-Material Practices of Organizing."

Navaro-Yashin, Y. (2009). Affective spaces, melancholic objects: Ruination and the production of anthropological knowledge. *Journal of the Royal Anthropological Institute*, 15(1): 1–18.

Nayak, A. (2008a). Experiencing creativity in organizations: A practice approach. *Long Range Planning*, 41(4): 420–439

Nayak, A. (2008b). On the way to theory: A processual approach. *Organization Studies*, 29(2): 173–190.

Nicholson, H. (2000). *Teaching Drama 11–18*. London: Continuum.

Osborne, T. (2003). Against "creativity": A philistine rant. *Economy and Society*, 32(4): 507–525.

Perry-Smith, J. E. (2006). Social yet creative: The role of social relationships in facilitating individual creativity. *Academy of Management Journal*, 49(1): 85–101.

Peters, M. A. (2009). Education, creativity and the economy of passions: New forms of educational capitalism. *Thesis Eleven*, 96(1): 40–63.

Peters, M. and Besley, T. (2006). *Building Knowledge Cultures: Education and Development in the Age of Knowledge Capitalism*. Lanham, MD and Oxford: Rowman & Littlefield.

Philo, C. and Parr, H. (2003). Introducing psychoanalytic geographies. *Social and Cultural Geography*, 4(3): 283–293.

Rehn, A. and De Cock, C. (2008). Deconstructing creativity. In T. Rickards, M. Runco, and S. Moger (eds.), *The Routledge Companion to Creativity* (pp. 222–231). Abingdon: Routledge.

Rorty, R. (1988). Unger, Castoriadis, and the romance of a national future. *Northwestern University Law Review*, 82(2): 335–351.

Rosanis, S. (2011). *The Birth of Democracy and Today's Crisis: Studies on Cornelius Castoriadis*. Athens: Eurasia (in Greek).

Shotter, J. (2008). Dialogism and polyphony in organizing theorizing in organization studies: Action guiding anticipations and the continuous creation of novelty. *Organization Studies*, 29(4): 501–524.

Shukaitis, S. (2008). Dancing amidst the flames: Imagination and self-organization in a minor key. *Organization*, 15(5): 743–764.

Simondon, G. (2005). *L'individuation: à la lumière des notions de forme et d'information*. Grenoble: Editions Jérôme Millon.

Simpson, B. and Marshall, N. (2010). The mutuality of emotions and learning in organizations. *Journal of Management Inquiry*, 19(4): 351–365.

Slutskaya, N. and De Cock, C. (2008). The body dances: Carnival dance and organization. *Organization*, 15(6): 851–868.

Tassis, T. (2007). *Castoriadis: A Philosophy of Autonomy*. Athens: Eurasia.

Taylor, C. (2002). Modern social imaginaries. *Public Culture*, 14(1): 91–124.

Thrift, N. (2004). Intensities of feeling: Towards a spatial politics of affect. *Geografiska Annaler: Series B, Human Geography*, 86(1): 57–78.

Thrift, N. (2008). *Non-Representational Theory: Space, Politics, Affect*. Abingdon: Routledge.

Tolia-Kelly, D. P. (2006). Affect—an ethnocentric encounter? Exploring the "universalist" imperative of emotional/affectual geographies. *Area*, 38(2): 213–217.

Tsoukas, H. (1996). The firm as a distributed knowledge system: A constructionist approach. *Strategic Management Journal*, 17: 11–25.

Tsoukas, H. (2009). A dialogical approach to the creation of new knowledge in organizations. *Organization Science*, 20(6): 941–957.

Tsoukas, H. (2013). Organization as ghaosmos. In D. Robichaud and F. Cooren (eds.), *Organization and Organizing: Materiality, Agency and Discourse* (pp. 52–65). New York: Taylor & Francis.

Unsworth, K. (2001). Unpacking creativity. *Academy of Management Review*, 26(2): 289–297.

Varela, F. J., Thompson, E., and Rosch, E. (1991). *The Embodied Mind: Cognitive Science and Human Experience*. Boston, MA: MIT Press.

Venn, C. (2010). Individuation, relationality, affect: Rethinking the human in relation to the living. *Body & Society*, 16(1): 129–161.

Voloshinov, V. and Bakhtin, M. (1929/1986). *Marxism and the Philosophy of Language*. Cambridge, MA: Harvard University Press.

Vygotsky, L. S. (2004). Imagination and creativity in childhood. *Journal of Russian and East European Psychology*, 42(1): 7–97. Reprinted from 1937.

Weick, K. E. (1979). *The Social Psychology of Organizing* (2nd edition). Reading, MA and London: Addison-Wesley.

Weick, K. E. (1989). Organized improvisation: 20 years of organizing. *Communication Studies*, 40(4): 241–248.

Wheatley, W. J., Anthony, W. P., and Maddox, E. N. (1991). Selecting and training strategic planners with imagination and creativity. *Journal of Creative Behavior*, 25(1): 52–60.

Woodman, R. W., Sawyer, J. E., and Griffin, R. W. (1993). Toward a theory of organizational creativity. *Academy of Management Review*, 18(2): 293–321.

Zhang, Z. (2007). Creativity, imagination and physicality in organizations. Paper presented at the Fifth Conference of Critical Management Studies (CMS5), Manchester.

5

Negotiating Novelty

How Cultural Psychology Looks at Organizational Dynamics

Jaan Valsiner

Abstract: Cultural psychology is a new area of general psychology that brings together developmental and social psychologies with cultural anthropology and history. It emerged at the intersection of developmental and social psychologies in the 1980s, combined with the interests of educational institutions. Within a set of different directions in cultural psychology, it is the semiotic dynamics direction that uniquely focuses on the processes of sign construction and use in irreversible time. Sign use guides actions, and actions feed forward to new construction and use of signs. This feed-forward loop involves the building and demolishing of sign hierarchies that control both continuity and innovation of general meaningfulness of the ongoing activities. The negotiation of *safety* in organizational discourses illustrates the general principles of sign-mediated processes of regulating organizational dynamics.

Organizations are open systems that therefore are capable of development. Furthermore, they are autopoietic systems that, through relating with their surroundings, construct their own development. In this regard, the study of organizational dynamics has much in common with developmental science (Carolina Consortium on Human Development, 1996). As cultural psychology has made its re-entrance into psychology over the past two decades (Valsiner, 2012), one can find common roots in the efforts to study organizational dynamics with a number of the trends present in the new effort to bring culture back to psychology. Thus, the work of George Herbert Mead, Charles Sanders Peirce, Magoroh Maruyama, Lev Vygotsky, and Mikhail Bakhtin figures prominently in both cultural psychology and organizational process research (Maruyama, 2004; Simpson, 2009, 2014). Questions of meaning-making in the context of organizational emergence are issues of common—or at least parallel—interest in cultural psychology and organizational processes research. Semiotic perspectives are becoming used in organization research starting from both the roots of Saussure (Musson, Cohen, and Tietze, 2007) and Peirce (Lorino, Tricard, and Clot, 2011), as well as Bakhtin (Lorino and Tricard, 2012; Shotter, 2008). *Novelty* is a key concept for both developmental science and organizational dynamics research—and it requires the introduction of *time* as a constitutive feature of developmental and organizational dynamics.

Time in development is *irreversible*—past and future are asymmetric. This creates the (seemingly) paradoxical status of processes of development that was captured by James Mark Baldwin over a century ago (as a "positive postulate"):

> that series of events is truly genetic which cannot be constructed before it has happened, and which cannot be exhausted backwards, after it has happened. (Baldwin, 1906, p. 21)

The "positive" nature of this postulate is in its focusing of the study of development on that of the unfolding novel processes, rather than their prediction, or retrospective explanation. As applied to the study of organizational dynamics, the postulate suggests the focus on the study of these processes as the location where outcomes are produced, rather than trying to reconstruct the processes based on the outcomes. The task of organizational management—whether it is a business firm, an institution, a family trying to bring up children, or a person oneself trying to develop—is the same: *how to organize the set of ongoing processes so that they can lead to the desired or best outcomes*. But since the outcomes cannot be pre-known, due to the uncertainty of moving towards the always indeterminate future, there is always uncertainty in what the outcomes of the present array of processes might be. Hence the study of process dynamics has the chance to clarify the emergence of novel outcomes (the forward look), but the reverse look from outcomes to emergence of novelty (the backward look) cannot reveal where novelty emerges. In human purposeful activities such novelty emerges in the context that is meaningful—what human beings do, and how they try to do it differently, are all concrete actions imbued with socially created meanings. The hard work by a start-up company to become successful in its business, or the efforts of parents to give their children the best education to make them secure for their futures—are all built here-and-now on the basis of imagination of what such futures should look like.

What can cultural psychology bring to organization studies that is not yet known, or used? Obviously not the central focus on affective meaning construction, or the importance of looking at the phenomena through a theatrical creativity lens—these perspectives are already in place (Cornelissen, 2004, 2006; Simpson and Marshall, 2010). Nor the focus on innovation—studies of the complexity of the dynamics of companies (e.g. Garud, Gehman, and Kumaraswamy, 2011) provide far richer and better grounded evidence of how companies set up conditions for sustained innovation than any analysis of a developing child or emerged adult can provide in the realm of psychology. However, maybe the innovative moment from cultural psychology could be in the careful look at the *relationships between signs* used in meaning construction? That such relationships are important is apparent from the increasingly common approach to organizational dynamics through semiotic and Bakhtinian lenses. Yet there is an assumption of equality inherent in the Bakhtinian focus on polyphony of "voices"—in the mind, in fiction, and in organizations. I start from the opposite assumption—signs (like sign makers) are in non-equal relations with one another—it is *dynamic sign hierarchies* that organize the dynamic flow of systemic phenomena. Equality in their relations is a temporary dynamic state that is transient, and can be temporarily stabilized only with special maintenance tactics. Borrowing George Herbert Mead's focus on the relations of "the Other" and "the Generalized Other" (Simpson, 2009) might be viewed as a step to looking at meaning-making in organizations as a hierarchic dynamic process. Both relating with the Others, and generalization, are relevant in the semiotic perspective elaborated here.

5.1 Looking Through the Lens of Semiotic Dynamics: How Signs Work

The basic model of the semiotic dynamics perspective is simple—human beings, while relating with their environment (acting upon it) create signs that regulate that very process of acting in irreversible time (Figure 5.1).

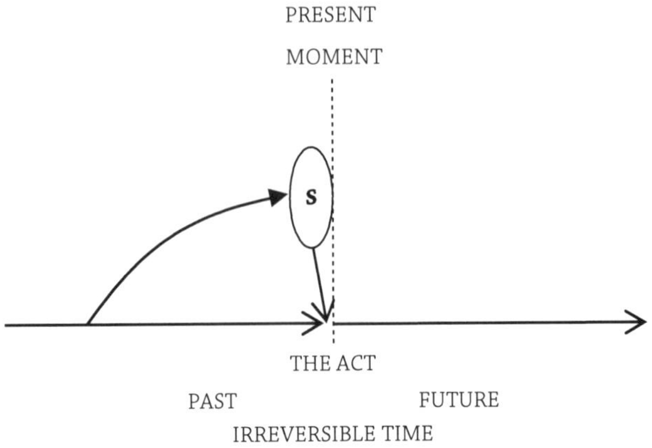

Figure 5.1 The core of the dynamic semiotic perspective: duality of the act

Within the flow of irreversible time, the sign (S) differentiates from the ongoing experience and becomes available at the present moment to guide that moment towards the future in two ways—immediate (at the locus of the Act) and through its relative extension over time—for the future (Sf). The act of meaningful social construction is thus always dual—involving action towards the future *through the context of the sign* (S), and vice versa (i.e. the sign has the act as its context). The phenomenon and its context cannot be separated from each other—by charting out a phenomenon its context is charted out dependently (according to co-genetic logic—Herbst, 1995). If we draw a circle on a blank piece of paper, such as:

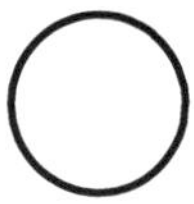

it is only our cognitive economy and language conventions that promote us to claim "this is a circle." In reality, we have created a triplet {outside<>border<>inside} that we label "circle" by selectively focusing on the inside of the figure (as if it were *one* "thing"), de-focusing from the ground. In reality it is a structure of three—all of the parts come into being simultaneously (as we draw "a circle") and vanish simultaneously (if we eliminate the border). One cannot eliminate the inside (nor outside) of the circle without eliminating the other parts. The "outside" is the inevitable context for the "inside," and the border is that which both separates and unifies them.

This double function of borders—to separate and unify at the same time—is a crucial feature for treating the notion of "context-boundedness" in cultural psychology (Marsico, Komatsu, and Iannaccone, 2013). The context is the ground for the figure and is inseparable from the latter. The context does not "act upon" the object (nor the object on the context), but *relates with it* as part of the system. The locus of such relating is the border—or, to use a biological metaphor—the *membrane*. The membrane of a cell is the location where one cell relates with its neighbors, leading to the functioning of the organism as a whole.

5.2 Irreversible Time and the Role of Signs

Our sign-making takes place in irreversible time. We act and reflect upon what we are doing. The duality of the act (in Figure 5.1) is given by the necessity of simultaneous acting (from present moment towards the future, which is to become present at the next moment) and some version of reflecting on what is going on. These processes are rapid, and cannot be retracted. The power of signs regulating human conduct is so obvious that under our ordinary conditions we hardly notice it.

In some pathological cases that power gives rise to dramatic and sometimes amusing examples. Thus, Pierre Janet (1919, p. 193) describes one of his patients (Nof, 19 years of age) who, walking around in Paris notices a hatmaker's shop and remarks to himself "*. . . c'est une boutique de chapelier où on achète des chapeaux*" [this is a hat shop where one buys hats]—after which he enters the shop and buys himself a hat that he does not need. Creating the meaning of the place activated a pattern of conduct that puts into practice the action *possibility* as if it were an action *imperative*. The same Nof, walking by the Gare de Lyon railway station, says to himself "*C'est une gare de chemin de fer, on y entre pour voyager*" [this is a railway station from where one starts to travel]—after which he enters the station, buys a ticket to Marseille, and travels—only realizing half-way to the destination that he had not planned to travel anywhere.

In these examples the power of the sign is not that of an inhibitor, but rather that of an unconditional determiner of the actions. Our naming of something leads us to immediately act upon it—rather than delay action. This is not automatically the case in our normal self-regulation. Here the determinative nature of the emerging sign generates its own limits (e.g. "this is a railway station, *but I have no intention to travel* anywhere" and "this is a hat shop *but I do not wear hats*"). In our ordinary lives the signs that create meaning of something simultaneously set up the field of action possibilities involving the object, and that of limits upon these possibilities. This is similar to the case of the circle that is actually a triplet (above)—signs create oppositions.

Let us consider a generic case—if I say "this is X" I actually create an opposition "X <> non-X" where the border (<>) plays a definitive role (Josephs, Valsiner, and Surgan, 1999). In German (the language in which psychology was predominantly written up to the 1920s) this is reflected by the notion of *Gegenstand* ("stand against something"—its English translation as "object" retains the notion if treated as a verb—"to object to something"). There is an inevitable, continuous construction of the *Gegenstand* between past and future in all processes that unfold in irreversible time.

A sign as *Gegenstand* in the context of irreversible time comes into being at the border of the triplet {PAST<border-which-is-present>FUTURE}. As signs emerge in the flow of experiencing and regulate that flow in the present, they can also set up a residual guidance of similar flow in some unspecifiable time in the future. Such feed-forward functions of the emerged sign may be explicit—fixing it in some form to be usable in the future, or implicit—carried forth to anticipate similar situations in the unpredictable future (see Figure 5.2—Future anticipated present moment). *The function of signs is always future-oriented*—both in their immediate impact (turning the next immediate future into a new present) and their general orientation towards encountering similar situations in some indeterminate future moment.

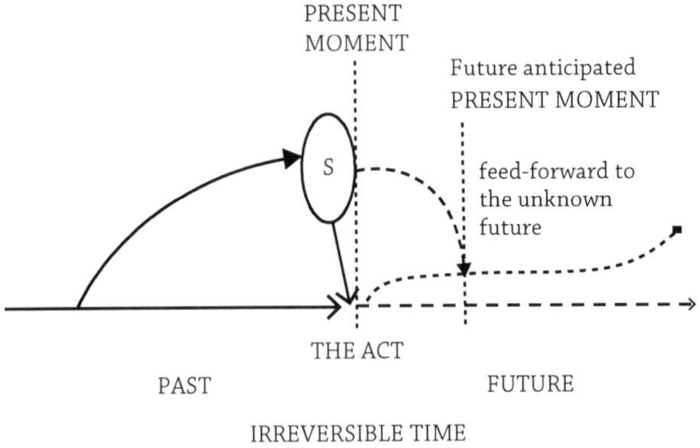

Figure 5.2 The emerged sign with functional longevity (feed-forward to the future)

This brings us to the curious question: if sign use is future-oriented, how can it be that the meaning-makers are constantly referencing the past—digging into one's memory, trying to recall relevant life moments of the past? Persons look for their "roots," organizations create their "corporate histories," and countries rewrite their histories in line with promoting patriotism. The meaning-maker at the present accesses different traces of the signs of the past—yet only those that can be accessed now as she or he is moving towards the future. What looks as if it entails "looking back" at the given moment is actually "looking forward"—thanks to the accessibility of different trace signs from the past. Within irreversible time one cannot reference "what was" without making it to be in the service of "what might come" (Figure 5.3). Frederic Bartlett's classic work that demonstrates the reconstructive nature of memory fits the consultation of the past at the present, while our imagination provides us simulation of the future (Zittoun et al., 2013).

The unity of presentation (*Vorstellung*)—referencing imagined future—and representation (*Darstellung*) in irreversible time—executed through signs—sets the stage for the principled uniqueness of every sign.

Understanding of the uniqueness of human experience is crucial. Our living—inevitably—within irreversible time sets limits on our ways of reflecting upon our experiences. Like these experiences themselves, signs that make it possible for us to reflect upon these experiences are constantly undergoing change. Signs—words here are a fitting example—are never the *same*, only *similar* (Sovran, 1992). We

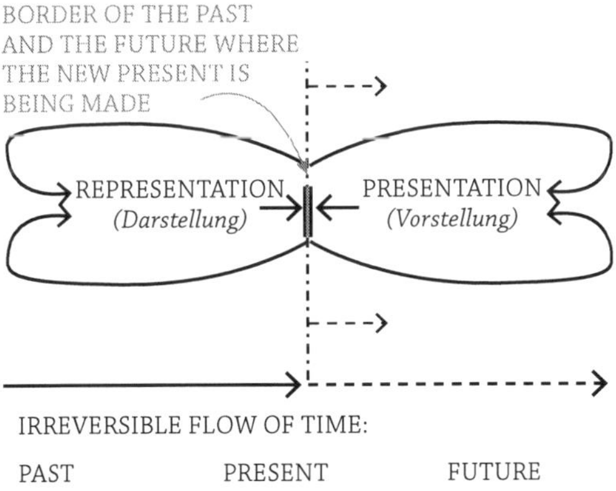

Figure 5.3 The unity of presentation (*Vorstellung*) and representation (*Darstellung*) in the case of processes in irreversible time

may easily forget the basic truth that this morning is different from yesterday's, or that giving birth to the first child is not the same as that of one's tenth child.

Yet in our everyday life, we are blind to the flow of novelties that are part of our development in irreversible time, glossing over *their similarity* with previous instances by considering them *the same*. Our capacity to categorize life events into homogeneous classes makes us "blind" to the dynamic processes that are involved. Such "blindness" has high "cognitive survival" value in making sense of our worlds in terms of stability. Yet such stability itself is our illusion of convenience.

5.3 From Duality of Signs to the Creation of Sign Hierarchies

How is stability created in the flow of dynamic uncertainty? A relevant feature of the emerging sign is its self-regulatory potential—it is ready to regulate something else, as well as itself. The latter guarantees dynamic stability of a sign. Each sign can be thought of as including two regulatory functions:

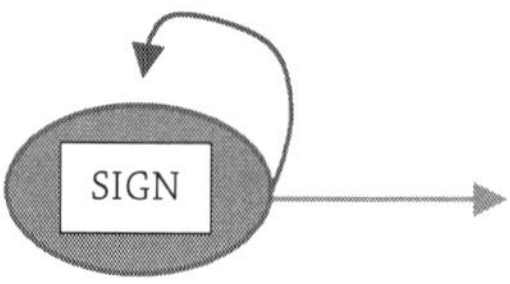

Examples of the coordination of these two sign functions abound. When your marginal acquaintance showers you with lavish praise for no apparent reason it is not you who is being praised, but she/he oneself who is doing the praising for one's own sake. We are eager to invent stable beliefs and convictions that keep us going even under most adverse external circumstances.

A sign's emergence can lead to the parallel emergence of another sign (see IN in Figure 5.4) the function of which is to regulate the first sign. A case reported by Vladimir Bekhterev—in the context of post-hypnotic suggestion—illustrates the work of inhibitory signs:

> I suggested to a person in hypnosis that when he wakes up he must take a postcard from the table. When he woke up, he almost immediately looked around on the table and his gaze became fixated on a certain spot. Do you see something—I asked. "I see a postcard." I said good-bye to him and prepared to

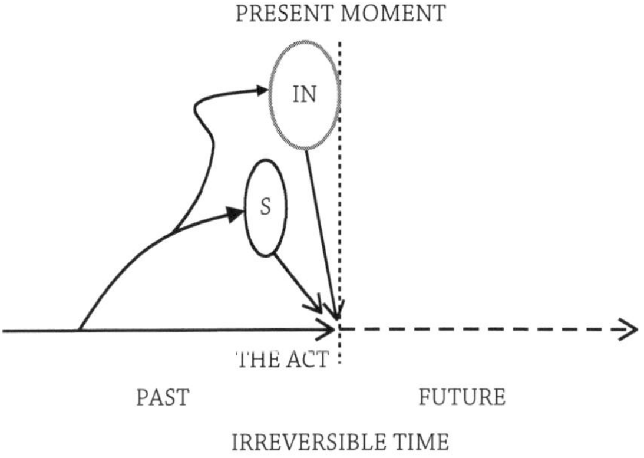

Figure 5.4 Sign hierarchy as an inhibitory sign (IN) emerges and blocks the meaning (S)

> leave, but he still keeps staring at the table. Don't you need to do anything?—I ask. "I would like to take that card, but I do not need it!"—answers the man, and leaves—not having fulfilled the suggestion and obviously fighting with it. (Bekhterev, 1903, p. 14)

The emerging meaning ("this is a postcard" and "I want to take it" [the suggestion]) is blocked by the inhibiting meaning ("I do not need it"). The example also illustrates the notion of circumvention strategies—meanings that override the previously constructed ones, to allow for new experience rather than be cycled in the middle of previous dilemmas.

What Bekhterev's example illustrates is that both activation and inhibition of the hypnotically suggested act ("take the postcard") are in action. The suggestion did not produce a behavior—a reaction—but rather a tension between two meanings: I FEEL I *WANT TO* TAKE THIS CARD and I *DO NOT NEED* THIS CARD. Both meanings are expressed in field-like generalized terms of WANTING—which specifies the direction of the act (in opposition to non-WANTING) and NEEDING—the negation of which neutralizes the former sign (Figure 5.4).

How would the inhibitor sign emerge in the sign-construction process? It is posited that each sign (A) simultaneously evokes its counter-sign field (non-A—Josephs et al., 1999). In this case, the emerging sign lets its counter-sign field "grow" an opposing sign—which could be the "inhibitor" (IN): S & non-S ➔ S & IN ➔ non-IN & IN (with elimination of S).[1] The meaning-making process produces both the meaning and its limit, allowing the latter to eliminate the former.

5.4 Preserving Signs Through Generalization

Not all signs are constructed anew. Many are maintained within our semiosphere—the field of meanings we create within our subjective internalized worlds—as well as in our environments. Meanings can be preserved through the acts of sign maintenance that happen in unique moments but that carry the meaning (and relevance) of a sign to the future. External aids for such maintenance can be created—our urban worlds are filled with reminders for getting rid of previously useful and meaningful objects (the presence of "garbage cans"), honoring the past (monuments and museums), as well as giving used objects and ideas a chance for a rebirth (flea markets and "recycling centers"). Such "management of memory" goes beyond objects—many acts of talking (or communication in general) that are dissociated from immediate action regulation perform such maintenance functions. For instance, gossiping about the reported (or suspected) sexual escapade by a celebrity (that has absolutely no bearing upon the real life of that celebrity) is an arena of maintaining the usability of generalized signs such as *trust, fidelity* (and *infidelity*), *cheating, morality, adultery,* etc. Subjecting oneself to theatre performances or cinema can maintain the uses of such general signs even further—the invention and performances of operas[2] like *Othello* may be the maintenance grounds for *jealousy,* and many other generalized (and hyper-generalized—Valsiner, 2007) signs. These are signs that carry intuitively understandable meanings shared by many people—yet are not specifiable in concrete terms. At the same time, these hyper-generalized meanings can be easily (and rapidly) deployed to make sense of events in new settings.

5.4.1 An Example: The Mutualities of CLEAN and DIRTY

Generalized signs operate in the mediation of basic social practices. Many of these include regular dynamic maintenance tasks. Consider the generalized notion of cleanliness—we are brought up with the understanding that washing our hands before every meal is a must, or that washing the feet before entering a mosque is a duty. Our dentists diligently prescribe various techniques for cleaning teeth. When we see a drop of water on an otherwise dry plate we are ready to "wipe it clean." The anticipation of the opposite—"my hands are likely to get dirty" can trigger the feeling in an action context that they now are dirty. The sign complex {CLEAN (good) <>> non-clean ("dirty")} guides us to wash our hands, clothes, floors, and

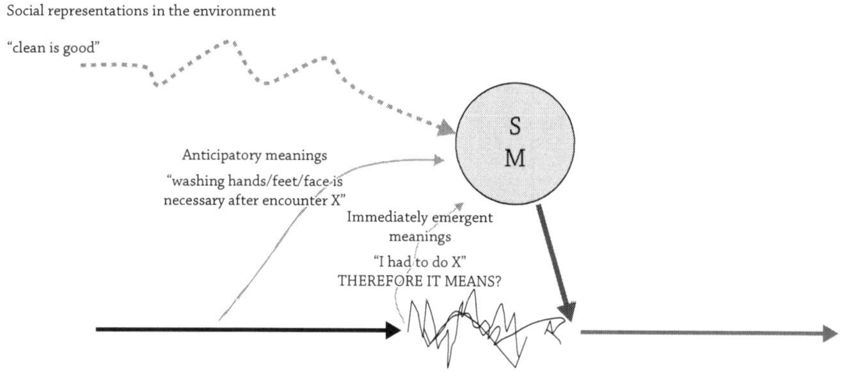

Figure 5.5 Social representations in the environment

cars, and any other "washables." The sign complex is a semiotic mediator in the context where *something is to become washed*—it is a combination of signs of different longevity and generality. As a result we can observe people all over the world in regular cleaning activities. *What* they clean may vary dramatically, but that *they feel they need to clean* is a human cultural universal (Figure 5.5).

The example of cleanliness illustrates a dynamic system that is proceeding in an eternal loop of movement between the temporary dominance of one of the two sides—anything that can become dirty can be made clean and become dirty again. This loop may be represented mathematically by Möbius strip, or in my terms of dynamics of meaning change by the growth of the opposite dominant meaning out of the sub-dominant (contextual) field of the present meaning (Figure 5.6). It is an example of lateral extension of the sign-regulation system—one state of meaning opposition flows into the other, and from there to the further state of the previous one, but no qualitative transformation of the system itself occurs. The "cleaning cycle" recurs over and over, without giving rise to the synthesis of a "final perpetually clean" state (at which the cycle could stop) or "final infinitely dirty" state—at which the cycle would stop as well, as cleaning would be considered an unnecessary or useless task.

Such closed reverberating cycles are substitutes for development. They keep the given system moving constantly between two opposite states, without qualitative novelty emerging. Relative novelty is rampant—each new state of CLEAN is a negation of previous state of DIRTY, and each CLEAN leads to new construction of DIRTY. Yet there is no synthesis of a qualitatively new state that would negate the previous negation.[3] Hence

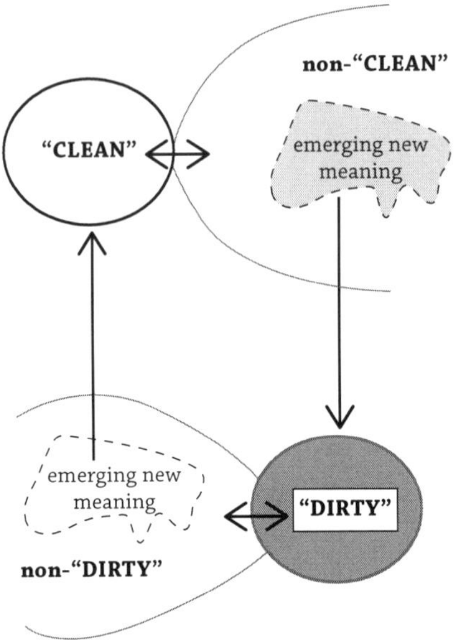

Figure 5.6 The eternal cycle of DIRTY and CLEAN

the focus on dynamic processes can be of two kinds—that of *dynamic stability* (as in Figure 5.6) and *dynamic innovation* (emergence of a new synthetic state). The latter includes the emergence of sign hierarchies and their self-regulation.

5.4.2 Growing Hierarchies of Signs: Potential for Dynamic Innovation

Building sign hierarchies guides human action—and it also creates psychological tensions. Figure 5.7 gives a schematic view of the ways dynamic sign hierarchies may unfold, be demolished, or proceed to a new qualitative level of organization. Our ordinary lives give us examples of dialogical negotiation within the emerging sign hierarchy (Figure 5.4). The inhibitor sign can itself be inhibited by yet another sign that gains a role higher up in the hierarchy.

The usual story of a weight-watching person on his or her birthday is an example of this internal dialogue: "I want that cake" (sign X) → "but I am on diet, I should not eat it" (sign X + 1) → "but today is my birthday" (sign X + 2). This hierarchical inhibition <> dis-inhibition process leads to

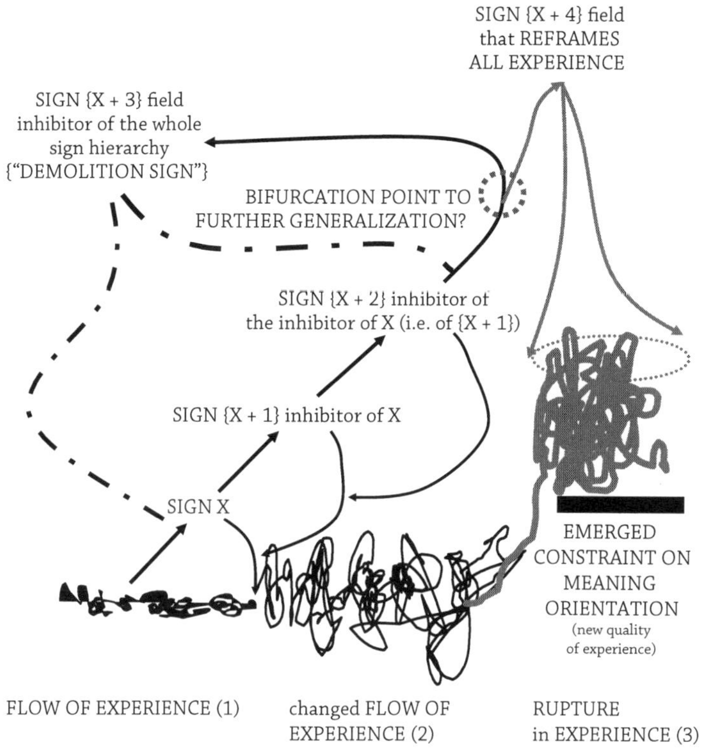

Figure 5.7 Emergence of a fixed dominant regulatory (FDR) sign

eating of the cake. This is a dialogical solution to the simple act of eating—prior to the act itself the anticipatory process of negotiation emerges. The act of eating can also emerge without such dialogicality—a person sees the cake, and eats it. The same act can be accomplished immediately, or going through a process of semiotic mediation. Immediacy is the general biological rule, while mediation emerges with the emergence of human beings as a species.

Alternatively, the negotiation about eating can be eliminated (sign X + 3 in Figure 5.7) by demolishing the whole sign hierarchy. Examples of such demolition abound—a previous meaning used to organize the current action can be suddenly abandoned. The meaning construction system operates by the principle of abundance—most of the signs we construct or bring over from past maintenance are abandoned—before, or after, use.

5.4.3 Tension between Innovation and Demolition

As the sign hierarchy expands towards generalization, at a certain moment our meaning-making system introduces a qualitative break—a "jump" in the affectively hyper-generalized meaning hierarchy—that reorganizes the current experience by giving it a qualitatively new flavor. The growth of such a sign—FDR (Fixed Dominant Regulator—{X + 4})—is the means through which rapid changes in generalized meanings come about. A "friend" may be rapidly turned into an "enemy," or a person undergoes religious or political conversion. This kind of generalized leap in the constructed meaning system is the target of any system of moral socialization.

Once the FDR emerges (in contrast to its opposite—Demolition Sign) at the bifurcation point to further generalization, it *changes the whole meaning field* of the meaning-maker, blocking the newly reconceptualized meaning system from intervention by previous meanings. This happens through establishment of a border—EMERGED CONSTRAINT ON MEANING ORIENTATION in Figure 5.7. The dynamically changing sign hierarchy becomes fixed through such constraint in a cycle of dynamic stability. Fixed and *affectively defended* meanings emerge—an *opinion*, rather than *thought*, starts to dominate the meaning field. The previously flexible meaning-maker turns into a rigid believer in an idea. All political and religious ideologies fixate themselves through this mechanism.

Such constraining of experience leads to the invention of new interpretations based on the constraint. A neighbor's gaze can become turned into an "evil eye," or into an act of spying for an "evil" empire, or made into a personalized demonic force. Likewise, the measurement of food qualities in neutral units (calories) becomes imbued with hyper-generalized meaning of *healthy* (or *non-healthy*). Political credos and fundamentalist exasperations are all set up by such constraints (e.g. *security* <> *non-security*). Claims that some act of inconvenience or limitation is forced upon us "for security reasons" are field-like signs used to legitimize assertions of institutional power *as if it is to the benefit* of the targets of such actions. Discourses on these ill-defined generalized notions are used constantly in organizations for regulating concrete action contexts. The world is filled with safety instructions, security guards, and policies to implement these in ever new areas of human living. From the perspective of cultural psychology of semiotic dynamics these human inventions are examples of materialized signs (called "safety instructions").

5.5 Organizational Dynamics: The Making of Safety in Skyscraper Construction

Erecting tall buildings—ranging from medieval church towers or minarets to modern skyscrapers—is an organizational effort that involves the differentiation of perspectives of the constructors and outside observers (Figure 5.8). The company that undertakes the construction work has its own differentiation of personnel into "office workers" (who might never visit the construction site, but who would create instructions for workers on the site) and "workers" (who do the job on the site, are recipients of all instructions—whether following or ignoring these—and who can end up in varied on-job accidents, and might never visit the "office"[4]). There are no serious accident concerns in the office conditions from where safety instructions for the construction site emanate. In contrast, there can be rampant dangers of new accidents, built into the construction conditions themselves (Lorino et al., 2011, p. 789)—especially as the high-rise building grows, floor by floor. The third set

Figure 5.8 Difference in perspectives: outsiders' view of a construction site

of perspectives is that of uninvolved bystanders who pass by the construction site, in awe at the enormous heights at which the construction work proceeds. They have no idea of the actual accident dangers inherent in the construction, nor of the efforts (from the "office") to prevent such undesirable events from happening. Their own fears may be limited to objects falling from the high-rise construction site. The three positions are strictly differentiated—by expertise, and by relation to the task. The ones who see most (the passers-by) are the most ignorant of the construction process. The ones who know (actual construction workers) do not have the luxury of enjoying the site from below (but have a perspective only from above, more distant with each meter of the upward growth of the building). While being (literally) up and above all other participants in the scene, they are in social power sub-dominant to the "office staff" (who create instructions, oversee working hours, pay salaries, order supplies, etc.).

Negotiations about work on skyscraper constructions are an example of the deep dialogicality of organizational dynamics and can proceed in ways coming close to the need to be relocated in a "boxing ring" (Lorino et al., 2011, p. 789). Under pressures of the construction timetable safety rules can be bypassed in practice. It is all the more remarkable that the construction company may decide to bring the accident report data to the level of symbolic importance on a "scorecard" used as a problem-solving tool in administration-to-site manager relations (Tricard and Lorino, 2013, table 2). The practice which lasted for six months may be abandoned as accidents did not diminish over that period of time.

Both the acts of introduction and elimination of the practice are relevant from the perspective of cultural psychology. It needs to be added that the mere *number* of accidents in the communicative messages between the partners who themselves were not accident-prone (office workers and foremen) is an institutional symbolic *value negotiation about* safety. It is not a means that would generate heightened safety orientation in the actual workplace (where violation of safety conditions is often the only way to get the job done).

What the episode of including (and later removing) the number of accidents for the given month on the "scorecard" reflects is the ambivalent nature of public disclosure of sensitive information in public documents. Accidents on construction sites are similar to casualties in a war—unavoidable, but better avoided. Reflection upon them (see Figure 5.1) is a necessary part of the planned actions to get the job done. Yet that reflection may lead to two opposites, both of which are functionally similar to the accidents themselves—displaying them in public, or hiding them from public view.

Of course accidents that have already happened cannot be reversed—but can only be used to try to prevent next ones. Examples of accidents—simulation of the dangerous moves that did lead to the example—can be viewed as signs guiding the practitioners towards preventing future ones. These are personal tools of working towards future accident prevention—through the worker's internalized use of simulation heuristics. In contrast, the organization provides an external counterpart for such personal reflection tools—by a form of communicative messages called "safety instructions."

Safety *instructions*—produced not by the actors themselves but by others who regulate the practice—operate as inhibitory signs (IN in Figure 5.2). The instructions are timeless—they are written down, and at times recited to the workers in oral "consciousness raising" ceremonies. In contrast, any accident is an emergent tragedy that happens in irreversible time (Gärling and Valsiner, 1985). The actual success (or failure) of any instruction in the here-and-now context depends upon its translation from the role of a timeless semiotic tool to the one needed at the present moment. Such translation can be blocked by the need of the given task, as was the case in the construction of a skyscraper (Lorino et al., 2011; Tricard and Lorino, 2013)—keeping the building process on schedule was possible only by violating safety standards.

5.5.1 The Role of the Promoter Sign

Based on the realities of the skyscraper construction, the appearance (and later disappearance) of the accident data on the "scorecard" can be interpreted as an effort to create a *promoter sign* (Valsiner, 2004) for the construction collective. The promoter sign is any semiotic tool that is brought into (or invented in) the given activity context with the goal of guiding the activity in some direction (in this case: awareness of the accident-proneness of the setting, the need to reduce the chances of accidents happening, etc.). By adding the accident data to the economic performance parameters on the "scorecard" the symbolic importance of the safety issues was to become treated similarly to the fulfilling of the construction tasks per se. Yet making the issue public through externalization (from the managers' minds to the "scorecard") can backfire—instead of *promoting* safety the data recorded monthly can show the realities of actual *declining* safety (if the accident numbers grow). Public visibility of

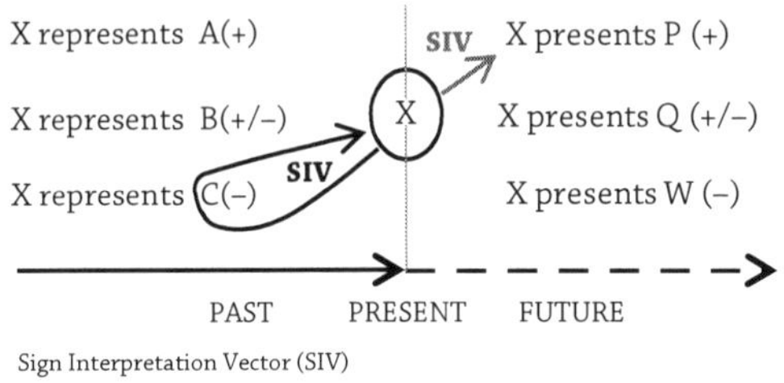

Figure 5.9 The multiple facets—due to added valuations—of a sign (X) in its ambiguous status between past and future (with Sign Interpretation Vectors—SIV)

such evidence can turn the safety-promotion act into non-safety display, thus undermining the future sign regulation of the processes. As a result, what was seen as a promotion possibility becomes a hindrance to the *self-presentation* of the construction company. Instead of public visibility as an organization concerned with safety it becomes publicly visible as an organization of worsening safety record. The same sign—accident data recorded on the "scorecard"—moves from the realm of future-oriented prevention guidance (presentation, *Vorstellung*) into a past-oriented representation (*Darstellung*) domain (Figure 5.3). The dynamic movement between past and future can become fixated—onto the past (and present—"this company is accident-prone"). Each sign—operating in irreversible time—references both the (reconstructed, at the moment) past and (desired) possible future (Figure 5.9).

5.5.2 Sign Interpretation Vector (SIV)

In the case of signs in irreversible time dynamics, each sign entails not only what it presents (about the future) or represents (reconstructing the past), but specific directional linkages (which I label Sign Interpretation Vectors, or SIVs) that guide the meaning-maker to the particular affective value-addition of the (re)presenting process. Thus, as depicted in Figure 5.9, the sign X "faces forward" (to the future) with a positive valuation ("X presents P and that is good") while at the same time it represents something else—with negative valuation. Introducing accident data onto the "scorecard" can be interpreted as "we have a poor safety record in our past but we are going to reach a good safety record in the future." As months go by, and the actual accident data reported fail to live up to the promises for the future, the sign can be abandoned. Institutional intentionality is encoded in the SIV—when needed, a select aspect of the past becomes linked with the direction for the future ("we were bad→ but now we will improve"). When undermining the symbolic construction of the future ("we were bad and we still are bad") the referencing of the past can be abandoned. Or redirected. In other terms—in institutional practices the linking of representation and presentation is strategically constructed. Hiding something from the past can function in similar ways to highlighting it (or something else).

Many such acts of institutional linking become encoded into operational documents. In terms of the legacy of George Herbert Mead (Simpson, 2014) the "scorecard" is a significant symbol that mediates meaning-making in the transaction between the "construction site" and the "office." I would add that such significant symbols mediate the process in a "two-faced" way—one of the perspectives facing the future (and being intentional as such), the other facing the past, selectively reconstructing selected aspects of it for the future. In this unity we can locate the inherent intentionality of the sign.

The adding of SIVs to the (re)presentational roles of the signs is an important step to make semiotics work in the case of dynamic processes. Traditionally, signs have been viewed solely as representing tools for something else—they "stand in" for that "something else." In the context of the cultural psychology of semiotic dynamics the signs function in the present to arrive at a new "settlement" between the past and the future (which is, by now, the immediately passing Present). Both utopian and progressive narratives ("PAST was bad but FUTURE will be good") as well as the "status quo" of fatalism ("PAST was bad and FUTURE will be bad too") emerge from the SIVs that are attached to linking the sign with the asymmetric past and future. *Each sign we construct in our irreversible meaning-making process has its SIVs with the past and with the future.* In other terms, each sign takes the form of duality of the core (sign) and its interpretation vectors—oriented towards the future, and referencing (selectively and reconstructively) the past. This idea provides further structure to Charles S. Peirce's notion of the interpretant.

5.5.3 Directionality of the Interpretant

What I do here is to add *double directionality* to C. S. Peirce's notion of the *interpretant*—the third in his triangular system of OBJECT–SIGN–INTERPRETANT. When set up in the context of irreversible time, the Interpretant is no longer abstractly located in the space (Peirceian triangle) but acquires concrete direction in the meaning-making processes that transiently are going on through-in the present. The same person—under different suggestions—can produce a life history narrative of "happy childhood" (A in Figure 5.9) or of the turmoils of being "emotionally abused" by bullying peers (B), or of the "negative life" under a totalitarian political regime (C). Likewise, the same person may project different valuations into the future. "Life has been hard, and will always be" can be contrasted with "I had a hard life but from now on I will live well." Independent of whether any of the future expectations actually materialize, they organize the person's life in the present.

5.5.4 Teleogenetic Actions

Organizations are constantly on the move—even if they seem to be stable. Planning by some of their members is put into practice by someone else, at a different time and location. Conditions for actualization of the plans, there-and-then, can be different from any planning, here-and-now. Organizing human life in any domain is no different from the empirical example of building a skyscraper—only the outcomes may be more variable and less visible.

Human activities are teleo*genetic*—future goals are constructed in the course of ongoing activities. These directions can be contested, stopped, renegotiated. The Shell Oil and Greenpeace confrontation about the decommissioning of an oil rig—the Brent Spar—in 1995 (Tsoukas, 1999) was an occasion of stopping the abandonment of the old oil rig in the sea based on negotiation of the symbolic futures (environmental pollution) while the plan of dumping the rig in the sea fitted with all the meaningfulness of safety as it was understood in the past.

The "David and Goliath" story of the fate of the oil rig acquires a different focus from the perspective of cultural psychology—with an emphasis on the double nature of the value insertion into the meanings that guide organizations' actions. The economic value (cost/benefit analysis) of the two options of getting rid of the rig (into the sea or on land) was clearly on the side of dumping it into the sea (together with full legal protection of that act). Yet the public symbolic value—built around the meanings constructed around environmental pollution—turned out to be the opposite. The tension between the double meanings led to specific actions (and cessation of planned actions) with that specific retired oil rig. As it was taken from one place to another, protesters moved also from one place to that other place to create a mass media dramatization (which all public protests are), and clients boycotted the company's products in third places, hence undermining the economic value of the planned act.

Importantly, all the negotiations around that very big object were in the realm of meaning projections into the AS-IF domain: What if the sunken oil rig pollutes the sea? What if all oil companies follow Shell if that plan for the first rig to be sunk is allowed to happen? What would all this mean for oil prices? The only object outside of these AS-IF (or AS-COULD-BE) discourses was the oil rig itself—no longer producing anything, but a bothersome "leftover object" (albeit a very big one) floating in the North Sea, no longer of any use, but a headache for the human beings in their organizational roles to get rid of in *meaningful* ways.[5] Similar tasks have recurred even more dramatically ever since the Brent Spar story—for example, dealing with nuclear energy issues after the Fukushima tsunami and earthquake disaster in Japan (2011), or the *Costa Concordia* accident (2012). In cases like that, grossly oversized industrial objects that were the responsibility of large corporate organizations were irrevocably damaged. The negotiations about the meanings given to the disasters—creating narratives of blame (for what happened) and of planning (what to do with such large dysfunctional objects)—are all in the symbolic domain.

5.6 Dynamic Social Geography of the Interpretant

I would here introduce the notion of Dynamic Social Geography of the Interpretant. Not only is the process of meaning-making happening in irreversible time (see Figures 5.1–5.6), but it also involves space—as objects about which meaningful decisions are to be made move around in space. As they move—or are moved by some agents—the movement becomes a meaning-triggering event for all the participants in the field. Obviously such movements are easy to detect in case of very large (and at times debilitated) objects like Brent Spar or *Costa Concordia*. Brent Spar is being towed in the North Sea at a slow pace in some direction, and the opponents of the deep sea dumping of the rig understand the plan is beginning to be put into practice. They act against it—and stop the move.

Less obviously—but more usually—we see such movements in our everyday environments in the movement of objects that acquire symbolic value. Finding a baby carriage with a baby inside in front of an American store (with the mother in the store shopping) can immediately evoke in passers-by the strange uneasy feeling of "child abandonment," while a similar scene in a Danish town passes the evaluative meaning-making lens as an ordinary part of "the mother is shopping," or "the baby is getting fresh air." In parallel, the decision made by the mother—*"can I leave my baby here for a few moments?"* is a sign-mediated decision in irreversible time, yet considerate of the social geography of the interpretant (estimation of the place—"here"). The precise "here" changes as the person moves in space, and the meaning constructed changes with the move.

The places in the Dynamic Social Geography of the Interpretant are saturated with social suggestions. A warning of caution at a specific location of an activity context creates a signified highlight for the very mundane activity, *presuming that there is some reason* for such caution in that setting. The authority of the inserter of such messages is accomplished—even if the precise identity of it is not directly revealed.

In these locations the various instructions for safety, or reminders of the obvious ("mind the step" one can see and hear in public places where trains stop or escalators end) signify the social guidance of organizational processes. The spatial locations for the display of such instructions create the spatial support for the meaning-making dynamics. Very often the instructions are displayed in places where they are quite unlikely to be read, but very likely to be seen. They are authority markers over the meaning-making fields. A hotel offering its guests lockable boxes—safes—for their valuables demonstrates its concerns for *safety* (while releasing itself from *responsibilities,* delegating those to the users of the safes). A researcher who contacts human beings is expected to ask them to sign a "consent form" that inserts the authority of the institution in between the researcher and the person.

5.7 General Conclusion: Can the Cultural Psychology of Semiotic Dynamics Contribute To Organization Process Studies?

After writing this chapter I have become cautiously optimistic to answer "yes" to this question. The problems of development are shared between all fields that look at processes—whether those of brains, persons, organizations, or societies—sharing the inevitable epistemological constraint set up by irreversibility of time.

What the semiotic dynamics perspective can provide to organization process research is the focus on the functional architectonics of sign assemblies that are used to regulate the organization processes. This regulatory system includes the erection of hierarchies of signs that can demolish themselves when necessary. It locates the functioning of sign hierarchies on the border of the Past and the Future. The sign hierarchies construct the relationship with the future, while reconstructing some of the past. It is probably time for the social sciences as a whole to restore the notion of the inherent intentionality of human acting—an idea developed by Franz Brentano in the second half of the nineteenth century—into twenty-first century human sciences. Signs that direct persons and organizations to face the future can be the vehicles of such inherent intentionality. Such intentionality-in-progress may be the basis for dynamic movements in business organizations. Can one develop an account of collective intentionality?

How would such application of cultural psychology look from the side of the study of organizational processes? Seemingly unimportant (and often ignored) organizational paperwork ("scorecards," safety instructions, elevator use rules, etc.) become the center of analysis of the dynamics of organizations, as well as arenas for intervention. Acts of elimination of extra unnecessary paperwork, or its opposite (generation of ever new standard forms to be filled out) become the places of analysis of the viability of the organization. Consider the difference between scenarios of problem-solving: if in one company that happens instantly when a problem emerges, and in another a long negotiation is needed to find the time for the relevant deciders to meet and start discussions (and filling out appropriate forms)—it becomes clear which of the two is better adjusted to the dynamic environments in which they operate. Signs of flexible informality in the working settings of organizations are not an indication of the invention of "Japanese management practices" but careful promoter signs for trusting one another in the pursuit of collectively shared goals. Cultural psychology brings to the study of organizational dynamics a perspective that allows the ways organizations do their jobs to change, without any explicit slogans of "intervention" or "trust building."[6]

Notes

1. The counter-sign that can grow out of the "non-A" field can have various functions—it can escalate the A, it can neutralize it. The important feature of the "non-A" field is that it carries multiple potentials for transformation of A.
2. Not always would operas remain maintenance arenas for generalized signs. On August 25, 1830 in Brussels, the performance of Daniel Auber's *La Mulette de Portici*—and especially the duet, *Amour sacré de la patrie* (Sacred love of Fatherland), triggered the riots that started the Belgian Revolution.

3. Known in dialectical philosophy as *second negation* in the scheme of *double negation*—the negation of a previous negation that results in synthesis of a qualitatively new level of organization (Valsiner, 2012, chapter 10).
4. In their own words—"when we go to the offices, we see it as a punishment!" (Lorino and Tricard, 2012, p. 228).
5. The continuing biography of the Brent Spar ("work years" 1976–1991) after the Shell/Greenpeace "war" (of 1995) is illustrative for a number of reasons. The Norwegian Stavanger Port Authority took it over from Shell in 1998 to make it a part of a quay extension at Mekjarvik. This meant finding it a new use precisely at the border of land and sea—rather than "dumping" it in deep sea or "disassembling" it on land. In the process of using it in construction the levels of pollutants were identified (and found to be in line with Shell estimates, revealing Greenpeace's gross overestimation of the amounts of remaining oil on the rig at the "war time"). Of course at war times all warring sides do their utmost to provide exaggerated messages of the atrocities of the opponent and the heroism of oneself. The battlefield in the Shell/Greenpeace war—as well as many other similar ones—was symbolic, and involved triggering peace time public sentiments that made it possible for the "David" to defeat the "Goliath." Peripheral participants—far from North Sea or issues of oil industry, or of nature conservation, but actively involved in symbolic public domains of worry—could be brought to action by way of their acceptance of the meaning presentations, which in this case led to the "win" by Greenpeace. As an event of nature's irony upon nature conservers, an endangered cold-water coral species was found growing on the legs of the platform—indicating that new symbiosis of nature and industrial interventions was already happening in the context of the sea. This created a paradoxical situation of doing damage to an endangered species by way of getting rid of a potential environmental pollution danger of industrial origin.
6. A preliminary version of this chapter was presented as a keynote lecture at the 5th International Symposium on Process Organization Studies—"Emergence of Novelty in Organizations"—in Chania, June 20–22, 2013. The preparation of the final version of this chapter was supported by the Danish Ministry of Science and Technology through a Niels Bohr Professorship grant.

References

Baldwin, J. M. (1906). *Thought and Things: A Study of the Development and Meaning of Thought, or Genetic Logic*. Vol. 1: *Functional Logic, or Genetic Theory of Knowledge*. London: Swan Sonnenschein & Co.

Bekhterev, V. M. (1903). *Suggestion and its Role in Social Life* (2nd edition). St. Petersburg: K. L. Rikker (in Russian).

Carolina Consortium on Human Development (1996). Developmental science: A collaborative statement. In R. B. Cairns, G. Elder, and E. J. Costello (eds.), *Developmental Science* (pp. 1–6). New York: Cambridge University Press.

Cornelissen, J. (2004). What are we playing at? Theatre, organization, and the use of metaphor. *Organization Studies*, 25(5): 705–726.

Cornelissen, J. (2006). Making sense of theory construction: Metaphor and disciplined imagination. *Organization Studies*, 27(11): 1579–1597.

Gärling, T. and Valsiner, J. (eds.) (1985). *Children within Environments: Towards a Psychology of Accident Prevention*. New York: Plenum.

Garud, R., Gehman, J., and Kumaraswamy, A. (2011). Complexity arrangements for sustained innovation: Lessons from 3M corporation. *Organization Studies*, 32(6): 737–767.

Herbst, D. (1995). What happens when we make a distinction: An elementary introduction to co-genetic logic. In T. Kindermann and J. Valsiner (eds.), *Development of Person-Context Relations* (pp. 67–79). Hillsdale, NJ: Lawrence Erlbaum Associates.

Janet, P. (1919). *Les medications psychologiques*. Paris: Felix Alcan.

Josephs, I. E., Valsiner, J., and Surgan, S. E. (1999). The process of meaning construction. In J. Brandtstätdter and R. M. Lerner (eds.), *Action & Self Development* (pp. 257–282). Thousand Oaks, CA: Sage.

Lorino, P. and Tricard, B. (2012). The Bakhtinian theory of chronotope (time–space frame) applied to the organizing process. In M. Schultz, S. Maguire, A. Langley, and H. Tsoukas (eds.), *Perspectives on Process Organization Studies*. Vol. 2: *Constructing Identity In and Around Organizations* (pp. 201–234). Oxford: Oxford University Press.

Lorino, P., Tricard, B., and Clot, Y. (2011). Research methods for non-representational approaches to organizational complexity: The dialogical mediated inquiry. *Organization Studies*, 32(6): 769–801.

Marsico, G., Komatsu, K., and Iannaccone, A. (eds.) (2013). *Crossing Boundaries: Intercontextual Dynamics Between Family and School*. Charlotte, NC: Information Age Publishers.

Maruyama, M. (2004). Polyocular vision or subunderstanding? *Organization Studies*, 25(3): 467–480.

Musson, G., Cohen, L., and Tietze, S. (2007). Pedagogy and the "linguistic turn": Developing understanding through semiotics. *Management Learning*, 38(1): 45–60.

Shotter, J. (2008). Dialogism and polyphony in organizing theorizing in organization studies: Action guiding anticipations and the continuous creation of novelty. *Organization Studies*, 29(4): 501–524.

Simpson, B. (2009). Pragmatism, Mead and the practice turn. *Organization Studies*, 30(12): 1329–1347.

Simpson, B. (2014). George Herbert Mead. In J. Helin, T. Hernes, and D. Hjorth (eds.), *The Oxford Handbook of Process Philosophy and Organization Studies* (pp. 272–287). Oxford: Oxford University Press.

Simpson, B. and Marshall, N. (2010). The mutuality of emotions and learning in organizations. *Journal of Management Inquiry*, 19(4): 351–365.

Sovran, T. (1992). Between similarity and sameness. *Journal of Pragmatics*, 18(4): 329–344.

Tricard, B. and Lorino, P. (2013). Habits and the semiotic emergence of organizational novelty. Paper presented at the 5th International Symposium on Process Organization Studies—"Emergence of Novelty in Organizations"—in Chania, June 20–22.

Tsoukas, H. (1999). David and Goliath in the risk society: Making sense of the conflict between Shell and Greenpeace in the North Sea. *Organization*, 6(3): 499–528.

Valsiner, J. (2004). The promoter sign: Developmental transformation within the structure of dialogical self. Paper presented at the Biennial Meeting of the International Society for the Study of Behavioural Development (ISSBD), Gent, July 12 (Symposium "Developmental Aspects of the Dialogical Self," Hubert Hermans, Convener).

Valsiner, J. (2007). *Culture in Minds and Societies*. New Delhi: Sage.

Valsiner, J. (ed.) (2012). *The Oxford Handbook of Culture and Psychology*. New York: Oxford University Press.

Zittoun, T., Valsiner, J., Vedeler, D., Salgado, J., Gonçalves, M., and Ferring, D. (2013). *Human Development in the Life Course: Melodies of Living*. Cambridge: Cambridge University Press.

6

Between Technology and Music

Distributed Creativity and Liminal Spaces in the Early History of Electronic Music Synthesizers

Trevor Pinch

Abstract: This chapter uses a case study of the development of the first commercial electronic music synthesizers to investigate creative activity. It focuses upon both engineers such as Robert Moog and sales people. Creativity can be described as a distributed process residing in the interactions between machines, materials, and people. The chapter argues that creativity involves not only producing new devices and artifacts but also new ways of socially organizing the production, distribution, and consumption of these artifacts and devices. In short it involves creating new sorts of users for these devices. The chapter advocates treating creativity as a process which is facilitated by the existence of "liminal spaces" which enable people to fantasize and play with new objects and possibilities. The opening up of a liminal space between engineering and art is what allows the new object of electronic synthesizers to emerge.

The first commercially produced electronic music synthesizers, developed by Robert Moog and Donald Buchla in the period 1964–1971, herald a rare moment in musical culture: the innovation of a whole new class of instruments. Inventors often come up with new designs of musical instruments but few of these designs get commercially produced and become innovations. In the twentieth century the application of electricity to instruments (Braun, 2000; Holmes, 2012) led to such instruments as the Theremin (Glinsky, 2005), the electric organ, the electric piano, and the most important new instrument of the twentieth century, the electric guitar (Waksman, 1999; Millard, 2004). The synthesizer with its novel way of producing sound[1] is the other major new instrument of the twentieth century (Théberge, 1997; Pinch and Trocco, 2002).

There is much interest in innovations such as the synthesizer which crosses between the worlds of engineering and the arts (in this case music). There is a big literature on creativity (e.g. Usher, 1954; Koestler, 1964; Csikszentmihalyi, 1996).[2] Here I will use the development of the synthesizer as a case study to examine the creative process, in an attempt to get a new handle on this old topic.

To jump ahead, there are three major points which I hope to establish: (1) *Creativity is a distributed process*. Edward Hutchins' studies of what he calls "distributed cognition" (Hutchins, 1995) is my way into this topic.[3] By examining complicated socio-technological systems such as aircraft carriers and airplanes, Hutchins shows the poverty of thinking about cognition in terms of an isolated Cartesian mind which comes up with and implements plans or cognitive acts. Cognition is better thought of as being distributed between teams of humans and as being shared with machines and technical devices (see also Suchman, 2007). The acts of creativity in developing a new technology can also be thought of as being part of a distributed process—the crucial actions cannot be pinpointed to the mind of one inventor but occur in processes that are distributed between several actors, devices, and tools. For example, one of the most important new interfaces on a synthesizer (and still a standard item found on synthesizers today) is something called the pitch wheel (see Figure 6.1). This is a controller for bending the pitch of a note in the same way as a guitarist or violinist can stretch a pitch by pulling the string slightly to the side on the fret board. The pitch wheel was first developed for the Minimoog synthesizer which premiered in 1970. I will show how the creative acts that led to this new synthesizer and its unique form of controller were distributed between a number of actors, devices, and tools.

The second major point to be argued here stems from thinking about the sorts of activity that count as being creative. (2) *Creativity involves not only producing new artifacts but also new ways of socially and materially organizing the production, distribution, and consumption of these artifacts*. This might include novel ways of organizing production (as famously Henry Ford did for the Model T) but also novel ways of demonstrating and selling products. One of the deepest points established in science and technology

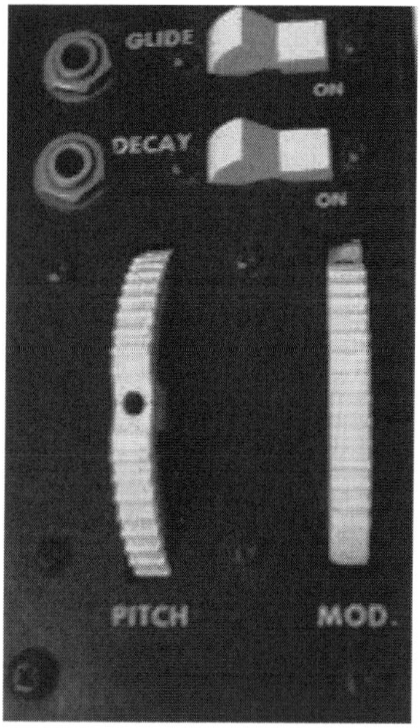

Figure 6.1 The pitch and modulation wheels on the Minimoog synthesizer

studies in recent years is that the creation of new artifacts also creates new sorts of human activities (Bijker, Hughes, and Pinch, 1987/2013; Latour, 1987). Novelty is an emergent process (Pickering, 1985). As I shall argue below, the success story of the synthesizer depended upon not only creative acts in designing new synthesizers, but also producing novel ways of demonstrating and selling synthesizers (Pinch, 2003, 2010). Furthermore the new sorts of performance synthesizers to emerge in 1970, such as the Minimoog, created a new sort of musician, who became known as the "keyboard hero." These mainly young male musicians—the better-known ones are rock stars such as Keith Emerson and Rick Wakeman, but there were countless others—used the synthesizer as a solo instrument enabling the keyboardist to get the same sort of limelight usually reserved for guitarists in rock bands.

The third and final issue I will address in this chapter is to think more generally about how art worlds (Becker, 1982) and engineering worlds come together. My thesis here is that: (3) *Liminal spaces enable creative acts.* I will argue that what I call liminal spaces, places "betwixt and between social worlds" (Turner, 1969; Pinch and Trocco, 2002), are particularly important because they enable people to fantasize and play with new objects and possibilities—to dream, to model, and tinker in new ways.[4] In talking about inventors at play, I am of course tapping into a big literature on hobbyists and enthusiasts (e.g. Douglas, 1992; Hughes, 1999; Haring, 2006). Here my focus is to think about the sorts of space where this play is carried out. I will chart the different career paths taken by the two major synthesizer pioneers, Robert Moog and Donald Buchla, and the different relationships each had with the world of art.

6.1 Creativity as a Distributed Process: The Minimoog and Invention of the Pitch Wheel

When Robert Moog was awarded the Polar Prize for music in 2001 (given every year by the King of Stockholm—a kind of Nobel Prize for music), followed by a technical Grammy in 2002 (he shared it with Steve Jobs for the Apple Macintosh), it was for his invention of the Minimoog synthesizer (Figure 6.2). The Minimoog was the first commercially produced, portable keyboard synthesizer. It became a classic and is widely desired and highly valued by synthesizer players even today. A digital form of the Minimoog,

Figure 6.2 Minimoog synthesizer

the Voyager, is currently made by Moog Music.[5] Unlike the larger and vastly more expensive modular moog synthesizer (which retailed for the price of a small house, about $15,000), the Minimoog has a built-in keyboard and uses knobs and switches rather than patch wires to control the sorts of sound made. The patch wires (complete with jack plugs and sockets), used to connect different modules together, gave the modular Moog synthesizer the appearance of an old telephone exchange (Figure 6.3). The huge number of possible patches facilitated exploration of a vast range of sounds, but made it cumbersome to operate. With no standard operating manual, musicians were forced to make their own maps of the instrument in order to repeat their favorite sounds. The few pioneering musicians who took this unwieldy beast on tour for live performance would often rehearse patch changes in advance, thus producing one of the most unusual sights in music—musicians rehearsing without producing a sound (because they were literally between sounds)![6]

All synthesizers have ways of producing and controlling sound. The main sources of sound on analog synthesizers are oscillators and noise sources (such as for producing "white noise"). The technology used in these early analog synthesizers is known as "voltage control." A varying

Figure 6.3 Moog modular synthesizer

voltage, such as a sine wave output from an oscillator, can be used as an input to vary the pitch of another oscillator (known as frequency modulation). The modular Moog possesses controls such as knobs and patch wires, keyboards, and a special device Moog designed known as the ribbon controller. The latter is essentially a resistance wire along which the performer can run his or her fingers thereby changing the voltage continuously, which in turn can be used continuously to control a parameter such as pitch. Much in the same way as a violinist or cellist controls pitch, this permits sweeps of sound to be made. The Minimoog, which also uses the same transistor technology of voltage control, is controlled by knobs and switches, a built-in keyboard, and by a totally new sort of controller, known as the pitch and modulation wheels (see Figure 6.1). These are two upright plastic wheels which protrude from the keyboard casing and are mounted perpendicular to the keyboard at the left end. The pitch wheel has a detente spring device fitted so that musicians, when turning the wheel, can "feel" its middle position. The Minimoog is a monophonic instrument, which means that it is capable of playing only one note at a time. The right hand is typically used for playing a melody on the keyboard (soloing), while the left hand adjusts the amount of pitch bend or modulation on individual notes.

Musicians immediately took to these new controls. Jan Hammer, whose trademark instrument in the rock jazz combo, the Mahavishnu Orchestra, was the Minimoog, is quoted as saying, "the pitch wheel really sets the min [sic] apart from any other keyboard synthesizer."[7] Roger Powell (a well-known mid-1970s synthesist) found that the pitch wheel and modulation wheel "are the most humanized controls that I have yet found on synthesizers."[8] Soon other synthesizer manufacturers, such as Moog's main rival, the Boston-based ARP company, had copied a form of the pitch and modulation wheels and it has subsequently become a staple of almost every keyboard synthesizer.

How did this new form of control get invented? The origins of the pitch wheel lie with the Minimoog itself. In a classic example of what can be called "bricolage" (Garud and Karnøe, 2003; Baker and Nelson, 2005) this classic synthesizer originated almost by accident, and its first version was built out of discarded modules and other pieces of junk found in the attic of Moog's factory in Trumansburg, upstate New York.

The year was 1969 and the Moog company for the only year in its brief life was actually turning a profit. The modular Moog synthesizer with its spacey sounds and unusual timbres had become part of the psychedelic revolution and had been used on hit records by the Doors, Byrds, and the Beatles. Furthermore the instrument had become a star in its own right with the 1968 release of Wendy Carlos' "Switched on Bach." This rendition of several classic Bach pieces, made on the modular Moog synthesizer with the aid of Carlos' recording skills (she had been a former engineer at Gotham studios in New York) and an early eight-track tape recorder, was an overnight sensation, and is still one of the best-selling Bach records. The modular Moog synthesizer became the latest gimmick for the recording industry and it sent its representatives to Trumansburg in droves to purchase the new instrument. After 1968 nearly every genre of music was "Moogified," with albums appearing under such titles as "Switched on Rock," "Switched on Country," "Switched on Bacharach," "More Switched on Bacharach," and "Switched on Santa."

None of these records had the artistry or commercial success of "Switched on Bach" but they did enable Moog to build his business. In 1969 he hired three new engineers and his business expanded to 42 employees. One of the new engineers to arrive was Bill Hemsath and it is Hemsath who originated the Minimoog and the pitch wheel. Bob Moog had hired Hemsath after he had made several visits to the factory in connection with electronic music projects he was involved with in Cleveland. Hemsath, like Moog himself, had got his start as a hobbyist building ham radio sets—he had learnt radio physics from a borrowed correspondence course during third grade. He was also a self-taught keyboardist. He studied electrical engineering at Case Western Reserve University where he took a course in the history of music. His electronic talents were spotted, and he was soon enlisted to help build an electronic music studio. He went on to work with Don Erb, a well-known electronic composer at the Cleveland Institute of Music, and this brought him into Moog's orbit. He was hired as engineer-in-chief at the Moog company in the spring of 1969. He was 26 years old at the time having finished his draft deferral at Cleveland Ordinance, building torpedoes.

The possibility of using a Moog synthesizer for live performance was just starting to emerge. A famous concert featuring live modular synthesizers for the first time (which turned into a "happening") took place in the sculpture garden at the New York Museum of Modern Art (MOMA) in the summer of 1969. One of Hemsath's first jobs was to modify the modular Moog synthesizers to be used for live performance by adding a special control box that enabled the synthesizers to be switched between several standard sounds. The modifications were carried out at the last moment and Hemsath and the other engineers were still soldering away at MOMA on the morning of the concert. Hemsath had become familiar with the standard sounds and patches (the configuration of patch wires) used to produce them after demonstrating the studio Moog on countless occasions to potential customers. He got the idea that it would be fun to have a Moog that just made the standard sounds—something he could tinker with:

> I got into a set routine. I would always use the same patching and I would always use the same settings. I would always play the same and so forth . . . And I got to thinking that I would like to have something like that just to tinker with on my own . . . something to play with.[9]

Moog's Trumansburg factory was a former furniture store. The ethos was very much "make do." As another of Moog's engineers, Jim Scott, described it:

> If I needed a niche in the wall to park my phone, I just went down and got a hammer and nail and pounded a hole in the wall and cut up some wood and put a shelf in.[10]

On entering the factory you walked straight into the assembly area (staffed mainly by local women who were quilters) consisting of several large tables in the middle of the room (see Figure 6.4). Work benches ran along both sides where the engineers designed, aligned, and tested

Figure 6.4 Moog's Trumansburg factory

new modules (later engineering moved to the second floor). There was a machine shop towards the rear of the building, a front office (first in the basement, later moved upstairs as the business grew), and a ramshackle studio at the rear of the building where visiting musicians and Moog's own studio musicians worked. Modules from this studio were often missing, having been filched to make up a new order. The overall atmosphere was described by one of Moog's former employees:

> They were pretty chummy and informal and excited about what they were doing and at the same time always a lot of talk and speculation about what Moog was up to, what the next invention would be, would it crash and burn, would it succeed.[11]

Hemsath's office was on the attic floor; the attic itself was unfinished and scattered with abandoned pieces of equipment. At lunchtimes Hemsath would take a walk through this attic. He describes what happened next:

> I would go through that every once a while in my lunch hour because I'm a pearl diver, and the thought started to gel . . . that there's a half case over there and all I have to do is saw the end off and glue . . . I loaded up my bottom desk drawer with cast off pieces . . . at noon I'd open up the drawer and chump on an apple while putting stuff together . . . the only piece that's in there that's a new part [the envelope generator]—I actually went down to the construction area and stole it . . . I found an old keyboard . . . I was able to slice that down to two and half or three octaves.[12]

By the time his lunch-time excursions had ended, Hemsath had collected most of the elements of what was to become the Minimoog. He found two abandoned oscillator modules and a module for shaping sound known as an envelope generator. He had made the key decision to get rid of the patch cords and hardwire all the modules together in the same box with a keyboard. The instrument he built is known as the Model A Min Moog (see Figure 6.5).[13] A primitive form of pitch bending could be achieved on the modular Moog by quickly turning one of the two knobs mounted on the five-octave keyboard. This knob's main function was to fine-tune the keyboard essentially by varying the voltage which the keyboard produced. Hemsath decided to make a pitch bender using a slide potentiometer (pot) rather than a rotary one and mounted it at the left side of the keyboard.[14] His decision was dictated by what he had available:

> In the original keyboards on the left [was] . . . a little control panel . . . all I was able to salvage was the left and right cheeks and one had a large notch

in it. So that's where I put the little slide pot . . . It's playable but it takes technique.[15]

Hemsath had initially built the new instrument for his own amusement (he was after all a keyboardist) and he took it home to play with it. "I had it at home for probably a couple of months. I played with it every night the first week, and two months later I brought it back to work because it's in the way."[16] For Hemsath the device was not particularly memorable; at that time he was "wading in synthesizers daily." As Bob Moog recalls, "Well Hemsath was always doing shit like that. And so was I. We were always putting stuff together. Nothing unusual about it."[17] The new synthesizer was referred to by the other engineers as "Hemsath's toy." None of the engineers could at that stage see the commercial potential for such an instrument. Moog himself thought it might conceivably be of use to session musicians as a replacement for the large modular instruments they dragged from session to session. Synthesizers at this time were not yet a mass-marketable item sold through retail music stores; they were expensive high-end pieces of audio-engineered equipment used by a few composers, famous rock stars, and academic studios. They were sold direct from the factory (although Moog did eventually hire a sales rep in New York and two in Los Angeles). The uncertainty as to a possible

Figure 6.5 Min Moog Model A

commercial market for the new instrument was nicely captured by engineer, Jim Scott:

> Nobody was going to buy these things . . . so what are we doing this for? And none of us really knew the market very well, none of us. We were a bunch of engineers, right, theorizing what the world out there wanted to buy.[18]

The close interaction between engineers and musicians which Moog's funky factory fostered now played a part. One of Moog's studio musicians was David Borden. Based at nearby Cornell University (where Moog had recently completed his PhD in engineering physics), Borden led the first ever live synthesizer ensemble, Mother Mallard. He was friends with Hemsath and saw the potential of the new instrument for his ensemble as a way of changing sounds quickly. Borden asked Hemsath if he could borrow the "Min" and it became such a standard part of the Mother Mallard set up that, to this day, it has Mother Mallard's trademark duck insignia plated onto its side.

In early 1970, it dawned on the engineers that their company was going under. Orders for modular synthesizers had dropped to one a month from ten a month, as none of the new "switched on" albums succeeded commercially. Moog was away most of the time looking for investors. Scott recollected:

> There was a sense of urgency we might not be able to meet payroll next week . . . Our credit was cut off . . . we were literally digging transistors out of cracks in the floor and testing them to see if they were any good or not.[19]

The engineers, with the support of Moog's business and marketing managers, decided that they would have to enter the mass-market to survive. And the most likely product looked to be the new Min. Hemsath decided that to win Moog over, he would build a new prototype with a sleeker look. This Model B version had many improvements including a new standardized front panel, easy to use layout, the addition of a third oscillator, and rocker switches to switch the control and audio signals between different parts of the synthesizer. The Model B had a particularly effective and elegant case that latched onto the synthesizer like a sewing machine case. Hemsath had given Art Phelps, who ran the woodshop, a drawing, and he came up with the details of the case design. It meant that musicians could actually carry the Model B to gigs—one such early user was the famous jazz musician, Sun Ra, who took a Model B after a visit to Trumansburg to use in his space spectacles.[20] He eventually sent his Model B back for repair by putting it on a flight to nearby Ithaca.

Moog was impressed with the progress his engineers had made, and hired an outside design team who came up with yet another distinctive feature of the Minimoog—its hinged control board which can be locked flat for transporting the instrument, but flipped upright at different angles for performance. Improvements were made in the electronics to stabilize the oscillators so that they did not go out of tune with changes in temperature (an annoying feature of the modular Moogs). The new design included an elegant walnut wooden case.[21] Known as the Model C, this served as the production model.

As the engineers finalized the design of the Model C, Hemsath was still not happy with the pitch-sliding device. He found it awkward to use with the left hand as the slider on the Min (later renamed the Model A) sometimes used to stick. He experimented by mounting the slider horizontally on the control panel of the Model B right over the center of the keyboard. The final form for the pitch wheel came from a totally different project. A customer had ordered a set of six calibrated joysticks to control two voltages at the same time (in the X and Y directions). Hemsath experimented with commercial joysticks but found he could not eliminate the backlash problem. So he decided to build his own joystick by connecting two potentiometers together with a metal angle bracket. This simple but effective design solved the backlash problem. The joysticks ended up looking like paddle wheels (Hemsath likes to refer to them as "rollers" that could be pushed smoothly either forward or backwards). Obviously the bigger the knob on the potentiometer, the more touch-sensitive it would be, but a big knob would look ungainly. Hemsath hit upon the idea of mounting the knob horizontally under the end of the keyboard so only a small part of it (enough to give it the needed range) would be above the surface. He decided to place his new device at the left end of the keyboard again because, "I just simply watched a lot of musicians and they could either play the ribbon [controller] with their left hand, or anything over here, just fine."[22]

To manufacture such a device with such a large wheel he turned to the help of Don Pakkla, whose official job at the Moog factory was buyer—he ordered everything from transistors to toilet paper. Pakkla had previously been a machinist, and he and Hemsath hit upon the idea of manufacturing batches of pitch wheels out of plexiglass (later the pitch wheels were injection molded). Hemsath and Pakkla worked closely together refining the design by adding a notch in the middle and experimenting with springs and a detente device so that the operator could "feel" in the dark when the pitch wheel was back in its center position. They were proud of what they had come up with, and showed it round the factory to their co-workers. They had no idea that they had created the "most humanized" control on a synthesizer, and that it would be used on synthesizers to this day.[23]

Now we can unpack a little more of the sort of creative effort involved in producing this new device. In one sense, there is very little new about the device—controlling pitch by a potentiometer has been a familiar technique since the beginning of analog synthesis (Holmes, 2012). The novelty lies not so much in the idea, as in its execution. As for most musical interfaces, it is the subtleties of feel, look, and sound which matter. For the pitch wheel, it is crucial that it feels good to performers in the context of the overall ergonomics of the instrument. Also, it must look like the sort of inviting control musicians want to use—and here, the etched knobs standing out at the end of the keyboard are just asking to be pushed. Lastly, the dramatic electronic pitch bending obtainable turns the piercing monophonic sound of the Minimoog in the hands of a Keith Emerson, Jan Hammer, or Rick Wakeman into a novel and useful musical effect (especially within the context of the genres of progressive rock and jazz rock). It enabled rock keyboardists to step out of the shadows and take some of the limelight guitarists generated with their solos. What the pitch wheel does paradoxically for a synthesized instrument is to turn it into a human instrument. It shows the machine is not doing everything and that the human can still exert and display his or her control and virtuosity (Bijsterveld and Pinch, 2003). The pitch wheel provides a direct and dramatic way to amplify the presence of the performer. For instance when rock performer Keith Emerson used the device in live performance with his band Emerson, Lake and Palmer (ELP) you not only heard the sonic shattering squeal of the pitch-bent note, but also saw his elbow bending to dramatic effect. The spectacle of the instrument for live performance was thus also enhanced.

What is the creative act in making this device? Where and with whom does it lie? These questions are related because, as we have seen, there is no one "place" just as there is no one "person." The pitch wheel did not arrive *de novo*, neither did any single engineer have an exact notion of what it would look, sound, and feel like before its creation actually materialized. The design started with a conventional potentiometer, and evolved over time with several prototypes in the context of the overall design of a new instrument.

The same is true of the Minimoog as a whole. Clearly Bob Moog who was awarded the Polar Prize for its invention had a role to play, but several other engineers played key parts including Bill Hemsath and Jim Scott. Yet other actors made significant contributions such as Art Phelps in the woodshop, Don Pakkla the machinist, and the anonymous outside design team who came up with the hinged control panel. Musicians such as David Borden played a crucial role too. In this case, what already exists heavily constrains what is possible in terms of the new instrument. Without a modular Moog synthesizer, live concerts, performing musicians, and an engineer such as Hemsath needing to demonstrate the instrument, none of this was possible. Also crucial are material factors such as an attic full of abandoned parts, the technologies of machine shops and wood shops, and the various materials from which the instrument was made.

The invention of the pitch wheel did not happen *de novo* either. An existing potentiometer was adapted to fit an existing keyboard, and over time and with each succeeding version, it was developed further (Usher, 1954). Also other projects such as the joystick project played a role. Non-human elements such as machines and plexiglass were crucial as well.

How individuals conceive of their work is also important. For Hemsath there was no clear distinction between work and play. The element of joyful tinkering using scrap parts strongly evokes the hobbyist ethos. That Hemsath could show and discuss and eventually enlist his fellow engineers and other personnel in the factory points to the importance of the social relations in the factory, and how these different groups interacted. The architectural "funky" layout of the factory also combined with the social arrangements in interesting and unexpected ways. Hemsath could be alone in his attic office to tinker, he could walk untroubled into the attic (or "graveyard" as he called it) for abandoned parts to use, and he could stroll down into the studio to talk with the musicians. Lastly, even the business economy played a role, with the engineers fully aware that Moog's business was going down the tubes (no Enron type structural secrecy in this small business!), thus providing them with that extra incentive to try to produce a new instrument to save the company (and their jobs).

There was no one creative act, and creativity did not solely reside in the minds or bodies of the engineers; it was also resident in the physical layout of the factory, and the material and social arrangements of machines, wood shops, materials, and so on. Creativity was, in short, distributed and distributed between humans and non-humans.

6.2 Creating a Novel Synthesizer Demonstration

Completely new sorts of musical instruments are hard to sell. Musicians like to try out an instrument before purchasing it—this is especially true if the instrument is an unfamiliar one. As a thought experiment, imagine the violin has arrived *de novo* and now violin makers have to sell it with hardly anyone being able to play it, and no repertoire of music developed for it. Would people see the potential in this strange scratching sound, which became musically useful only after a lot of practice?

Retail music stores were well aware of this problem with new instruments. Electric organ manufacturers and retailers had developed slick demonstrations (known as "demos" or "clinics") to show off the standard sounds and potential of the new organs. Keyboardists were hired by organ companies to showcase the new instruments by playing popular pieces of music particularly suited to their electric timbres.

The Minimoog keyboard synthesizer, when it was first introduced, faced a similar problem. Synthesizers had never been sold in retail music stores before. The 44 knobs and switches made the Minimoog look complicated and there was no easily available orchestral or instrumental sounds to be conjured up at the flip of a switch as with organs. Unless you knew what you were doing it was hard to get the instrument to make any sound at all. Salesmen, hoping to sell the Minimoog and ARP's keyboard synthesizer, the Odyssey, reported going into music stores and being thrown out because no one could yet see how to sell such a complicated instrument.

One legendary Moog salesman, David Van Koevering, was responsible for changing the prospects of the Minimoog by devising a new way of demonstrating them. David Van Koevering is a former TV evangelist (he was known as "little David") who has a background playing in his father's novelty musical instrument show (the show not only brought kids to music but also to God). Van Koevering eventually took over his father's show and was always on the lookout for new instruments to include. He showcased a Theremin,[24] and as soon as he got word of the Moog synthesizer, he incorporated that as well. Van Koevering describes his first encounter with the Moog in an almost spiritual and visionary way. He had accompanied Moog to an early live modular Moog performance at Carnegie Hall in January 1970:

> I saw something . . . the power of the sound, the sonic energy, and I believed it could become common, and I imagined it as powerful as the electric guitar to the first guys who ever played that thing.[25]

What Van Koevering realized was that this new instrument had the same potential to transform musical practice as the electric guitar had. But exactly how this potential would be realized was still unclear to him. He knew the effect of the Moog on live audiences, but what genre of music was best suited to it? It seems he initially conceived of the Moog as a form of instrument to play popular tunes on, a kind of Hammond organ. He even teamed up for a short while with a Florida business acquaintance, Glen Bell, the founder of Taco Bell. Van Koevering presented his novelty musical show in schools and afterwards handed out vouchers to the kids for free tacos at their local newly opened Taco Bell restaurant. There, they would find Van Koevering later that evening playing popular music on his modular Moog synthesizer (see Figure 6.6). Tacos in Florida have never tasted better!

Van Koevering's next venture was more ambitious. He leased from Glen Bell a man-made island off the coast of Florida at St Petersburg, renamed it "The Island of Electronicus," and used it to stage Moog spectacles. It seems he wanted to realize the potential of the Moog for making soundscapes and spacey effects (the same sort of sounds and effects used in psychedelia). He built a massive sound system in a glass domed rotunda and offered cushions for the audience to lie on in front of the "Love and Peace" stage as they listened to live and recorded Moog music. The shows

Figure 6.6 Coupon advertising Taco Bell using Moog synthesizer

involved a mix of Van Koevering's preacher's rap and soundscapes where he talked about the spiritual uplifting effects of the sounds, describing the Moog as an "eternity" and heralding the "dawn of a new enlightenment." He would use sounds to create the impression of motorbikes and a four-cylinder sports car roaring around the rotunda. "And you'd hear the motorcycle going one way and you'd hear the sports car go the other way, and a horrendous crash would happen over the stage . . . And the audience would go nuts. They'd stand and they'd cheer and they'd clap."[26]

The shows were a huge success. He even persuaded Moog himself to make a guest appearance at the Island (Figure 6.7). As soon as the new Minimoog synthesizers came off the production line, he ordered three and incorporated them into his show. He encouraged young people from the audience to solo on the Minimoogs, with a spotlight on them. It was the perfect way of satisfying the sixties ethos of audience participation.

We can think of Van Koevering's Island as a novel kind of sound test laboratory.[27] Van Koevering was experimenting on his audience to find the sorts of Moog sounds and music that were effective and how to set

Figure 6.7 The Island of Electronicus

up and operate Minimoogs to produce these sounds. He also was able to observe the popularity of the Minimoog amongst the younger members of his audience.[28] With the much cheaper portable Minimoog, Van Koevering became even more convinced that the world was ready for live performance synthesizers and he resolved to go out on the road and sell them. He set up a company in partnership with a local music store and in classic American salesman fashion he loaded up his Cadillac with Minimoogs and confidently set off on a tour of Florida to try and convince retail music stores to sell the new synthesizer.

He quickly discovered that music stores had other plans. They were just not interested in stocking the new instrument because of its complexity. Van Koevering could demo the instrument but it looked hard for a sales assistant to do likewise. Also it was still a comparatively expensive piece of equipment. Retailing at $1,195, it was about the price of a rock group's van. To get stores interested, he discovered that the best thing to do was to bring customers to the store—that *demonstrated* the demand. To get musicians interested he would find young rock keyboardists in clubs and lend them an instrument to use in their shows. He showed them the power the Minimoog could have in turning them into stars:

> The Minimoog could make, because of its sonic energy, it could make the keyboard guy a superstar—a monophonic, piercing sound coming out or four or five . . . amplified speaker stacks, could give him some energy and he could compete with the guitar, and he wanted to do that.[29]

But first the keyboardist had to learn to play the new instrument. He devised a quick and easy way to help them set up sounds they wanted using little pieces of colored tape to mark the sounds:

> I would create a sound that he liked, and we'd put red slivers on all the 44 knobs and switch positions that meant all the red is sound red, and all the yellows are sound yellow . . . these are the presets. "But on the way from one preset to the other, anything you find that's musical, play it, experiment, create a song for the sound" . . . . I was teaching them synthesis and they would get it.[30]

This idea of marking the different sorts of sounds later was incorporated by the Moog company into the instruction manual they wrote for the Minimoog. Different sounds were described in "sound charts" that marked the positions of all 44 controls to produce sounds such as "trumpet," "xylophone," or later "Emerson's Fat Bass From Brain Salad Surgery" (a popular ELP album where Keith Emerson uses the Moog). Van

Koevering would post the word MOOG in big silvery letters on the back of the Minimoog, and would instruct his musicians to ask the audience whether they liked the sound of the Moog. He was even known to take the slow-blow fuse out of instruments between sets so that musicians and their audience would experience what it was like suddenly *not* to be able to use the Moog. Van Koevering would often wait in his car outside the club with the loan papers ready to be signed and then take his prospect to the music store the next day to demonstrate to at least one interested customer. Van Koevering did this for countless Florida music stores, and then later spread his network wider to other states. At the same time well-known performers on the Minimoog such as Rick Wakeman and Keith Emerson were touring the US creating even more demand for the instrument. Orders would arrive from the last city where ELP had played.

Word of Van Koevering's success spread to the Moog company. In a bitter-sweet moment for Moog, in 1971 he finally found a venture capitalist, Bill Waytena, to buy him out—thus losing control of his company. One of Waytena's first acts was to take Van Koevering out of the field and hire him for the new company where he eventually rose to become vice president of marketing. Van Koevering now started to attend musical instrument trade shows such as the National Association of Music Merchants (NAMM). As performers became familiar with the new instrument and its sound, Van Koevering was able to train a sales force to demo the instrument. They widened the sorts of musician to whom the instrument would appeal to include other genres of music and also started building the global market for the new instrument. ARP was doing similar things to sell its portable keyboard instruments, and gradually, retail music stores everywhere started stocking performance synthesizers—where they have remained to this day.

In discussing creativity and technology, it is important to recognize the novel way whereby Van Koevering developed a means of persuading retail music stores to stock the instrument. Like other acts of creativity, this one is distributed over time, actors, and materiality. Van Koevering did not get his ideas *de novo*, but through the backing of people like Moog and Glen Bell and retail music store owners; he began to develop new sales practices; and the experience he gained from setting up his "sound lab" at the Island of Electronicus was invaluable. He depended upon the skills of musicians to play the new instrument and extract new sounds from it. Even the mystic tape and scissors he always carried with him were part of the creative act. It was the potential in these materials that he enacted which served as a way of stabilizing sounds; helped persuade musicians of the merits of the instrument; and provided the template for the sound charts which came later. Van Koevering also seemed to be the first person to realize that the new instrument in effect could create a new form of musician, the "keyboard hero." Of course, it was the rock keyboardists (and their fellow band members) who had to create and play the songs and music to be effective, but without the new performance synthesizer in their hands, they could not do it. Again, all of this is best talked about as distributed creativity shared between musicians, instruments, and salesman. Van Koevering and other pioneering salesmen's legacies were enormous. The boundaries of what counted as musicianship and the boundaries of sound were forever changed by their activities.

6.3 Liminal Spaces for Creativity

I would like to conclude this chapter by thinking a bit about the sorts of spaces and places where creative acts occur. There is a danger in any such discussion that we overemphasize one place at the expense of others. As I have shown for the case of the Minimoog, creative work occurs over many casual interactions. Nevertheless it is useful to try and generalize about these sorts of spaces.

The origin of the commercial electronic music synthesizer lies in the coming together of two fields: engineering and music. It is possible to trace this "coming together" in the careers of the two main synthesizer pioneers, Robert Moog and Donald Buchla. Moog was trained as an engineer. After graduating from Bronx High School for Science in 1952, he obtained a joint degree in physics at Queens College and electrical engineering at Columbia University in 1957, before entering the PhD program in engineering physics at Cornell. It was while he was at Cornell that Moog first started to develop his modular synthesizer. Equally important as Moog's formal engineer training, was his hobbyist background. Moog's father was an engineer for Con Edison and had a well-equipped basement workshop where Bob loved to tinker as a young man. He and his father founded R. A. Moog and Co. in 1953—they sold coils for Theremins and designed Theremin kits (one of Moog's designs appeared on the front cover of the hobbyist magazine *Electronics World*) and later they sold fully assembled Theremins as well as kits. Moog also had some musical background. His mother insisted on him receiving piano lessons as a kid and he even played for a while in a college band but apparently showed little talent as a musician. Despite Moog's lifelong involvement with music and musicians, he always thought of himself as above all an engineer. All the early pictures of him show him with a pen protector in place. As he himself said, "I'm an engineer. I see myself as a toolmaker and the musicians are my customers. They use my tools."[31]

The moments of creative impulse in Moog's life seem to have stemmed from two sources: (1) his tinkering and futzing around with electronics—a lifelong interest which started with his hobbyist background, and (2) his encounters at key moments with musicians. Moog hung out with musicians a lot because of his Theremin hobbyist business. He employed a sales rep for his Theremins in New York, Walter Sear (who later became his synthesizer sales rep in New York). Sear himself had an unusual career, starting off playing tuba in the pit at Radio City New York, later manufacturing tubas and guitar amplifiers (in a short-lived ill-fated venture with Moog); he then turned to audio engineering, and built a well-known all tube recording studio in New York (Sear Sound). It was Walter Sear who introduced Moog to the musician who turned out to be the most significant for the future of the synthesizer, Herbert Deutsch. It was Deutsch who first saw the need for a new more portable electronic music studio, finding the off-the-shelf oscillators he used to make experimental electronic music cumbersome and expensive. But Moog's encounter with Deutsch was not just a matter of cerebral interaction, although their first meeting was marked by a three-hour conversation over the possibilities of building new sorts of electronic music devices. They soon found they could help each other.

One of the formative events in Moog's life was a concert Deutsch put on in the artist Jason Seley's Manhattan loft. Moog was there ostensibly to record the event. The loft was full of Seley's large automobile bumper sculptures and occasionally Deutsch would bang these sculptures accompanied by taped music. The event was an early "happening" (the avant-garde art scene was developing in New York at this time with the Fluxus group) and Moog reports that he had "his mind blown." It was his first real experience with the avant-garde music scene. Later Moog invited Deutsch to take a summer holiday staying in a cabin on Lake Cayuga near Trumansburg, and it was during these few weeks in the spring of 1963 that Moog and Deutsch worked together and produced their first synthesizer modules. "Worked together" implies work, but both Moog and Deutsch stressed that what they were doing was as much fun as anything. They simply had no idea that a new instrument was being developed and that this would lead to a gigantic new industry. As Moog recalled: "I've always had trouble with differentiating business from hobby . . . It was fun, it was interesting, maybe it would lead somewhere who knows?"[32]

The clues in this story of invention are the references to play and fun (recall also the creation of Hemsath's Min Moog). It seems that creative engineering involves this element of playfulness and fun. Now we have most of the parts in place for the theory of creativity with which I want to conclude this chapter.

Creativity comes from bringing together two separate social worlds—in this case, the world of engineering and the world of music—but it does so in a special sort of space, what I will call a liminal space. In a liminal space the social worlds and the concomitant identities become less important. It is like a fantasy world where the imagination can run free to imagine possibilities, which the normal social world would constrain. The imaginative and fantasy part is similar to children playing their typical imaginary games where they choose and build elaborate characters. But this liminal space is not an unreal space—it is populated by real social relationships, materials, and skills. It is a space where real work is done. In short, when Moog entered this liminal space, he did not leave behind all his engineering skills to suddenly become a musician with all the skills and experience that musicians accumulate. Ultimately he remained an engineer, and he took what he had created and ran with it in the world of engineering and eventually manufacturing. What happened is that the boundaries and identities around these two separate social worlds for a while blurred a little, enabling musicians and engineers to work together on a common project. That Moog had some familiarity with music helped a lot. Deutsch too was familiar with the world of engineering having built his own equipment since an early age. Moog later ran into other musicians such as Wendy Carlos and Keith Emerson who were important, and with whom he had an almost "telepathic" rapport. In our book *Analog Days* (Pinch and Trocco, 2002), we describe Moog as a "boundary shifter"—someone who enters a liminal space and reconfigures the boundaries around the object he creates. We describe the synthesizer itself as a liminal entity—one that has the power to cross social worlds and reconfigure and transform boundaries. The very materiality of the synthesizer is part of the liminal possibilities. It allows what we have elsewhere called "interpretative flexibility" (Pinch and Bijker, 1984)—for radically different meanings of the synthesizer to be actualized.

The liminal quality of the early modular synthesizers is best seen in the problems people had with describing the skills needed to operate them. On the early albums the people who operated the synthesizers were sometimes described as programmers, sometimes as engineers, sometimes as keyboardists and musicians, and in one case as a "mad cap scientist."

This notion of liminality also applies to Van Koevering's activities. Van Koevering has a constantly shifting persona. At one moment, he was a preacher, then an educator and entertainer, then a musician, then an impresario, before finally ending up as a salesman. The account of his achievements selling Minimoogs is replete with visionary semi-religious talk of his "mission" to bring the Moog to musicians. Is this just salesman's bluster, or something more significant? If liminal spaces are important for creative acts, then it can be argued that visionary talk provides just such a liminal space. In such talk, the person imagines a different world, a world of possibilities. Like the world of possibilities found in play, visions too can provide a space away from the usual social worlds we inhabit. Van Koevering saw before anyone else how young rock keyboardists could take to the new instrument and what it could do for their music and star potential.

It is also interesting to consider the career of Moog's fellow synthesizer innovator, Donald Buchla, in the light of the above considerations about creativity. Buchla is of the same generation as Moog, and like Moog had a science degree (at the University of Berkeley in physics). Buchla met avant-garde composers Morton Subotnick and Ramon Sender at the mind-blowing San Francisco Tape Center in the middle of Haight Ashbury, almost at the same time Moog was meeting Deutsch. Buchla too developed a voltage-controlled modular synthesizer, and started manufacture from his small garage-like workshop in Berkeley. But unlike Moog, Buchla had aspirations as a musician. He made his own electronic music, and throughout his career, considered himself an artist who happened to be skilled at electronics rather than an engineer. As Suzanne Ciani, a pioneering synthesizer musician, who was one of Buchla's closest collaborators, put it: Buchla was "an artist who lived off his art."[33] Buchla himself expressed the dilemma of art and commerce:

> I don't regard it as important to be a commercial success . . . It's a fine line to tread, but you want to stay in the arts at the creative end of it and not mass produce anything, and yet you still have to make a living if you choose to do it.[34]

These differences between the identities of Moog and Buchla were crucial for the future of the synthesizer. Buchla rejected keyboard interfaces and was influenced by the more radical experimental musical ethos of John Cage and David Tudor (David Tudor was Buchla's first ever customer). Buchla was also part of the emerging San Francisco counterculture and friends with the Grateful Dead (for whom he made some synthesizer models). He refused to call his synthesizers "machines" and always referred to them as instruments—one-off creations, which contain all the little resonances and uncertainties which make a traditional instrument especially valuable. He rejected standard names for the white noise source found on synthesizers—preferring to call it "the source of uncertainty." He refused to call his work space a "factory" and employed "like minded friends, philosophers, artists and Zen Buddhists" who stuffed circuit boards in total silence. A more different ambience to Moog's funky upstate factory could not be imagined. Moog was ambiguous about the counterculture, preferring to watch from a distance (smoking pot but never inhaling); he let his West Coast sales reps Paul Beaver and Bernie Krause deal with what he called the "hippies." Moog was also uneasy about the take-up of his synthesizer in psychedelia, preferring to see it used for the classical creations of Wendy Carlos. In short, despite his boundary-crossing Moog's identity remains firmly rooted in fifties engineering values. He wanted to manufacture a robust, reliable product—he once told us he might as well have been manufacturing drills as synthesizers. Moog's synthesizers are famously reliable on the road while Buchla's are more delicate.

I do not want what I am saying here to be misunderstood. Professions and the identities that go with them are remarkably stable and are only rarely reconfigured. Inventive creativity seems to flourish in the sorts of liminal spaces which allow the boundaries around social worlds to blur a little, but it does not happen often. Identities can change but it is very hard in a world with a rigid institutional ecology to manage hybrid identities in a career which continually crosses two worlds. In the end, despite the similarity of their creative acts, neither figures are able to sustain careers as hybrid figures. Moog keeps his identity as an engineer and Buchla as an artist. Both men were equally creative and equally passionate and both made significant devices which changed our soundscapes and our notion of musicianship (Pinch and Trocco, 2002). In the world of synthesizer manufacturing Moog's name is better known because he became a synthesizer manufacturer rather than an artist.[35] But Buchla is still out there doing his art and making as beautiful and evocative instruments with as amazing sounds as ever.

6.4 Conclusion

In thinking about novelty and where it comes from one of the main themes of this chapter has been to point to the importance of materiality and objects as sources of novelty. Whether it be the material of the new controller the pitch wheel, or the sound itself which is made in a new way, or the novel spaces such as the "Island of Electronicus" sound laboratory, it is clear that an important component of novelty is the ability to reconfigure material objects. But our story of novelty goes beyond this; human actors, whether inventors, musicians, sales people, or consumers of the new electronic sounds, too must be reshaped or reconfigured. The actions we have documented which produce novelty are themselves distributed over time, space, community, and different materialities and institutions. New sorts of social actions arise, such as new ways to demonstrate synthesizers, new sorts of markets are born, as are new sorts of consumers, and last, but by no means least, a new form of electronic soundscape is also produced.

Notes

1. Unlike the electric organ, the synthesizer gives ways to produce and control the fundamental components of sound.
2. Koestler considers mainly how individuals are creative whilst Csikszentmihalyi comes closer to the distributed approach towards creativity argued for in this chapter. The difference is that in this chapter it is argued that artifacts themselves can be a source of creativity.
3. The argument here resonates with the active approach towards "path creation" developed by Garud and Karnøe (2001).
4. Another related strand of work here is Jim March's notion of a technology of foolishness (March, 1971).
5. Moog's company was revitalized in the 1990s as he recovered the right to use his own brand name, became a cult legend, and musicians increasingly found value in analog synthesizers.
6. In other words setting up unique sounds with unique patches was a time-consuming process as for each new piece many wires had to be replugged and switches and dials adjusted. How it is possible for sounds to be stabilized and valued in such a technology is discussed in Pinch (2014).
7. Jan Hammer in interview with Tom Rhea, *Imooginations* II (Lincolnwood, IL: Norlin Music, 1977), p. 9.
8. Roger Powell in interview with Tom Rhea, *Imooginations* II (Lincolnwood, IL: Norlin Music, 1977), p. 12.
9. Interview with Bill Hemsath, August 8, 1998.
10. Interview with Jim Scott, October 26, 1997.
11. Interview with Ken Fung, April 24, 1996.
12. Interview with Bill Hemsath, August 8, 1998.
13. The prefix Mini came later.

14. ARP synthesizers (a rival of Moog's based in Boston) notably used slide pots for many of their controls.
15. Interview with Bill Hemsath, August 8, 1998.
16. Interview with Bill Hemsath, August 8, 1998.
17. Interview with Bob Moog, November 15, 1997.
18. Interview with Jim Scott, October 26, 1997.
19. Interview with Jim Scott, October 26, 1997.
20. Sun Ra used the Minimoog on his recordings "My Brother the Wind" Volumes 1 and 2—for more details see Szwed (1996).
21. The outside designers had suggested molded plastic cases. Fortunately Moog couldn't afford to get these made; and the much more classic wood look was preserved.
22. Interview with Bill Hemsath, August 8, 1998.
23. They had no inclination to patent the device.
24. An early electronic instrument invented by the Russian scientist Leon Theremin in the 1920s which could be controlled by no direct physical touch (Glinsky, 2005).
25. Interview with David Van Koevering, January 30, 1999.
26. Interview with David Van Koevering, January 30, 1999.
27. Such spaces, like festivals, are important places for technologies to be discovered, experimented with, and valued (Schulte Romer, 2013).
28. Van Koevering's movement from the wider world to his test lab and back again into the world to sell synthesizers is reminiscent of Bruno Latour's (1983) story of Pasteur's lab in the pasteurization of France.
29. Interview with David Van Koevering, January 30, 1999.
30. Interview with David Van Koevering, January 30, 1999.
31. Quote is from Wikipedia entry on Bob Moog.
32. Interview with Bob Moog, June 5, 1996.
33. Interview with Suzanne Ciani, August 23, 1998.
34. Interview with Don Buchla, April 4, 1997.
35. Here the wider story of capitalism and the culture industries enters. The story line is familiar—there was money to be made from best-selling records and mass producing and selling synthesizers—not that Moog himself ever made much of it. But some sorts of activities are valued in our society more than others.

References

Baker, T. and Nelson, R. E. (2005). Creating something from nothing: Resource construction through entrepreneurial bricolage. *Administrative Science Quarterly*, 50(3): 329–366.

Becker, H. (1982). *Art Worlds*. Berkeley: University of California Press.

Bijker, W., Hughes, T. P., and Pinch, T. (1987/2013). *The Social Construction of Technological Systems*. Cambridge, MA: MIT Press.

Bijsterveld, K. and Pinch, T. (2003). Should one applaud? Breaches and boundaries in the reception of new technology in music. *Technology and Culture,* 44(3): 536–559.

Braun, H. (ed.) (2000). *"I Sing the Body Electric": Music and Technology in the Twentieth Century.* Hofheim: Wolke.

Csikszentmihalyi, M. (1996). *Creativity.* New York: HarperCollins.

Douglas, S. J. (1992). Audio cultures: Radio and phonograph enthusiasts. In J. C. Wright (ed.), *Possible Dreams: Enthusiasm for Technology in America.* Dearborn, MI: Henry Ford Museum and Greenfield Village.

Garud, R. and Karnøe, P. (2001). Path creation as a process of mindful deviation. In R. Garud and P. Karnøe (eds.), *Path Dependence and Creation* (pp. 1–38). Hillsdale, NJ: Lawrence Erlbaum Associates.

Garud, R. and Karnøe, P. (2003). Bricolage vs. breakthrough: Distributed and embedded agency in technology entrepreneurship. *Research Policy,* 32(2): 277–300.

Glinsky, A. (2005). *The Theremin: Ether Music and Espionage.* Urbana: University of Illinois Press.

Haring, K. (2006). *Ham Radio's Technical Culture.* Cambridge, MA: MIT Press.

Holmes, T. (2012). *Electronic and Experimental Music: Technology, Music, and Culture* (4th edition). New York: Routledge.

Hughes, T. P. (1999). *American Genesis: A Century of Invention and Technological Enthusiasm, 1870–1970.* New York: Viking.

Hutchins, E. (1995). *Cognition in the Wild.* Cambridge, MA: MIT Press.

Koestler, A. (1964). *The Act of Creation.* New York: Macmillan.

Latour, B. (1983). Give me a laboratory and I will raise the world. In K. Knorr Cetina and M. Mulkay (eds.), *Science Observed: Perspectives on the Social Study of Science* (pp. 141–170). London and Beverly Hills: Sage.

Latour, B. (1987). *Science in Action.* Cambridge, MA: Harvard University Press.

March, J. G. (1971). The technology of foolishness. *Civiløkonomen* (Copenhagen), 18(4): 4–12.

Millard, A. (ed.) (2004). *The Electric Guitar: An American Icon.* Baltimore: Johns Hopkins University Press.

Pickering, A. (1985). *The Mangle of Practice.* Chicago: University of Chicago Press.

Pinch, T. (2003). Giving birth to new users: How the Minimoog was sold to rock & roll. In N. Oudshoorn and T. Pinch (eds.), *How Users Matter: The Co-Construction of Users and Technology* (pp. 247–270). Cambridge, MA: MIT Press.

Pinch, T. (2010). Performativity and economic demonstrations: Pitching quality and quantity. In M. Akrich, Y. Barthe, F. Muniesa, and P. Mustar (eds.), *Débordements: Mélanges Offert à Michel Callon.* Paris: L'Ecole des Mines Presse.

Pinch, T. (2014). Moments in the valuation of sound: The early history of synthesizers. In A. B. Antal, M. Hutter, and D. Stark (eds.), *Moments of Valuation: Exploring Sites of Dissonance* (pp. 15–36). Oxford and New York: Oxford University Press.

Pinch, T. and Bijker, W. (1984). The social construction of facts and artifacts: Or how the sociology of science and the sociology of technology might benefit each other. *Social Studies of Science*, 14(3): 339–441.

Pinch, T. and Trocco, F. (2002). *Analog Days: The Invention and Impact of the Moog Synthesizer*. Cambridge, MA: Harvard University Press.

Schulte-Romer, N. (2013). Fair framings: Art and culture festivals as sites for technological innovations. *Mind & Society*, 12(1): 151–165.

Suchman, L. (2007). *Plans and Situated Actions*. Cambridge and New York: Cambridge University Press.

Szwed, J. F. (1998). *Space is the Place: The Lives and Times of SUN RA*. New York: Da Capo Press.

Théberge, P. (1997). *Any Sound You Can Imagine: Making Music/Consuming Technology*. Hannover and London: Wesleyan University Press.

Turner, V. W. (1969). *The Ritual Process: Structure and Anti-Structure*. Harmondsworth: Penguin.

Usher, A. P. (1954). *A History of Mechanical Inventions* (revised edition). Cambridge, MA: Harvard University Press.

Waksman, S. (1999). *Instruments of Desire: The Electric Guitar and the Shaping of Musical Experience*. Cambridge, MA: Harvard University Press.

7

Taking Advantage of Emergence

Deborah Dougherty

Abstract: Innovators in complex innovation systems can more productively generate new products if they deliberately take advantage of emergence. Focusing on drug discovery, the chapter develops three abductive learning routines through which innovators take advantage of emergence and generate knowledge for new drugs, despite very incomplete understandings of human biology. Abduction concerns what may be, and provides the logic of discovery through which innovators develop novel hypotheses about configurations of interdependencies among product elements, evaluate hypotheses by staying open, and accumulate knowledge by reframing models. The chapter explains how these abductive learning routines are enacted in different sub-systems of the overall innovation system (project, process, strategic, and ecological) to fit particular problem contexts. Finally, it discusses how the sub-systems can adapt to the emergence of other sub-systems, and continually weave together their understandings.

Emergence is the central dynamic in systems of complex product innovation, such as drug discovery, alternative energy, economic renewal, and many pressing societal challenges from poverty to economic development. Emergence means that new products arise from the actions of interdependent agents who are purposely pursuing individual plans based on local knowledge, but are also continuously adapting to feedback about the actions of others (Chiles, Meyer, and Hench, 2004). New products cannot be imposed by a central authority, since they arise from the circumstances spontaneously as innovators create new knowledge and recombine it with existing knowledge (Snowdon and Boone, 2007). While emergence is familiar (the economy is an emergent system, for example), its unpredictability and ambiguity make it disconcerting. Emergence contradicts the managerial logic based on "Newtonian" thinking (Tsoukas and Dooley, 2011), which privileges universal principles, hierarchical decomposition, and uncertainty reduction. Moreover, organization scholars have not developed clear processes for effectively enabling emergence, while many processes exist for enabling linear control. In our research on the complex system of innovation in pharmaceuticals, we find that innovators and their managers confront many challenges, from declining R&D productivity to shifting market demands. But they do not know how to deal with emergence, so they tend to rely on conventional managerial logic to deal with these challenges of complexity, which dampens rather than enables emergence.

The purpose of this chapter is to sketch out a framework for taking advantage of emergence and thus innovating more effectively in systems of complex product innovation. I integrate insights from a number of research papers from our study of drug discovery in pharmaceuticals into a coherent view of the whole system (Dougherty and Dunne, 2011, 2012; Dougherty et al., 2013; Dunne and Dougherty, 2013). Drug discovery is a good empirical setting for understanding how to take advantage of emergence, because product innovation in this system is truly complex (Pisano, 2006). Fundamental causal mechanisms in biology remain unknown (West and Nightingale, 2009), but innovators nonetheless seek to materialize a molecular compound that can enter the body, travel through the bloodstream, ameliorate the disease, and not affect any other systems in the body. In addition, pharmaceutical innovation is troubled because of the complexity. Despite enormous public and private investment in biomedical sciences, the number of new drugs produced per $billion spent continues to decline (Scannell et al., 2012). The translation of basic biomedical research into safe and effective drugs remains slow, expensive, and failure prone (Collins, 2011); the average product cycle time is 13 years, the failure rate still exceeds 95 percent, and the cost per successful drug exceeds $1 billion, after adjusting for all the failures. Because of these challenges, many pharmaceutical firms are closing R&D labs, which only further reduces their innovative capabilities.

Because the stakes are so high, industry, university, and governmental entities are working hard to overcome these challenges of complexity. I synthesize all their efforts into an intermediary model for taking advantage of emergence in complex innovation systems. In keeping with learning under emergence, my model merely captures some of the insights that many others and I have developed for complex innovation, and it can provide the basis for further exploration and analysis. But I fully expect that, like all intermediary models, this one will be reframed and reworked to take into account additional understandings from ongoing research.

My goal is to understand the everyday, ordinary social practices through which people can collectively deal with emergence for drug discovery, and by extension, in some other systems of complex innovation. Interested readers are directed to the listed studies for citations to the nature of complexity in this innovation system. However, we find that some think that new technologies would solve these problems, so I briefly point out a few misunderstandings. First, Henderson and Cockburn (1994) suggest that rational drug design can enhance drug discovery. Rational drug design uses algorithms based on knowledge of the biological target to design a molecule to bind to that target. While technologies like rational drug design are very useful, they are also limited. Scientific advances have actually enhanced the ambiguity of the work. Until recently, drug development was based on just a few hundred targets with a great depth of understanding about them, so algorithms could be developed to model their behavior (Collins, 2011). The new science has identified thousands of new potential drug targets with limited understanding about their mechanisms, so algorithms for rational drug design are much more limited. In addition, Scannell et al. (2012) argue that the focus on high affinity binding to a single target, what rational drug design does, may not be best because many drugs derive their benefits from interactions with multiple proteins. Moreover, many scientific breakthroughs remain undeveloped because of the complexity of human biology. For example, some estimate that 50 percent of studies on targets published in academic journals cannot be replicated because so much of the knowledge is tacit. And while the map of the human genome in 2000 is also a major scientific breakthrough, it has not yet led to any new cures (Cohen, 2011). The assumption was that a limited number of common genetic variants underlie diseases, but it seems now that even common heritable diseases are linked to many genetic variants, each relatively rare (Singer, 2009). There are no magic bullets from single technologies, but Scannell et al. (2012) suggest that there may be magic shotguns from integrating various knowledge systems and practices. Integrating knowledge into possible magic shotguns is the topic of this chapter.

The research studies that I synthesize in this chapter each focus on a distinct learning context of innovation that addresses a distinct problem: exploratory searching for clues to develop specific drugs;

innovation-wide processes that leverage new sciences; strategic management that directs innovation; and ecology-wide orchestration of all the institutions and agencies that contribute to drug discovery. In this discussion I integrate these different learning contexts by explaining how each sub-system emerges in its own right, but also works interdependently with the other sub-systems. In addition, the four learning contexts are not hierarchically nested. Rather, they are heterarchical with many to many links, and they interpenetrate each other. Effective new drug discovery is an emergent property of the overall system, based on ongoing interactions among the four sub-systems.

The framework that I sketch out in this chapter centers on learning. All product innovations depend on learning, or the creation, combination, and recombination of knowledge into novel configurations. However, as many as 90 percent of new products that businesses develop concern just one or a few novel parts (Adams, 2004), so most of the learning for innovation leverages existing product architectures and immediate feedback using clear, a priori metrics for expected product performance (Denrell, Fang, and Levinthal, 2004). Dunne and Dougherty (2013) argue that emergence changes learning for complex innovation. Complex learning is based on abductive reasoning, not on quick feedback. Most elements in complex product innovation are novel and there are no existing architectures, so innovators must discover necessary product elements and how they go together, with no immediate feedback and no clear metrics. According to Peirce (Locke, Golden-Biddle, and Feldman, 2008, p. 908), abduction is the best answer we have to problems of discovery, since abduction alone among the forms of reasoning originates possible explanations and introduces new ideas. Locke et al. (2008, p. 907) quote Peirce to explain: "[d]eduction proves that something *must* be; induction shows that something *actually is* operative; abduction merely suggests that something *may be*" (emphasis in original). Also quoting Peirce, Boisot and McKelvey (2010) add that abduction consists of examining a mass of facts and allowing those facts to suggest a theory. Weick describes the abductive process as "clues giving rise to speculations, conjectures, and assessments of plausibility rather than a search among known rules to see which ones might best fit the facts" (quoted in Locke et al., 2008, p. 906).

Bartel and Garud (2009) and Garud, Dunbar, and Bartel (2011) develop similar insights about learning about unusual experiences, and emphasize narratives that can be incorporated into abductive reasoning. In addition, abduction is part of a trio of abduction, deduction, and induction (Nesher, 2001). Clinical trials, for example, depend on the inductive logic of evaluation, which depends in turn on the deductive logic of specifying logical consequences. However, I deliberately emphasize the abduction of novel concepts and hypotheses for three reasons. One is that abduction is especially important in the earlier discovery phases of drug innovation. Another is that this logic of discovery is overlooked by many organization scholars, or conflated with induction. Third, the very high failure rate of clinical trials in pharmaceuticals (Collins, 2011) suggests that the scientist may not have adequately abducted good hypotheses to be evaluated through induction.

I develop three general abductive learning routines for taking advantage of emergence by matching the dynamics of emergence with abductive reasoning (see literature review on emergence in Dougherty and Dunne, 2011; on abduction in Dunne and Dougherty, 2013). One dynamic of emergence is making enough connections among elements to generate fluctuations outside the norm, and initiate emergence. Innovators can take advantage of this dynamic of emergence by using abductive reasoning to focus on searching for plausible configurations of interactions among drug elements (e.g. compounds, disease processes, and the rest of the human body). The abductive routine of searching for and surfacing configurations of interactions differs from the conventional learning routine that focuses on separate elements, not interactions (e.g. hierarchical decomposition (Yayavaram and Ahuja, 2008), modularity (Baldwin and Clark, 2000)). A second dynamic of emergence involves deviation amplifying activities such as positive feedback to move emerging configurations to a new order. Innovators can take advantage of this dynamic of emergence by using abductive reasoning to anticipate possibilities rather than predict outcomes (Boisot and McKelvey, 2010). Anticipation helps innovators stay heedfully poised to spot configurations that might emerge, especially minor perturbations that can escalate into major problems or opportunities, and open to serendipity (Garud, Gehman, and Kumaraswamy, 2011). A third dynamic of emergence enables new orders to come into being by recombining elements into a new order with enhanced capacity. Innovators can take advantage of this dynamic by using abductive reasoning to rethink and reframe their emerging models. They cannot confirm or validate models in the early stages of discovery, but they can judge how well these models account for what they know, and reformulate them to create new performance objectives.

Table 7.1 lists the three dynamics of emergence and matches each with a general routine for abductive learning. Then in the columns under the heading "Four sub-systems of complex innovation: distinct learning

Table 7.1 Learning routines for taking advantage of emergence in systems of complex product innovation

Dynamics of emergence	**Abductive learning routines**	**Four sub-systems of complex innovation: distinct learning contexts**			
		Project context of learning	**Innovation process context of learning**	**Strategic management context of learning**	**Ecology context of learning**
Many connections: generate fluctuations outside the norm	Surfacing configurations of interactions, interdependencies	Surfacing configurations of compounds, disease, body that create a new drug	Surfacing configurations among digital sciences to create problem space for project search	Surfacing configurations among learning events that create new business models	Surfacing configurations of new collaborations to create new knowledge
Deviating amplifying processes that move configurations to a new order	Anticipating to stay heedfully poised to spot emergent perturbations	Anticipating new clues by asking good questions, keeping open	Anticipating new thrusts by modeling further out in the search space	Anticipating new patterns across learning events to see new business opportunities	Anticipating new ways to develop new drugs by exploring industry-wide failures
Coordinating mechanisms that recombine into a new order	Recombining, reframing elements, problems with new performance objectives	Iteratively integrating clues by crossing boundaries, jointly making sense	Reframing partial models of drug possibilities to encompass all the new insights	Reframing ways to deal with ambiguity by combining diverse temporal structures	Creating new rules of the game that provide more common ground for knowledge integration

contexts," I specify how these general learning routines (searching for configurations, staying open to possibilities, reframing) can be enacted in the four distinct sub-systems to fit the particular problems of those sub-systems. In the first section below, I summarize the unique problems that each sub-system addresses, and explain how people in each can enact abductive learning routines for taking advantage of emergence in ways that fit their particular context and problem. In the second section, I discuss how people working in each sub-system can adapt to the learning from people in other sub-systems by aligning their abductive learning. Possible patterns in one sub-system reveal more about patterns in the others, and also help shape and constrain the emergent learning. The ongoing alignment of the sub-systems produces what Henderson and Cockburn (1994) refer to as "architectural competence," and generates the needed integration described by Pisano (2006).

7.1 Emergence within Four Sub-Systems of the Complex Product Innovation System

7.1.1 Project Level Sub-System of Learning for Complex Product Innovation

The project level sub-system of contextual learning addresses the problem of actually building the product, by ferreting out the many specific parts and components, figuring out how these may go together to generate some desired functionality, and exploring innumerable possibilities as effectively as possible. This sub-system is the heart of drug discovery, where teams of biologists, chemists, and others focus on synthesizing a molecule that can enter the body, travel through the bloodstream to the disease site, and ameliorate that disease. Developing an understanding of these interactions emerges unpredictably (Dunne and Dougherty, 2013), as innovators leverage their science to figure out what might work. The work is very hands-on, very concrete, and very embodied in the full sense of the scientists in their labs, as described by Knorr Cetina (1999). Project scientists are uniquely able to see how particular configurations of elements might work, explicate how mechanisms function, and assess the plausibility of approaches. The challenge of learning in this sub-system is that the possibilities for configurations and interactions are virtually infinite (see Scannell et al., 2012 for details). Project scientists need to search with "forward looking intelligence" (Gavetti and Levinthal, 2000) that enables them to use their science to avoid random searching and select more promising paths (Fleming and Sorenson, 2004). The central challenge that this context of learning confronts is: are we navigating well in this multi-dimensional labyrinth?

Dunne and Dougherty (2013) develop abductive learning routines that provide this forward-looking intelligence for project level scientists. The first routine focuses attention on searching for configurations of interdependencies among elements that make up a new drug—among possible compounds, disease processes, and the rest of the human body. Surfacing these configurations is a common objective. By always looking at the interdependencies, scientists can leverage more of the information that is available despite its noisy nature. Project scientists use their extensive background knowledge and experience to spot clues to configurations or patterns, and to negotiate the meanings of these clues.

The second abductive learning routine enacts the ability to anticipate and stay poised to spot even minor perturbations by keeping possibilities open. This routine leverages anticipation by asking good questions, not driving to answers. Since the path of science in complex innovation is convoluted (Grinnell, 2009), scientists cannot confirm expected outcomes in the early stages of work. Instead, they use science-based causal hypotheses to develop new and useful ideas and questions (Dunne and Dougherty, 2013), which is the essence of abduction. They also of course apply deductive logic to specify consequences, and inductive logic to evaluate the expected relationships. However, they continually cycle through abduction, deduction, and induction to build an understanding, not simply to test an expectation (Nightingale, 2004)—they "tinker," as Nightingale explains.

The third abductive learning routine enacts reframing by iteratively integrating, which is how project scientists make sense of their learning so far. Iteratively integrating is a coordinating mechanism that gives some closure to the searching. Iteratively integrating involves continually crossing various knowledge boundaries to pull in insights from different perspectives. With iterative integration, scientists are trying to understand if they have identified a workable pattern of interactions that comprise a potential drug.

The outcome of the ongoing enactment of these abductive learning routines is what we have labeled "learning events" (Dougherty et al., 2013). A learning event occurs when scientists learn enough about the configuration of interdependencies between the disease, chemical compound, and the rest of the human body system to indicate the next thrust of work. Each learning event reflects deeper learning about the emerging configuration. Discovery scientists anticipate these learning events, but they cannot predict when learning events will occur. Learning events are milestones, but they emerge unpredictably over time, and do not occur in a single step at a specific point in time. Our studies find that scientists rely on subjective negotiations, sensemaking, and intuition as they attempt to sort through all the tacit understandings and ambiguous experimental results to find that workable configuration of interdependencies that would constitute a good drug (Dunne and Dougherty, 2013). Abductive reasoning relies on facts from experimentation, but it also relies on sensemaking to figure out what those facts might signify.

This strong reliance on abductive sensemaking also makes project level learning fragile and easily disrupted, as explicated by Dunne and Dougherty (2013), for three reasons. First, this learning does not leverage enough of the massive amounts of biomedical knowledge that is available, so project level abduction is necessary, but not sufficient. Second, because project scientists work locally, they may muddle through myopically rather than explore alternatives systematically. Project scientists' emergent approach has no automatic means of closure, so they may explore too many blind alleys, they may persevere too long with unviable courses of action, and they may not spot enough of the interactions in the body that can be seen only from a distance. Third, rather than help shape emergent project learning, other scientists and managers try to constrain the potentially unproductive aspects of emergent project learning, and end up dampening emergence. Managers push project scientists to eliminate unpredictability by looking for clear facts and weeding possibilities out quickly. Digital scientists attempt to police the learning rather than actively participate in it (Dougherty and Dunne, 2012). Managers also worry that project scientists focus on interesting science for its own sake, and so try to narrow the search space (Dougherty et al., 2013). Managers also try to reduce uncertainty, which is not possible.

The end result of this fragility is that people tend to lose sight of the collective learning objective, which is to discover possible configurations that can become products. However, if the other three sub-systems of learning also enact the general abductive learning routines in a way that specifically addresses their own critical problems of innovation, the overall innovation system can overcome the fragility of project learning, and more productively take advantage of emergence. My key point: project learning cannot work alone, and requires effective abductive reasoning in these other sub-systems as well.

7.1.2 Innovation Process Level Sub-System of Learning for Complex Product Innovation

The next sub-system of contextual learning can help frame project learning, and overcome these fragilities. This context of learning works at the level of the innovation process overall that encompasses multiple projects. This sub-system deals with the problem of developing and integrating all knowledge systems into the drug discovery process. In most industries, the innovation process involves familiar functions such as R&D, marketing, and manufacturing, and pharmaceuticals does as well. However, pharmaceuticals also must integrate the explosion of new sciences in biomedical disciplines that have arisen around the complexity. These new sciences support general questions that span therapy areas, such as how well compounds bind or whether they are efficacious. Pisano (2006) explains why all these new sciences need to be integrated into the innovation process, pointing out that each one alone serves only to enlarge the exploratory landscape. The director of the National Institutes of Health (NIH) in the US also argues that these new sciences need to "shift from a series of one off solutions toward a more comprehensive strategy" (Collins, 2011, p. 1). The central challenge of this sub-system is: are we integrating all the knowledge well enough?

These new capabilities merge digital technologies and computation power with biological and chemical sciences to create what we term "digital sciences" (Dougherty and Dunne, 2012). Pisano (2006) explains that new digital sciences can enhance drug discovery in three main ways (consult Pisano, 2006 and Ng, 2004 for more explication). One way to enhance drug discovery is to develop new modes of synthesis that expand the types of potential drugs. An example is computational or "synthetic" chemistry that uses algorithms for assembling organic compounds to generate a large variety of virtual compounds digitally, and perform *in silico* (i.e. using computers) experiments to find compound types that might work in certain diseases (Barry, 2005). Structural data for compounds and receptors are generated from X-ray crystallography or nuclear magnetic resonance imaging (NMR), and then digitized for modeling to assess probable 3-D structures. A second way to enhance drug discovery is to generate new knowledge about biology and targets. For example, proteomics studies the structure and function of the proteins expressed by genes, to discover the patterns of proteins associated with various diseases. And, since few diseases are caused by a single gene, systems biology integrates knowledge from genomics, proteomics, cell biology, chemistry, physics, mathematics, and computer science to study the behavior of complex biological systems. A third way to enhance drug discovery is new design and screening methodologies. For example, in rational drug design, compounds are designed to fit that target's receptor using accumulated science to create computerized models of receptors and compounds (Ng, 2004). High throughput screening is an automated approach to test thousands of compounds with a multitude of assays for activities in specific diseases.

However, drug discovery has not improved during the past 20 or more years as these useful digital sciences have been introduced on a massive scale (FDA, 2004; Cohen, 2011), for four reasons. First, most digital sciences are still immature, and continue to evolve. Second, digital sciences were originally expected to *replace* older project bench sciences, and "industrialize" separate steps in the discovery process. Despite claims that new sciences can replace old ones (e.g. Powell, Koput, and Smith-Doerr, 1996), traditional sciences as well as project contextual learning remain necessary (Scannell et al., 2012). We show how scientists and managers we interviewed recognize this mistake, but are struggling to manage the integration (Dougherty and Dunne, 2012). Third, the complexity of this innovation was overlooked.

The fourth reason for the failure to effectively leverage all this new knowledge, articulated by Dougherty and Dunne (2012), is that a major knowledge boundary exists between project science and digital sciences. We argue that this boundary needs to be deliberately and continuously worked on, just as is done for the boundary between functions in conventional innovation management (Dougherty, 1992), but the presence of this boundary in drug discovery has been overlooked. These two sciences are based on different "machineries of knowing," the term used by Knorr Cetina (1999) to describe the epistemic cultures in science. Project scientists work hands-on, are very intuitive and engaged deeply in searching as they explore more immediate interactions among the compounds, disease, and rest of the body. Digital scientists work more abstractly from the immediate functioning of the living body, and develop systematic measures of entire biological systems like the genome or cell systems, map rather than search. Each type of science also has a different understanding of what constitutes robust science and good data, and how to deal with ambiguity. There are, no doubt, other knowledge boundaries, but the therapy/digital divide stood out in our analysis, and signifies different machineries of knowing which lead to different practices for approaching problems and making sense of results.

I suggest that the digital scientists can also enact the abductive learning routines to resolve their core problem of integrating the new sciences with the projects more productively. The first innovation process learning routine enacts searching for configurations at the level of the innovation process overall, by searching for configurations of digital sciences to define the search spaces for projects. Simon (1977) points out that for some real-world problems, algorithms are unknown, so people need to select problem spaces to explore based on initial goals, constraints, and processes for generating and evaluating alternatives. Digital sciences can be integrated around disease areas to shape an open but promising space where the science suggests that learning events are more likely. They can find "good" possibilities for interdependencies that the project scientists can delve into using their hands-on techniques. For example, a director of digital sciences explained how they have learned to stop generating "super huge" numbers of compounds with combinatorial chemistry, and instead combine this digital science with other algorithms to cluster the chemical structures around the activity they are trying to achieve (see Dougherty and Dunne, 2012). Then they more systematically choose places for project scientists to begin their work.

The second learning routine enacts anticipation at the innovation process level by integrating digital sciences to anticipate possible problems and opportunities further out in the development. Pickering (1995) suggests that scientific practice emerges around unpredictable problems, called "resistances," that arise and must be accommodated. Drug discovery is fraught with resistances that invoke the need to create accommodations to circumvent the obstacles. The digital sciences can create partial models about what is known so far in searching for clues in particular projects and then extend those models out along particularly promising dimensions that can suggest better possibilities. For example, according to Scannell et al. (2012), pharmaceutical firms now whittle down the thousands of "hits" (possible bindings) generated by high throughput screening techniques using a single outcome—potency. But the authors argue that a better approach would be to develop a more complete understanding of the full biological profile of the hits, since by focusing only on potency they may be throwing away very good possibilities. Developing a fuller biological profile requires the integration of digital sciences. Another example comes from our study. One scientist said that computational chemistry helps them to jump from leaf to leaf, but also to look for next generation type compounds that do not have the negative effects of the current compounds they are working with.

The third abductive learning routine enacts reframing the problem space by integrating digital sciences into partial models of the progress in the projects. By creating drug models that are open to additional transformations, the scientists together can capture learning more systematically. These models shift over time, but at any one point in time they are robust understandings that allow multiple alternatives to be explored. The articulation of models accumulates new insights and results in a more complete understanding about how this molecule behaves in the body, by developing possible architectures that reveal what they all know so far.

7.1.3 Strategic Management Sub-System of Learning for Complex Product Innovation

The third sub-system of contextual learning addresses the problems of developing and maintaining decision processes that support projects and knowledge development, and making sure that business models accommodate the streams of innovation. However, in systems of complex innovation, both the strategic management of innovation and the business models for deploying innovations continually emerge. In addition, strategic managers must muster the staying power to persevere and learn from the years of twists and turns and unpleasant surprises (Lynn, Morone, and Paulson, 1996, p. 32). The central challenge of this context of learning is: are we using all these knowledge assets available to us as effectively as we can?

Dougherty et al. (2013) suggest that the challenges faced by the strategic management of drug discovery concern time: how to map out the very long future flows of innovation yet also deal with immediate demands for reports on profitability and progress. Projects average 13 years in development, which means that everyone must develop points of reference for understanding and anticipating very long-term emergent events. Without the ability to map out long-term futures, people focus on current activities. However, managers also must deal with a short-term institutional environment where investors and others demand weekly, quarterly, and annual reports. We find that managers try to pace innovation—regulate people's attention and efforts—with clocks and calendars, which highlight near-term and predictable outcomes. Drug discovery cannot be clocked since the configurations of interdependencies that comprise a drug emerge unpredictably over many years. Scientists pace their work by working towards anticipated but unpredictable learning events. The literature on time and organizing distinguishes between *chronos* or clock time (the serial time of succession measured by the chronometer), and *kairos* or event time (the subjective, living time of intention, or people's sense that the time is right; Orlikowski and Yates, 2002; Garud, Gehman, and Kumaraswamy, 2011).

I suggest that strategic managers can also enact the abductive learning routines to address the problems they face. The first strategic abductive learning routine enacts surfacing configurations by focusing on finding new configurations that suggest new business models or opportunities. Strategic managers can measure how quickly consortia are formed, how many options are explored effectively at once, and how effectively scientists uncover more alternatives and useful consequences. Managers can develop improved processes by examining which activities can be done more efficiently to surface configurations, and what are the barriers to learning that can be overcome.

The second strategic abductive learning routine enacts anticipation by staying open to new patterns across all the learning events. Managers can look further into the future by synthesizing the various next thrusts among the projects and anticipating new business models or applications that make better use of drug possibilities that are emerging from the innovation. Managers can also plan ahead to offer a broader array of drugs for a particular disease in collaboration with other firms, and open opportunities for small market drugs, where projects might be canceled otherwise. And managers can work with industry partners and regulators to develop more flexibility in clinical trials.

The third strategic abductive learning routine enacts reframing by creating new ways to deal with ambiguity and evaluate plausibility. Perhaps the biggest opportunity to deal with ambiguity is to combine and recombine the two trajectories of clock time and event time to create a rich set of reference points that people can use to anticipate more possibilities further into the future, and understand more emergent patterns. To employ both temporal structures for pacing work, Dougherty et al. (2013) suggest a common orientation to milestones for assessing progress. When progress cannot be scheduled or timed by the clock, as is the case with complex innovation, people can still orchestrate future trajectories of events, anticipate activities that need to be accomplished, and coordinate attention and effort to carry out those activities. Event-time pacing structures the inherently exploratory searching and helps to constrain the short-term nature of clock time by keeping the future open to emergent possibilities. Clock-time pacing helps to constrain the potentially expansive searching, and marshals the development of resources that can be clocked.

7.1.4 The Ecology Sub-System of Learning for Complex Product Innovation Systems

The final sub-system of contextual learning addresses the problems of orchestrating the many organizations, institutions, regulators, and other agents that all generate essential knowledge for innovation. Ecologies that support innovation are increasingly vital for many industries, because competitive pressures and rapid technological changes have reduced the ability to rely on in-house R&D. Instead, more firms rely on open innovation (Chesbrough, 2003). Systems of complex product innovations rely even more heavily on ecologies, because no one organization, no matter how large, can possibly generate all the knowledge necessary for innovations like new drugs, or new kinds of energy or materials. In the case of new drugs, the basic science is created in many public and private R&D organizations around the globe, including universities and government labs, and alliances and other consortia. In addition, public safety in drugs and health care is heavily regulated by government offices such as the FDA in the US. The central challenge in the ecology context of learning is: are we using society's resources (all that knowledge and all that investment in infrastructure) well?

Dougherty and Dunne (2011) suggest that the ecology for drug discovery is already organized, but not organized to enable emergence. For example, patent systems encourage the monetization of knowledge that fragments capabilities rather than helping to integrate them (Pisano, 2006); very large firms grab first-mover advantages rather than collaborate; knowledge does not flow very well from universities to industry (Su, 2013); and regulations prevent iterative learning.

I suggest that people in the ecology can also enact abductive learning routines to address their specific problem in this innovation system. The first ecology abductive learning routine seeks to surface new kinds of collaborative arrangements among the various institutions that are involved, in order to create new ways to integrate knowledge. These new kinds of collaborations can overcome the avoidance of the enormous risks by enabling groups of participants to merge their abilities to create new understandings of particular diseases. Many collaborations are arising, such as new standards setting bodies, not for profit ventures based on diseases (e.g. the Michal J. Fox foundation), and new associations between industry and academia. The ecology may also need to sponsor new associations and create new laws, as was the case with eminent domain to foster the expansion of railroads, or the public monopoly to foster public utilities.

Some collaborations may need new rules for dampening competition so that firms can work on small market therapies. Other ways to generate collaboration include sponsoring precompetitive research on biomarkers, better life-system models, and other assays that everyone can use.

The second ecology abductive learning routine enacts anticipation by taking advantage of the 95 percent failure rate in clinical trials. It seems that many perturbations are overlooked, or at least not noticed across the ecology. A systematic analysis of failures may help reveal why, and point to new approaches for drug development and testing that may be more promising. Now, participants do not share data on failures or pool their knowledge to figure out how to enhance the innovation process overall and anticipate failures more fully. Relatedly, clinical trial regimes can be changed to fit different kinds of drugs. At present, if a drug is found to have an effect that is not the one that was precisely predicted, it is a failure. The iterative nature of drug discovery extends into the trial phase, and can be enabled provided public safety is addressed.

The third ecology abductive learning routine enacts reframing by enhancing ecological coordinating mechanisms with new institutional rules. At present, participants create and share knowledge using patents and publications, which are limited (Pisano, 2006). One possibility is to institutionalize a common goal: everyone works on surfacing configurations of interdependencies among various drug elements. Academics tend to zero in on a specific element and do not investigate interrelationships with disease systems. Many "biotechs" try to sell specific tools without explicating how those tools surface configurations. Su (2013) finds that academic and industry collaborators now emphasize the development of a drug possibility into "the best shape possible" for hand-off to industry. This best shape possible changes the objective from discovering or selling unique novelties to examining the configurations of interdependencies that would constitute a viable drug product.

7.2 Integrating Sub-Systems of Contextual Learning

Each sub-system of the overall system of complex innovation that is outlined above plays an essential role. The sub-systems of learning contexts are also mutually interdependent since the work carried out in one context helps to shape and inform the work to be carried out in another context. Therefore it is necessary to enable the ongoing integration of the sub-systems, so that the local innovation work in each can continually adapt to feedback about the actions in other sub-systems. I suggest that there are three ways to enable ongoing integration of the sub-systems: (1) recognizing the unique role each sub-system plays; (2) aligning the abductive learning routines across each sub-system; and (3) creating spaces of innovation that combine all contexts.

The first way to integrate the sub-systems is to differentiate them. This may seem odd, but as Tsoukas and Dooley (2011) argue, the ecological style of complexity emphasizes the diverse contexts of emergence. Innovation management scholars have also articulated different problems or sub-systems of product innovation (e.g. Van de Ven, 1986), and we find the same kinds of problems to be managed in their own right for the complex innovation of drug discovery. However, my research suggests that the four learning contexts are not fully recognized as unique kinds of problems that need to be addressed in their own right in pharmaceuticals. The ecological, strategic management, and knowledge integration problems are not fully acknowledged and are not being adequately addressed. Differentiating the distinct learning contexts highlights the distinct kinds of configurations that need to be abductively developed, evaluated, and continually reframed. Differentiating the different kinds of problems would also help untangle the complexity into distinct sub-systems that can emerge separately, provided the other sub-systems are emerging.

The second way to integrate the sub-systems is to align the four sets of abductive learning routines for searching for configurations, staying open to possibilities, and reframing. Looking across the first row in Table 7.1 regarding surfacing configurations, the four specific enactments of this abductive learning routine frame each other. Surfacing configurations among the digital sciences helps project scientists look for configurations among compounds, diseases, and the human body. Surfacing configurations across project learning events at the strategic level leads to new business models, which identifies projects that are more likely to be commercially successful. Enabling the emergence of more collaborative associations in the ecological context creates more shared knowledge of diseases and therapies.

Looking at the second row in Table 7.1 regarding anticipation and staying poised to spot emerging perturbations, the specific enactments of this abductive learning routine also frame each other. Anticipating new clues by asking good questions keeps the searching open, while anticipating new thrusts in the sciences by modeling further out highlights better clues. Scientists can jointly assess what might be useful to manipulate by bringing to bear digital science's careful measures of various human bio-systems with therapy scientists' intimate understandings of how compounds operate. Staying poised to see new business opportunities applies more project possibilities, while systematically exploring failures to spot perturbations in the ecology helps to improve overall approaches.

Looking at the third row in Table 7.1 regarding reframing, project level iterative integration leverages the hands-on knowing of the scientists, and shapes the development of partial models among digital sciences that can reformulate what is known. Framing the exploratory searching by partial models can reduce the myopia of local search, help scientists avoid unviable options, and enable them to work through alternatives systematically. The work by strategic management to integrate different temporal structures enhances everyone's ability to deal with the ambiguity by comprehending more possibilities. Reframing institutional rules in the ecology context of learning enables the combination of new knowledge across the various agents and organizations. Everyone's professional practice is to engage in emergent, exploratory learning in a rational, systematic fashion. Everyone seeks to learn how interactions can form patterns, and focuses on learning about what may be.

The final way to integrate the sub-systems is to create a variety of unique spaces that combine all four contexts of learning. I do not anticipate giant programs that combine all the contexts fully. I do anticipate a variety of more focused projects that connect several players and combine all four contexts of learning around particular diseases or possibilities. For example, one large pharmaceutical company has created a strategic alliance with a large university hospital and academic researchers around the possibilities for re-engineering human white cells to kill off a certain kind of cancer. The university scientists are working with the company scientists to create a way to scale up the re-engineering of the cells safely and more effectively, while hospital patients are treated and clinical trials are developed for this new approach. Other kinds of collaborations leverage all four contexts of learning to address global challenges such as searching for vaccines to malaria and HIV. I anticipate that a variety of projects and niches of value creation will emerge to integrate learning in a variety of ways.

7.3 Discussion

This brief summary of a framework for taking advantage of emergence attempts to make a few points. The first point is to pull together a variety of conceptual ideas about complexity, emergence, abduction, and the need to "complicate" (Weick, 1979) managerial thinking, and apply them to the very real challenges of innovation management in complex systems. My goal is to use these ideas to extend innovation management. Emergence is all about novel configurations of interdependencies—surfacing them, staying open to spotting them, and rethinking them to create better ones based on exploratory learning—and so is complex innovation. Innovation management still privileges decomposition, drawing on Simon's (1977) idea of near decomposability, and on modularity, but these ideas do not apply either to complex systems or to the various chemical and biomedical sciences that underlie drug discovery (Barry, 2005; Grinnell, 2009; Mayr, 2000). I have outlined a few very simple, observable, and doable learning routines that apply abductive reasoning in four different contexts of innovation learning. The framework indicates that people can work very systematically, as Grandori (2010) explains, despite the ambiguity and incomplete state of the knowledge. Together, these abductive learning routines enable people working in complex systems of product innovation to deal with the fundamental uncertainty, and more productively generate new products—at least this is the working hypothesis that needs to be examined, rethought, and reframed. I also propose that perseverance over the long term with the development of these complex innovations is an emergent outcome of the entire innovation system.

The second point is that this framework is only a beginning model to be reworked, but it is a beginning. It triggers a variety of possible research efforts to further develop possibilities for more effectively enabling complex product innovation. One is to take a hard look at various emerging programs like the cancer project outlined above, and see if they indeed integrate the four contexts of learning, and then see how they do so. A second research thrust is to examine the ecological context of learning more fully. New rules for the game are needed at this ecological or market level, but which new rules are more likely to emerge and how needs study. I propose a new orientation in science to looking for configurations rather than only exploring separate elements, but how such an orientation might emerge is unclear—it conflicts with the current institution of academic publication, which emphasizes finding novelties about elements. However, universities need to develop better ways to connect with industry to generate new streams of revenues, without destroying fundamental research. I hypothesize that new social mechanisms developed by universities to connect better with industry will develop the abductive learning routines for this context of learning, and also interrelate with other contexts as suggested here. Exploring this hypothesis by examining the various efforts now underway would flesh out and rework this framework. The challenges of developing multi-focused temporal structures also need much more work, especially because much of the research in management and innovation about time (see Dougherty et al., 2013 for literature summaries) are actually about clock time.

The third point is to think about how this framework might apply to other systems of complex product innovation. For example, if we consider social innovations intended to enhance economic development in blighted cities, we can see a variety of innovation projects, but not much in knowledge development and integration. The behavioral, economic, and social sciences in academe may be too disconnected from social innovation projects, much more than is the case in drug discovery. In addition, the strategic management problem is likely to be addressed by city governments, while the ecological problem is more likely to be subject to strong political pressures that may dampen the whole system if not addressed somehow. If we consider financial services, clearly a system of complex innovation, we might find that the four problems of emergent learning themselves are not well addressed or even acknowledged.

In conclusion, people can take advantage of emergence in complex innovation rather than avoid it or work around it. Abductive reasoning suggests some sensible, doable approaches for taking advantage of emergence. Because so much money is at stake in pharmaceuticals and other health care programs, many people are trying to work out how to improve innovation in these systems. Perhaps ironically, these money-driven efforts may lead the way for solving other very pressing societal problems that are also complex systems of innovation.

References

Adams, M. (2004). PDMA Survey. Report, Product Development and Management Association.

Baldwin, C. and Clark, K. (2000). *Design Rules: The Power of Modularity*. Cambridge, MA: MIT Press.

Barry, A. (2005). Pharmaceutical matters: The invention of informed materials. *Theory, Culture and Society*, 22(1): 51–69.

Bartel, C. and Garud, R. (2009). The role of narratives in sustaining organizational innovation. *Organization Science*, 20(1): 107–117.

Boisot, M. H. and McKelvey, B. (2010). Integrating modernist and postmodernist perspectives on organizations: A complexity science bridge. *Academy of Management Review*, 35(3): 415–433.

Chesbrough, H. (2003). *Open Innovation: The New Imperative for Creating and Profiting from Technology*. Boston: Harvard Business School Press.

Chiles, T., Meyer, A., and Hench, T. (2004). Organizational emergence: The origin and transformation of Branson Missouri's musical theaters. *Organization Science*, 15(5): 499–519.

Cohen, J. (2011). The human genome a decade later. *Technology Review*, 114(1): 40–56.

Collins, F. (2011). Re-engineering translational science: The time is right. *Science Translational Medicine*, 3(90): 1–5.

Denrell, J., Fang, C., and Levinthal, D. (2004). From T-mazes to labyrinths: Learning from model-based feedback. *Management Science*, 50(10): 1366–1378.

Dougherty, D. (1992). Interpretive barriers to successful product innovation in large firms. *Organization Science*, 3(2): 179–202.

Dougherty, D., Bertels, H., Chung, K., Dunne, D. D., and Kraemer, J. (2013). Whose Time is It? Understanding Clock-Time Pacing and Event-Time Pacing in Complex Innovations. *Management and Organization Review*, 9(3): 233–264.

Dougherty, D. and Dunne, D. D. (2011). Organizing ecologies of complex innovation. *Organization Science*, 22(5): 1214–1223.

Dougherty, D. and Dunne, D. D. (2012). Digital science and knowledge boundaries in complex innovation. *Organization Science*, 23(5): 1467–1484.

Dunne, D. D. and Dougherty, D. (2013). Navigating in the labyrinth of complex product innovation: Routines of abductive learning. Working paper, Fordham University.

FDA (2004). Innovation or stagnation: Challenge and opportunity on the critical path to new medical products. March. US Health and Human Services, Food and Drug Administration.

Fleming, L. and Sorenson, O. (2004). Science as a map in technological search. *Strategic Management Journal*, 25(8–9): 909–928.

Garud, R., Dunbar, R., and Bartel, C. (2011). Dealing with unusual experiences: A narrative perspective on organizational learning. *Organization Science*, 22(3): 587–601.

Garud, R., Gehman, J., and Kumaraswamy, A. (2011). Complexity arrangements for sustained innovation: Lessons from 3M Corporation. *Organization Studies*, 32(6): 737–769.

Gavetti, G. and Levinthal, D. (2000). Looking forward and looking backward: Cognitive and experiential search. *Administrative Science Quarterly*, 45(1): 113–137.

Grandori, A. (2010). A rational heuristic model of economic decision making. *Rationality and Society*, 22(4): 477–504.

Grinnell, F. (2009). *The Everyday Practice of Science*. New York: Oxford University Press.

Henderson, R. and Cockburn, I. (1994). Measuring competence? Exploring firm effects in pharmaceutical research. *Strategic Management Journal*, 15(S1): 63–84.

Knorr Cetina, K. (1999). *Epistemic Cultures: How the Sciences Make Knowledge*. Cambridge, MA: Harvard University Press.

Locke, K., Golden-Biddle, K., and Feldman, M. (2008). Making doubt generative: Rethinking the role of doubt in the research process. *Organization Science*, 19(6): 907–918.

Lynn, G., Morone, J., and Paulson, A. (1996). Marketing and discontinuous innovation: The probe and learn process. *California Management Review*, 38(3): 8–37.

Mayr, E. (2000). Biology in the 21st century. *BioScience*, 50: 895–897.

Nesher, D. (2001). Peircian epistemology of learning and the function of abduction as the logic of discovery. *Transactions of the Charles S. Peirce Society*, 37(1): 23–57.

Ng, R. (2004). *Drugs: From Discovery to Approval*. Hoboken, NJ: John Wiley.

Nightingale, P. (2004). Technological capabilities, invisible infrastructure and the un-social construction of predictability: The overlooked fixed costs of useful research. *Research Policy*, 33(9): 1259–1284.

Orlikowski, W. and Yates, J. (2002). It's about time: temporal structuring in organizations. *Organization Science*, 13(6): 684–700.

Peirce, C. (1935). *Collected Papers, Vol. 5*. (ed. C. Hartshorne and P. Weiss). Cambridge, MA: Harvard University Press.

Pickering, A. (1995). *The Mangle of Practice*. Chicago: University of Chicago Press.

Pisano, G. P. (2006). *Science Business: The Promise, the Reality, and the Future of Biotech*. Boston, MA: Harvard Business School Press.

Powell, W., Koput, K. and Smith Doerr, L. (1996). Interorganization collaboration and the locus of innovation: Networks of learning in biotechnology. *Administrative Science Quarterly*, 41(1): 116–145.

Scannell, J. W., Blanckley, A., Boldon, H., and Warrington, B. (2012). Diagnosing the decline in pharmaceutical R&D efficiency. *Nature Reviews Drug Discovery*, 11: 191–200.

Simon, H. (1977). *Models of Discovery and Other Topics in the Methods of Science*. Dordrecht: D. Reidel.

Singer, E. (2009). Interpreting the genome. *Technology Review*, 112(1): 48–53.

Snowden, D. and Boone, M. (2007). A leader's framework for decision making. *Harvard Business Review*, November: 69–76.

Su, Y. (2013). Transforming academic knowledge for drug innovation: A practice-based view of objects, entrepreneurs, and institutions. Dissertation submitted to the Graduate School, Newark Campus, Rutgers University.

Tsoukas, H. and Dooley, K. J. (2011). Introduction to the Special Issue: Towards the ecological style—embracing complexity in organizational research. *Organization Studies*, 32(6): 729–735.

Van de Ven, A. (1986). Central problems in the management of innovation. *Management Science*, 32(5): 590–607.

Weick, K. E. (1979). *The Social Psychology of Organizing*. New York: McGraw-Hill.

West, W. and Nightingale, P. (2009). Organizing for innovation: Toward successful translational research. *Trends in Biotechnology*, 27(10): 558–561.

Yayavaram, S. and Ahuja, G. (2008). Decomposability in knowledge structures and its impact on the usefulness of inventions and knowledge base malleability. *Administrative Science Quarterly*, 53(2): 333–362.

8

How Organizational Innovation Emerges Through Improvisational Processes

R. Keith Sawyer

Abstract: This chapter begins with the observation that innovation emerges through improvisational processes. Innovation is never generated by a single individual, but always by groups, networks, and organizations; innovation emerges from diffuse and distributed social networks. The chapter argues that an explanation of innovation requires an analysis of the processual and interactional mechanisms whereby innovation emerges, and explores the exact interactional nature of improvisational encounters, and what specific mechanisms allow improvisational encounters to generate surprising and original innovations. This explanatory framework is used to analyze the stage theater dialogues that emerged improvisationally during performances of several different Chicago improvisational theater groups. The chapter aims to develop the view that organizational innovation is improvisational, by contributing detailed and specific methods for understanding the underlying mechanisms that account for the creative power of improvisation. The chapter concludes by drawing out the implications of this framework for business organizations.

In an influential 1988 article, the legendary management guru Peter F. Drucker argued that the "new organization" of the future would be like "the hospital, the university, the symphony orchestra." These organizations have in common a flat management structure rather than a many-leveled hierarchy. Yet Drucker realized that the scored symphonic work was not a perfect metaphor, because his "new organization" would be improvisational: "a business has no 'score' to play by except the score it writes as it plays . . . The performance of a business continually creates new and different scores" (Drucker, 1988, p. 49).

In the years since Drucker's article, many influential organizational theorists have elaborated on his ensemble metaphor by emphasizing that organizations are improvisational, like jazz groups (Bastien and Hostager, 1992; Crossan and Sorrenti, 1997; Eisenberg, 1990; Kao, 1996; Miner, Bassoff, and Moorman, 2001; Moorman and Miner, 1998; Perry, 1991; Weick, 2001) or like improv theater (Crossan et al., 1996; Crossan and Sorrenti, 1997; Moorman and Miner, 1998; Weick, 2001). An improvisational group is a better metaphor for organizational innovation than Drucker's orchestra, because in organizations there is no script; individuals are often surprised by their collaborators; and interaction can result in the emergence of creative insights and solutions. In the writings of these contemporary organizational theorists, we find the jazz metaphor used to emphasize the key characteristics of group creativity: improvisation, emergence, and interaction. The team works without a script, and thus its activity is collaboratively improvised; and the outcome is uncertain (in many cases it cannot be known, by definition, because the goal is to generate an innovation) and thus is emergent from the group dynamic. In this new organizational paradigm, the team manages itself through a collective, emergent process. Many of the descriptions of *self-managed teams* are reminiscent of an improvisational jazz group: "multiple leaders emerge and a dynamic pattern of shared team leadership evolves" (Belasen, 2000, p. 259) and "this collaborative action is informal, emergent, and dynamic" (p. 262).

In this chapter, I share with this line of scholarship the observation that innovation emerges through improvisational processes. I follow the current organizational studies consensus in holding that innovation is never generated by a single individual, but always by groups, networks, and organizations; innovation emerges from diffuse and distributed social networks. Furthermore, I align with a recent strand of organizational scholarship that argues that an explanation of innovation requires an analysis of the processual and interactional mechanisms whereby innovation emerges (Feldman and Pentland, 2003; Simpson, 2009; Stacey, Griffin, and Shaw, 2000). But then I go beyond this existing management scholarship, and extend it by exploring the exact interactional nature of improvisational encounters, and what specific mechanisms allow improvisational encounters to generate surprising and original innovations.

I contrast my innovation-as-emergent-improvisation account with two alternative explanations for organizational innovation:

(1) Innovation is generated by the wise and careful leadership of a strong executive, who guides the organization toward a successful new process or product. This explanation associates innovation with a single person who is in charge.
(2) Innovation is generated by the careful application of routinized business processes, which consistently and predictably generate successful new processes and products. This explanation associates innovation with the scripted and routinized processes that generate it.

In contrast, in the emergent processual account of innovation that I advocate, innovation emerges from appropriately guided and channeled bottom-up processes. As such, innovation is unpredictable; it cannot be channeled into a repeatable and routinizable business process. A necessary corollary of this emergentist and processual view of innovation is that the innovation process is improvisational. The essence of jazz and theater improvisation is the absence of a central controlling individual and the absence of a guiding script or score (Sawyer, 2003a). Of course, improvisational performances vary in the degree to which they are routinized versus improvised (as I elaborate below in my discussion of Table 8.1). Perhaps the most improvisational extreme of musical performance is *free jazz*, where the musicians do not pre-select any structuring features of the performance—not the rhythm, nor the key, nor even which instruments will play and when. And yet, even in free jazz, the musicians share many implicitly structuring elements, such as their understandings of rhythm, harmony, and melody developed during years of musical training, and their interactional history in prior performances with the same ensemble. But most musical improvisation occurs with much more explicit forms of guiding structure.

I begin this chapter by presenting an account of emergence that draws on processual and interactional theories that were originally developed to study socially situated language use, both in linguistic anthropology and in microsociology. Such theories hold that human interaction and organizational dynamics are fully explained in terms of the actions and interactions of participating individuals. I then argue that a fully interactional account is insufficient to explain action in organizations, because these social interactions lead to the emergence of collective group properties that cannot be explained in terms of the actions and interactions of the participants.

Consequently, I combine these micro-level perspectives with a second theoretical perspective drawn from complexity theory and theories of social emergence, to present a hybrid account that I call *collaborative emergence*. In this account, I argue that micro-level perspectives are inadequate to fully explain symbolic interaction in organizations, because those interactions generate autonomous emergent social frames and structures, that once having emerged, constrain and enable participants' future actions. This is why a hybrid theoretical account is required, one that combines processual theories of interaction with multi-level theories of social emergence.

I then demonstrate the benefit of this explanatory framework by using it to analyze the stage theater dialogues that emerged improvisationally during performances of several different Chicago improvisational theater groups. My goal is to further develop the strong intuition that organizational innovation is improvisational, by contributing more detailed and specific methods for understanding the underlying mechanisms that account for the creative power of improvisation. A second goal is to argue that accounts of underlying mechanisms must be combined with accounts at the collective emergent level of analysis, to develop a full explanation of socially situated action.

I conclude by drawing out the implications of this framework for business organizations. The grounding insight here is that even in improvised performance genres like jazz and improv theater, the improvisational processes take place against a backdrop of guiding structures. Similarly, organizational innovation emerges most effectively when an organization determines the most appropriate degree of guiding structures, those that result in the most consistently innovative emergent processes. The challenge for organizational innovation is to enable the innovative power of improvisational, emergent, bottom-up innovation, while guiding and channeling it toward desired business outcomes, without going so far that these guiding structures end up removing the emergent potential of collaborative improvisation.

8.1 The Improvisational Processes of Emergence

Innovation emerges from distributed, diffuse, interactional processes that I have characterized as improvisational. This central observation led me to an exploration of various theoretical accounts of emergence (Sawyer, 2005). Most of this work has taken place in sociological theory, with some important work in the philosophy of science.

Sociological theories of emergence align with a strong contemporary strand in sociology today, the belief that social theory must be centrally concerned with process and mechanism (Abbott, 1995; Archer, 1995; Giddens, 1984; Hedström and Swedberg, 1998). Nonetheless, sociologists have found it difficult to develop an adequate theory to capture social processes; and even more difficult has been the empirical study of social processes. As a result, much of modern sociology neglects process (cf. Cederman, 2002; Gilbert, 1997, para. 3.3). This parallels a neglect in organization theory that I attempt to address in this chapter.

Process theories have much in common with the recent interdisciplinary turn to complexity theory, in both the natural sciences and the social sciences. Complexity theory developed to provide accounts of *complex dynamical systems*. Complex dynamical systems are "dynamical" because processes of change over time are of central interest. In the most general sense, complex phenomena are those that reside between simplicity and randomness, at "the edge of chaos," in Kauffman's (1993) terms. When the laws governing a system are relatively simple, the system's behavior is easy to understand, explain, and predict. At the other extreme, some systems seem to behave randomly; there may be laws governing its behavior, but the system is highly nonlinear—small variations in the state of the system at one time could result in very large changes to the later state of the system. Such systems are often said to be *chaotic*. Complex systems are somewhere in between these two extremes; the system is not easy to explain, but it is not so chaotic that understanding is completely impossible (as argued by researchers associated with the Santa Fe Institute including Murray Gell-Mann and Stuart Kauffman).

Many sociologists have drawn on earlier variants of systems theory to analyze human social organizations—including Talcott Parsons' structural functional theory (1951), and the systems theories of Buckley (1967), Bertalanffy (1968), and Miller (1978) (see Sawyer, 2005, for an extended discussion of this history). However, these sociological systems theories were relatively static, tended to focus on the macrosocial and structural level of analysis, and consequently did not incorporate the processual, interactional, and mechanistic elements associated with contemporary complexity theory. Contemporary complex systems approaches have potential implications for organization theory, because they start with the core observation that social organizations are complex configurations of many people, engaged in overlapping and interlocking patterns of relationship with one another. Some key questions raised by these society-as-system metaphors are: How do complex social systems originate, when they are not consciously designed by anyone? What do social relations and configurations look like? Which societies are the most effective, and which are stable and long-lasting? How could a stable complex system ever change and evolve, as societies often do? What is the role of the individual in the system? These questions have long been central in sociology.

More so than societies, business organizations tend to be more consciously designed toward explicit intentions. Many business organizations are, in fact, explicitly designed by people to accomplish specific goals. And in this, business organizations are somewhat different from the emergent and undirected historical processes of emergence that lead to sociological structures—but, I will argue, not qualitatively different. Business organizations experience these same processes over time—particularly in a rapidly changing business environment in which adaptability and innovation become necessary. Contemporary organizational theory is deeply concerned with how organizational structure influences individual action, how organizational processes unfold over time, and how individual behavior results in the emergence of global organizational properties (Carley and Gasser, 1999; Cyert and March, 1963; Marion, 1999). In addition, neoclassical microeconomics—which has provided substantial insights to our understandings of business organizations—is centrally concerned with the processes whereby aggregated individual actions lead to macroeconomic phenomena. In sociology, this relationship is known as the *micro–macro link* (Alexander et al., 1987; Huber, 1991; Knorr-Cetina and Cicourel, 1981; Ritzer, 2000). Theories of the micro–macro link are central, if implicit, in many twentieth-century sociological paradigms, including structural functionalism (Parsons, 1937/1949, 1951), exchange theory (Blau, 1964; Homans, 1958, 1961), and rational choice theory (Coleman, 1990).

8.2 What Emerges? Complexity Theory and the Micro–Macro Link

It is in this theoretical context of complexity, process, and the micro–macro link that theories of emergence have become of interest. Emergence refers to processes whereby the global behavior of a system results from the actions and interactions of agents. Philosophers of science, who have been concerned with emergence for almost a century (as documented in

Chapter 3 of Sawyer, 2005), refer to properties of system components as being "lower-level properties," and emergent properties of the entire system as "higher-level properties." In both psychology and sociology, the relation between lower-level and higher-level properties has often been theorized in terms of emergence.

In complex systems, higher-level structures "emerge" from complex lower-level processes. Canonical examples of emergence include traffic jams, the colonies of social insects, and bird flocks. For example, the "V" shape of the bird flock does not result from one bird being selected as the leader, and the other birds lining up behind the leader. Instead, each bird's behavior is based on its position relative to nearby birds. The "V" shape is not planned or centrally determined; it emerges out of simple pair-interaction rules. The bird flock demonstrates one of the most striking features of emergent phenomena: Higher-level regularities are often the result of simple rules and local interactions at the lower level.

In the social sciences, a comparable example of an emergent phenomenon is language shift. Historians of language have documented that languages have changed frequently throughout history, with vocabulary and even grammar changing radically over the centuries. Yet until the rise of the modern nation state, such changes were not consciously selected by any official body, nor were they imposed by force on a population. Rather, language shift is an emergent phenomenon, arising out of uncountable everyday conversations in small groups scattered throughout the society (Sawyer, 2001). In this social system, the "lower level" are the individual speakers, their interactions are the individual conversations, and the "higher level" is the collective social fact of language as a group property.

Common to both of these examples is that patterns, structures, or properties emerge at the global system level that are difficult to explain in terms of the system's components and their interactions. Whether or not a global system property is emergent, and what this means both theoretically and methodologically, has been defined in many different ways. For example, in some accounts system properties are said to be emergent when they are *unpredictable* even given a complete knowledge of the lower-level description of the system—a complete knowledge of the state of each component and of their interactions. In other accounts, system properties are said to be emergent when they are *irreducible*, in any lawful and regular fashion, to properties of the system components. In yet other accounts, system properties are said to be emergent when they are *novel*, when they are not held by any of the components of the system.

In all of these accounts, there is agreement that explanations at the system level cannot be easily reduced to descriptions of the constituting elements at the lower level. Sociologists have often used complex dynamical systems theory to argue against methodological individualism, the attempt to explain groups in terms of individuals (Sawyer, 2005). Methodological individualism refers to any attempt to explain group, system, and organization phenomena by reducing them to explanation in terms of the individual members of the system. In current scholarship, there are two broad variants of methodological individualism. The first is *psychology*, as practiced in academic departments of psychology with controlled laboratory experiments. Psychologists, for example (and many organizational behavior scholars as well) have attempted to explain organizations by reducing them to properties of individuals, such as personality traits, motivations, or cognitive styles. The second is *rational actor theory* (RAT) as practiced by microeconomists. RAT attempts to explain organizational phenomena in terms of the optimizing rational choices made by members of groups; microeconomists use statistical methods to aggregate many individual choices to group-level phenomena.

Complex systems theorists have discovered that emergence is more likely to be found in systems (1) which have many components interacting in densely connected networks; (2) in which global system functions cannot be localized to any one subset of components, but rather are distributed throughout the entire system; (3) in which the overall system cannot be decomposed into sub-systems, and those into smaller sub-sub-systems, in any meaningful fashion; (4) in which the components interact using a complex and sophisticated language (Bechtel and Richardson, 1993; Sawyer, 2003a). Not all complex systems have all of these features; for example, interaction between birds in a flock does not involve a symbolic language—instead, it involves very simple rules—but the flock manifests emergence nonetheless because of the large number of birds. Conversely, the complex musical communication among the four musicians in a jazz group leads to emergent properties, even though there are only four participants (Sawyer, 2003a). All four of these properties are found in social systems, including business organizations, perhaps to an even greater extent than in natural systems:

(1) Social systems have many components—the individual people participating in the system—interacting in densely connected

networks. In business organizations, these include the formal ties documented explicitly on an organizational chart, as well as the informal ties that result from extracurricular activities, school alumni networks, or membership in neighborhood organizations or churches.

(2) In social systems, global system functions cannot be localized to any one subset of components. One of the most important system functions, as Parsons noted long ago, is that of *reproduction*—as individuals enter and leave the system, the system nonetheless continues to maintain itself in roughly similar structure. In many social systems, the reproductive function is distributed throughout the system rather than associated with any one sub-system (although in Parsons' model, a key player in the reproductive function was the formal educational system, societal reproduction also depended on parents and communities).

(3) In many social systems, the overall system cannot be decomposed into sub-systems. This may seem less true of business organizations, which are classically designed in hierarchical fashion, with exactly the intent to make them decomposable. But today, in the most innovative organizations, these structural forms are fading away.

(4) And of course, human beings interact using highly sophisticated languages. Human language enables much more complex interaction patterns than are found in any other system in nature.

These four properties are interrelated in most complex systems. For example, social systems with a densely connected network are less likely to be decomposable or localizable. In modern societies, network density has become progressively greater as communication and transportation technology has increased the number and frequency of network connections among people. Several hundred years ago, a farmer in a small village had an extremely small social network. Cities, with the opportunity for more diverse and broader social networks, were typically the location of societal innovation (see Florida, 2002). Today, in many advanced industrial countries, individuals are able to move geographically and frequently change professions, hence developing broad and diverse social networks. The Internet has enabled social ties even between people who have not physically met. Some complexity theorists suggest that the greater network density of today's social systems is enabling what has been called *swarm intelligence* (Kennedy and Eberhart, 2001).

8.3 Improvisation as the Processual Mechanism of Emergence

In complex systems that manifest these four properties, emergence processes are more likely to be *improvisational*. The degree of improvisationality of emergence processes varies along a dimension from *ritualized* to *improvised* (see Table 8.1). All socially situated genres of interaction and performance can be located at a point along a continuum from more structured, more fixed, and more ritualized—such as a 1920s-style hot jazz performance—to more improvised, fluid, and unpredictable—like the free jazz I described earlier. Just as with the wide range of degrees of improvisationality in jazz sub-genres, in many cultures around the world, some musical and verbal performance genres are characterized by more fixity and stability over time, and others characterized by more improvisationality and freedom, as documented by linguistic anthropologists and ethnomusicologists (see the ethnographies discussed in Sawyer, 1996, 2003a).

As in many complex systems, the global behavior of an improvising group emerges from the interactions among the individual parts of the system. And as with other complex systems, the properties of the group—including the performance that emerges—is at a higher *level of analysis* than the system's components, the members of the group. I use the term *collaborative emergence* to refer to emergence in small groups, to call attention to how these emergence processes differ from those in physical and natural complex systems (Sawyer, 1999, 2003a). Most analyses of emergence assume that it is associated with complex systems with large numbers of many simple units, such as ant colonies and bird flocks. Cognitive scientists have argued that the human brain manifests emergence, because of its 100 billion neurons, and also because of the large number of connections between those components—each neuron connects with between 1,000 and 10,000 other neurons at connections called *synapses*. Obviously, an improvising ensemble is a very different sort of system—with only four

Table 8.1 Contrasting dimensions of emergent processes, from ritualized to improvised

Ritualized	Improvised
Predictable	Unpredictable
One person in control	Control is distributed
Focus on product or outcome	Focus on process
Communication of intended meaning	Meaning is retrospectively determined

or five components (the individual musicians) and with a correspondingly limited number of connections among those individuals. In my account of collaborative emergence (Sawyer, 2003a), I argue that a system with a small number of elements—such as the four members of a jazz ensemble—can exhibit complex behavior in spite of the small number of components and small number of connections among components, because the individual elements (the musicians) are complex (human beings are much more complex than a single neuron or a single ant) and the communication language is complex (human language is much more complex than the neurotransmitters that cross a synapse). These complexities can result in collaborative systems that manifest emergence, even though they do not have the large number of system components found in natural systems, like an ant colony or a human brain, that manifest emergence.

Because improvisation in groups is emergent, the unfolding process that the group will follow is difficult to predict in advance. The flow of the performance cannot be predicted even with unlimited knowledge about the skills, motivations, and mental states of the individual performers. Even with this knowledge, there is simply too much potential variability in what might emerge during the performance; the multiplying moment-by-moment combinatorics make advance prediction practically impossible.

8.4 Exploring the Mechanisms of Improvisational Emergence

Example 1 is an example of emergent improvisation, taken from my own ethnographic study of Chicago improvisational theater (Sawyer, 2003b). The performance is constructed turn by turn; one person proposes a new development, and others respond by modifying or embellishing that proposal. Each new proposal for a development in the performance is the creative inspiration of one person, but that proposal does not become a part of the shared understanding until it is evaluated by the others. In the subsequent flow of dialogue, the group collaborates to determine whether to accept the proposal, how to weave that proposal into the understanding of the performance that has already been established, and then how to further elaborate on it.

Example 1 is the first few seconds of dialogue from a scene that the actors knew would last about five minutes. The audience was asked to suggest a proverb, and the suggestion given was "Don't look a gift horse in the mouth."

EXAMPLE 1

Lights up. Dave is at stage right, Ellen at stage left. Dave begins gesturing to his right, talking to himself

	Speaker	Utterance	Action
1	Dave	All the little glass figurines in my menagerie, The store of my dreams. Hundreds of thousands everywhere!	Turns around to admire.
2	Ellen		Slowly walks toward Dave.
3	Dave	Yes, can I help you?	Turns and notices Ellen.
4	Ellen	Um, I'm looking for uh, uh, a present?	Ellen is looking down like a child, with her fingers in her mouth.
5	Dave	A gift?	
6	Ellen	Yeah.	
7	Dave	I have a little donkey?	Dave mimes the action of handing Ellen a donkey from the shelf.
8	Ellen	Ah, that's=I was looking for something a little bit bigger . . .	
9	Dave	Oh.	Returns item to shelf.
10	Ellen	It's for my Dad.	

By turn 10, elements of the performance are starting to emerge. We know that Dave is a storekeeper, and Ellen is a young girl. We know that Ellen is buying a present for her Dad, and because she is so young, probably needs help from the storekeeper. These dramatic elements have emerged from the creative contributions of both actors. Although each turn's incremental contributions to the performance can be identified, none of these turns fully determines the subsequent dialogue, and the emergent performance is not chosen, intended, or imposed by either of the actors. (Also note that the dialogue is not obviously derived from the audience's suggestion, either, although the actors will later integrate it with the performance.)

The emergence of the performance cannot be reduced to actors' intentions in individual turns, because in many cases an actor cannot know the meaning of her own turn until the other actors have responded. In turn 2, when Ellen walks toward Dave, her action has many potential meanings; for example, she could be a co-worker, arriving late to work. Her action does not carry the meaning "A customer entering the store" until after Dave's query in turn 3. In improvised dialogues, many actions do not receive their full meaning until after the act has occurred; the complete meaning of a turn is dependent on the flow of the subsequent dialogue. This sort of retrospective interpretation is quite common in improvised dialogue, and it is one reason that the emergent frame is analytically irreducible to the intentions or actions of participants in individual turns of dialogue.

Emergent properties often result from the *unintended effects* of action; effects that are intended are, by definition, not emergent because their origin can be traced to the individual motivations and advance plans of specific individuals. In improvised dialogues like Example 1, the actors do not use language to express an internal mental state; rather, mental states are attributed to individual actions retrospectively as the dialogue evolves. In spite of their lack of plans and intentions, actors are able to coordinate their actions to generate a plausible, coherent dialogue, and a coherent interactional frame emerges.

8.4.1 Metapragmatics

Following conversation analysis, I refer to the emergent improvised performance as an *interactional frame*. In conversation analysis, the "frame" refers to the various aspects of the encounter that are determined in advance, often by the physical and social context, and that are implicitly shared by the participants. For example, when purchasing groceries at the grocery store, the conversational exchange between the customer and the checkout clerk takes place within an interactional frame that is fairly highly specified, thus falling at the ritualized extreme of Table 8.1. In contrast, in a staged improvisational theater performance, all elements of the frame emerge from the collaborative efforts of the entire group. No single participant creates the frame; it emerges from the give and take of conversation. Just as with everyday framed encounters like the grocery store, emergent improvised interactional frames also include all of the elements of a small group encounter: the socially recognized roles and practices enacted by each participant, the publicly shared and perceived motives of those individuals, the relationships among them, and the collective definition of the joint activity they are engaged in. Linguists refer to these elements as the *pragmatics* of linguistic interaction, and thus *metapragmatics* refers to conversation about the unfolding pragmatics of an encounter (Silverstein, 1993). When an utterance functions "metapragmatically," it is reflexively commenting on the pragmatic features of the encounter—the social roles being performed or occupied by the participants, the contested and negotiated understanding of what type of encounter is happening, the status and relationship between the participants.

In improvised dialogues, each conversational turn functions on two levels simultaneously. First, each turn functions on a *denotational* level—the explicit meaning of the words and the sentence formed. For an example, take turn 3 of Example 1: "Can I help you?" The denotational function of this conversational turn is rather straightforward: An offer to help. And yet, the turn also functions on the second, *metapragmatic* level, by functioning to project a new understanding of the shared interactional frame. Prior to turn 3, the two actors were not yet in a relationship in which Dave was occupying a role in which it would be socially appropriate to offer help to Ellen. The metapragmatic function of turn 3 is to project, and potentially create, a new understanding of the emergent interactional frame, within which Dave and Ellen occupy socially understood roles and a corresponding relationship.

In the examples below, I argue that it is this second functional level, the metapragmatic function of language, that is the key to understanding how collaborative emergence results from improvised dialogue. In an improv performance, what emerges is a constantly changing interactional frame. It emerges from individual actors' turns and then constrains the future actions of those actors. Because of the demands of intersubjective interaction, there is slippage among the mental models of the actors. Consequently, for a coherent interaction to emerge, the actors have to be able to negotiate among their distinct representations. However, actors do not step out of character to talk about how their scene will develop; this would break the dramatic illusion and lose the continuity of the scene. Instead, actors have to negotiate their intersubjectivity while enacting the ongoing scene. Thus, every actor's turn of dialogue both enacts a character within the frame (the denotational function of language), and at the same time negotiates this intersubjectivity implicitly, by proposing an additional elaboration or transformation of that frame (the metapragmatic function of language). Most often, the metapragmatic function is *implicitly metapragmatic* because it is not stated explicitly, and its indirect pragmatic effect is to further define the nature of the ongoing interaction itself. Again, to take turn 3 from Example 1, Dave could have accomplished the same metapragmatic function explicitly, by saying "Let's pretend that I am a storekeeper and you are my customer." In such an utterance, the denotational and metapragmatic functions of the utterance are aligned. But it is much more common in everyday conversation—and, particularly, in improvisational theater, where actors are taught rules like "Show, Don't Tell"—for the metapragmatic function to remain implicit. Improv communications—like all human discourse—thus function on two levels: an enacted, or denotational level, and a metapragmatic, or negotiatory pragmatic level (Silverstein, 1993).

An offer that is stated more directly and explicitly is more powerful and more constraining than an offer that is more indirect and implicit. An implicit strategy has greater ambiguity and thus leaves a wider range of potential options for the addressee.

In turn 2 of Example 1, Ellen's nonverbal offer—walking into the store—is maximally implicit (as are many nonverbal offers). This action has many possible meanings; one of them is "a customer arrives." To construct a more explicit interactional move, Ellen could have said, as she walked towards Dave, either (1) or (2):

(1) I've got to have today's newspaper, do you sell them?
(2) I'm looking for some milk for my newborn baby.

Note that both (1) and (2) are compatible with Ellen's actual nonverbal move in turn 2, although neither are anything like the eventual meaning that the scene attributed to turn 2, and none of the three alternatives are compatible with one another. This indicates a general property of denotational explicitness: an implicit offer has a wider range of possible meanings than an explicit offer. This is why implicit metapragmatic strategies are more likely to result in unpredictable outcomes and creative emergence.

Denotational explicitness is closely related to the amount of dramatic information provided in the offer. A turn can offer a lot of dramatic information or a small amount of information. (1) and (2) are big offers, because they offer many details about the frame. In contrast, (3), an early turn from a 60-minute long-form performance analyzed later in this chapter, is a small offer:

(3) Here are those papers. Handing a "stack of papers" to addressee.

Big offers often propose fundamental frame properties, such as a character, activity, or location; small offers are rather subtle modifications or qualifications of a frame property: a character's personality quirk, a detail of an unfolding event, or specifics about the location. Big offers are more interactionally powerful, and constrain the range of creative options available to the addressee simply by virtue of providing more information for the addressee to respond to. Small offers are weaker, and provide the addressee with a wider range of creative options.

At the same time that they are enacting characters, actors use metapragmatics to negotiate the emerging frame. Metapragmatics have an effect like a narrator or a director's voice, which occurs simultaneously with the in-character dialogue of the play. Bakhtin (1981) used the term "dialogism" to refer to this two-leveled nature of improvised dialogue:

> Behind the narrator's story we read a second story, the author's story . . . We acutely sense two levels at each moment in the story; one, the level of the narrator . . . and the other, the level of the author. (p. 314)

Bakhtin argued that the "central problem" in studies of dialogue was "the problem of the double-voiced, internally dialogized word" (p. 330). The theory of metapragmatics is an attempt to solve this problem.

I will show that collaborative emergence is more likely to be found in interactions that use implicit metapragmatics. This is because such acts are less directive and provide the other participants with a broader range of potential responses.

8.4.2 Frame versus Process

In improvisation, the frame is always in flux—it never becomes fixed and static. I believe that sociological theories of emergence can help interaction scholars to theorize the interactional frame as a collective social fact. Conversation analysis is potentially helpful, because it is foundationally based on a view of conversation as a collaboratively improvised, joint accomplishment of shared meaning in interaction. In this, conversation analysts draw on the symbolic interactionists' emphasis on "human group life [as] an ongoing process" (Blumer, 1966, p. 538) and on joint action as "the fitting together of the lines of behavior of the separate participants" (p. 540).

Conversation analysis emerged out of 1960s ethnomethodology, a rejection of structuralist macro-level sociology associated with Talcott Parsons (1951). Rather than structure, symbolic interactional processes are the fundamental unit of social life: "the essence of society lies in an ongoing process of action—not in a posited structure of relations" (Blumer, 1966, p. 541). Because situations are unstructured and improvised, "it is necessary to trace and study the emerging process of definition" of the situation (Blumer, 1962, p. 188). And yet, this rejection of structuralism led conversation analysts to reject the ontological status of the emergent interactional frame. In the hybrid theoretical account here that I call "collaborative emergence," I argue that these strictly processual accounts would be enhanced by reintegrating some elements of structural emergence theory.

The studies of improvisational theater dialogues that I present below show that a dramatic frame emerges from the dialogue turns of individuals as an unintended consequence of those turns. I show that they are emergent, unintended collective facts, and I argue that they are analytically irreducible to facts about individuals. Thus, they cannot be completely analyzed within the paradigm of conversation analysis, ethnomethodology, or action theory, because those paradigms focus on the conscious decisions of actors, their strategic displays of subjective understandings, and their expectations of future events.

8.4.3 A Comparison of Metapragmatic Patterns in Two Improv Theater Performances

In an extended study of metapragmatics and social emergence, I compared emergence processes in two different 60-minute improvised plays, both performed by professional groups in Chicago in the early 1990s (Sawyer, 2003b). The first group, called The Family, used a format that they called "The Movie"; in The Movie, actors are allowed to step out of character and to explicitly metacommunicate about the ongoing drama, using "director talk" as if they were the director or playwright. The second group, called Jazz Freddy, did not allow their actors to step out of character at all. As a result, all of their metapragmatic negotiation had to be accomplished while speaking in character. Both groups created their 60-minute play from a combination of two- to four-minute scenes. The edits between these short scenes were not timed or planned in advance; these were emergent and collaboratively accomplished by the actors. I found that in The Movie, all scene edits were done with director talk; of course, in Jazz Freddy, all scene edits had to be done while remaining in character.

I pursued this comparison to determine whether the metapragmatic level of interaction could help to explain processes of social emergence. Upon analyzing the two emergent frames, I found major differences. The Jazz Freddy frame that emerged over the course of the one-hour performance emphasized character and relationship development, but its plot was not very complex. In contrast, The Movie's emergent frame had multiple, interwoven plot lines, but had weak characters and relationships.

Could these differences in socially emergent outcomes be attributed to the differences in the metapragmatic communications used? To answer this question, I used interaction analysis (Sawyer, 2006) to identify the step-by-step processes of this emergence. I found that the metapragmatic differences were indeed responsible for these different emergent outcomes, largely due to the dramatic demands associated with scene edits. The actor initiating a scene edit has to metacommunicate which other actors should join him or her on stage to start the new scene. The Movie actors would simply state explicitly which actors were to participate in the next scene:

EXAMPLE 2

"We now see John and Mary, sitting in a coffeehouse, talking about what just happened." (After which, the actors playing John and Mary would walk onstage, pull up chairs, and sit down and mime the act of drinking coffee, and the actor initiating the edit would leave the stage and allow the scene to begin.)

In contrast, the Jazz Freddy actors had to execute their scene edits while remaining in character. Unlike in The Movie, the actor initiating the scene edit had to be in the new scene; otherwise, there would be no dramatically plausible reason for him or her to be onstage in the first place. The most effective way for an actor to implicitly metacommunicate who should join him or her on stage was to address another character (the one meant to come on stage) by name. To execute the same edit as the Movie did in Example 2, the actor playing the character of Mary would have to walk on stage, pull up a chair and sit down, and say something like:

EXAMPLE 3

"John, could you bring some creamer over with our coffees?"

My interaction analyses showed that because Jazz Freddy was required to accomplish scene edits in character, they tended to use metapragmatic strategies like these relationship-focused edits, and these had the unintended effect of causing a frame to emerge that was rich in relationship and character information.

I also found that once these frames emerged—about one-third of the way through each performance—they then began to constrain and enable the later communication strategies that actors used in scene edits. This influence became progressively stronger as the frames became increasingly elaborated and complex. For example, as The Movie's plots became progressively more complex, actors used edits that drew on these plots, and as Jazz Freddy's characters and relationships become more developed, the actors used edits that invoked those characters and relationships. In other words, edits like Example 3 became easier and thus more common after a rich set of relationships had emerged.

8.4.4 Lack of Conscious Awareness

There is rarely conscious awareness of such emergence processes in small groups, in part because dialogue exchanges happen so quickly. For example, actors in The Family (who were performing The Movie) and in Jazz Freddy were not aware of these contrasts between their performances. In improvised dialogue, people act without conscious awareness or reflection.

It can be difficult to study these forms of indexical creativity because these are "aspects of behavior that participants never report on and do not attend to" (Kendon, 1992, p. 333). In an influential series of papers on linguistic ideology, Silverstein demonstrated that "it is extremely difficult, if not impossible, to make a native speaker aware of . . . relatively creative formal features, which have no metapragmatic reality for him" (1976, p. 49; also see 1979, 1981). We often don't notice the indexically creative metapragmatics of everyday conversation because most properties of the frame are fixed before we start talking. We usually know our assigned role in the participation framework and we usually talk to people that we already have established relationships with. We typically talk in a symbolically meaningful location which is culturally obvious to all participants, like a retail store or a conference room. We know when we spoke last with this person, and what we talked about. Because participants are so skillful at formulating indexical entailments as if they are simply indexical presuppositions of states of affairs that already obtain, analysts and participants alike are often misled into considering these creative interactional ploys as attributable to preexisting context (Silverstein, 1979, p. 232; 1981).

It is particularly difficult for speakers to become consciously aware of *implicit metapragmatic strategies*. Most of the indexical creativity in improvised dialogue is implicitly metapragmatic because the speaker, without stating the metapragmatic intent directly, manages nonetheless to communicate a metapragmatic message, in a sense "piggy backed" on top of a message that may on first glance seem to carry only unproblematic denotational content. Implicit metapragmatic strategies studied by past researchers include *keying* (Hymes, 1972; Goffman, 1974), *register shifts* and other *contextualization cues* (Gumperz, 1982), *pronoun selection* (Brown and Gilman, 1960; Friedrich, 1971), stylistic variables such as the *vagueness* or *ambiguity* of an utterance (Errington, 1985, on Javanese; Inoue, 1979, on Japanese), *non-referential indices* (Ochs, 1992, pp. 338–339), and the implicit management of participant structures (Goodwin and Goodwin, 1992). The presence of implicit metapragmatic strategies—which speakers are rarely conscious of—is one reason that improvised dialogues have unintended effects that result in emergent properties.

There can be no conscious awareness of these interactional phenomena because they happen so quickly. As Sacks was perhaps the first to point out (1992, p. 11), during conversation people respond so fast that they could not conceivably have consciously planned and decided their action. The psychological processes underlying conversational behavior are largely preconscious, and are difficult to explain with the action theory that is dominant in contemporary sociology (e.g. Joas, 1997). For example, Giddens claimed that people know pretty much everything that is sociologically relevant about social life, and that since people know what they're doing we should just ask them (1984). Even sociologists that reject structuration theory nonetheless generally believe that the causal impact of macrosocial forces must be mediated through individual's perceptions of them. However, in improvised dialogue, people act without conscious awareness or reflection. In particular, prior research has demonstrated that speakers have great difficulty becoming aware of the metapragmatic function of their own utterances, even when they consider an interaction in retrospect (Silverstein, 1979, 1981).

Implicit metapragmatics can only be effective when participants share the same cultural knowledge about "how particular linguistic forms can be used to perform particular pragmatic work" (Ochs, 1992, p. 342). Implicit forms are invisible to participants because they are *unmarked* behaviors; explicitly creative offers are marked and can be used to create frames that are not so familiar. This contrast could lead us to expect that improvised dialogues would use more marked, more explicit talk, because they so often attempt to create unfamiliar situations to mine them for their humor.

In interactions in which improvisational emergence is due in large degree to implicit metapragmatics, the emergent interactional frame is difficult to fully explain using action theories that focus on the intentions, subjective understandings, and actions of individuals in the encounter. This is because the individuals themselves are typically unaware of the creative function of implicit metapragmatic strategies—typically, believing after the fact that the denotational content of each utterance fully accounted for the frame that emerged, even when ethnographic analysis has documented that this could not have been the case. The metapragmatic mechanisms that lead to the emergence of an interactional frame require that we analyze that emergent frame as a collective social fact, not reducible to the intentions, subjective understandings, and actions of the participating individuals. To fully explain improvisational encounters that lead to the emergence of innovation, we need a hybrid social theory that integrates the best insights of microsocial, processual accounts, and those of macrosocial structural accounts.

8.5 Improvisational Emergence in Organizations

> The newfound urgency in organizational studies to understand improvisation and learning is symptomatic of growing societal concerns about how to cope with discontinuity, multiple commitments, interruptions, and transient purposes that dissolve without warning. (Weick, 2001, p. 297)

Improvisational theater dialogues represent the improvisational extreme of the contrast dimension presented in Table 8.1. They are more emergent and less reducible to the two non-emergentist explanations I presented earlier in the chapter: explanation in terms of an individual guiding leader, or explanation in terms of a guiding structure or routinized process. These super-creative groups may seem quite different from business teams and structured organizations, and yet, as I stated at the beginning of this chapter, many influential organizational theorists have emphasized that organizations are improvisational, like jazz groups or like improv theater.

Human societies and cultures emerge, over historical time, without being explicitly and consciously designed. The explanation for how they came to be falls in the realm of cultural history, or perhaps sociology or anthropology. In contrast, business organizations are explicitly designed. In the most simple sense, in an organization the lower level contains the individuals working for the organization, and the higher level is the organizational chart combined with the organization's codified business processes. If an organization's structures and processes are explicitly and consciously designed, then in what sense is emergence taking place? Where is the space for improvisation?

In fact, emergence happens every day in all human organizations, even those that are highly structured and designed. For example, organization scholars have long recognized the existence of *informal organization*. Social network analysis (SNA) is a valuable methodology specifically because it has the potential to document these informal relationships. But most organizations have not yet determined how to utilize the informal social network to help achieve desired business ends.

Improvisation provides a theoretical lens to integrate the formal organization and the informal organization. Achieving this integration is particularly important for organizations that need to adapt and innovate. If there is no improvisationality, if an organization is fully specified by the codified structures and processes, then there is no emergence, and there can be no innovation, no adaptability, and no change. Very few organizations—even the most rigidly structured—can survive for long with this high degree of rigidity. As a result, all organizations that survive over time have retained some degree of improvisationality and emergence.

Earlier in the chapter, I identified four organizational characteristics that are more likely to result in higher-level emergent properties:

(1) If the organization has many individuals and sub-systems interacting in densely connected networks, it is more likely to manifest emergent properties.
(2) If organizational functions cannot be localized to any one subset of components, but rather are distributed throughout the entire system, it is more likely to manifest emergent properties.
(3) If the organization cannot be decomposed into sub-systems, and those into smaller sub-sub-systems, in any meaningful fashion, the organization is more likely to manifest emergent properties.
(4) If the components of the organization interact using a complex and sophisticated language, the organization is more likely to manifest emergent properties.

One reason that open source innovation has received so much attention from organization scholars (e.g. Chesbrough, 2003) is because the networks of individuals that participate in the creation of open source software generally possess these four properties, to a much greater extent than traditional business organizations. This is the core insight of scholars who have applied lessons of "swarm intelligence" to business organizations (e.g. Bonabeau, Theraulaz, and Dorigo, 1999). Swarm intelligence is thought to be uniquely powerful due to its ability to generate emergent innovation, through unstructured processes that are essentially improvisational. Advocates of swarm intelligence are complexity scientists who draw on the analogy of eusocial insects, such as ants, bees, and termites, which generate higher-level complex structures without top-down guiding leaders or structures. It is no accident that one of the earliest theorists of emergence, William Morton Wheeler (author of the 1928 book *Emergent Evolution and the Development of Societies*) was an insect biologist famous for his studies of ants, as for example in his 1911 article "The ant colony as an organism."

More generally, the diffuse networks of suppliers, freelancers, and subcontractors that characterize the twenty-first century advanced Western economies likewise share these network characteristics, to a greater extent than more traditional models of the firm, where all critical functions are brought within the same organizational structure to reduce transaction costs (Pink, 2002; Williamson and Winter, 1993).

These diverse scholars share the belief that the contemporary economy is shifting toward newer, more diffuse organizational and transactional models, within which emergence and improvisationality are likely to be more prominent and more frequent.

More improvisational teams are a common source of technical innovation (Belasen, 2000, pp. 252–258; Eisenhardt and Tabrizi, 1995; Lanzara, 1983; Moorman and Miner, 1998; Weick, 2001). This explains the burst of interest in *self-directed* or *self-managed teams* (Belasen, 2000; Evans and Sims, 1997; Lanzara, 1983, p. 86; Weick, 2001). Such teams represent a paradigm shift from the more traditional hierarchical organization, with management exerting control from the top down. Many organization theorists have argued that these empowered teams lead to a flat organizational structure that is more agile, flexible, efficient, productive, and adaptive (Belasen, 2000, p. 252).

Many theorists have emphasized the improvisationality of such teams (Crossan and Sorrenti, 1997; Eisenberg, 1990; Kao, 1996; Miner et al., 2001; Weick, 2001). In organizations as in improvisational theater, "people are able to accomplish collectively what they could not do individually . . . The design that produces this complex mixture tends to be emergent and visible only after the fact" (Weick, 2001, p. 58). Improvisational organizations are emergent and self-organizing, and lead to solutions that have an emergent orderliness, in that small initial structures and decisions can eventually generate a more complex, larger design (p. 67). This recent paradigm shift in organization theory shows that much organizational behavior involves improvisational creativity.

8.5.1 What Organizations Benefit From Emergence?

The business press is enamored with innovative organizations such as Google, Apple, and smaller startups, many of which share the organizational characteristics I have been describing. For example, Google famously has a "20 percent" rule, where each employee can spend one day each week on a project of their own choosing. These 20 percent projects are not directed or selected by senior management; rather, they emerge from the bottom up. As such, these innovation practices tend to result in improvisational and emergent processes.

However, in many industry sectors and for some tasks, it is much harder to survive with an organization that holds the above characteristics. If a task is very large and involves many interdependent parts, the groups that design each of the parts must work closely with many other groups. The necessity of this interdependent work means that the interactions among the groups must be codified, and the processes managed from the top down, in such a way that emergence and improvisation in any one of the groups is dramatically reduced. This is the case, for example, in the sport of American football, where each of the eleven players engages in a task that is highly interdependent with the other ten players on the team. As a result, teams in such sports require many layers of coaching staff, and extensive practice on carefully scripted plays.

Contrast this case with W. L. Gore and Associates, maker of the famous waterproof fabric Gore-Tex. Gore's organizational culture is highly improvisational (Sawyer, 2007) and they frequently innovate new products through an emergent, improvisational process. And yet, each of their new products is almost completely independent of the others. For example, a group of Gore engineers worked for two years to develop a new brand of guitar strings; when released as the Elixir guitar string brand, they soon became the top-selling acoustic guitar string in the US. But the Elixir guitar string project had no interdependencies with the Gore-Tex waterproof fabric line, nor with the many medical devices that Gore sold to hospitals, nor with Gore's line of dental floss, Glide.

Some projects and some industry sectors require more structure than others; differing degrees of emergence and improvisation are appropriate. An organization cannot design and build a new aircraft carrier through completely bottom up, improvisational, emergent processes. And yet, if an organization is rigidly structured from the top down, there can be no emergence and thus no adaptability and no innovation. The challenge of organization design is getting the balance exactly right: enough structure to guide the organization more effectively toward desired business ends, and at the same time, leaving enough flexibility and play in the organization so that there is still room for improvisation and emergence—because that is always the source of adaptability and innovation.

This is where the insights from improvisational theater are particularly helpful. All improv ensembles begin a performance with an agreed-upon set of guiding rules and structures. This community of practicing actors realized, long ago, that completely unstructured improvisation tends not to result in an interesting and viable stage performance. Instead, their performances are guided by a set of structures that tend to result in more dramatically effective performances, in large part by enabling and guiding the emergent interactional processes of dialogue. In the performances that I analyzed above, by Jazz Freddy and by The Family (performing using The Movie set of rules), the actors have developed a shared set of guiding structures that allow them to improvise a fairly elaborate 30- to 60-minute play.

A second lesson from these two theater performances is that different structures result in different emergent outcomes, and that these differences can be explained in terms of the metapragmatic functions that each set of rules tends to foster. The actors themselves tend not to be aware of these relationships; they are unintended effects of the guiding rules, and these unintended effects emerge as a result of the implicit metapragmatic features of language. These mechanisms and relationships are complex, and are rarely possible to identify simply by interviewing the members of the group (because they remain implicit and unintended). Instead, an extended ethnography is almost always required (see Moeran, 2005, for methodological insights) to identify these processual mechanisms, and their relationship with the consequent emerging higher-level structures.

Talcott Parsons was the first sociologist to apply systems theory to analyze social organizations. And given his social and historical context of 1950s post-war America, it is perhaps not surprising that his theory analyzed hierarchical and decomposable systems—the sorts of organizations that dominated America during the 1950s, both in business and in government. Decomposable systems are modular, with each component acting primarily according to its own intrinsic principles. Each component is influenced by the others only at well-defined input points; its function (its internal processing of those inputs) is not itself influenced by other components (Simon, 1969). In such a system, the behavior of any part is *intrinsically determined*: it is possible to determine the component's properties in isolation from the other components, despite the fact that they interact. The organization of the entire system is critical for the function of the system as a whole, but that organization does not provide constraints on the internal functioning of components. This was the concept of system that Parsons borrowed from cybernetics; his structural functionalism assumed decomposability, in its elaborate identification of systems and sub-systems, and in its focus on status-role sets as decomposable components of systems (Parsons, 1951).

Decomposable systems are less likely to manifest emergence than non-decomposable systems. In non-decomposable systems, the overall system organization is a significant influence on the function of any component; thus, component function is no longer intrinsically determined. Dependence of components on each other is often mutual and may even make it difficult to draw firm boundaries between components (Bechtel and Richardson, 1993, pp. 26–27). Systems that are not *nearly decomposable*

(Simon, 1969) are more likely to have emergent system properties that are difficult to explain in reductionist fashion, by working up from analyses of the components and their relations.

Parsons' theory also assumed *functional localizability* in social systems. In Parsons' AGIL (Adaptation, Goal attainment, Integration, and Latency) scheme, each of the four major systems is defined in terms of its function. Likewise, the lowest-level components—roles—are defined in terms of the function they serve for the system: "There is the same order of relationship between roles and functions relative to the system in social systems, as there is between organs and functions in the organism" (Parsons 1951, p. 115). Organizations are likewise conceptualized in role terms, and are also defined in terms of their functions (Parsons and Shils, 1951, pp. 190–197). The allocation process—which together with the integration process allows systems to maintain equilibrium—serves the function of allocating functions to roles and to sub-systems (Parsons and Shils, 1951, pp. 108, 198).

In functionally localizable systems, emergence is less likely to occur. A system is localizable if the functional decomposition of the system corresponds to its physical decomposition, and each property of the system can be identified with a single component or sub-system. If system functions or properties cannot be identified with components, but are instead distributed spatially within the system, that system is not functionally localized (Bechtel and Richardson, 1993, p. 24). Many social functions and properties are not localizable. For example, "being a church" cannot be localized to any of the individuals belonging to the church, nor to any sub-network of those individuals. In an improvising collaborative group, the topic, tone, style, and genre cannot be localized to any one individual nor to any specific moment in the dialogue (Sawyer, 2003a).

Parsons' concept of system was perhaps appropriate for highly structured bureaucracies typically found in mid-century American hierarchical organizations such as large corporations and government agencies. However, in the latter part of the century, due to a range of changes in the economy, new forms of organization emerged to challenge hierarchical organization (Bell, 1973). Many writers in organization theory and management science have noted the flattening of the modern corporation; hierarchy is out, and heterarchy—structures with multiple lines of reporting and with flexibly reconfiguring task groups—is increasingly embraced (Weick, 2001). The structures of many contemporary organizations have become more similar to informal social groups such as social movements, improvised ensembles, and ephemeral organizations, and these shifts require an updated systems theory in social science.

An unresolved challenge for organization design and organization theory is to further explore and document what balance of structure and improvisation is best matched to each different industry and project type. The current intellectual dominance of bottom-up innovation models has made it difficult to determine how to best apply these underlying processual understandings to industry sectors that do not align with emergence characteristics—those that of necessity require ritualized business processes and a higher degree of top down guidance and control.

8.5.2 Group Flow

With the goal of identifying the most appropriate balance of structure and improvisation to attain desired business goals, I propose a model of *group flow* that is meant to align an organization's goal with the degree of emergence and improvisationality. My model of group flow is derived from Csikszentmihalyi's theory of individual flow. Csikszentmihalyi's (1990) term "flow" refers to a state of heightened consciousness that occurs in individuals during peak experiences:

> It is what the sailor holding a tight course feels when the wind whips through her hair, when the boat lunges through the waves like a colt—sails, hull, wind, and sea humming a harmony that vibrates in the sailor's veins. It is what a painter feels when the colors on the canvas begin to set up a magnetic tension with each other, and a new thing, a living form, takes shape in front of the astonished creator. (p. 3)

Over two decades of research with people from many walks of life, Csikszentmihalyi identified the common characteristics of the flow experience:

> The best moments in our lives are not the passive, receptive, relaxing times . . . The best moments usually occur when a person's body or mind is stretched to its limits in a voluntary effort to accomplish something difficult and worthwhile. (1990, p. 3)

When in flow, "people are so involved in an activity that nothing else seems to matter; the experience itself is so enjoyable that people will do it even at great cost, for the sheer sake of doing it" (1990, p. 4). In flow, the individual feels a sense of control over their own actions, their self-awareness vanishes, and time feels warped.

When a group is performing at its peak, I refer to the group as being in *group flow*, in the same way that an individual performing at his or her peak often experiences a subjective feeling of flow. The concept of group flow is related to Csikszentmihalyi's flow, but with a critical difference. Csikszentmihalyi intended flow to represent a state of consciousness within the individual performer, whereas group flow is a property of the entire group as a collective unit. When studying group creativity we need a way of characterizing the collective experience of the entire group. Based on my observations of performing ensembles, I have developed the concept of *group flow* to characterize those groups that are collectively in a flow state. Group flow has been neglected in studies of flow, which have focused on how individuals attain flow through their own actions. In *group flow*, everything seems to come naturally; the performers are in interactional synchrony. In this state, each of the group members can even feel as if they are able to anticipate what their fellow performers will do before they do it.

Many Chicago improvisers refer to the ensemble flow using the term *groupmind*. Groupmind is "the entire troupe working intuitively together toward the same goals. The perfect working of groupmind is a magical kind of high, akin to perfect teamwork in sports or even great sex; comedian Jim Belushi famously said that the high that comes from ensemble flow was 'better than sex' " (Seham, 2001, p. 64; compare Berliner on jazz, 1994, p. 389). Actor Alan Alda referred to this state, saying "you're actually tuned into something that's inside the actor's mind and there's a kind of mental music that's played and that everybody shares" (Sweet, 1978, p. 326). Improv actors often speak of ensemble flow as "a state of unselfconscious awareness in which every individual action seems to be the right one and the group works with apparent perfect synchronicity" (Seham, 2001, p. 64). Performers often talk about the groupmind in spiritual terms, and believe it channels "a truth beyond their own conscious reasoning" (Seham, 2001, p. 64).

But there is not one universal way that groups attain the peak performance that I refer to as group flow. Group flow is attained in different ways, depending on the organizational context. Group flow requires the group to develop an appropriate number of *pre-existing structures* to match the *extrinsic collective goal* imposed by the organizational leadership, strategy, and culture (Sawyer, 2003a; see Figure 8.1).

By an "extrinsic collective goal," I mean, for example, the task facing a business team when they know that by the end of the meeting they have to come up with a resolution of a budget shortfall, or the task facing an

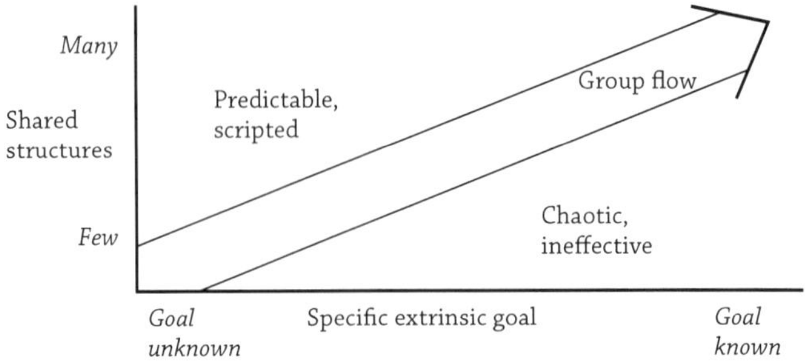

Figure 8.1 Group flow

engineering design team when they know that the purpose of the meeting is to fix a software bug that threatens to spiral out of control. In jazz groups, in contrast, there is no such extrinsic collective goal; the only goals are intrinsic to the performance itself—to perform well and to entertain the audience.

By "pre-existing structures," I mean the performance elements that are associated with a ritualized performance. These include at least four types of structure:

(1) An overall flow or outline of the performance that all participants know in advance (although the exact length of each segment, and the timing of transitions, must still be improvised).
(2) A shared repertory of ready-mades, with a knowledge of how they typically sequence in order.
(3) Clearly defined roles for each of the performers. In product-oriented ensembles, roles tend to be more clearly defined and distinct, and efficiency is a major concern. In improvisational ensembles, the emphasis is on process and open communication, and there is a more flexible division of roles.
(4) Common agreement on the conventions—the set of tacit practices governing interaction in the ensemble.

If there are many shared structures when there is no specific goal, then the business process will be too predictable and scripted. Shared structures interfere with the generation of new insights. For example, a corporate brainstorming session in which everyone in the group comes from the same corporate culture and has very similar ideas about what counts as a good idea will be so predictable that it will not serve its function of generating new insights.

At the other extreme, if there is a specific goal and the participants do not share enough common structures, then it will be very difficult for the group to accomplish its goal. The interaction will be chaotic and ineffective—both ineffective at attaining its goal, and ineffective in its own right as a performance. When a jazz ensemble is hired to perform what's known as a "society gig"—a wedding reception or a corporate party—they will tend to play relatively straight. In a society gig, there is more of a specific goal than in a late-night jam session performance—the goal of enhancing the experience of the attendees and conforming to their perhaps simplistic notions of what jazz is. Society gigs only work if all of the musicians are well-trained in the standard jazz repertoire; a young player who has spent his short musical career at the Berklee School of Music in Boston, playing technically demanding open-ended free jazz, will not share the necessary structures, and the resulting performance will not effectively attain its goal.

The "extrinsic goal" dimension parallels the distinction made in creativity research between *problem finding creativity* and *problem solving creativity* (Csikszentmihalyi and Sawyer, 1995; Getzels, 1964). When the group has a specific goal in mind, they are "problem solving"—the purpose of the group is to come up with a solution to the problem. When the group has no goal in mind, they are, in a sense, seeking out a goal or looking for a goal—they are trying to "find the problem." Improvisational ensembles are engaged in problem finding—they are not faced with a specific problem to solve, but instead, part of the enjoyment of the performance is in the unexpected moment-to-moment goals that the performers create for themselves. For example, during an extended improvisation of a jazz group, the music may stray quite far from the 32-bar song form that initially inspired the improvisation. By straying from the form, the musicians have collectively created a problem for themselves—how will they return back to the "head," the unison performance of the straight melody?

In a 60-minute performance of a fully improvised play, the ensemble spends the first half of the performance finding problems that they will solve in the second half. At the beginning, actors are encouraged to offer new material, and toward the end, to resolve and connect items that have already been introduced. By the second half of the scene, a variety of dramatic material has been introduced, including some conflict and contradictions. After the early work of introducing dramatic material, the performance then requires collaborative work to construct a feasible dramatic frame within which all of this material makes sense. The actors must collectively solve a problem that they have created for themselves, solving a puzzle of which they have created the pieces. The actors don't know how everything will be resolved and connected; the resolution of these problems is an emergent group process, and no one actor can know what will emerge from the subsequent dialogue.

The most improvisational ensembles fall in the lower-left quadrant of Figure 8.1, having intrinsic goals and fewer shared structures. But in organizations, groups are more likely to be located in the center and the upper-right quadrant of Figure 8.1. Such groups can also attain group flow, but for maximum effectiveness, appropriate pre-existing structures must be in place.

8.6 Summary

I began this chapter noting that it has become almost a truism in the management literature that organizational innovation is improvisational, citing a host of articles and books comparing innovative organizations to jazz ensembles or improv theater groups. What has not been widely studied in the management literature is the exact interactional nature of improvisational encounters, and what specific mechanisms allow improvisational encounters to generate surprising and original innovations.

I then developed a theoretical framework, collaborative emergence, that combines elements of processual and interactional microsociological approaches, with micro–macro accounts of social emergence that are more typically associated with structural sociology. I argue that elements of both theoretical approaches must be combined to fully account for interaction in organizations.

I then drew on theories from linguistic anthropology, and argued that improvisational processes result in the emergence of an unintended and collective frame, due to the metapragmatic function of language, rather than the denotational function of language. Further, I identified two very different types of metapragmatic strategies, implicit and explicit. Even though participants are not consciously aware of their use of these strategies, their use nonetheless results in different emergent group outcomes.

I then turned a more critical eye on the improvisation metaphor, and argued that for many business organizations, the jazz analogy is misleading because it overemphasizes freedom and improvisationality, while neglecting the equally important role of structure, convention, and guidance. In all jazz, and also in all improv theater, there is a constant tension between freedom and structure. Each organization will warrant a differing balance of the two, depending on a complex array of factors related to the nature of the project. I presented the framework of *group flow* as a way to balance this tension. The key to organizational success is finding the ideal balance between structure and improvisation, such that emergent social processes optimally occur to deliver desired business outcomes.

References

Abbott, A. (1995). Things of boundaries. *Social Research*, 62(4): 857–882.

Alexander, J. C., Giesen, B., Münch, R., and Smelser, N. J. (eds.) (1987). *The Micro-Macro Link*. Berkeley, CA: University of California Press.

Archer, M. S. (1995). *Realist Social Theory: The Morphogenetic Approach*. New York: Cambridge University Press.

Bakhtin, M. M. (1981). Discourse in the novel. In *The Dialogic Imagination* (pp. 259–422). Austin, TX: University of Texas Press.

Bastien, D. T. and Hostager, T. J. (1992). Cooperation as communicative accomplishment: A symbolic interaction analysis of an improvised jazz concert. *Communication Studies*, 43(2): 92–104.

Bechtel, W. and Richardson, R. C. (1993). *Discovering Complexity: Decomposition and Localization as Strategies in Scientific Research*. Princeton, NJ: Princeton University Press.

Belasen, A. T. (2000). *Leading the Learning Organization: Communication and Competencies for Managing Change*. Albany, NY: SUNY Press.

Bell, D. (1973). *The Coming of the Post-Industrial Society: A Venture in Social Forecasting*. New York: Basic Books.

Berliner, P. (1994). *Thinking in Jazz: The Infinite Art of Improvisation*. Chicago: University of Chicago Press.

Bertalanffy, L. von (1968). *General System Theory: Foundations, Development, Applications*. New York: G. Braziller.

Blau, P. M. (1964). *Exchange and Power in Social Life*. New York: Wiley.

Blumer, H. (1962). Society as symbolic interaction. In A. M. Rose (ed.), *Human Behavior and Social Processes: An Interactionist Approach* (pp. 179–192). Boston: Houghton Mifflin.

Blumer, H. (1966). Sociological implications of the thought of George Herbert Mead. *American Journal of Sociology*, 71(5): 535–544.

Bonabeau, E., Theraulaz, G., and Dorigo, M. (1999). *Swarm Intelligence: From Natural to Artificial Systems*. New York: Oxford University Press.

Brown, R. and Gilman, A. (1960). The pronouns of power and solidarity. In T. A. Sebeok (ed.), *Style in Language* (pp. 253–276). Cambridge: MIT Press.

Buckley, W. (1967). *Sociology and Modern Systems Theory*. Englewood Cliffs, NJ: Prentice-Hall.

Carley, K. M. and Gasser, L. (1999). Computational organization theory. In G. Weiss (ed.), *Multiagent Systems: A Modern Approach to Distributed Artificial Intelligence* (pp. 299–330). Cambridge: MIT Press.

Cederman, L. E. (2002). Computational models of social forms: Advancing generative macro theory. Paper presented at the conference "Agent 2002: Social agents: ecology, exchange, and evolution," Chicago, Oct. 11–12.

Chesbrough, H. (2003). *Open Innovation: The New Imperative for Creating and Profiting from Technology*. Boston, MA: Harvard Business School Press.

Coleman, J. S. (1990). *Foundations of Social Theory*. Cambridge, MA: Harvard University Press.

Crossan, M. M., Lane, H. W., White, R. E., and Klus, L. (1996). The improvising organization: Where planning meets opportunity. *Organizational Dynamics*, 24(4): 20–35.

Crossan, M. M. and Sorrenti, M. (1997). Making sense of improvisation. In J. P. Walsh and A. Huff (eds.), *Advances in Strategic Management, Vol. 14* (pp. 155–180). Greenwich, CT: JAI Press.

Csikszentmihalyi, M. (1990). *Flow: The Psychology of Optimal Experience*. New York: HarperCollins.

Csikszentmihalyi, M. and Sawyer, R. K. (1995). Creative insight: The social dimension of a solitary moment. In R. J. Sternberg and J. E. Davidson (eds.), *The Nature of Insight* (pp. 329–363). Cambridge, MA: MIT Press.

Cyert, R. M. and March, J. G. (1963). *A Behavioral Theory of the Firm*. Englewood Cliffs, NJ: Prentice-Hall.

Drucker, P. F. (1988). The coming of the new organization. *Harvard Business Review*, 66(1): 45–53.

Eisenberg, E. M. (1990). Jamming: Transcendence through organizing. *Communication Research*, 17(2): 139–164.

Eisenhardt, K. M. and Tabrizi, B. N. (1995). Accelerating adaptive processes: Product innovation in the global computer industry. *Administrative Science Quarterly*, 40(1): 84–110.

Errington, J. J. (1985). On the nature of the sociolinguistic sign: Describing the Javanese speech levels. In E. Mertz and R. J. Parmentier (eds.), *Semiotic Mediation: Sociocultural and Psychological Perspectives* (pp. 287–310). Orlando, FL: Academic Press.

Evans, K. B. and Sims-Jr., H. P. (1997). Mining for innovation: The conceptual underpinnings, history and diffusion of self-directed work teams. In C. L. Cooper and S. E. Jackson (eds.), *Creating Tomorrow's Organizations: A Handbook for Future Research in Organizational Behavior* (pp. 269–291). New York: Wiley.

Feldman, M. S. and Pentland, B. T. (2003). Reconceptualizing organizational routines as a source of flexibility and change. *Administrative Science Quarterly*, 48(1): 94–118.

Florida, R. (2002). *The Rise of the Creative Class and How It's Transforming Work, Life, Community and Everyday Life*. New York: Basic Books.

Friedrich, P. (1971). Structural implications of Russian pronominal usage. In W. Bright (ed.), *Proceedings of the UCLA Sociolinguistics Conference, 1964* (pp. 214–259). Los Angeles: Center for Research in Languages and Linguistics.

Getzels, J. W. (1964). Creative thinking, problem-solving, and instruction. In E. R. Hilgard (ed.), *Theories of Learning and Instruction* (pp. 240–267). Chicago: University of Chicago Press.

Giddens, A. (1984). *The Constitution of Society: Outline of the Theory of Structuration*. Berkeley: University of California Press.

Gilbert, N. (1997). A simulation of the structure of academic science. *Sociological Research Online*, 2(2) <http://www.socresonline.org.uk/2/2/3.html>.

Goffman, E. (1974). *Frame Analysis: An Essay on the Organization of Experience*. New York: Harper & Row.

Goodwin, C. and Goodwin, M. H. (1992). Context, activity, and participation. In P. Auer and A. D. Luzo (eds.), *The Contextualization of Language* (pp. 77–99). Amsterdam: John Benjamins.

Gumperz, J. J. (1982). *Discourse Strategies*. New York: Cambridge University Press.

Hedström, P. and Swedberg, R. (eds.) (1998). *Social Mechanisms: An Analytical Approach to Social Theory*. New York: Cambridge University Press.

Homans, G. C. (1958). Social behavior as exchange. *American Journal of Sociology*, 63(6): 597–606.

Homans, G. C. (1961). *Social Behavior: Its Elementary Forms*. New York: Harcourt, Brace, & World.

Huber, J. (1991). *Macro-Micro Linkages in Sociology*. Newbury Park, CA: Sage.

Hymes, D. (1972). Models of the interaction of language and social life. In J. J. Gumperz and D. Hymes (eds.), *Directions in Sociolinguistics: The Ethnography of Communication* (pp. 35–71). New York: Basil Blackwell.

Inoue, K. (1979). Japanese: A story of language and people. In T. Shopen (ed.), *Languages and their Speakers* (pp. 241–300). Cambridge, MA: Winthrop Publishers.

Joas, H. (1997). *The Creativity of Action*. Chicago: University of Chicago Press.

Kao, J. (1996). *Jamming: The Art and Discipline of Business Creativity*. New York: HarperCollins.

Kauffman, S. A. (1993). The sciences of complexity and "origins of order." In J. Brockman (ed.), *Creativity: The Reality Club 4* (pp. 75–107). New York: Simon & Schuster.

Kendon, A. (1992). The negotiation of context in face-to-face interaction. In A. Duranti and C. Goodwin (eds.), *Rethinking Context: Language as an Interactive Phenomenon* (pp. 323–334). New York: Cambridge University Press.

Kennedy, J. and Eberhart, R. C. (2001). *Swarm Intelligence*. San Francisco, CA: Morgan Kaufmann Publishers.

Knorr-Cetina, K. D. and Cicourel, A. V. (eds.) (1981). *Advances in Social Theory and Methodology: Toward an Integration of Micro- and Macro-Sociologies*. Boston: Routledge & Kegan Paul.

Lanzara, G. F. (1983). Ephemeral organizations in extreme environments: Emergence, strategy, extinction. *Journal of Management Studies*, 20(1): 71–95.

Marion, R. (1999). *The Edge of Organization: Chaos and Complexity Theories of Formal Social Systems*. Thousand Oaks, CA: Sage.

Miller, J. G. (1978). *Living Systems*. New York: McGraw-Hill.

Miner, A. S., Bassoff, P., and Moorman, C. (2001). Organizational improvisation and learning: A field study. *Administrative Science Quarterly*, 46(2): 304–337.

Moeran, B. (2005). *The Business of Ethnography: Strategic Exchanges, People and Organizations*. London: Bloomsbury Academic.

Moorman, C. and Miner, A. S. (1998). The convergence of planning and execution: Improvisation in new product development. *Journal of Marketing*, 62(3): 1–20.

Ochs, E. (1992). Indexing gender. In A. Duranti and C. Goodwin (eds.), *Rethinking Context: Language as An Interactive Phenomenon* (pp. 335–358). New York: Cambridge University Press.

Parsons, T. (1937/1949). *The Structure of Social Action*. New York: Free Press.

Parsons, T. (1951). *The Social System*. Glencoe, IL: The Free Press.

Parsons, T. and Shils, E. A. (1951). Values, motives, and systems of action. In T. Parsons and E. A. Shils (eds.), *Toward a General Theory of Action* (pp. 47–275). Cambridge, MA: Harvard University Press.

Perry, L. T. (1991). Strategic improvising: How to formulate and implement competitive strategies in concert. *Organizational Dynamics*, 19(4): 51–64.

Pink, D. H. (2002). *Free Agent Nation: The Future of Working for Yourself*. New York: Business Plus.

Ritzer, G. (2000). *Modern Sociological Theory* (5th edition). Boston: McGraw-Hill.

Sacks, H. (1992). *Lectures on Conversation, Volume 1*. Cambridge, MA: Wiley-Blackwell.

Sawyer, R. K. (1996). The semiotics of improvisation: The pragmatics of musical and verbal performance. *Semiotica*, 108(3/4): 269–306.

Sawyer, R. K. (1999). The emergence of creativity. *Philosophical Psychology*, 12(4): 447–469.

Sawyer, R. K. (2001). *Creating Conversations: Improvisation in Everyday Discourse*. Cresskill, NJ: Hampton Press.

Sawyer, R. K. (2003a). *Group Creativity: Music, Theater, Collaboration*. Mahwah, NJ: Lawrence Erlbaum.

Sawyer, R. K. (2003b). *Improvised Dialogues: Emergence and Creativity in Conversation*. Westport, CT: Greenwood.

Sawyer, R. K. (2005). *Social Emergence: Societies as Complex Systems*. New York: Cambridge University Press.

Sawyer, R. K. (2006). Analyzing collaborative discourse. In R. K. Sawyer (ed.), *The Cambridge Handbook of the Learning Sciences* (pp. 187–204). New York: Cambridge University Press.

Sawyer, R. K. (2007). *Group Genius: The Creative Power of Collaboration*. New York: Basic Books.

Seham, A. E. (2001). *Whose Improv Is It Anyway? Beyond Second City*. Jackson, MS: University Press of Mississippi.

Silverstein, M. (1976). Shifters, linguistic categories, and cultural description. In K. Basso and H. Selby (eds.), *Meaning in Anthropology* (pp. 11–55). Albuquerque: University of New Mexico Press.

Silverstein, M. (1979). Language structure and linguistic ideology. In P. R. Clyne (ed.), *The Elements: A Parasession on Linguistic Units and Levels* (pp. 193–247). Chicago: Chicago Linguistic Society.

Silverstein, M. (1981). *The Limits of Awareness*. Austin, TX: Southwest Educational Development Laboratory.

Silverstein, M. (1993). Metapragmatic discourse and metapragmatic function. In J. A. Lucy (ed.), *Reflexive Language* (pp. 33–58). New York: Cambridge University Press.

Simon, H. A. (1969). *The Sciences of the Artificial*. Cambridge, MA: MIT Press.

Simpson, B. (2009). Pragmatism, Mead and the practice turn. *Organization Studies*, 30(12): 1329–1347.

Stacey, R. D., Griffin, D., and Shaw, P. (2000). *Complexity and Management: Fad or Radical Challenge to Systems Thinking?* London: Routledge.

Sweet, J. (1978). *Something Wonderful Right Away: An Oral History of the Second City & the Compass Players*. New York: Avon Books.

Weick, K. E. (2001). *Making Sense of the Organization*. Malden, MA: Blackwell.

Wheeler, W. M. (1911). The ant-colony as an organism. *Journal of Morphology*, 22: 307–325 (A lecture prepared for delivery at the Marine Biological Laboratory, Woods Hole, MA, August 2, 1910).

Wheeler, W. M. (1928). *Emergent Evolution and the Development of Societies*. New York: Norton (Portions originally presented at the symposium on emergence held at Cambridge, MA, September 14, 1926).

Williamson, O. E. and Winter, S. G. (eds.) (1993). *The Nature of the Firm: Origins, Evolution, and Development*. New York: Oxford University Press.

9

Creativity at Work

Generating Useful Novelty in Haute Cuisine Restaurants

Isabelle Bouty and Marie-Léandre Gomez

Abstract: Creativity is an essential foundation of value creation in contemporary organizations and environments. As a specific phenomenon, distinct from innovation, it has, however, received only partial attention in prior management literature. This chapter investigates the dynamics and complexities of creativity within a process perspective accounting for flows of activities and events, the actors involved, and the material, spatial, and temporal entanglements of their work within the focal organizations and the institutional field. It builds on the empirical study of three fine-dining restaurants in haute cuisine to identify three distinct threads in the creative process, to show that creativity is a developing social process in which the different threads dynamically interrelate. The chapter highlights that despite its generative nature, the creativity process is highly organized, and demonstrates the importance of time and space in the process. Chefs play with time and space to nourish and structure the creativity process.

> The real problem is to explain novelties. The crux of my problem [. . .] is to explain how novelties are possible and how they are formed
>
> (Piaget, 1971, p. 1)

9.1 Introduction

Creativity and novelty are systematically proposed as essential foundations of value creation in contemporary organizations and environments

(Amabile et al., 1996; George, 2007; Oldham and Cummings, 1996). Creativity is taken to be the ultimate source of value and innovation in products, services, work, and social progress. Both individuals and organizations are increasingly required to be creative. It is therefore no surprise that scholars have more and more directed their efforts towards developing a better understanding of creativity, the conditions under which it flourishes, and the benefits that accrue.

In the management literature, creativity is most commonly defined as "the production of novel and useful ideas" (Amabile et al., 1996, p. 1155). As suggested by George (2007, p. 442) "considering that both novelty and usefulness must be present for ideas to be considered creative helps to distinguish what is creative from what is not." In particular George (2007) and Runco (2004) insist that although wild thinking and problem-solving are often considered forms of creativity, this is not necessarily the case, as what emerges may simply be new useless ideas or old useful ideas.

Creativity in organizations has only been partially investigated. There are two reasons for this. First and foremost, creativity has often been subsumed into wider innovation or problem-solving concerns. Innovation is "the successful implementation of creative ideas within an organization" (Amabile et al., 1996, p. 1155) and is indeed related to creativity, but creativity has often been restricted to the initial step of innovation processes, and previous research on innovation has tended to consider the specific investigation of creativity as a secondary preoccupation. However, creative work also can happen outside innovation processes (George, 2007; Runco, 2004).

Second, those scholars who did direct their attention towards creativity as a distinct phenomenon primarily focused on predictors of creativity and the organizational conditions that (directly or through intrinsic motivation) favored and influenced its flourishing (Driver, 2008; Montag, Maertz, and Baer, 2012). Some studies do address creativity as an individual experience in organizations (e.g. Mainemelis, 2001, 2010; Mainemelis and Ronson, 2006), but despite the significant contributions made by such earlier research, our understanding of creativity in organizations remains incomplete. We suggest that a process approach offers new ways to improve our knowledge. In particular, because literature has mainly investigated the sources, influences, and outputs of creativity, the dynamics and complexities of creativity as a process remain relatively unexplored (Arjaliès, Lorino, and Simpson 2013; Mainemelis, 2002). A process perspective can outline the social interactions and the progressive development of activities in creativity: "The fundamental goal of process theorizing in organization studies is to come to grips with organizations as a continuous process of becoming, as opposed to seeing them as stable entities that change in a step-by-step fashion" (Hernes, Simpson, and Soderlund, 2013, p. 3). A fairly simple question therefore remains to be further investigated: how does creativity happen in organizations; how is creative work actually carried out? We contribute to answering this question with the study of the creativity process in haute cuisine restaurants. For this purpose, and based on prior literature (Townley, Beech, and McKinlay, 2009; McLeod, O'Donohoe, and Townley, 2011), a process view (Langley, 2007; Langley and Tsoukas, 2010) should capture the emergence and dynamics of creative working, and enrich our understanding of the process by which creativity is achieved over time. Our focus is on a flow of activities and events (Tsoukas and Chia, 2002), on detailing the specificities of creative work. This will include the actors involved and the material, spatial, and temporal entanglements of their work within the specific context of the focal organizations and the institutional field of haute cuisine.

Haute cuisine is the cultural field made up of agents and organizations engaged in the world of elite gourmet restaurants and fine dining (Parkhurst-Ferguson, 2004; Rao, Monin, and Durand, 2003). It is highly institutionalized (Rao et al., 2003). The overall success of restaurants depends on the ratings of major gastronomic guidebooks (Parkhurst-Ferguson, 2004) and, in particular, that of the Michelin Red Guide (Durand, Rao, and Monin, 2007; Karpik, 2010). In rating restaurants, Michelin grants essential importance to their day-to-day operational excellence and the inventiveness of their cuisine (Karpik, 2000). Creativity is therefore vital in gourmet restaurants: chefs and their teams are expected to create new dishes and menus on a regular basis to defend their position. In addition, however, creativity is also shaped by chefs' interpretation of Michelin criteria for novelty. We conducted a qualitative and comparative analysis of three French restaurants that are particularly renowned for their creativity and have been singled out by Michelin. We base our analysis on both secondary and primary data. Our secondary data consist of press articles and long video documentaries. Our primary data include formal interviews with chefs and their teams, and more informal conversations.

We identify three distinct threads in the creative process, which correspond to different activities, different people involved, and different times and spaces: working on ideas, creative teamworking, and naming. These threads are not sequential, but rather form an ebb and flow in their continuous interweaving. Creativity is a developing social process in which the different threads dynamically interrelate. We exemplify that creativity entails both personal and social influences for the generation of new and useful ideas, and specifically show how institutional pressure and evaluation surface with each thread. Finally, we highlight that despite its generative nature, the creativity process emerges as highly organized; we specifically put forward the importance of time and space in the process. We show how chefs permanently play with time (rhythm, deadline, and cycles of activity) and space (varying the location of activity) to nourish and structure the creativity process.

9.2 Literature: From Creativity as the Capacity of a Unique Genius to a Process Perspective on Creativity

Describing and explaining the genesis of creativity and the development of new ideas has become a crucial issue for social science. Research conducted to this end has mostly been linked to psychology and has studied individual cases of creative geniuses, such as Darwin, Einstein, Pierre and Marie Curie, and Picasso (Wallace and Gruber, 1989; Simonton, 1997). Management and organization literature has also adopted this perspective and has primarily focused on the psychological characteristics and engagement of creative people (Drazin, Glynn, and Kazanjian, 1999), and on detailing the cognitive steps of the creative process. Amabile (1983), for example, conceived creativity mainly as an individual cognitive process and put forward different stages: task representation, preparation, response generation, response validation, and outcome. In a review of past studies adopting such an orientation, Montag et al. (2012, p. 1367) identified four types of tasks that indeed received wide support in the literature: problem formulation/definition, preparation/information gathering, idea generation, and idea evaluation/validation. All these tasks are based on individual engagement and are sustained by (desirable) contextual conditions (Feldman, Csikszentmihalyi, and Gardner, 1994; Simonton, 1997). Feldman (1999) considered the dimensions that explain creativity should include family aspects, education and preparation, characteristics of the domain and the field, and historical forces. Organizational conditions that sustain individual creativity have been proposed and include, for example, mindless activities (Elsbach and Hargadon, 2006), a different work focus and a wide high-attention scope (Runco, 2004; Simonton, 1997; Uzzi and Spiro, 2005; Amabile et al., 2005), as well as low workload pressure (Amabile et al., 1996).

Previous research also highlighted, however, that the social context and the organizational dimension are more than simply conditions that stimulate creativity, but that they are strong influences that actually shape creative work and its output. For Csikszentmihalyi (1990), creativity in art, for example, must be placed in its specific historical and social context: "Rembrandt's contemporaries did not believe he was that creative and preferred the work of several painters less well known to us. Rembrandt's 'creativity' was constructed after his death by art historians who placed his work in the full context of the development of the European painting" (Csikszentmihalyi, 1990, pp. 198–199). The recognition of non-individual elements in creativity has also been echoed by scholars investigating the development of creativity in organizations. Most studies define creativity as "the production of novel and useful ideas" (Amabile et al., 1996, p. 1155). Underlying is the assumption that both novelty and usefulness are socially assessed, but little research has investigated this dimension so far.

Process approaches can better outline the social interactions and the progressive development of activities in creativity (Tsoukas, 2009). Drazin et al. (1999) subsequently developed an alternative multi-level model that views creativity as a sense-making process that is sustained by individual sense-making, intersubjectivity, and a negotiated belief structure that may shift as a result of crisis. Hargadon and Bechky (2006) investigated creativity as a collective activity that not only emerges from single individuals, but also involves the interactions of multiple actors in the creative process. They showed that problem-solving sometimes shifts from being individual to becoming collective as the result of social interactions that are precipitated by help seeking, help giving, reflective reframing, and reinforcing. Townley et al. (2009) insist on the necessity to integrate the practical dimensions that may exist in creative work: creativity and collective creative work are based on, shaped, made possible, and constrained by interdependent aesthetic, economic, social, and material factors (Moeran, 2009). Mainemelis (2001) highlighted the temporal and experiential nature of creative work and showed how timelessness favored the creative flow. However, his model remains purely theoretical and mainly individual. In organizations, creativity makes sense within a specific social group (McLeod et al., 2011), by whose rules and networks it is both framed and sustained (Kern, 2006; Tschang, 2007). Within a pragmatist perspective, Arjaliès et al. (2013) find creativity to be a collective process in a non-creative industry field: a finance services company. They outline the role of abduction as the form of reasoning that generates creative ideas, and the transactional nature of this process where participants, situations, and meaning are continuously influenced, altered, and reconstructed. Despite these seminal contributions, much exploratory work remains to be conducted in order to develop a process perspective on creative work, a perspective which is "sensitive to context, interactivity experience, and time; and it acknowledges non-linearity, emergence, and recursivity" (Langley and Tsoukas, 2010, pp. 5–6). In particular we still need to develop an in-depth understanding of how creative work emerges and develops in organizations, within a social context that gives it value and meaning. This involves understanding its dynamics and temporal arrangements; how it actually takes place; and what are its minutiae. To do so, we have conducted an empirical study on creative work in kitchens of gourmet restaurants in the field of haute cuisine.

9.3 Haute Cuisine and Gourmet Restaurants

Haute cuisine is the field made up of agents and organizations engaged in the world of elite gourmet restaurants. This includes the restaurants themselves, their chefs, employees, clients, gastronomic critics, journalists, specialized journals, suppliers, contractors, some cooking schools, and, last but not least, guidebooks. It has become highly institutionalized (Fauchart and Von Hippel, 2008; Rao et al., 2003) and internationalized (Parkhurst-Ferguson, 2004; Svejenova, Mazza, and Planellas, 2007; Svejenova, Planellas, and Vives, 2010): the expectations that weigh on chefs, the rules and the stakes of haute cuisine are institutional conditions that strongly shape the work and trajectories of elite chefs worldwide.

A central tenet in the haute cuisine field is the fact that overall success is institutionally defined according to the restaurants' ratings by major gastronomic guidebooks (Parkhurst-Ferguson, 2004; Rao et al., 2003). In France, Michelin is the most important culinary guidebook (Durand et al., 2007; Ottenbacher and Harrington, 2007). It is also acknowledged internationally as the most rigorous (Karpik, 2000) and the underlying understanding of haute cuisine that it carries has become influential throughout the world. More specifically, the Michelin stars are the criterion most valued by all agents (Karpik, 2000; Parkhurst-Ferguson, 2004), be they restaurants, clients, or critics. It is, however, worth mentioning that although the number of stars is a highly social criterion, it also has a significant impact on the revenue of the restaurants that are rated. According to Johnson et al. (2005, pp. 173 and 179), moving from a two- to a three-star ranking generates a 30 percent increase in revenue and losing a star can result in a fall in revenue of up to 50 percent.

The gastronomic quality of the restaurant is central to Michelin's evaluations and stars (Karpik, 2000). It includes two aspects: daily operational excellence (quality of products, cooking, and wine) and cuisine inventiveness (creativity in the menu, new dishes, new ideas, and gastronomic advances). Daily operational excellence is compulsory in starred restaurants, but it is clearly not enough to maintain a three-star ranking. As is the case in haute couture, chefs are expected to create new dishes and menus on a regular basis. Creativity has become a prerequisite to maintaining a restaurant's position in haute cuisine, particularly in three-star restaurants (Beaugé, 2008; Gomez and Bouty, 2011). A high level of technical excellence is necessary yet insufficient (Parkhurst-Ferguson, 2004; Rao et al., 2003). Over time, it has also become increasingly important for most elite chefs to be considered as a reference for particular cooking techniques, or for specific food products or a gastronomic universe (Durand et al., 2007). The notoriety that comes with such recognition is also useful to maintain visibility, to value innovation, and to attract international clients.

New dishes are therefore an occasion for the chefs to demonstrate their expertise (Ferguson, 2005) and defend the rating of their restaurant. At the same time, three-star chefs and their kitchen teams are expected to create dishes that maintain a consistently high level of sophistication and perfection (Beaugé, 2008). Creativity is not required simply to propose newness, as the introduction of misjudged novelties in a menu can be detrimental to a restaurant's rating (Bouty and Gomez, 2010). Consequently, only a few new dishes are introduced each year. They are the result of significant efforts and, though vital, their creation is a very demanding practice (Ottenbacher and Harrington, 2007).

Today, only 26 restaurants in France, and fewer than 60 in Europe are awarded Michelin's maximum grade of three stars out of a total number of around 600 and 2,000 starred restaurants in France and Europe respectively. We chose our cases among them.

9.3.1 Method

We conducted a qualitative and comparative analysis (Langley, 1999, 2007) of creative processes in French restaurants awarded three Michelin stars. The Michelin rating institutionally testifies to high creativity and therefore permits comparison. Among this population, we selected chefs who were acknowledged as creative icons, on the basis of their unique personal culinary universe. Finally, as previous research highlights the role of individual and contextual factors in creativity, we introduced variations in terms of the career trajectories of the chefs chosen and with regard to the specific context of the restaurants. Table 9.1 summarizes our sampling criteria and the main characteristics of the three cases we selected.

Table 9.1 Characteristics of the three cases studied

	Restaurant A	Restaurant B	Restaurant C
Michelin rating	**3 stars**	**3 stars**	**3 stars**
Creativity, inspiration, culinary universe	Extremely creative; a "*cubist*" chef* Modern art, constructivism, gastronomic chemistry Unexpected combination of flavors and textures, permanent transgression	Extremely creative Jazz music, graphic arts, seasons Vegetal, colored, sober, and based on low heat roasting techniques	Extremely creative, a "*gastronomic explorer*"** Natural countryside, local products, plants and herbs, photography Visual, minimalist, emotional
Chef's trajectory	Born 1950 Son of cooks; grew up in the family restaurant and did an apprenticeship in French high-end restaurants Launched his first restaurant in 1981, awarded 3 stars in 1993. Went bankrupt in 1995	Born 1956 Grandson of cook and son of musician Apprenticed at 3-star restaurants from age 14. Became head chef in 1980, and was the youngest French chef ever awarded two stars at the age of 26	Born 1946 Son of a cook and of a blacksmith farrier Did not take apprenticeship in other restaurants and always cooked in the family restaurant; now runs this restaurant
Restaurant context	Founded by chef A in 1996 Capacity: 55 guests Located in Paris, Champs Elysées area Restaurant in a hotel Awarded 3 stars since 1998	Bought by Chef B in 1986 Capacity: 30 guests Located in Paris, near ministries Restaurant only Awarded 3 stars since 1996	Run by Chef C since 1978 Capacity: 60 guests Located outside Paris Restaurant with a hotel; closed from November to March due to snow Awarded 3 stars since 1999
Data	Interviews with Chef A, and second chef 43 min video documentary on creative work (with chemist partner and with kitchen team) Menus Recipes Drawings Press articles selected from Factiva (40)	Interviews with Chef B, and second chef 60 min video documentary on creative work (alone, with gardeners, and with kitchen team) Menus Recipes Drawings, collages Press articles (77)	Press interviews with Chef C Two video documentaries (52 min and 86 min) on creative work (alone, and with kitchen team) Menus Recipes Drawings Press articles (29)

Notes: * *Le Monde des Livres* (July 7, 2011); ** *Le Monde* (September 28, 2006).

We collected both secondary and primary data as multiple sources of evidence (Denzin, 1989; Lincoln and Guba, 1985), and as a means to understand the specificities of cooking and gastronomy. We collected secondary data from media sources, as texts are a highly pertinent source to analyze haute cuisine as a field (Parkhurst-Ferguson, 1998; Rao et al., 2003, p. 816). We also gathered crucial secondary data in the form of long video documentaries showing the three chefs' creative work (Bensadoun, 2006; De Maistre, 2005; Lacoste, 2002, 2011). In France, elite chefs are now considered prominent cultural actors and the initial purpose of film directors with these documentaries was to document the gastronomic, technical, and creative work of some of these leading figures. The documentaries have been broadcast on national television networks and are now sold to the public as DVDs. For the purpose of our study, these visual data were especially useful as they documented various aspects of creative work, such as chefs working alone or working with their teams. As Heath, Hindmarsh, and Luff (2010, p. 6) insist, such visual data offer "opportunities for 'time-out', to play back in order to re-frame, re-focus and re-evaluate the analytic gaze. [. . .] They allow multiple takes on the data—to explore different issues on different occasions or to consider the same issue from multiple standpoints." Such possibilities were absolutely crucial from our process perspective. By playing and replaying the videos, we could investigate a wide range of different aspects that make up the "here and now" of creative work, from conversations to tools, gestures, faces, places, people, and dishes. Video documentaries thus represent a particularly rich data source allowing the examination of detailed aspects that are difficult to observe in real time. In addition, they include accounts of work that happens outside of the kitchen, in particular when chefs are alone. They allowed us to access material that direct observation methods would not have enabled us to unearth. Although there are also limits to such a data collection strategy, we considered that they were less subject to observation biases than direct on-the-spot observations at the restaurants. Establishing relationships with participants is central to gaining their agreement to being filmed (Heath et al., 2010), and the video documentaries are the consequence of film directors building a strong relationship with the chefs over a period of several months. To use the videos as observation material, we selected specific sections and fully transcribed them in detail (conversations, tools, gestures, faces, places, people, and dishes) in order to integrate these data in our analysis. In the following pages when we use these data, we refer to the name of the film director and the year of documentary as the source. We supplemented these elements with interviews of chefs and press articles.

This qualitative material resulted in a rich data set, which we analyzed with the view that creative work is something that people do (Langley, 1999). We conducted our analysis in two phases. In the first analytical phase, based on our process perspective, we coded our data for each restaurant based on which actors were involved in creative working, where and when they were involved, and for which purpose. On this basis we identified three creative threads: three flows that include distinct activities, different time and space boundaries, different people involved, and different purposes. In a second phase, we investigated each of these creative threads further and compared them across the three restaurants in order to refine our understanding and highlight iterative dynamics.

9.4 Results: Cases Analysis

Our data indicate that creativity at the restaurants is a specific process with three distinct threads: working on ideas, creative teamworking, and naming. Each of these threads is organized in time and space, and involves different actors as presented in Figure 9.1. In this section we examine each of these three threads in turn.

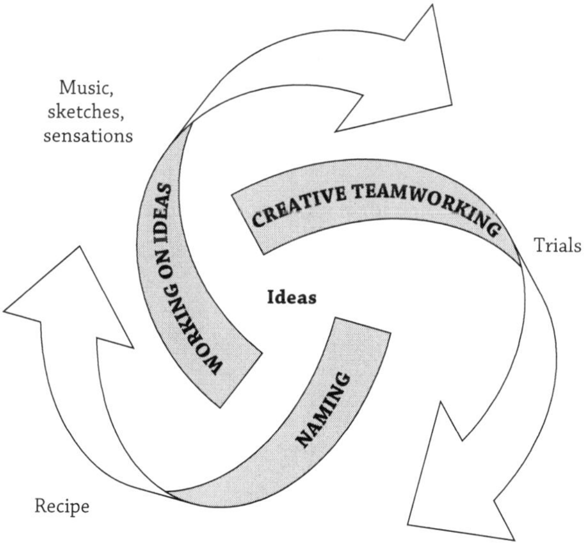

Figure 9.1 Creative threads

9.4.1 *Working on Ideas*

Firstly, we observed that creativity in the kitchen is mainly based on working on ideas. This is a matter of pure idea generation performed by chefs alone or with non-cook mates (people from other sectors) from outside the kitchen.

In restaurant A, Chef A saves his mornings to *"think about [his] personal work"* (interview). It is in fact the moment he devotes to working on ideas. *"You need to be organized to throw yourself into creative situations. Even though you do not cook at the time, you need situations when you dream up your cuisine"* (Chef A quoted in Colan, 2005). Chef A finds inspiration in modern contemporary art, travel, and his regular exchanges with a chemist friend of his, with whom he investigates chemistry in food ingredients. This latter activity illustrates how organized Chef A is in relation to working on ideas. Chef A and his chemist friend regularly meet in quiet Parisian cafés and intellectually challenge each other on a variety of themes. They play a "creative game" (as they call it) and explore products, textures, combinations, and colors. They debate for example the case of oysters, which are both *"ugly and good"* (Documentary film, DeMaistre, 2005); or they discuss how the display of products makes them taste differently, and how and why the taste of a dish differs if the crunchy element is located on the top or at the bottom. Together they take a constructivist approach to sensations and refer directly to the work of such artists as Kandinsky. Recently, from a similar perspective, they have started to investigate and challenge popular adages in the culinary field. During these sessions, they take personal notes, and write joint texts summarizing their discussions. Chef A explains that these exchanges set his imagination running. In the mornings, Chef A also works alone in his personal office located in the basement of his restaurant, and takes further notes of his ideas and draws sketches that may or may not be very sophisticated and that represent possible dishes, emotions, or associations (Documentary film, De Maistre, 2005).

In restaurant B, Chef B tries not to be in the kitchen before mid-mornings and to save the quiet early hours to distance himself from his kitchen work. He finds most of his inspiration in arts (sculpture, paintings, music), through exchanges with creators from other fields (for example perfume designers) and in his market gardens. In the market gardens, Chef B talks with gardeners and seeks out seasonal products, new varieties, or even vegetables with which he is not yet familiar (Documentary film, Bensadoun, 2006). He is especially sensitive to the subtle and infinite variations in the tastes, smells, colors, and textures of vegetables. *"With the gardeners, we talk of vegetables as we would talk of types of wines. The yellow beetroot is a chardonnay and the red one is the pinot noir"* (*Libération*, December 18, 2010). In the gardens, he also carries out experiments such as building a fire to smoke onions. Chef B also spends time working in his personal office or at home, especially on such themes as colors and textures. He selects images or pictures that inspire him from magazines and arranges them artistically into personal collages and drawings to evoke sensations and associations. *"At the beginning I used to cut out everything that came to hand according to my desires and moods. One day, in a hotel in Tokyo, I asked for scissors and I started to play with ideas of warm and cold, matt and gloss. I longed for color too. My paper compositions have influenced my dishes . . ."* (*Le Figaro Magazine*, April 19, 2013). *"I started with the four seasons and then I got hooked. It wasn't planned, that's what makes it even stronger"* (*Libération*, December 18, 2010).

Chef C similarly saves special moments to work on ideas alone. During the season when the restaurant is open from April to October, his preferred location is the surrounding remote and harsh countryside. Up on the green desert of high pasturelands, Chef C spends long, almost mystical moments observing the ever-changing colors of nature, and the light playing on the landscape. He stops and quietly observes the surroundings through a square glass, as a photographer would do with his camera; and he draws quick sketches on the glass that he uses as tracing paper noting the perspectives, brightness, shades and shadows, and textures that catch him (Documentary film, Lacoste, 2002). He also carries his notebook, to sketch other contrasting shapes: *"I draw sketches of everything that catches my eye"* (Documentary film, Lacoste, 2002). *"I know each parcel of land, each tree . . . But no matter how often you'll wander around; smells, lights, and sensations will always be different"* (*L'Express*, November 15, 2004). Entrenched in his rural and remote native region, and referring to the painter Pierre Soulages, he insists that his form of expression is actually strengthened by the limited means that nature offers him: *"Abstraction is important to me, I want to go into things, to identify with them"* (Documentary film, Lacoste, 2002). Chef C is also a marathon runner, and he describes his training as moments of osmosis when Mother Nature whispers to him. When the restaurant is closed, from November through March, Chef C also travels throughout the world with his family, mostly avoiding luxurious resorts and favoring backpacking and trekking. These travels, he says, also nourish his relationship to the spirit of "terroir": *"In India, in China, in Latin America, I am moved by geographical similarities, by gestures, by daily cuisines rooted in the soil and climate; exactly like I am moved by herbs, flowers, and the skin on milk here in my region"* (*Sud Ouest*, November 22, 2004).

Overall, we observed that in our three cases, a significant share of creativity is individual and the time and space, when and where it occurs, is organized by the chef. Although each chef has his own inspirations and universe, all of them work on ideas in a quite organized manner. First and foremost, they dedicate specific time and efforts to such work; they extract themselves from the rush of daily cooking to engage in this particular activity separately. This does not mean that ideas cannot emerge during sittings but rather that specific dedicated moments are necessary to nourish personal thinking. Second, they work on ideas outside the kitchen; working on ideas benefits from different non-kitchen environments, from exposure to different contexts, and from non-cooking activities. Lastly, chefs always work on ideas without their kitchen teams; they are alone or with partners external to the restaurant. From this perspective, working on ideas is to some degree inherently individual. However, it does not only consist of genius chefs working on their own; chefs do collaborate at this stage but only with external non-cooking partners, such as creators, scientists, and people in the street, with whom they share sensations, emotions, and ways. They base their working on objects, activities, and influences that span a scope that is far wider than that of their restaurants and kitchens.

9.4.2 Creative Teamworking in the Kitchen

The second thread of creativity that we identified is that which happens in the restaurants' kitchens, with a small team of cooks. As with working on ideas, this creative teamworking is organized in time and space: chefs and selected cooks meet during quiet hours, when they can be alone and undisturbed in the kitchen. Our data also indicate that it is a regular activity, happening once a week on average, although chefs can hold additional ad hoc sessions if they have a particular inspiration. In each of the three restaurants the creative team is composed of the chef, the second-chef, and some station chefs (meat and fish chefs at A, garde-manger/vegetable chef at B, and sometimes the meat or pastry chefs at C). We found that a significant amount of creative work happened at this stage as the chefs' initial ideas have remained quite open. Discussions and creative teamworking challenge and enrich them. They lead to revisions, refinements, adjustments, and further elaborations in a variety of directions such as products, textures, proportions, and aesthetics. This teamworking is highly creative and constitutes an important complement to the chefs' working on ideas.

In all three kitchens, creative teamworking is triggered by chefs bringing up their ideas and trying to share them and their vision with the team. To do so, they make use of the elements that they produced when working on ideas: sketches, texts, pictures, collages. Chef A, for example, uses his written notes where he mixes pencil sketches, short literary texts, indications of some ingredients, and sometimes descriptions of some of the techniques he imagined. Chef B evokes his ideas with verbal elements but also paintings, drawings, collages, and music pieces. *"Let's take, for example, something I had in mind [. . .] It was a harmony of spinach, oranges, carrot, sesame oil, lemon with a light caramelized deglazing of langoustines. I tell them: 'the carrot mousseline takes the orange flavor'. Just to have a hint, just like a guess. Spinach just lightly cooked in salted butter. Sesame oil, a zest of candied lemon"* (interview). With this particular idea for a dish, Chef B also showed us the card he drew with his color pencils. Although the dish was not represented, the contrast of the pastel colors and the overall sketch rendered the freshness, the harmony, and the happiness of his idea: a dish that suggested springtime yet based on wintertime ingredients. At restaurant C, creative teamwork sessions are organized in the kitchen. The chef sets his notebook on the table, leafs through pages, and points to sketches as he evokes the sensations that he wants to convey (Documentary film, Lacoste, 2002). The chef also talks about sensations, memories, feelings, and poetry. *"He produces pictures that he took in India, the expression of a child or the vermilion of a dress"* (*Libération*, April 23, 1999).

On this basis creative teamwork consists of ideation around concrete elements and the relationship to products and senses is especially central to creative teamwork. We observed that chefs' monologues are, in fact, quite short and that rapidly, all three chefs and their creative teams start cooking. Mutual exchanges within the team develop directly over intermediary products and sensations. For example at restaurant C (Documentary film, Lacoste, 2002): the kitchen is quiet with only Chef C, his kitchen-chef (his son) and second-chef attending. Chef C explains his thinking about potato chips: simply that he would like to interpret them differently but has no specific idea. His notebook is open. First, he sketches a horizontal strip, and then a rose-shaped figure while explaining that he doesn't know which shape to explore further. They start peeling and slicing potatoes. The kitchen-chef arranges a strip of potato slices. Chef C watches and frowns, not fully convinced: *"You need a shape and it has to be long. [pause] Yeah . . . [unconvinced] perhaps . . . We need to try . . ."* They start aligning potato slices on a cooking tray. Chef C: *"No it doesn't work . . . We should slice it . . ."* He picks up a potato and cuts thinner slices with the mandolin. They place them on a corrugated cooking tray: potato slices overlapping and forming about 10 centimeter-long strips. Then they place the tray directly into the oven. Sometime later, the potato strips are cooked. The strips have taken a U-curved shape; they are roasted on the edge and still bright yellow in the middle. Chef C delicately appreciates them with his fingertips: *"it's beautiful, it's soft and crunchy; I think we have everything there."* Kitchen-chef: *"but we lost the shape . . ."* Chef C: *"Yes I think . . . but it's not a problem. I find it an enhancing accident. [he calls on the second-chef while examining both sides of the potato strip] Look Regis, look how nice it is . . . And all in all, we lost it [the initial shape] but we have two textures of potato, soft and crusty, and it's beautiful . . . It's the magic of creation; sometimes you start with an idea and suddenly boom . . . But it doesn't mean that it denaturizes it."*

As shown in this illustrative video extract, creative teamwork largely revolves around products, tastes, and aspects. Conversations, drawings, and idea abstractions are quickly abandoned in favor of preparations and trials. The chef and his team are focused on doings, using ingredients and tools. They are attentive to sensitive aspects: they touch products and preparations, they look at them and smell them, and they try to appreciate them. They also include tools in their trials (in the last example, they adjust the blade of the mandolin, and discuss the shape of the cooking tray for instance). Creative teamworking is deeply embedded in the kitchen universe, and chefs and their cooks often refer to previous sessions and use them as examples, illustrations, or counter-examples during their exchanges.

As chefs further explain, creative teamworking is a very important thread of creativity. It is about refining ideas through materialization: cooking is taken as another way of cultivating ideas, complementing more intellectual and individual working on ideas. As Chef A puts it: *"alone, you remain too close"* (interview). In fact, all three chefs indicate that none of these materializing ideas are definite yet. Sometimes, trials are kept running on a regular basis until the chef is satisfied and he decides to include a new dish in the restaurant's menu. Then, as all three chefs explained, a new and different challenge needs to be dealt with: the implementation of the dish in daily kitchen work, with the full team of cooks. As often as not, however, trials are suspended because the chef finds them inconclusive; he does not like the taste or the aesthetics; or he finds that they are too far from the initial project that was central to his idea. Trials end up in additional notes in chefs' notebooks; further trials will happen later, with different ingredients, and different techniques, though around the same general idea. These further sessions can happen over the following days, weeks, or months, depending on how mature the ideas are and on the chef's additional inputs. All chefs agree that this is, in fact, a natural and inherent thread of creative work. At other times, chefs find trials "interesting" or "satisfying" but they do not feel the necessity for further exploration; trials are documented in the personal notes or notebooks until further sessions. They may or may not be pursued, at different times, and in potentially different directions. This is for example quite often the case at restaurant A, when the chef wants to experiment on the basis of conversations/creative games with his chemist friend, and to cultivate ideas and play with them. Creative teamwork and trials are mostly echoed in literary accounts, personal notes, and individual memories. They nonetheless will potentially resurface at other occasions, and nourish later sessions on different themes.

9.4.3 Naming

The third aspect of creative practice that we recorded happens after innovation, and is in relation to finding the dish's name. In our three restaurants it is considered critical because the dish's name contributes to creating gastronomic experiences and emotions. It evokes the chef's and dish's universes and the sensations that the chef intended to convey. Chef A explains the importance that this aspect has for him: *"Long ago, Chef Alain Chapel's menu left a mark on me. It was beautiful: to look at, to touch, and to read. The layout was meticulous and words had been carefully chosen. [. . .] Everything was in perfect harmony. Sometimes, when I see certain restaurants' menus, I think to myself that some chefs are lazy with writing"* (Pinay-Rabaroust, 2012).

In the three restaurants, it is the chefs and their seconds that specifically conduct this creative work. To name dishes, they use metaphors, literary descriptions, and evocations. For instance in restaurant A there is a two-level system of naming. The first level of naming of the dish refers to the main ingredient, such as for example "Lozère Lamb." The text of 4 to 6 lines that follows indicates the various components, their preparation ("tartar"; "deboned") and hints at the idea, the sensations, and the evocations ("abstract"; "modest"). As a result, the complete name of this dish in the restaurant's menu is:

LOZÈRE LAMB

Seared saddle of Lozère lamb rubbed with oregano.
Crispy sweetbreads, black rice, home-made harissa sauce.
Cooking juice thickened with tamarin.
Chop cooked à la milanaise, chard with pine kernels.
Kidneys cooked with vaudouvan, a basket of agria potatoes.
Crepinette of lamb's foot, red onion scampi.

At restaurants B and C, the dishes' names are shorter but they remain a matter of creativity and attention for the chef. At restaurant B, they generally consist of two lines: the first line indicates the dominant preparation and the second refers to supporting elements. For example:

Corrèze sweetbreads with licorice root aroma.
Young leeks.

At restaurant C names are different again and include an average of three lines. The first line indicates a short name for the dish based on central sensations or conceptual elements. The second line refers to the main ingredient and the third one to key accompaniments. For example:

Light and shades;
monkfish poached in black oil;
mustard stalks and stems, garlic flowers.

These variations in sophistication reflect the chefs' sources of inspirations and the way they conceive their cuisine. Chef A confesses that his creative universe is mostly mental and that he needs to reflect this in the names of his creations. Names are sophisticated because they refer to his complex intellectual elaborations. Recently, he has been experimenting with another way of expressing such complexity, by using shorter names and adding punctuation effects, such as the use of slash signs. Chef B's universe is more strongly related to colors and it surfaces in the contrasts that the names of his dishes evoke: the brown of roasted meat and the fresh green of young vegetables. Chef C's universe is contemplative, entirely based on emotions and a nearly mystical fusion with the surrounding land, and his dishes' names convey these sensations first. They are meant to appeal to diners' feelings as they face the landscape through the huge dining-room windows.

Dishes' names are vectors of creativity and vehicles of ideas and experiences. As such, they are an integral part of the dishes and naming constitutes a key creative practice to which chefs devote a lot of time and attention. This aspect of creativity supports Fine's observation (1996) that wording, cooking vocabulary, and rhetoric are of special importance to cooks' professional identities. Given the importance granted to creativity by the chefs we observed, this rhetorical dimension appears inherent to their creative status.

9.5 Discussion

Our study of creative processes in three French haute cuisine restaurants showed that creativity involves efforts, hard work, and commitment, and is far more demanding and structured than often pictured. Our analysis specifically delved into the process of creativity and identified three threads, each of which is highly organized in terms of team, time, and space.

9.5.1 Creativity as a Three-Thread Process

Our comparative analysis showed that creativity is multi-threaded and involves: working on ideas, creative teamworking, and naming. By working on ideas, chefs generate ideas, and they may do this with non-cooking partners outside the kitchen. Our study confirms the key role of creative individuals put forward by past literature (e.g. Amabile et al., 2005), but also highlights how these creative individuals are not alone and how they choose and interact with external partners to nourish this specific work. Even though the chef is central to working on ideas, it does not mean that this thread is purely individual; it is a collective and most of all social activity. A chef's choices and orientations reflect his trajectory in haute cuisine. This is nonetheless completely tacit. Chefs have integrated what is haute cuisine compared to other types of catering; what is acceptable and valued in this field. Working on ideas is socially embedded. As such, our study emphasizes how the institutional dimension structures this work. Kern (2006) or McLeod et al. (2011), for example, explained how creativity made sense within a specific social group and we contribute to this work by illustrating how the specificities of the field shape working conditions. Moreover, we show how the rules of haute cuisine not only allow the chef to be the key individual creative person, but also require that he/she be creative. It is both a position in the team, and a matter of role expectation forged at the field level. This institutional dimension in creativity has, to date, been relatively neglected.

Creative teamworking is refining ideas on the basis of cooking as part of a reduced team in the kitchen. By identifying such a thread in the creativity process, we highlight that creativity is not merely a matter of individual serendipity, intuition, or sensitivity and we show that such sensory and emotional dimensions are also salient in the collective working process. This result contributes to, and advances, past literature on group creativity, which has mostly emphasized cognitive and rational aspects of creativity (e.g. Drazin et al., 1999; Hargadon and Bechky, 2006). Nonetheless, we concur with Drazin et al.'s (1999) perspective on partial inclusiveness. As sensations and emotions are deeply rooted in individuals, creative teamworking is a matter of inter-individual dynamic combination, rather than simply the addition of individual ideas.

Naming is evoking the dish's universe and the sensations that chefs intended to convey. This is a key aspect in the creative process, which has not been highlighted so far. In naming what is novel, chefs are engaging in a poetic process that reflects both their own universe, and the specific dish, with the emotions and aesthetics it carries, as well as some key features such as ingredients, or a cooking technique that the chefs want to highlight. Through naming, chefs enter into a dialogue with the future client. They begin a discussion that is pursued with customers during the sitting. This extends the dialogical approach (Bakhtin, 1981; Tsoukas, 2009) as the chef invites the future client into creative work, both in the kitchen and in his personal universe. This dialogue is prepared and expected, and mixes existing written texts and conversations that will take place in the future. With naming, we illustrate how novelty is constrained as ingredients and preparation will have to fit in, and yet how incremental emergence can still develop through this dialogue (Tsoukas, 2009) because at each sitting, dishes remain open to further adjustments. Further process-oriented research could fruitfully investigate this dialogical dimension.

Our study also enriches process research by understanding how the three threads we identified are articulated in the creative process. We specifically suggest that they are not organized in a linear manner and cannot be considered steps in a linear process. While it is true that creative teamworking generally follows on from working on ideas (it develops on the basis of chefs' ideas), our study shows, however, that creative teamworking can also feed back into working on ideas as in the case when idea generation occurs following failure during teamworking, and it can also lead to additional teamworking, or indeed lead to another type of activity (implementation). Similarly, naming can happen before, during, or after working on ideas or creative teamworking. More generally, we show that creativity does not develop in a linear way, moving through different stages, but needs to be understood as an ebb and flow, that represents an emerging phenomenon in which different threads interrelate in a dynamic way. Such a perspective also challenges the common perception that evaluation acts as a gateway at the end of the creative process. We show instead that evaluation is part of the whole process and flows through each thread. This is particularly true because Michelin's evaluations, the haute cuisine rules, the organizational context, and restaurant customers are immanent in the day-to-day running of such restaurants. Creativity is thus intrinsically shaped by these external stakeholders. Because they have been involved in the field for a long time and have already been granted three stars, chefs are aware that there is a creative requirement in haute cuisine, and they also take into account what their own clients specifically expect from them, given their career trajectories, and the style of their cuisine. While they are aware that they can evolve or even change radically, they also anticipate that they will have to explain, motivate, and present these changes. We consider this a form of assessment of the "usefulness" of creativity (George, 2007; Montag et al., 2012), which has not been detailed so far. Harvey and Kou (2013, p. 367) have recently reached similar conclusions in the healthcare sector. Further research is still required, however, to develop a more refined understanding of how evaluation and creativity are actually intertwined.

9.5.2 A Highly Organized Process in Terms of Team, Time, and Space

Our data also indicate that despite its generative nature, creativity is a highly organized process, in terms of team, time, and space.

First, creativity is organized with regards to who participates and who does not. This aspect has rarely been addressed in previous research as the composition of a creative team has most often been considered as given. We show that who participates and who does not is a key aspect in the creativity process that depends both on the chefs' preferences and more importantly, on institutional rules that give priority to second and station chefs. For these actors, being selected to be involved in the creative process also represents a unique opportunity to learn and develop their creative abilities progressively and is particularly important in the making of future elite chefs. In this light, the integration of subordinates also plays a role in a long-term perspective on creativity. Through this contribution to the making of future haute cuisine chefs, current chefs project themselves over the long term in gastronomy as they become masters with disciples and their kitchens become schools of thought.

Second, the creative process is organized in time with specific moments dedicated to this activity. It is difficult, if not impossible, for cooks to be creative during regular work hours, with the rush of the sitting. During sittings, chefs can improvise around already known phrases, mixing together elements from different dishes, or proposing some new dishes to the clients that have not yet been completely defined. However, all this activity can be considered improvisation, as defined by Vera and Crossan (2005), as the chefs and cooks are working from pre-existing schemes that they rearrange. To conduct creative work per se, chefs need to extract themselves from this kind of pressure and work at a different pace, which they choose in a calmer environment where they are not disturbed. This shows that there is a specific relationship between creative work and time. In addition to the personal preferences of chefs who manage their own time differently, there is an organizational need to distinguish between time that is dedicated to operational work and time that is set aside for creative work. Chefs play with speed and slowness and, as such, exemplify the evolution of our societies (Czarniawska, 2013). This need by chefs to extract themselves from their daily workload and its associated time pressure is coherent with the work of Amabile et al. (1996), and Elsbach and Hargadon (2006). In her study of information agencies, Czarniawska (2013, p. 9) shows that the demand for speed may be an obstacle to experimentation and creative thinking. Our analysis also stresses the role of timelessness as put forward by Mainemelis (2001). However, the creative process in haute cuisine exemplifies other aspects of time too, notably cyclical time (Mainemelis, 2002). The field of haute cuisine imposes an institutional rhythm and a seasonality that infuse creativity: chefs need to offer new dishes each year, and to renew their menu each season. Moreover, whereas Mainemelis (2001, 2002) pictures time as something that is often given to, or imposed on, we see that actors can actually play with the various temporalities, question them, and navigate between them throughout the creative process. Chefs, for example, can base some of their creative teamwork in timelessness, whereas in other situations they can engage their team in a more pressured and cyclical perspective. The chefs we studied are permanently involved in multiple time frames, in a way that scarcely appeared in prior empirical studies, but echoes the temporality features defined in theoretical process approaches, such as G. H. Mead's vision of both the past and the future being involved in a socially constructed present (Simpson, 2009; Hernes et al., 2013). Further empirical research could extend this specific relationship between creativity and time, and in particular investigate how the notion of the present (and in particular the specious present, in Mead's words) affect the creative process.

Third, the spatial dimension of creativity is another salient aspect in our study. We specifically show that each thread of creativity is related to specific spaces: chefs work on ideas outside the restaurant; creative teamwork happens in the kitchen; naming is related to the chef's office. These spaces are not specifically dedicated to creativity though; we find that, as suggested by Mainemelis and Ronson (2006, p. 88), a given place can become a place of creativity at some times and not at others. This space and time combination structures and bounds each thread of creativity, and provides meaning and rules for the actors, in a way that is similar to the symbolic effects outlined by Moeran (2009) in his study of a shooting studio. Our study also exemplifies the theoretical insights of Mainemelis and Ronson (2006) who used the metaphor of play to highlight the material, spatial, and temporal boundaries for creativity. Given the importance of time and space that emerges here, future research on the creative process should investigate these dimensions further, particularly inside organizations, as most studies have focused on geographical aspects of territories in creativity (Kornberger and Clegg, 2004). In this respect, the concept of heterotopia, suggested by Michel Foucault (1984) as the spaces of *otherness* that, among others, physically and symbolically house deviation, imagination, and creativity, could also prove a useful line of inquiry. In particular, a process perspective could illuminate how actors navigate between heterotopia and other spaces in organizations, and how these movements feed the creative process.

9.6 Conclusion

We have examined how creativity occurs through the analysis of high-end, three-star kitchens. Based on in-depth studies at Michelin starred restaurants to analyze the creative process, we show that creativity does not develop linearly by passing through different stages; it is more correctly viewed as an ebb and flow, a developing phenomenon in which different threads (working on ideas, creative teamworking, and naming) interrelate dynamically. We also illustrated how creativity involves both personal and social influences for the generation of new and useful ideas, and specifically show how institutional pressure and evaluation permeate each thread. Finally, we highlight that, despite its generative nature, the creativity process is highly organized and we specifically emphasize the importance of temporal and spatial dimensions in the process. These dimensions are not only constraints for chefs. They also are material arrangements they use in creative work. Chefs permanently play with time (rhythm, deadline, and cycles of activity) and space (varying the location of activity) to nourish and structure the creativity process.

References

Amabile, T. (1983). The social psychology of creativity: A componential conceptualization. *Journal of Personality and Social Psychology*, 45(2): 357–376.

Amabile, T. M., Barsade, S. G., Mueller, J. S., and Staw, B. M. (2005). Affect and creativity at work. *Administrative Science Quarterly*, 50(3): 367–403.

Amabile, T. M., Conti, R., Coon, H., Lazenby, J., and Herron, M. (1996). Assessing the work environment for creativity. *Academy of Management Journal*, 39(5): 1154–1184.

Arjaliès, D.-L., Lorino, P., and Simpson, B. (2013). Understanding organizational creativity: Insights from pragmatism. In M. Kelemen and N. Rumens (eds.), *American Pragmatism and Organization: Issues and Controversies* (pp. 131–145). Burlington, VT: Gower Publishing.

Bakhtin, M. M. (1981). *The Dialogic Imagination: Four Essays* (ed. M. Holquist). Austin, TX: University of Texas Press.

Beaugé, B. (2008). Comment dire qu'un talent est nouveau? In *Les Annales de l'EPM*, Vol. XIV. Paris: Maison des Sciences de l'Homme.

Bensadoun, S. (2006). *Alain Passard: Le Solfège du Légume*. Documentary film. Paris: La Huit Distribution.

Bouty, I. and Gomez, M.-L. (2010). Dishing up individual and collective dimensions in organizational knowing. *Management Learning*, 41(5): 545–559.

Colan, G. (2005). La créativité: Donner un sens à sa vie. *Le Chef*, 173 (December): 30.

Csikszentmihalyi, M. (1990). The domain of creativity. In M. A. Runco and R. S. Albert (eds.), *Theories of Creativity* (pp. 190–212). Newbury Park, CA: Sage.

Czarniawska, B. (2013). Is speed good? *Scandinavian Journal of Management*, 29(1): 7–12.

De Maistre, G. (2005). *Les Alchimistes aux Fourneaux*. Documentary film. Strasbourg: ARTE France.

Denzin, N. K. (1989). *The Research Act* (3rd edition). Englewood Cliffs, NJ: Prentice-Hall.

Drazin, R., Glynn, M. A., and Kazanjian, R. R. (1999). Multilevel theorizing about creativity in organizations: A sensemaking perspective. *Academy of Management Review*, 24(2): 286–307.

Driver, M. (2008). New and useless: A psychoanalytic perspective on organizational creativity. *Journal of Management Inquiry*, 17(3): 187–197.

Durand, R., Rao, H., and Monin, P. (2007). Code and conduct in French cuisine: Impact of code changes on external evaluations. *Strategic Management Journal*, 28(5): 455–472.

Elsbach, K. D. and Hargadon, A. B. (2006). Enhancing creativity through "mindless" work: A framework of workday design. *Organization Science*, 17(4): 470–483.

Fauchart, E. and Von Hippel, E. (2008). Norms-based intellectual property systems: The case of French chefs. *Organization Science*, 19(2): 187–201.

Feldman, D. (1999). The development of creativity. In R. J. Sternberg (ed.), *Handbook of Creativity* (pp. 169–186). Cambridge: Cambridge University Press.

Feldman, D., Csikszentmihalyi, M., and Gardner, H. (eds.) (1994). *Changing the World: A Framework for the Study of Creativity*. Westport, CT: Greenwood Press.

Ferguson, P. (2005). L'ostentation culinaire. Naissance du champ gastronomique. In J. Dubois, P. Durand, and Y. Winquin (eds.), *Le Symbolique et le Social: La Réception Internationale de la Pensée de Pierre Bourdieu* (pp. 93–102). Liège: Editions de l'Université de Liège.

Fine, G. A. (1996). Justifying work: Occupational rhetorics as resources in restaurant kitchens. *Administrative Science Quarterly*, 41(1): 90–115.

Foucault, M. (1984). Des espaces autres. *Architecture Mouvement Continuité*, 5 (October): 46–49.

George, J. M. (2007). Creativity in organizations. *Academy of Management Annals*, 1(1): 439–477.

Gomez, M. L. and Bouty, I. (2011). The emergence of an influential practice: Food for thought. *Organization Studies*, 32(7): 921–940.

Hargadon, A. B. and Bechky, B. A. (2006). When collections of creatives become creative collectives. *Organization Science*, 17(4): 484–500.

Harvey, S. and Kou, C.-Y. (2013). Collective engagement in creative tasks: The role of evaluation in the creative process in groups. *Administrative Science Quarterly*, 58(3): 346–386.

Heath, C., Hindmarsh, J., and Luff, P. (2010). *Video in Qualitative Research*. London: Sage.

Hernes, T., Simpson, B., and Soderlund, J. (2013). Managing and temporality. *Scandinavian Journal of Management*, 29(1): 1–6.

Johnson, C., Surlemont, B., Nicod, P., and Revaz, F. (2005). Behind the stars: A concise typology of Michelin restaurants in Europe. *Cornell Hospitality Quarterly*, 46(2): 170–187.

Karpik, L. (2000). *Le Guide rouge Michelin. Sociologie du Travail*, 42(3): 369–389.

Karpik, L. (2010). *Valuing the Unique: The Economics of Singularities*. Princeton, NJ: Princeton University Press.

Kern, A. (2006). Exploring the relation between creativity and rules: The case of the performing arts. *International Studies of Management and Organization*, 36(1): 63–80.

Kornberger, M. and Clegg, S. (2004). Bringing space back in: Organizing the generative building. *Organization Studies*, 2(7): 1095–1114.

Lacoste, P. (2002). *L'Invention de la Cuisine; Michel Bras—Laguiole*. Documentary film. Paris: La Huit.

Lacoste, P. (2011). *Entre Les Bras—La Cuisine en Héritage*. Documentary film. Paris: Jour2Fête.

Langley, A. (1999). Strategies for theorizing from process data. *Academy of Management Review*, 24(4): 691–710.

Langley, A. (2007). Process thinking in strategic organization. *Strategic Organization*, 5(3): 271–282.

Langley, A. and Tsoukas, H. (2010). Introducing "Perspectives on process organization studies." In T. Hernes and S. Maitlis (eds.), *Process, Sensemaking, & Organizing* (pp. 1–26). Oxford: Oxford University Press.

L'Express (2004). Les hauts plateaux de Michel Bras. November 15.

Le Figaro Magazine (2013). Passard en pince pour le homard. April 19.

Le Monde (2006). Le coulant au chocolat. September 28.

Le Monde des Livres (2011). Conversations avec Catherine Flohic, Pierre Gagnaire: Un jazzman aux fourneaux. July 7.

Libération (1999). Michel Bras—Profil. April 23.

Libération (2010). Entretien: Le légume a ouvert la porte. December 18.

Lincoln, Y. S. and Guba, E. G. (1985). *Naturalistic Inquiry*. Newbury Park, CA: Sage.

McLeod, C., O'Donohoe, S., and Townley, B. (2011). Pot noodles, placements and peer regard: Creative career trajectories and communities of practice in the British advertising industry. *British Journal of Management*, 22(1): 114–131.

Mainemelis, C. (2001). When the muse takes it all: A model for the experience of timelessness in organizations. *Academy of Management Review*, 26(4): 548–565.

Mainemelis, C. (2002). Time and timelessness: Creativity in (and out of) the temporal dimension. *Creativity Research Journal*, 14(2): 227–238.

Mainemelis, C. (2010). Stealing fire: Creative deviance in the evolution of new ideas. *Academy of Management Review*, 35(4): 558–578.

Mainemelis, C. and Ronson, S. (2006). Ideas are born in fields of play: Towards a theory of play and creativity in organizational settings. *Research in Organizational Behavior*, 27: 81–131.

Moeran, B. (2009). The organization of creativity in Japanese advertising production. *Human Relations*, 62(7): 963–985.

Montag, T., Maertz, C. P. Jr., and Baer, M. (2012). A critical analysis of the workplace creativity criterion space. *Journal of Management*, 38(4): 1362–1386.

Oldham, G. R. and Cummings, A. (1996). Employee creativity: Personal and contextual factors at work. *Academy of Management Journal*, 39(3): 607–634.

Ottenbacher, M. C. and Harrington, R. J. (2007). Institutional, cultural and contextual factors: Potential drivers of the culinary innovation process. *Tourism and Hospitality Research*, 9(3): 235–249.

Parkhurst-Ferguson P. (1998). A cultural field in the making: Gastronomy in nineteenth-century France. *American Journal of Sociology*, 104(3): 597–641.

Parkhurst-Ferguson, P. (2004). *Accounting for Taste: The Triumph of French Cuisine*. Chicago: University of Chicago Press.

Piaget, J. (1971). The theory of stages in cognitive development. In D. R. Green, M. P. Ford, and G. B. Flamer (eds.), *Measurement and Piaget* (pp. 1–11). New York: McGraw-Hill.

Pinay-Rabaroust, F. (2012). Le f(l)ou artistique <http://www.atabula.com/pierre-gagnaire/>.

Rao, H., Monin, P., and Durand, R. (2003). Institutional change in Toque Ville: Nouvelle cuisine as an identity movement in French gastronomy. *American Journal of Sociology*, 108(4): 795–843.

Runco, M. (2004). Creativity. *Annual Review of Psychology*, 55: 657–687.

Simonton, D. K. (1997). *Genius and Creativity: Selected Papers*. Greenwich, CT: Ablex.

Simpson, B. (2009). Pragmatism, Mead and the practice turn. *Organization Studies*, 30(12): 1329–1347.

Sud Ouest (2004). Le goût de l'Aubrac et de l'universel. November 22.

Svejenova, S., Mazza, C., and Planellas, M. (2007). Cooking up change in haute cuisine: Ferran Adrià as an institutional entrepreneur. *Journal of Organizational Behavior*, 28(5): 539–561.

Svejenova, S., Planellas, M., and Vives, L. (2010). An individual business model in the making: A chef's quest for creative freedom. *Long Range Planning*, 43(2–3): 408–430.

Townley, B., Beech, N., and McKinlay, A. (2009). Managing in the creative industries: Managing the motley crew. *Human Relations*, 62(7): 939–961.

Tschang, F. T. (2007). Balancing the tensions between rationalization and creativity in the video games industry. *Organization Science*, 18(6): 989–1005.

Tsoukas, H. (2009). A dialogical approach to the creation of new knowledge in organizations. *Organization Science*, 20(6): 941–957.

Tsoukas, H. and Chia, R. (2002). On organizational becoming: Rethinking organizational change. *Organization Science*, 13(5): 567–582.

Uzzi, B. and Spiro, J. (2005). Collaboration and creativity: The small world problem. *American Journal of Sociology*, 111(2): 447–504.

Vera, D. and Crossan, M. (2005). Improvisation and innovative performance in teams. *Organization Science*, 16(3): 203–224.

Wallace, D. B. and Gruber, H. E. (eds.) (1989). *Creative People at Work: Twelve Cognitive Case Studies*. New York: Oxford University Press.

Part II
Process Studies

10

The Paradox of Stability and Change

Elias' Processual Sociology

Chris Mowles

Abstract: This chapter draws on the oeuvre of the process sociologist Norbert Elias further to extend the canon of process-oriented scholarship concerned with organizations and organizing. It reflects upon his aversion towards abstract ways of thinking about social change in favor of an interest in human interdependence, manifested in processes of inclusion and exclusion, cooperation and competition, stability and change. The chapter considers how Elias' articulation of dynamic social paradoxes underlying the flux and change of social life adds original insights to the process perspective. The author argues that Elias' work goes beyond both "weak" and "strong" versions of process scholarship. The chapter goes on to discuss the implications of taking Elias' perspective seriously in organizational research, which would involve taking an interest in informal as well as formal manifestations of human interdependence, including power, affect, and identity.

10.1 Introduction

There are a number of broad themes which arise again and again in the work of scholars who consciously adopt a process view of organization studies, and something of an emerging canon of philosophers, sociologists, and organizational theorists who underpin their work. Hernes (2008), Langley et al. (2013), Langley and Tsoukas (2012), and Hernes and

Maitlis (2012) give a helpful overview of the kinds of themes which interest scholars who identify with process-oriented perspectives, although as a group they still constitute a broad church. To put it briefly, process scholars are concerned with how organizations become and change over time, that is to say in organizational evolution and emergence; they are interested in the fluctuating relationships which form and are formed by individuals and groups; they focus on the importance of language, sense-making, and narrativity; they often draw on dialectic, ambiguity, and paradox; and they are often concerned to problematize a linear understanding of time. As one prominent process scholar puts it, organizations are "always in a state of creation, of emergence, of becoming" (Hernes, 2008, pp. xvii–xviii) and what they become could have been otherwise. A typology of process scholarship is still evolving, but Van de Ven and Poole (2005), drawing on Chia and Langley (2004), make a distinction between weak and strong versions of process studies, where the former still gives priority to stable entities which undergo periods of change, while the latter regards entities as temporary stabilizations of processes of change.

Central to the canon of process-oriented scholars are philosophers such as Heraclitus, the pragmatists William James (1842–1910) and sometimes John Dewey (1859–1952), Alfred North Whitehead (1861–1947) and Henri Bergson (1859–1941), Wittgenstein (1889–1951), and more contemporary scholars such as Latour, Weick, and Deleuze. These scholars promote and explore the Heraclitan tradition of flux and change and the centrality of time from a variety of different perspectives.

However, one major sociologist with potentially important contributions to process thinking appears to have been neglected. In this chapter, I would like to reintroduce the work of Norbert Elias with a view to adding his name and work to the emerging canon of process-oriented scholars. I do so because I think he makes an important contribution to thinking about organizational emergence and how it can be accounted for in social terms. This is because he makes highly social, interdependent human beings and what they are doing central to his theorizing about social flux, which in my view is missing from both "weaker" and "stronger" theories of process, particularly when the latter tend towards the abstract. In Elias' work, embodied, feeling human beings form intentions and act on them but do so within a web of other people's actions and intentions, the precise outcome of which can never be predicted. He also works deftly with dualisms, such as stability and change, individual and group, refusing to choose one pole over the other because he recasts them as paradoxes, a method which I explore more fully below. Elias' socio-anthropological oeuvre reinstates humans into what might otherwise be a depopulated landscape, a form of abstraction which C. S. Peirce (1958, 8.112) warned against: "We must not begin by talking of pure ideas—vagabond thoughts that tramp the public roads without any human habitation—but must begin with men and their conversation."

As Elias' student, commentator, and translator Stephen Mennell (1992) has pointed out, Elias' theories bring together both micro and macro perspectives within a temporal framework that takes in the broad sweep of history and which gives central importance to the inherent unpredictability of social life. In doing so they pose particular challenges for organization studies, problematizing as they do more managerialist interpretations of predictability and control, and raising questions even for critical or process perspectives in organizational scholarship.

Although Elias' ideas have been taken up by organizational scholars and sociologists previously (Bogner, 1987; Burkitt, 1996, 1999; Dopson, 2001, 2005; Layder, 1986; Newton, 2001, 2003, 2004, 2010; Smith, 2001; Van Iterson, Mastenbroek, and Soeters, 2001; Van Iterson et al., 2002) both to support and critique them, his work is still not widely adopted in theorizing about organizational life. In particular I pay attention to a number of paradoxes that Elias frames to describe the stable instability of social life, and how it is possible for both order and disorder, routine and novelty to arise at the same time. As I do so I engage briefly with some of the critiques of his work to identify how what I am claiming adds to, or differs from, what other scholars have said more broadly in the organizational and sociological literature.

10.1.1 Outline of the Chapter: Introducing Paradox

In what follows I explore the main themes of Elias' work in four main areas: process, power and interdependence, time, and emergence. For each theme, I explain his principal ideas and illustrate how they might apply, or are already taken up, in organizational scholarship. I then discuss the distinctive contributions of Elias to process thinking over and above other writers from the canon and conclude with an assessment of the potential for future scholarship. Throughout I will be drawing attention to the paradoxes that arise in his thought which, interestingly, he never directly addressed as a concept even though he deployed them time and again.

So, to offer my own explanation, by paradox I am pointing to the ability, noticed by both Kant and Hegel, of human thought to veer round to its opposite (Kainz, 1988, p. 66). Two, mutually negating, self-referencing ideas arise simultaneously producing the potential for meaning-making which is not confined to one pole of the paradox or the other: for example, regular irregularity is considered to be a property of complex systems because they are predictably unpredictable. I am attending to what I consider is Elias' reliance on paradox in the generative sense noting that this same phenomenon can manifest more destructively as a double bind (Bateson, 1972), as chiasm (Shotter, 2005), or what is known as a vicious paradox, where a negative dialectic between the poles of the paradox simply blocks thought and action. A wide variety of organizational scholars have also taken up paradox as a way of drawing attention to contradictory pressures in organizational life (Quinn, 1988; Poole and van de Ven, 1989; Leana and Barry, 2000; Clegg et al., 2002; Beech et al., 2004; Smith and Lewis, 2011; Jay, 2013), although they sometimes mix up paradox in the strict sense I have used above with a dilemma, two opposing choices both with criteria for and against, or a simple contradiction. There can also be a tendency to suggest that leaders and managers can harness paradox for the good of the company, or can choose to adopt a meta-position in relation to them. Paradox appears almost unconsciously in Elias' thinking as a complex description of dynamic social processes: there is no assumption in his work that they can in any way be resolved or instrumentalized.

10.2 Elias and Process

In a similar vein to scholars oriented towards process, Elias was also troubled by what he termed "process reduction" (1978) in theories about the social. Just as Dewey (2005) and Bergson (1911/1998) before him were critical of philosophical traditions which regarded the fixed and the immutable as more important than things which change, so Elias was critical of sociology which, in his view, is dominated by a form of abstraction which appears to deal with isolated objects in a state of rest. This perspective is informed by a philosophical ideal of science and sometimes dominated by vocabulary borrowed from the natural sciences:

> In other words, present forms of sociological analysis make possible the separation of interrelated things into individual components—'variables' or 'factors'—without any need to consider how such separated and isolated

> aspects of a comprehensive context are related to each other. At all events, the relationship appears to be an afterthought, an addition, tacked on later to intrinsically unrelated and isolated objects. (Elias, 1978, p. 116)

Perhaps the parallels between what Elias is saying about the limitations of some approaches in sociology and with particular variation-oriented traditions (Mohr, 1982) within organizational and management research do not need pointing out. Process reduction occurs, Elias argues, because of inherited structures of speech and thought, our tendency to turn processes into entities. He gives as an alternative example four people sitting round a table playing cards. One of them might remark that "the game" is very slow, thus endowing it with a life of its own. But Elias observes that there is no game without the moves and counter-moves of the individual players. Our natural tendency to abstract and synthesize turns a social process, which only exists in the interdependencies, the varying strategies of the four card players, into an entity. Nor would one attempt to understand the game by studying the moves of each individual player, abstracting the characteristics which several players have in common, and then theorizing about an ideal average player. Instead we might pay attention to the changing pattern between the players. To privilege process is to notice and describe relationships and functions as they evolve over time. Elias points out that process reduction does not just lead to a favoring of particular sociological methods, but it also carries with it an inherent value judgment: that anything which changes must be more ephemeral, less significant, and therefore of less value than something static and "eternal." As both Elias and Dewey conclude, this hints at a much older metaphysics of the Unmoved Mover.

This is not to deny that societies and organizations have particular structures which can endure over periods of time, but they are structures of a special kind which are dynamically maintained and affect psychological development as much as they influence relationships. To talk of organizations as though they were entities is a helpful shorthand, but the abstraction can sometimes cover over what we most need to be focusing on. For Elias there would be no organization unless people turned up every day to work and created and recreated it moment by moment. There are many very good examples of organization scholars in the process canon and beyond who also assume that organizations are created and recreated moment by moment in conversation and practice (Boden, 1994; Shaw, 2002; Tsoukas and Chia, 2002; Hernes, 2008; Hernes and Maitlis, 2012; Mowles, 2011; Mowles, 2015; Langley and Tsoukas, 2012; Sandberg and Tsoukas, 2011; Stacey, 2012).

10.3 Elias, Power, and Interdependence

To what does Elias attribute the constant fluctuations in social life? Paradoxically we are both formed by, and form interdependencies with others, he argues, because we are social through and through. Our need for love, respect, recognition, care, money, a career means that we are dependent on others, as, paradoxically they are dependent on us. Together we are bound by relations of power: as long as I need something from someone else more than they need it from me, or they are in a position to direct me, then power is temporarily tilted in their favor. Elias understood power as a structural characteristic of all human relating, neither good nor bad (and it may be both), but a relationship which, paradoxically, both constrains and enables. In highly differentiated societies we are tied together as though by bonds of elastic in what Elias termed "figurations" (the card game example above is a minor example of this), where the movement of one person affects, and is affected by, the network or web of relationships, the figuration of which they are part.

This analogy may be particularly helpful for reflecting on organizational life, particularly larger organizations with tiered hierarchies and divisions where large numbers of games are possible.

> At the core of changing figurations—indeed the very hub of the figuration process—is a fluctuating, tensile equilibrium, a balance of power moving to and fro, inclining first to one side then the other. This kind of fluctuating balance of power is a structural characteristic of the flow of every figuration. (Elias, 1978, p. 131)

As a way of breaking away from static representations of bodies at rest, Elias turns instead to ideas of networks (2001), where there is an incessant and changing interweaving of threads, or game analogies (1978), where the changing strategies of one player respond to, and are responded to in their turn by, other players. As the game of social or organizational life becomes more and more complicated, Elias argues, it begins to separate out into different "levels," or into a game of games, the overall patterns of which become more and more opaque to individual players. From the individual's perspective, it becomes harder to predict the outcome of the game. Players are also members of groups, in which they are both cooperating and competing to get things done, and at the same time these groups may be both cooperating and competing with other groups. The players become more and more aware that the game has taken on a life of its own independent of the moves of any individual player, or group of players.

In Elias' major work, *The Civilizing Process* (2000), he argues that there can be no surprise that social life is both paradoxically predictable and unpredictable at the same time. As groups of people form plans and intentions and try to implement them, these interweave with the plans and intentions of others to form a web, or a tissue of outcomes which no single person or group has planned or intended:

> It is simple enough: plans and actions, the emotional and rational impulses of individual people, constantly interweave in a friendly or hostile way. This basic tissue resulting from many single plans and actions of people can give rise to changes and patterns that no individual person has planned or created. From this interdependence of people arises an order *sui generis*, an order more compelling and stronger than the will and reason of the individual people composing it. (Elias, 2000, p. 366)

I want to draw attention to what I consider to be a number of important points from Elias' central observation about the difficulty of predicting the outcome of the interweaving of intentions. The first is to note, using Stephen Mennell's formulation, that in highly differentiated societies more and more people are more dependent on more others, more of the time. This interdependency produces social stability, in terms of the kinds of regularities which result from such a tightly bound web of interwoven threads where people must "attune their conduct to that of others, the web of actions must be organized more and more strictly and accurately" (Elias, 2000, p. 367). But this attunement, the day-to-day improvisation which is necessary to reproduce stability, also accounts paradoxically for its elasticity and sometimes its fragility if the web of interdependencies is subject to shocks or disruptions, which can be felt throughout the figuration.

Second, it is interesting to note the way that Elias links social control with self-control: "every individual is himself or herself regulating his or her behaviour with the utmost exactitude in accordance with the necessities of this network" (Elias, 2000, p. 368). Control which used to be imposed externally and as a consequence of the state's increasing monopoly of violence from medieval times onwards, has developed over many hundreds of years into self-control, as highly differentiated societies socialize their children to take up their roles in society. As court society became more and more settled, so social advantage was gained by the ability of courtiers to take what Elias refers to as a "detour via detachment," which I take to mean the increasing ability to become detached about one's role in the social game. The paradoxical ability to become detached about one's involvement (Elias, 1987a) in the flux of social life has also brought about structural changes in the psyche, a much more pronounced sense of an "I" distinct and separated from others "I's." The idea that we are rational, autonomous selves is a fairly recent social phenomenon according to both Elias and the Canadian philosopher Charles Taylor (1992) (the latter makes the distinction in his hermeneutic treatise on the development of the self, between our prior "permeable" sense of self and our current idea of a "buffered self" cut off from others as though by an invisible membrane). Nonetheless, Elias argues, the socialization process of children creates scars and contradictions which means that we are still guided by affect, "a wall of deep-rooted fears" which operate blindly and by habit and as a consequence often create "collisions with social reality" (Elias, 2000, p. 368). We are governed, he argues, by rising tides of guilt, shame, and anxiety which inevitably impact upon our relations with others.

One example of how this plays out is the way we are drawn into paradoxical processes of collaboration and competition within groups and between groups, driven by questions of identity, status anxiety, and social advantage, as described in the study Elias co-wrote with his MA student John Scotson. *The Established and the Outsiders* (1994) is an empirical study of the relationships between two communities in a Leicestershire village, where the established community, which is of a similar social background to a housing estate of more recent incomers, works to exclude residents from the estate from village resources and opportunities. Although the "established" villagers work alongside the "outsiders" in the same factory and are similarly educated, they nonetheless talk of them as being lesser. They create what Elias and Scotson refer to as a heroic "we identity" which they use to aggrandize their own achievements and to denigrate the social mores of the incomers. One of the ways they do this is through the use of gossip, which is deployed both to keep incomers at a distance and to police their own community, despite the fact that some individual members of both communities were sometimes on quite good terms with each other. Processes of inclusion and exclusion, fueled by the more powerful group's strong status anxieties and underpinned by gossip, enhanced the ability of the established to retain their more powerful social positions through twin effects: it boosted the self-image of the established group, but in addition the outsider community came to believe in their own negative self-image. The latter were thrown into an antagonistic relationship with their neighbors without wishing to be, and through no fault of their own.

10.3.1 *Power and Interdependence in Organizational Research*

One way of taking up Elias' insights about the paradoxes of inclusion and exclusion, cooperation and competition in terms of organizational research would be to think that his observations apply to special situations such as mergers and acquisitions as explored by Monin et al. (2013) from a process perspective. Undoubtedly, a merger between two groups with different identities is highly likely to produce some of the complex dynamics which Elias described. However, I think he also meant us to understand his ideas in an everyday sense. In most organizations different departments have varied reputations: the marketing department might develop a heroic "we" identity in relation to those working in sales, for example. Gossip, strong affect, and the development of identity are the everyday currencies of organizational life simply because we are interdependent members of different, fluctuating groups.

From an Eliasian perspective let us critically evaluate a piece of process-oriented research to see if it adds anything. Garud, Gehman, and Kumaraswamy's (2011) interesting account of innovation and change in the 3M corporation directly alludes to the complexity of arrangements within the firm to sketch out an understanding of the emergence of innovation. As a research approach, Garud and his colleagues pursue many of the things that would matter to Elias—they take a long-term view of the company, they argue that innovation arises as a result of the particular practices of groups of people over time, and they point to the way that the company socializes people into the 3M "way." It is a subtle account of organizational complexity which works against more heroic and simplified understandings of organizational innovation. The authors also point to the importance of a complex understanding of time, which I treat later on in the chapter, and the appropriateness and relevance of company narratives for understanding the unfolding stable instability of innovation over different phases in a company setting.

However, and at the same time, by neglecting the theme of power, interdependence, and processes of inclusion/exclusion, in my view the authors produce an over-orderly account of innovation, and by doing so they overstate the potential for managers to "design" it. From an Eliasian perspective new knowledge emerges from fluctuating interdependencies between groups of people. There are likely to be winners and losers, as people compete and cooperate, gossip about each other, praise and blame each other, and become heated about things that matter to them.

As examples of work which more directly address power and figurations, Dopson (2001) adopts Eliasian game theory explicitly in her analysis of change in the National Health Service. Power figurations also inform both Stacey's work (2009, 2012) and that of Mowles (2011, 2015). From a slightly different perspective, drawing on Bourdieu and Foucault rather than Elias, Flyvbjerg (2001) and Flyvbjerg, Landman, and Schram (2012) recommend putting both *phronesis*, everyday practical judgment, and power at the heart of research.

More generally in organizational research there is a greater interest in affect and informal "shadow" organizational processes, and how anxiety, guilt, shame, gossip, and informal power relationships shape outcomes and lead to changes which are otherwise inexplicable in more formal and orthodox accounts. There is a growing thread of research concerned with affect (Cascón-Pereira and Hallier, 2012; Coupland et al., 2008; Samra-Fredericks, 2004) and how it might be possible to take these into account when analyzing processes of change in organizations. An example of research which I think demonstrates a number of Elias' concerns without ever mentioning him (although he does draw on the professor who supervised Elias' *Habilitation*, Karl Mannheim) is Robert Jackall's *Moral Mazes* (2010). Jackall investigates how affect is provoked in the relationships between groups and notes processes of inclusion and exclusion, and game playing as they cooperate and compete. Just as in Elias' *The Established and the Outsiders*, dominant groups in North American corporate life justify their actions by the creation of what Elias referred to as heroic "we" identities.

10.4 Elias and Time

Time is a central concept for Elias and he takes a long-term view of its increasing importance in sociological terms. Precise time-oriented coordination is a relatively recent phenomenon which has developed within a much longer intergenerational process of knowledge development.

He draws a contrast between the comparatively slow development of changes in the natural world and human biology, in comparison with the rapid changes in human societies. Physiologically we are much as we were thousands of years ago, but the way our societies are structured has altered dramatically. These developments have brought about new knowledge and an alteration in what Elias terms the paradox of the I/we balance in human personality structure (1987b). Greater social integration and longer and longer chains of interdependency have also produced a pronounced tendency to individualization, weakening the sense of we in favor of a more marked sense of an I. Elias decries what he sees as a kind of sociological forgetting and hubris when we treat our own stage of development as a given and assume that we have always known what we now know. For him it is important to remember the long and sometimes painful development of human knowledge, which has no beginning. Developments in knowledge always arise from previous developments and "a very long line of human generations handing on knowledge and learning from one another" (Elias, 1998, p. 254).

Since social changes are so rapid, Elias argues that it is unhelpful to rely on research methods derived from the natural sciences, like physics and chemistry, which are in search of timeless rules applicable in all contexts. The dynamics and structure of human groups can change relatively quickly so time and context become important considerations:

> They are different at different times and in different places. To orient oneself on this integration-plane of the universe it is of little help to look around for laws, or concepts functioning as laws, applicable to the human world in the same way in all times and places. The task which this integration level sets human beings seeking orientation is to discover the order of change in the course of time, the order of successive events, and to seek concepts with which people can communicate about individual aspects of this order. (Elias, 1987b, p. 174)

There is little doubt in Elias' mind that there is a development process involved in the social which is broadly progressive, and that societies do in general become more civilized, although he remains agnostic about whether this has made human beings happier. This process is not coterminous with the idea of "progress" for him. The civilization process has, in his view, resulted in a much greater control over Nature, though much less control over human nature.

In his essay offering a sociological treatment of the development of our concept and use of time to coordinate within highly integrated societies, Elias notes that here too there is a tendency to turn time into an entity. In doing so we lose the idea that it has complex implications for the coordination of effort amongst human beings. In previous times we would have relied upon natural and less precise methods of coordinating using the tides or the changing of the seasons. Only in comparatively advanced societies, he argues, would it be possible to develop as highly sophisticated means of measurement as are required to coordinate a complex and differentiated society:

> the word 'time', one might say, is a symbol of a relationship that a human group, that is, a group of beings biologically endowed with the capacity for memory and synthesis, establishes between two or more continua of changes, one of which is used by it as a frame or standard of measurement for the other (or others). (Elias, 1998, p. 259)

Elias cleaves to the idea of change continua to stay true to his idea that social life is subject to constant flux and change. Time, then, is not a thing for Elias but a complex integrating activity which allows for the ever more precise coordination of effort between different change continua. Increasingly we regulate ourselves and our social lives according to abstract symbols of our own making.

10.4.1 Time and Organizational Research

There are a number of researchers who focus attention on the importance of time in organizational research (Wiebe, 2012; Purser et al., 2005; Tsoukas and Chia, 2002; Pettigrew, 2001) and how organizations are instantiated in particular places at particular times with particular practices. Taking account of time involves, in Elias' terms, adopting the paradoxical perspective of both the airman and the swimmer, bringing together particular phenomena and locating them in their longer-term history. But in addition to this it also points to who wins and who loses, and how the relations between groups change over time. A good example of organizational scholarship which takes a long-term view of the development of organizational theory (the perspective of the airman) and at the same time points to changes in power relationships between groups is Rakesh Khurana's *From Higher Aims to Hired Hands* (2010) which charts the rise, and in his opinion, the fall, of American business schools. Wiebe (2012), taking the perspective of the swimmer and drawing on Mead (1932), links narrative and temporal sense-making to argue that clock time is of limited use in making sense of organizational change processes.

10.5 Elias and Emergence

Perhaps it is time to pause to consider some of the fluctuating paradoxes in which, from Elias' perspective, our thoroughly social selves are caught in our relationships with others. These include the paradox of forming while being formed by the social; the paradox of interdependency which leads to the paradox of the enabling constraint of power; the paradox of the I in the we; the paradox of inclusion and exclusion, cooperation and competition; the paradox of involvement and detachment; the paradox of stable instability; and the paradox of the perspectives of the airman and the swimmer, or the particular and the general.

On the one hand, increased competition and longer and longer chains of interdependencies have resulted in our enhanced ability to "take a detour via detachment," which has led to the production of knowledge about ourselves and about Nature. It has given rise, Elias would argue (1972), to the discipline of science where humans have been able to develop knowledge which is relatively independent from the groups who have produced it. We have a far greater ability to predict and control natural phenomena, which in turn has amplified the civilizing process. Social differentiation and the production of knowledge contributes to the accretion of power of certain groups over others, but also provokes concerns over status as well as semi-automatically operating affect which can govern our behavior. Groups can unwittingly get drawn into relationships of antagonism and opposition with other groups, driven as they are by anxieties about status and group belonging, privilege and power chances.

The increasingly complex web of human interactions gives rise to emergent patterns and trends which tend in a particular direction, sometimes for decades, but which can then change abruptly and appear to take on a life of their own. There is a social dynamic which results from the combined effect of myriads of plans and intentions, which is nonetheless above and beyond each of them separately considered. This means that no individual or group can entirely control the way that society develops. Equally, social developments can go into reverse, and the civilizing process can produce barbarism, as Elias shows in his treatise on the rise of Nazism entitled *The Germans* (1997). In social life, he argues, we constantly encounter the unintended consequences of our best intentions:

> Over and over again the deeds and works of individual people, woven into the social net, take on an appearance that was not premeditated. Again and again therefore, people stand before the outcome of their actions like the apprentice magician before the spirits he has conjured up and which, once at large, are no longer in his power. They look with astonishment at the convolutions and the formations of the historical flow which they themselves constitute but do not control. (Elias, 2001, p. 62)

Our increasingly dispassionate ability to detach ourselves from our previously affect-driven involvement with nature, which is itself a product of the civilizing process, has not been matched by our ability to be detached about our engagement with other human beings. According to Elias the degree of fantasy content of our knowledge about the social is almost as high as it used to be about the natural world. This is partly because of the tendency to reduce process, as noted previously, and to introduce natural scientific ideas and methods inappropriately into the social domain, but also because of our inability to reflect purposefully on affect, which guides our actions irrespective of our attempts to control it. The task before us, then, is to try to become more detached about our involvement in the social, which, because we are socially formed, there is no position outside of, no view from nowhere as Nagel formulated it (1986).

In sum and according to Elias, we develop a sense of self because there are other selves, and our individual identity arises from our membership of the groups to which we belong. We are both constrained and enabled by others, with whom we cooperate and compete, caught up in the dynamics of inclusion and exclusion, within a group and between groups. We form intentions and make plans and pursue these, but so do other groups. What emerges, then, is the interweaving of intentions, a tissue of activity that creates itself *sui generis*. Because of the patterning that arises from the interweaving of intentions, there can be no guarantee that what we plan will come to pass. The increasing competition between both individuals and groups in highly differentiated societies causes constant fluctuations in relations, including changing power chances, which are reflected in the production of knowledge. This is an uncertain process, however, which often leads to unintended consequences, perhaps outcomes which lead to the opposite of what we intended, the paradox of stability and change:

> It is perfectly possible that by their own actions, groups of people consciously orientated towards preserving and maintaining the present figuration in fact strengthen its tendency to change. It is equally possible for groups of people consciously oriented towards change just to strengthen the tendency of their figuration to remain as it is. (Elias, 1978, p. 147)

As we mentioned earlier, in order better to understand the unique flow of social life, Elias argued (2001) that we must adopt the perspective of both the airman and the swimmer: this is a formulation for suggesting that we need to bring together both the particular and the general. In setting out this paradox, he puts forward the idea that it is only from the perspective of the airman that we are able to gain some detachment, a relatively undistorted view of the order of the long course of historical changes and the way we are forming and are formed by them. These long-term historical trends are extremely hard to resist even by very powerful coalitions of people or groups. However, there is nothing inevitable about our actions and reactions to the processes in which we find ourselves participating. But only by adopting the perspective of the swimmer, who is obliged to take action in the moment itself, is it possible to see how varied are the different pressures that are brought to bear on the particular circumstances in which find ourselves acting, in order that we might create opportunities to bring about outcomes of a different kind.

10.5.1 Emergence and Organizational Research

It is my view that Elias' perspective potentially helps enrich our current theorizing about organizational life as well as guiding us to pose further research questions for understanding the problematic of the emergence of the novel in the social, particularly if it is pursued as an organizational goal. This is an idea explored in a recent article by Mackay and Chia (2013), where they develop the idea of "unowned" change processes, i.e. ones which are neither the product of rational autonomous individuals, nor the outcome of deterministic environmental processes, but the interweaving of both.

There is also a clear link between Elias' work and the organizational literature on complexity. A number of organizational scholars have made the connection between the sciences of complexity and the stable instability of organizational life, including scholars in the process canon (Tsoukas, 2004; Hernes, 2008) and perhaps the most consistent of these is Ralph Stacey. In a body of work stretching back to the early 1990s (1991, 1995, 2001, 2011, 2012) Stacey has taken up insights from the complexity sciences understood by analogy, and developed and explained them in social terms drawing extensively on Elias and G. H. Mead (1934) amongst others to do so. Referring directly to the theory of complex adaptive systems (CAS), models of complex evolutionary behavior developed to run as agent-based computer simulations, Stacey notes how CAS are unpredictable over the long term. Stacey makes a link between insights from CAS models and the work of Elias. Emergence, Stacey argues (2011, p. 309) drawing on Elias, is not the opposite of intention, nor can anyone stand outside of the interactions which are a result of everyone acting with intention. It is what arises from the interweaving of intentions as everyone acts, and responds to the actions of everyone else. Change occurs in "self-organising, emergent processes of perpetually constructing the future as continuity and potential transformation at the same time" (2011, p. 309). Stacey notes that Elias is unlikely to have been aware of the development of thinking arising from what he terms the nonlinear sciences, but he anticipated them with his theories of emergence in the social by 40 years.

10.6 Discussion: How Elias Contributes to Process Organizational Scholarship

Newton (2001) gives a helpful overview of Elias and his relevance for organizational research, citing examples in a variety of research categories where scholarship might be deepened taking his perspective, or where scholars have already done so. He argues that Elias is relevant for thinking about strategy because of his concern with game models, time, and the interweaving of intentions. Equally, he points to how Elias' oeuvre might encourage further interest in bodily interaction and concomitant emotions and their development in figurational contexts. He suggests that drawing on Elias helps point to power and violence in organizations, particularly how changes in discourse are often related to changes in the power chances between groups. Elias' ideas are helpful for intensifying research into globalization, the environment, industrial relations, and studies of organizational history. He makes the case that, although a variety of scholars have drawn on Elias' work, in the main it remains a resource in the potential and is relatively unexplored.

To this list and in this chapter I have added the insight that although his work can sometimes shade into sequential dualisms, Elias is otherwise constantly working with paradoxes which generate the "continuous structured flux" (1987c, p. 340) of social life. From these paradoxes emerge the social and the development of knowledge. I have indicated above some of the ways in which his ideas concerning the radically social nature of the self and about process, power, time, and emergence might be mobilized in organizational scholarship.

In what follows I try to bring insights from Elias alongside some of the work of scholars contributing to the process orientation in organizational scholarship in an attempt to highlight similarities in differences, and to see how they refract. There are clearly common areas of overlap of interest, but I try to elucidate the distinctive contributions that Elias' view of process brings to process organizational studies.

10.6.1 *Human Interaction Rather Than Abstractions*

Elias considered philosophy to be a hollowed-out discipline dependent upon abstractions, and at the same time he was wary of the wholesale importation of models derived from the natural sciences to understand the social. He was extremely skeptical of abstract philosophical statements of a transcendental kind (Kilminster, 2007), which might posit, for example, the "primacy of process over fact" (Chia, 1996). For this reason it is likely that he would have been critical of the tendency towards abstract thinking in the intellectual informants of, for example, Hernes' (2008) volume on organizational process, particularly Whitehead, March, and Luhmann. Elias might have engaged robustly with the emphasis of the first two on atomism, as well as with March and Luhmann's understanding of the social in systemic terms. For Elias, figurations emerge from the moment by moment interactions of human bodies which produce no "entities," "parts and whole," or "levels" outside of themselves. Process is not an abstraction independent of what human beings are doing, nor does it produce social wholes. To an extent, Hernes recognizes what he refers to as "the fallacy of levels of analysis" (Hernes, 2008, p. 68) and adduces Latour to help him resolve it, but to my mind in this volume, and where he draws on Latour here and elsewhere (2012), he is unable to let go of the idea of parts and whole. For Elias the idea of wholes is a concept borrowed from the natural sciences, particularly informed by biology, which in Elias' terms is using "a mystery to explain a mystery" (1978, p. 73) when applied to the social. If there is no whole and no boundary, then how is the idea of a system helpful, Elias asks?

My guess is that Elias would have been suspicious both of a weak form of process ontology, one which privileges substance or entities, as well as a strong form, one which tends towards an essentialist view of process, since he took a strong line against what he termed nominalism (1978, p. 23). He tried to steer between what he considered to be the twin poles of philosophical absolutism, on the one hand, where concepts take on a foundational status, and relativism on the other (Elias, 1971). I see this as an attempt to maintain a paradoxical position.

10.6.2 *Emergence Through Shifting Interdependencies*

From an Eliasian perspective, the discussion of power relationships in the process canon is generally quite understated. Power, of course, is a highly contested concept, but figures mostly tangentially in the work of the broad cohort of process scholars with albeit some notable exceptions (Clegg, Courpasson, and Phillips, 2006; Hardy and Leiba-O'Sullivan, 1998). Without an account of power it is difficult to account for social emergence in Elias' terms. I do not underestimate the difficulty of writing about power in organizations, particularly in studies where researchers are given privileged access to personnel and documents.

Elias assumes that people act within webs of other people's actions and therefore contingency, chance, and unintended consequences are the norm rather than the exception in social life. Human intentions are also impelled by semi-automatically operating affect, caused by imperfect socialization processes, so that intention and action can never be fully conscious, never fully controlled. What transpires in the social are the intended and unintended consequences, consciously and unconsciously developed, which take on a patterning in and of themselves. Acting with intention to achieve particular changes in the social can paradoxically bring about the opposite of what one intends, just as resisting particular social changes can result in a speeding up of the change one is resisting. Engaged bodily interaction between thoroughly social selves produces profoundly emotional responses in human beings as identities are formed by being members of groups. Figurations produce our sense of we as well as a pronounced sense of I. There is some process literature which pays attention to emotion and identity, for example Howard-Grenville, Metzger, and Meyer (2013).

There is a general tendency in organizational research to overstate the capacity of leaders and senior managers to bring about the changes they intend. Although in the main the process canon could hardly be accused of contributing to this, from an Eliasian perspective human interdependency, affect and unintended consequences can sometimes be understated in process scholars' account of social change.

10.6.3 A Radically Relational View of Space and Time

A variety of process scholars (Chia, 1999; Chia and Holt, 2009; Hernes and Maitlis, 2012; Hernes, 2012; Shotter, 2012) draw on phenomenological theories of time, mostly via Bergson and sometimes Heidegger, as a way of problematizing more linear conceptions of organizational emergence and as a counter to what Sandberg and Tsoukas refer to as "variance theorizing" (2011, p. 342). As we noted above, time is also a central concept for Elias. He argues that humans' capacity to conceptualize and mediate time has evolved alongside social development, and is a manifestation of our ability to develop and manipulate symbols (1991). The more highly differentiated a society becomes, the more central time and ways of measuring it become important for synchronizing and standardizing human behavior, for regulation and self-regulation.

However, Elias argues against the idea that time is some kind of substance with a regular flow pointing out that it was Einstein who reconfigured time as a form of relationship. In the same way, he takes issue with the Western philosophical metaphysical tradition, including Bergson and Heidegger, which views time as a universal of human consciousness. Time for Elias is not a concept that has always been understood everywhere the same, but implies a large fund of knowledge and social learning to become meaningful:

> Time-relations, as one can see, are many-layered relationships of considerable complexity. One may experience some difficulty in distancing oneself from the homely metaphors which make 'time' appear as a thing, or the widely accepted notion that time can be used as a football for philosophical fantasies, since nothing definite can be said about it. But in the long run one will find it more rewarding to adopt a mode of thinking which reveals 'time' to be a conceptual symbol of advancing synthesis, a setting-up of fairly complex relationships between continua of changes of various kinds. (1998, p. 260)

The idea of time is not excluded from Elias' account of socio-genesis, but is central to it. The sophistication of our sense of time and timing has gone hand in hand with the particular phase of social development in which we find ourselves and the particular problems we have found ourselves facing. The denser the web of interdependencies between human beings the more refined and constricting becomes our sense of time.

It is hard to imagine that Elias would have been much exercised by abstract discussions that take place in much organizational literature. In general, his work draws on historical accounts of the development of, say, manners in court society, and in his empirical work, such as *The Established and the Outsiders*. He had a marked distaste for spatial metaphors, particularly ones which understood human beings as having an inside or an outside (2000, p. 480). In Elias' work there is nothing "outside" the figuration of historically formed, interdependent people nor are people "outside" of the natural world which they strive to comprehend.

10.6.4 Summary

There are common interests between the loose affiliation of process-oriented scholars and researchers whose work has been informed by Norbert Elias. Both are concerned about process reduction, show an interest in complex social emergence over time, and consider stability and change to be mutually constitutive. However, there are also some important differences of emphasis and theoretical understanding.

Informed in particular by Hegel, Darwin, Marx, and Freud, Elias is centrally concerned with human beings and what they are doing in their daily practice with others, as well as how this produces and reproduces social life over time. In this sense he answers directly Langley et al.'s (2013) appeal for accounts of organizational processes which include more micro accounts of people and what they are doing. Elias introduces questions of interdependence, explicitly power, at the heart of his inquiry and grounds human experience in affect, involving guilt, shame, and anxiety. Without considering the role of emotion and our psychological development, he argued, our theories of the social will always be incomplete. Unlike many process-oriented scholars, it seems to me that Elias was much less interested in developing a metaphysics of process. Rather he was concerned to generalize from the way that groups of human beings have behaved, and do behave towards each other, shaped and conditioned, pushed and pulled by broader social developments which emerge as a result of no overall plan or intention.

10.7 Conclusions

This chapter has revisited a variety of concepts developed by Norbert Elias to explain the emergence of novelty and change in the social as a way of broadening the canon of process-oriented scholarship. I have argued that Elias' work is infused with paradoxes which attempt to bring together the particular and the general, stability and change, continuity and renewal, all topics which interest scholars in the process tradition. For Elias we are both in control and not of social development since our plans and intentions interweave in surprising ways with those of others. As we anticipate the anticipations of others, small differences can become amplified and produce outcomes which surprise and perhaps disappoint us. In this way Elias straddles both "weak" and "strong" tendencies of process scholarship, privileging process at the same time as arguing for regularities, "structures," in social life.

Of course, Elias is not without his critics. Elias' implicit rather than explicit adoption of paradox, and the inconsistencies in his oeuvre, have left him open to a thread of critique that he is insensitive to the simultaneous operation of contradictory social trends, for example civilizing and barbarizing social processes. Burkitt (1996) reads Elias broadly sympathetically, but still suggests that Elias can sometimes present mutually constitutive social processes as sequential and negating, rather than two sides of the same coin. He can therefore lose their inherent ambivalence. Equally, in his exploration of the development of credit, Newton (2003) examines Breuer's (1991) view that Elias was unable to describe the dialectic of history and ultimately finds against him, but nonetheless expresses some support for his critique because of a variety of ambiguities in Elias' argument in relation to the development of money and its social consequences. Layder (1986) argues that Elias creates, then demolishes, straw men in separating out functional from phenomenological perspectives in social research doing justice to neither. Meanwhile Mouzelis (1995) argues that Elias' discussion of figuration and the emergence of institutions privileges the former over the latter, thus giving the impression that social relations are more mutable than they are.

All in all, there are a variety of scholars who have pointed to inconsistencies in Elias' arguments, more or less substantive, where Elias seems to create the very dualisms that he claims to oppose. However, my task here is to continue with what Burkitt (1996) refers to as an imaginative and sympathetic reading of Elias's texts to explain how it seems to me that although he sometimes struggles to maintain them his work is infused with paradoxes which could be helpful to developing a process perspective in organizational research as I hope I have shown.

In an editorial for the journal *Strategic Organization* in 2007, Ann Langley encourages organizational researchers to adopt qualitative research methods, particularly narrative, to produce rich, process-oriented research which she feels is underrepresented in this particular journal and many others. To take up Langley's invitation and to take Elias' insights seriously, organizational researchers need to reconsider power relationships, figurations, as central to understanding the flux and change of organizational life.

Of course, such themes present their own particular ethical difficulties as well raising questions of confidentiality for the organizations involved in such research. Nonetheless, for accounts of organizational change to be more reality-convergent, in Elias' terms, they might rely less on abstract and sometimes idealized accounts of purposeful, or purposeless change, and more on research which focuses on how flux and change is directly experienced by those caught up in the game of organizational life.

Finally, Szackolczai (2001) argues that Elias is a highly reflexive sociologist. This is partly because he resisted attempts to translate his work into English for 30 years in some cases. Eventually, when invited to write an introduction to an English edition of his previous work this led him to reappraise his thinking. One could make a strong argument, then, that an organizational researcher drawing on Elias would also be interested in reflexive scholarship, which Tsoukas (2009) calls "self-distanciation," and is a strong theme of interest for a variety of process-oriented and non-process-oriented researchers (Alvesson, Hardy, and Harley, 2009; Cunliffe, 2003). Scholars recommend a variety of research methods from simple problematizing of the researcher's assumptions through to auto-ethnographic narratives (Humphreys, 2005). Reflexive and narrative-based research (Tsoukas and Hatch, 2001) would be one way of realizing Elias' observation that we can never be totally removed from the social life which has formed us, nor are we ever totally immersed. A reflexive organizational researcher is, in Elias' terms, trying to become more detached about their involvement.

References

Alvesson, M., Hardy, C., and Harley, B. (2009). Reflecting on reflexivity: Reflexive textual practices in organization and management theory. *Journal of Management Studies*, 45(3): 480–501.

Bateson, G. (1972). *Steps to an Ecology of Mind*. Chicago: University of Chicago Press.

Beech, N., Burns, H., de Caestecker, L., MacIntosh, R., and Maclean, D. (2004). Paradox as invitation to act in problematic change situations, *Human Relations*, 57(10): 1313–1332.

Bergson, H. (1911/1998). *Creative Evolution*. New York: Dover.

Boden, D. (1994). *The Business of Talk: Organizations in Action*. Cambridge: Polity Press.

Bogner, A. (1987). Elias and the Frankfurt School. *Theory, Culture & Society*, 4: 249–285.

Breuer, S. (1991). The denouements of civilization: Elias and modernity. *International Social Science Journal*, 128: 401–416.

Burkitt, I. (1996). Civilization and ambivalence, *British Journal of Sociology*, 47(1): 135–150.

Burkitt, I. (1999). *Bodies of Thought: Embodiment, Identity and Modernity*. London: Sage.

Cascón-Pereira, R. and Hallier, J. (2012). Getting that certain feeling: The role of emotions in the meaning, construction and enactment of doctor managers' identities. *British Journal of Management*, 23(1): 130–144.

Chia, R. (1996). The problem of reflexivity in organizational research: Towards a postmodern science of organization. *Organization*, 3(1): 31–59.

Chia, R. (1999). A "rhizomic" model of organizational change and transformation: Perspective from a metaphysics of change. *British Journal of Management*, 10(3): 209–227.

Chia, R. and Holt, R. (2009). *Strategy Without Design: The Silent Efficacy of Indirect Action*. Cambridge: Cambridge University Press.

Chia, R. and Langley, A. (2004). The First Organization Studies Summer Workshop on Theorizing Process in Organizational Research. June 12–13, 2005, Santorini, Greece: Call for papers <http://www.egosnet.org/journal/os_summer_workshop.html>.

Clegg, S., Courpasson, D., and Phillips, N. (2006). *Power and Organizations*. London: Sage.

Clegg, S., Vierra da Cunha, J., and Pinha e Cunha, M. (2002). Management paradoxes: A relational view, *Human Relations*, 55(5): 483–503.

Coupland, D., Brown, A., Daniels, K., and Humphreys, M. (2008). Saying it with feeling: Analysing speakable emotions. *Human Relations*, 61(3): 327–353.

Cunliffe, A. (2003). Reflexive inquiry in organizational research: Questions and possibilities. *Human Relations*, 56(8): 983–1003.

Dewey, J. (2005). *The Quest for Certainty: A Study of the Relation of Knowledge and Action*. New York: Kessinger Publishing.

Dopson, S. (2001). Applying an Eliasian approach to organizational analysis. *Organization*, 8(3): 515–535.

Dopson, S. (2005). The diffusion of medical innovations: Can figurational sociology contribute? *Organization Studies*, 26(8): 1125–1144.

Elias, N. (1971). Sociology of knowledge: New perspectives. *Sociology*, 5(2): 149–168 and 5(3): 355–370.

Elias, N. (1972). Theory of science and history of science. *Economy and Society*, 1(2): 117–133.

Elias, N. (1978). *What Is Sociology?* New York: Columbia University Press.

Elias, N. (1987a). *Involvement and Detachment*. Oxford: Blackwell.

Elias, N. (1987b). Changes in the We–I balance. Reprinted in Elias, *The Society of Individuals* (pp. 153–258). New York: Continuum Books, 2001.

Elias, N. (1987c). On human beings and their emotions: A process-sociological view. *Theory, Culture & Society*, 4(2–3): 339–361.

Elias, N. (1991). *The Symbol Theory*. London: Sage.

Elias, N. (1994). *The Established and the Outsiders*. London: Sage.

Elias, N. (1997). *The Germans*. Cambridge: Polity Press.

Elias, N. (1998). *Norbert Elias: On Civilization, Power and Knowledge* (ed. S. Mennell and J. Goudsblom). Chicago: University of Chicago Press.

Elias, N. (2000). *The Civilizing Process.* Oxford: Oxford University Press.
Elias, N. (2001). *The Society of Individuals.* New York: Continuum Books.
Flyvbjerg, B. (2001). *Making Social Science Matter: Why Social Inquiry Fails and How it Can Succeed Again.* Cambridge: Cambridge University Press.
Flyvbjerg, B., Landman, T., and Schram, S. (2012). *Real Social Science: Applied Phronesis.* Cambridge: Cambridge University Press.
Garud, R., Gehman, J., and Kumaraswamy, A. (2011). Complexity arrangements for sustained innovation: Lessons from 3M Corporation. *Organization Studies,* 32(6): 737–767.
Hardy, C. and Leiba-O'Sullivan, S. (1998). The power behind empowerment: Implications for research and practice. *Human Relations,* 51(4): 451–483.
Hernes, T. (2008). *Understanding Organization as Process: Theory for a Tangled World.* London: Routledge.
Hernes, T. (2012). Actor network theory, Callon's scallops, and process-based organization studies. In T. Hernes and S. Maitlis (eds.), *Process, Sensemaking, & Organizing* (pp. 161–184). Oxford: Oxford University Press.
Hernes, T. and Maitlis, S. (2012). Process, sensemaking and organizing: An introduction. In T. Hernes and S. Maitlis (eds.), *Process, Sensemaking, & Organizing* (pp. 27–37). Oxford: Oxford University Press.
Howard-Grenville, J., Metzger, M., and Meyer, A. (2013). Rekindling the flame: Processes of identity resurrection. *Academy of Management Journal,* 56(1): 113–136.
Humphreys, M. (2005). Getting personal: Reflexivity and autoethnographic vignettes. *Qualitative Inquiry,* 11(6): 840–860.
Jackall, R. (2010). *Moral Mazes: The Corporate World of Managers.* Oxford: Oxford University Press.
Jay, J. (2013). Navigating paradox as a mechanism of change and innovation in hybrid organizations. *Academy of Management Journal,* 56(1): 137–159.
Kainz, H. (1988). *Paradox, Dialectic and System: A Contemporary Reconstruction of the Hegelian Problematic.* University Park, PA: Pennsylvania State University Press.
Khurana, R. (2010). *From Higher Aims to Hired Hands: The Social Transformation of American Business Schools and the Unfulfilled Promise of Management as a Profession.* Princeton, NJ: Princeton University Press.
Kilminster, R. (2007). *Norbert Elias: Post-Philosophical Sociology.* London: Routledge.
Langley, A. (2007). Process thinking in strategic organization. *Strategic Organization,* 5(3): 271–282.
Langley, A., Smallman, C., Tsoukas, H., and Van de Ven, A. (2013). Process studies of change in organization and management: Unveiling temporality, activity, and flow. *Academy of Management Journal,* 56(1): 1–13.
Langley, A. and Tsoukas, H. (2012). Introducing "Perspectives on process organization studies." In T. Hernes and S. Maitlis (eds.), *Process, Sensemaking, & Organizing* (pp. 1–26). Oxford: Oxford University Press.

Layder, D. (1986). Social reality as figuration: A critique of Elias's conception of sociological analysis. *Sociology*, 20(3): 367–386.

Leana, C. and Barry, B. (2000). Stability and change as simultaneous experiences in organizational life. *Academy of Management Review*, 25(4): 753–759.

MacKay, R. B. and Chia, R. (2013). Choice, chance, and unintended consequences in strategic change: A process understanding of the rise and fall of Northco Automotive. *Academy of Management Journal*, 56(1): 208–230.

Mead, G. H. (1932). *The Philosophy of the Present*. Chicago: Open Court Publishing.

Mead, G. H. (1934). *Mind, Self and Society from the Standpoint of a Social Behaviorist*. Chicago: University of Chicago Press.

Mennell, S. (1992). *Norbert Elias: An Introduction*. Dublin: University College Dublin Press.

Mohr, L. B. (1982). *Explaining Organizational Behavior*. San Fransisco: Jossey-Bass.

Monin, P., Noorderhaven, N., Vaara, E., and Kroon, D. (2013). Giving sense to and making sense of justice in postmerger intergration. *Academy of Management Journal*, 56(1): 256–284.

Mouzelis, N. (1995). *Sociological Theory: What Went Wrong?* London: Routledge.

Mowles, C. (2011). *Rethinking Management: Radical Insights from the Complexity Sciences*. London: Gower.

Mowles, C. (2015). *Managing in Uncertainty: Complexity and the Paradoxes of Everyday Organizational Life*. London: Routledge.

Nagel, T. (1986). *The View from Nowhere*. Oxford: Oxford University Press.

Newton, T. (2001). The relevance and the limitations of Elias. *Organization*, 8(3): 467–495.

Newton, T. (2003). Credit and Civilization. *British Journal of Sociology*, 54(3): 347–371.

Newton, T. (2004). From Freemasons to the employee: Organization, history and subjectivity. *Organization Studies*, 25(8): 1363–1387.

Newton, T. (2010). Knowledge and practice: Organization studies within a historical and figurational context. *Organization Studies*, 31(9&10): 1369–1395.

Peirce, C. S. (1931–35 and 1958). *Collected Papers of Charles Sanders Peirce* (vols. I–IV, 1931–35, ed. C. Hartshorne and P. Weiss; vols. VII–VIII, 1958, ed. A. Burks). Cambridge, MA: Belknap Press.

Pettigrew, A. (2001). Management research after modernism. *British Journal of Management*, 12, Special Issue: S61–S70.

Poole, M. S. and Van de Ven, A. (1989). Using paradox to build management and organization theories. *Academy of Management Review*, 14(4): 562–578.

Purser, R. E. and Petranker, J. (2005). Unfreezing the future: Exploring the dynamic of time in organizational change. *Journal of Applied Behavioral Science*, vol. 41(no. 2): 182–203.

Quinn, R. E. (1988). *Beyond Rational Management: Mastering the Paradoxes and Competing Demands of High Performance*. San Fransisco: Jossey-Bass.

Samra-Fredericks, D. (2004). Managerial elites making rhetorical and linguistic "moves" for a moving (emotional) display. *Human Relations*, 57(9): 1103–1143.

Sandberg, J. and Tsoukas, H. (2011). Grasping the logic of practice: Theorizing through practical activity. *Academy of Management Review*, 36(2): 338–360.

Shaw, P. (2002). *Changing Conversations in Organisations: A Complexity Approach to Change*. London: Routledge.

Shotter, J. (2005). Bringing corporeal life back in: Chiasmic relations and poetic understandings. In W. Doll, M. Fleener, D. Trueit, and J. St. Julien (eds.), *Chaos, Complexity, Curriculum, and Culture: A Conversation* (pp. 195–208). New York: Peter Lang.

Shotter, J. (2012). Adopting a process orientation . . . in practice: Chiasmic relations, language and embodiment in a living world. In T. Hernes and S. Maitlis (eds.), *Process, Sensemaking, & Organizing* (pp. 70–101). Oxford: Oxford University Press.

Smith, D. (2001). Organizations and humiliation: Looking beyond Elias. *Organization*, 8(3): 537–560.

Smith, W. K. and Lewis, M. W. (2011). Toward a theory of paradox: A dynamic equilibrium model of organizing. *Academy of Management Review*, 36(2): 381–403.

Stacey, R. D. (1991). *The Chaos Frontier: Creative Strategic Control for Business*. Oxford: Butterworth Heinemann.

Stacey, R. D. (1995). The science of complexity: An alternative perspective for strategic change processes. *Strategic Management Journal*, 16(6): 477–495.

Stacey, R. D. (2001). *Complex Responsive Processes in Organizations: Learning and Knowledge Creation*. London: Routledge.

Stacey, R. D. (2009). *Complexity and Organizational Reality: Uncertainty and the Need to Rethink Management after the Collapse of Investment Capitalism*. London: Routledge.

Stacey, R. D. (2011). *Strategic Management and Organisational Dynamics: The Challenge of Complexity to Ways of Thinking about Organisations* (6th edition). London: Prentice-Hall.

Stacey, R. D. (2012). *Tools and Techniques of Leadership and Management: Meeting the Challenge of Complexity*. London: Routledge.

Szackolczai, A. (2001). *Reflexive Historical Sociology*. London: Routledge.

Taylor, C. (1992). *Sources of the Self*. Cambridge, MA: Harvard University Press.

Tsoukas, H. (2004). *Complex Knowledge: Studies in Organizational Epistemology*. Oxford: Oxford University Press.

Tsoukas, H. (2009). A dialogical approach to the creation of new knowledge in organizations. *Organization Science*, 20(6): 941–957.

Tsoukas, H. and Chia, R. (2002). On organizational becoming: Rethinking organizational change. *Organization Science*, 13(5): 567–582.

Tsoukas, H. and Hatch, M. J. (2001). Complex thinking, complex practice: The case for a narrative approach to organizational complexity. *Human Relations*, 54(8): 979–1013.

Van de Ven, A. H. and Poole, M. S. (2005). Alternative approaches for studying organizational change. *Organization Studies*, 26(9): 1377–1404.

Van Iterson, A., Mastenbroek, W., Newton, T., and Smith, D. (2002). *The Civilized Organization: Norbert Elias and the Future of Organization Studies*. Amsterdam: John Benjamins.

Van Iterson, A., Mastenbroek, W., and Soeters, J. (2001). Civilizing and informalizing: Organizations in an Eliasian context. *Organization*, 8(3): 497–514.

Wiebe, E. (2010). Temporal sensemaking: Managers' use of time to frame organizational change. In T. Hernes and S. Maitlis (eds.), *Process, Sensemaking, & Organizing* (pp. 213–241). Oxford: Oxford University Press.

11

After Mastery

Insights from Practice Theorizing

Dvora Yanow

Abstract: Much of the practice studies literature, especially in a phenomenological vein, focuses on novices learning, acquiring what the master "has." This leaves two under-theorized areas: a "life-cyle" of practitioner and practicing phases, including pre-novice and post-mastery; and forms of practice-learning across these, including that characteristic of mastery itself. In conceiving of themselves as all-knowing and then "rushing to judgment" or making "premature diagnoses," for instance, masters seem to lose their ability to inquire. Might learning to become a master contribute to some things being "unlearned" which are key to good practicing in being a master, thereby generating problems in the practice? This chapter elucidates the characteristics of novice-learning in organizational settings of various sorts. It then frames several problems in need of further theorizing, including the changing character of practitioners' awareness of "tools" across the practice life-cycle and the need for work-practice studies to theorize about practices entailing human "tools."

In memory of Michael Cohen:
long engaged with these sorts of ideas, he was taken from us all too quickly, and too soon

In *Return of the Jedi* when Luke is training
and his fighter has been mired in the swamp,
he tells Yoda, "I don't think I can, but I'll try."
Yoda says, "Try!? There is no Try! Do or Do Not!"
Less objective thinking and trying, more instinctive doing.
For me that applies to the way I sing Sacred Harp,
but not to the way I sing choral music.

—Judy Mincey (2009; emphasis added)

"I didn't do it *intellectually*," Ms. Streisand said
[regarding how she figured out how to prolong the intensity
of the sound while fading her voice to *piano*].
"I did it *intuitively, unconsciously*. I kind of like that."

—Quoted in Tommasini (2009; emphasis added)

I use my clinical judgment—my *intuition*—
to decide whether [the patient] should undergo surgery,
be kept in the hospital for observation, or be sent home.

—Atul Gawande (2002, p. 42; emphasis added)

"How do I get to Carnegie Hall?"
"Practice!"

—Old joke, variously attributed to a New York taxi driver or to renowned pianist Arthur Rubinstein answering a tourist's question

Working "instinctively," "intuitively," "unconsciously," as in these epigraphs, rather than "intellectually," through "objective thinking," is a key characteristic of practices and their mastery, according to practice theory of a phenomenological bent (e.g. Dreyfus, 1991; Dreyfus and Dreyfus, 2005; Heidegger, 1962; Knorr Cetina, 2001; Nicolini, 2012; Nicolini, Gherardi, and Yanow, 2003; Schatzki, 2005; Schatzki, Knorr Cetina, and von Savigny, 2001; Yanow and Tsoukas, 2009). Practices are learned—none of us is born knowing how to sing in operatic or Western choral fashion, how to diagnose patients, how to manage others, how to teach—and theorizing learning processes of novices becoming masters is central to practice studies. Hands-on "learning on the job" is fundamental: lab, clinic, and other forms of nonformal education join more formal book and lecture learning; novices develop practice-related skills, becoming competent in manipulating practice-related tools and related body movements, in the process becoming masters of them, and it. As many practices are conducted in organizational settings, practice-learning is a matter for organizational studies, especially when work practices are distinguished from more general social practices.

Comparative analysis of three key taxonomies of practice-learning stages highlights the drive toward the acquisition of mastery: the general novice-master language, the medieval guilds' apprentice-journeyman-master system, and Dreyfus and Dreyfus' (2005) five-stage novice, advanced beginner, competence, proficiency, and expertise model. Lave and Wenger's (1991) "legitimate peripheral participation," in which novices move from the peripheries of practices to their centers, parallels these. In recognition of the learning *processes* unfolding across what is recognized as "a practice," we might better speak of "practicing" (cf. Weick, 1979, on the move from "organization" to "organizing").

Key in this learning process is a change in the character of the practitioner's attention to component parts of practicing. Novices begin with a more focused, conscious engagement with the practicing's material elements and kinesthetics. A master would be less engaged with the practicing's "objective," "intellectual" work—rational, cognitive, detached—and more with the "flow" of its actual doing (cf. Czikszentmihalyi, 1990), as rapt attention to its "tools" shifts to subsidiary awareness (Polanyi, 1962), including developing "clinical judgment" or intuition concerning their use. To remain with the initial epigraphs' vocal settings, in mastering her practice, a singer's attention shifts to the shaping of a musical line, for instance, away from sounding the precise notes on the musical stave. (Although more could be said about bodily engagement, for purposes of this discussion, I subsume related bodily movements within "tools," in the sense that the blind man's cane, for example, can be seen as an extension of his tapping hand; Bateson, 1972.)

Practice theorizing appears to frame the novice-to-master transition in terms of repairing a "deficit": masters "have" something (knowledge, in the form of expertise) that novices lack and need to develop. It is this learning that is theorized; the stage model is implicit. "Practice" is equated with mastery: novices learn, they do not practice; masters practice—implying that they no longer learn. This distinction illuminates three uses of the term, two verbs, one noun: masters "practice"—perform—"the practice"—the recognized, acquired, embodied know-how with its rules and evaluative standards; when novices "practice"—repeating acts over and over, as a musician does in articulating a set of notes—they are learning "the practice," trying to get it right, to get, metaphorically, to the Carnegie Hall of the fourth epigraph. Moreover, an unspoken assumption undergirding studies of practice-learning is that the supply of novices is unending. Novelty in the practice system arrives in the person of the novice, who is to be absorbed into the ongoing practice. Practicing itself, that is, including its transmission to newcomers, is a conserving affair: neither "the practice" nor the know-how passed on to novices is theorized in terms of introducing novel ways of seeing and doing.

This treatment positions learning in a particular way both in "practice time" and in character, as if the "novitiate" on the road to mastery were the only phase during which learning takes place. Introducing the concept of novelty into the discussion brings out several aspects of practice-learning. For one, the possible locus of novelty points to differences between practitioner-learning and the practice itself "learning" (e.g. to accommodate new members; this parallels distinctions concerning organizational learning; see Cook and Yanow, 2011 [1993], pp. 363–366). Second, asking where novelty might be introduced in different practitioner-practice stages highlights potential variations in the character of learning across these. Considering a fourth taxonomy, the conscious competence model, raises the question of a pre-novice stage, with its own form(s) of learning. This notion, in turn, suggests an arc of "lifelong learning"[1] in practices and practicing, including a possible post-mastery stage at its other end—a phase of other bodily, mental, and/or emotional ways of being, whether resulting from illness or aging, with retirement a subset—entailing still other forms of learning, as well as learning modes particular to mastery itself. These added dimensions call for theorizing the kinds of learning that might characterize different phases of a practitioner's life-cycle and their intersections with the "life-cycle" of a practice.

Consider novices (and pre-novices), for one, who learn things that are new to them, but not to the practice. And then consider established practices working to conserve themselves—something Kuhn (1970) observed in theorizing knowing and practicing in scientific communities—suggesting maintaining expertise as a form of mastery-learning. Contemplating maintenance-learning points to problems characteristic of mastery, including error-making. Although distinctive by practice arena, these appear to share the character of masters' "rushing to judgment" or making "premature diagnoses," closing off pathways to inquiry—at times with catastrophic results—based on the assumption that masters know all there is to know. Re-engaging learning in this phase would require countering the subsidiary-focus, rote character of masters' engagement with the tools of their practicing. Might it be that in mastery's requisite shift of tools from focal to subsidiary awareness, certain learning processes are "unlearned," thereby generating problems in and for the practice, including master-practitioners not recognizing their error-making or their practicing's lost effectiveness? Additionally, considering mastery-learning highlights a feature of many work practices—managing, teaching, doctoring, nursing, lawyering, and so forth: by contrast with practice theorizing's engagement with inanimate tools, these practices entail human "tools."

This chapter introduces the idea of practitioner and practice life-cycles, seeking to frame several questions (more than to pose answers) that a more robust account of practice-learning might explore. Because this theorizing is based on a particular view of practice-learning, section 11.1 illustrates that at length, empirically, moving from novice-ry to mastery. This extended illustration lays the groundwork for section 11.2's discussion of the mastery-errors and -learning, including human "tools," which are my main concern. I engage an issue central to several literatures, framed in the language of practice theorizing: how and why some masters are more or less likely to interrupt their regularized practices in ways that return certain aspects to focal awareness, in order to address problems.

This theorizing was inspired by analysis of others' thickly observed, thickly narrated (participant-) observational data, presented primarily in four reflective accounts by practitioners and/or teachers of the practice in question—Henry Petroski (2002) on being a paperboy; Atul Gawande (2002, 2007a) and Jerome Groopman (2007) on surgery and related medical practices; David Cohen (2011) on school-teachers and teaching—supplemented by examples from other accounts. This method parallels Karl Weick's secondary analysis (1993) of Norman Maclean's investigative reportage on the Mann Gulch disaster, to which Maclean brought his own prior firefighting experience. The original texts' ample detail, Petroski's in particular, enable section 11.1's extended discussion of what it means to learn a practice, not only illustrating the complexities that practice theorizing seeks to explicate, but also providing an observational "thickness" sufficient to support both comparative analysis and theorizing (Schwartz-Shea and Yanow, 2012; Yanow, 2014). I might have begun by simply reiterating the theoretical literature's claims about practice-learning; but this would have produced too "thin" a description to support the subsequent theorizing and problem-framing. These field narratives demonstrate the utility—indeed, the necessity—of thickly observed and narrated data of an ethnographic sort for describing practices in ways that open them up for inquiry. (For additional methodological reflections, see the Appendix.)

11.1 On the Road to Mastery: Practice-Learning Processes

What does learning look like, phenomenologically, in work practices? Professor of civil engineering Henry Petroski's autobiographical account (2002) describes learning how to deliver newspapers for *The Press*, a now defunct newspaper. Being a "paperboy" was a common practice in many mid-twentieth century US suburban settings (girls came later), entailing hauling folded papers in bicycle baskets and landing them on subscribers' doorsteps (ensuring the tossed paper missed the empty bottles waiting on the stoop for the milkman to retrieve; Karl Weick, personal communication, December 12, 2011). Petroski articulates, vividly and precisely, the very material, bodily, and social elements practice theorizing identifies as central to practice-learning: newspapers, bicycles, and delivery routes; balancing bike, papers, and body; delivery boys and customers. His narrative demonstrates that non-"professional" practices can also be useful settings for practice theorizing,[2] and it moves us beyond automobile gear-boxes and eyeglasses (Dreyfus, 1991; Heidegger, 1962; Knorr Cetina, 2001) closer to organization-based work practices involving human "tools" (see section 11.2). I compare these extended paperboy accounts with briefer ones of other practices—learning how to be a doctor, a surgeon, an anaesthesiologist, all engaged with human "tools"—taking them up further in section 11.2.

11.1.1 Becoming a Press Paperboy and Other Practice-Learning: Practice Theorizing, Empirically

Practices are learned. But how? Petroski makes remarkably transparent the characteristics of practice-learning as he moves from novice to master. He describes the kind of knowledge-in-practice a master-paperboy needs:

> In theory, all a *Press* boy had to have was a route book full of house numbers and special delivery instructions, a bicycle with a big basket, and a reliable source of newspapers. In practice, he had to have stamina and resolve. And he had to have hands and a plan and the willingness to learn how to fold and how to pack and the savvy to learn when to double-fold and when to stuff. He had to have rules of thumb. He had to have an arm. He had to learn why his papers were exploding over the lawn, or why they were missing their targets. He had to analyze his failures and he had to learn from them. He had to read not the weather forecast but the weather, and he had to know when to put the papers in out of the rain. (p. 354; all paperboy-related passages are from Petroski 2002)

This passage illustrates a central characteristic of practicing: the distinction between explicit knowledge (what a paperboy knows he needs) and tacit knowledge (Polanyi, 1966), in part embodied—having hands, an arm, an orientation toward learning, and rules of thumb. Several of the components of paperboy practicing can be seen, here and in other passages, in the technical language of the practice:

folding
packing
double-folding
stuffing (circulars into the main paper; papers into paper-bag)
balancing (papers on bike; bike and self while flipping)
memorizing (the route; special requests: e.g. paper placed under mat, not flipped)
flipping
doorknobbing
collecting
reading the weather.

Several of these have weather variations (rainy day, windy day), as well as paper size variations. And then there is bike maintenance and repair, and knowing how to re-establish your reputation after delivering soggy wet papers, to regain the customer or the tip.

Note the utter commonplaceness of the verbs. "Ordinary language" terms, they disassemble the practicing such that we can begin to see its components. Similarly ordinary language populates David Cohen's (2011, pp. 40–41) study of teaching practices in classroom settings:

explaining
demonstrating
writing (on the board)
repeating (things)
detecting variations (from prescribed procedures)
imagining
unpacking problems
repeating the same idea in different ways
discriminating (between key ideas and procedures)
responding
organizing inquiry
sustaining inquiry
managing social interactions.

Why these (and other) activities might usefully be called "practices" becomes clear in reading their descriptions against what practice theorizing tells us about practice-learning. I explore seven characteristics.

1. *Prior knowledge.* Practice-learning starts from prior, but inchoate, unexamined knowledge. Here is Petroski's, and its experiential source:

> Before I became a paperboy, I thought little about how a paper looked or how it was delivered. . . . To me, papers had always come in the disarray my father had put them in, their pages misaligned, their corners torn, their ink smudged. . . . Now, after having seen virgin papers counted out at the circulation office, I realized that a newspaper read is a different thing: dirty rather than clean, soft rather than crisp, curled rather than flat. (pp. 86–87)

He signs up for the job and decides to practice before his starting day:

> I had brought home with me a single folded copy of the *Press*. . . . I knew that once I unfolded the paper, I might not get it back together, so I put it down on the bed and studied it. I picked it up with care, turning it around and around in my hands . . . looking for clues in its balance. . . . The inside revealed nothing that I could not see from the outside. (p. 87)

His learning is sight-based, tactile, and kinesthetic, after heft and feel (cf. McClintock's "feel for the organism," Fox Keller, 1983; Cook and Yanow, 2011 [1993]):

> I . . . tried to practice folding a bunch of stale newspapers that I took from the pile in the garage. . . . I hardly knew what I was doing, trying to mimic what I had watched the silent paperboys do with the speed of a party clown twisting long thin balloons. . . . I had to practice folding something, so that I could also practice throwing—flipping, as *Press* boys would say—papers onto stoops and porches. (p. 89)

Trying to practice, he is not yet "practicing." He has an image in mind, which he tries to replicate. But his context is not the practicing itself, and he is stuck trying to imitate what for others has moved to subsidiary awareness.

2. *Moving tool-attention from focal to subsidiary awareness.* Petroski is initially fully focused on the hand motions required to fold. He needs "practice," Carnegie Hall style: learning from repeated movement, over time, under "controlled"—regularized, unsurprising—circumstances:

> This near-constancy in size [from Monday's paper through Wednesday's] gave me a chance to improve my folding technique, which in turn increased

> greatly the chance of my papers reaching the stoop without unfurling. . . . Thursday's paper was twice the size of Monday's, but my hands had already come to know their task and my fingers had developed some strength. (p. 97)

Still, he can't flip; the papers come undone; giving up on the bike, he tucks them, flat, under the doormat; and he ends up short two papers, which he buys at the corner store and brings back to those customers.

> [By Saturday] my folding and packing style was beginning to look . . . almost as good as my neighbors' at the bench. The papers in the bag were nearly as uniform as cigarettes in a freshly opened pack. My flipping success rate had also improved since I had begun tossing the papers with the seam of the fold down. . . . I had also learned to give the papers a slight rotation when folding them and to give them a good cross crease before packing them in the bag. (p. 98)

The more practiced he becomes at folding, packing, and flipping, the less attention the motions require. Gawande makes parallel observations about surgeons, who, he says, "believe in practice, not talent" (2002, p. 19):

> Practice is funny that way. For days and days, you make out only the fragments of what to do. And then one day you've got the thing whole. Conscious learning becomes unconscious knowledge, and you cannot say precisely how. . . . You don't think. You don't concentrate. Every move unfolds effortlessly. . . . At such moments, it is more than easy; it is beautiful. (2002, pp. 21, 22)

This is the shift in focus in the relationship between the novice and her "tools." At the beginning stages of practice-learning, the novice is primarily focused on mastering the manipulation of the materials central to enacting the practice. How do I use my voice, shape my mouth, pitch my sound, work with the overwhelming echo in this old hall? How do I handle my body in relation to this scalpel, this jury, this chalk? As a practice is learned, such *focal awareness* shifts to *subsidiary awareness* (Polanyi, 1962): the tools themselves and what is required in handling them, physically (and perhaps mentally or emotionally; theory is nearly silent on these topics, but see Gherardi, 2009), fade into the background. One becomes less mindfully oriented toward them and more oriented toward other aspects of the practice; one attends *from* one's background knowledge of the tools *to* the content of one's intended action (Polanyi, 1966, p. 10). Here is clinical judgment, "an unconscious form of pattern recognition" (Gawande, 2002, p. 248).

The more he can shift his attention away from the basics, "backgrounding" them, the more Petroski can refocus on mastering the next level of detail (the rotation and cross crease of his last sentence, previous quote). The Sunday paper, however, presents a surprise: huge size, enormous weight. He can't get all the papers up the hill on his bike; he can't flip them; they unravel; he delivers them by hand, walking. Then, Tuesday's paper is very thin, needing new learning for folding, stuffing, and flipping:

> Here I was being confronted by still another variation on preparing the paper for delivery, and I had not yet been on the job ten days. Newspapers that once looked all the same to me now seemed to come in too many variations. (p. 100)

Encountering "surprises" or "puzzles"—variations that add nuance to practicing—interrupts his newly-acquired sense of regularity, requiring focus again on the practice's "tools"—the paper fold, its heft, the bike, and so on. As new variations insert themselves into the landscape of what had been becoming "mindless," Petroski's "tool attention" shifts back from subsidiary to focal awareness, shifting again as he internalizes new knowledge.

3. *Tacit knowledge: out of sight and out of mind.* Petroski starts trying to learn from what he sees and what others tell him. His learning moves from the rational-intellectual to the kinesthetic, via explicit instruction, mimicking, trial and error (cf. Dreyfus and Dreyfus, 2005):

> My efforts at folding were in imitation of the folded product. What I needed to understand was not *its form* but *how it was formed*. I tried to remember the *Press* boys folding their papers at the bench, but understanding how their hands manipulated the papers was as difficult as following the fingers of a prestidigitator. I had listened to my mentor begin to explain the process, but his instructions were of no help. "Take this part and slide it into here," he said, "like this," his hands moving faster than his tongue and covering up the very act that I wanted to see. "Then pull the sides out and flatten it," he continued, "like this," which concluded the trick. By the time he had said the presto words he had already picked up the next paper and formed it into a tube. He was soon lost in a rhythm of his own devising, in silent and thoughtless folding that excluded me. (p. 90, emphasis added)

He attends to the wrong object initially, needing more "verb" than "noun," more body knowledge than product knowledge; and he needed to know still more:

> What I wasn't taught was how to fold the bulk of the papers properly and toss the typical paper from my bicycle onto the stoop intact. Dan demonstrated these skills, but he only let me watch. . . . He did not explain to me how he did

> what he did. I had been on my own to learn to ride a bike up a hill with fifty pounds of papers in the basket . . . and . . . to balance my unbalanced bike against a tree while I walked from house to house. (p. 91)

His bedroom practice had not helped, nor did other paperboys, who could not articulate what they knew:

> To be sure, they themselves had mastered the act, but they could hardly describe it. All they could do was say, over and over, "Take this end and put it into here, like this," and do it. But they did it so fast, lest their own hands freeze at the thought, that I could not follow the sequence of movements. It was only by trying as best I could to imitate their movements and imitate their product that I would do it myself. (p. 94)

Repeated over time, practice-knowing—the bodily and other ways of relating to practice-tools—becomes not only "out of sight" (as it moves from focal to subsidiary awareness), but "out of mind," tacit: what "all paperboys know" (else they would not call themselves paperboys) but have so internalized that they can no longer make it explicit; they "know more than they can tell" (Polanyi, 1966, p. 4; cf. Tsoukas, 2011). Dan "did not explain . . . how he did what he did" probably because he could not explain it, like the paperboys who kept repeating the same procedural mantra instead of detailing step by step what needed to be done. That had long ago become part of their common sense, taken-for-granted, unspoken, unwritten, everyday, tacit know-how, removed from focal awareness. The two verb lists above make visible a key aspect of practicing's tacit dimensions: reading either list, no novice could then go deliver papers or teach school.

Petroski later reflects on this:

> How could I have expected all of the tricks of the trade to be transmitted in one day from a practiced paperboy to a novice like me? Dan Healey, my predecessor on the route that was now mine, so emphasized the special delivery instructions and foibles of cranky and crotchety customers that I missed the fundamentals, which he took for granted. None of the boys on Sunday morning, for all their good intentions, could . . . tell me what I needed to know. They folded their papers mechanically, not able to think about what they were doing lest their hands lose their own train of thought. The boys' discussions focused on the exceptions to the rule, the paper that was too light or too thick, the man who wanted his paper flat, the woman who wanted hers rolled. (p. 90)

The "practiced" experts have mastered paperboy-ing. Knowledge now tacit needs no attention; it is the exceptions, the surprises, that demand focal awareness.

4. *Practicing is social.* Petroski is also learning that he cannot learn the practice on his own. Practicing is social; practice-knowing can only be learned—and demonstrated—within the practicing itself:

> On Monday, I drew my daily allotment of newspapers. . . . Following the example of the boys beside me, I put the pile of papers on the shelf below . . . The boy to my right slowed his hands down to where I could see what he was doing, and the boy to my left did the same thing. They were competing to teach me to fold, and the mirror-image twins gave me a good look at the process from two points of view. . . . Between the two boys, I had a complete picture of the process, and I began to follow these guides as if they were instructors for folding paper airplanes.
>
> My papers were not nearly as neat as those piling up in the bags beside me. . . . Like split firewood, they were of uncertain size and uneven shape. Nevertheless, each successive paper resembled increasingly a properly folded one, and the more papers I folded the more uniform they became. My neighbors finished and . . . left the folding bench before I was half through. But I had gotten the hang of it by then. . . . When I finished, I could see an improvement from the bottom to the top rows in the bag. (pp. 94–95; cf. Sudnow, 1978, pp. xi–xiii, 12–33)

Reporting on a surgeon learning to make diagnoses, Jerome Groopman (2007, p. 168) describes a similarly social, in-practice learning process:

> [N]o one had ever really taught him how to 'think of it' [what is missing in a diagnosis]. Instead, he learned how to observe senior surgeons closely . . . and then began to imitate those who worked with 'clarity and effectiveness'.

Moreover, both novices, paperboy and surgeon, are being guided by experienced members of each practice. (Note that *how to observe* is also learned!)

5. *What is learned is context-specific.* Groopman's surgeon-in-learning is explicit about choosing his models with care. This signals the idea that there is more than one way to be a surgeon—or any sort of practitioner. That the same practice is not conducted universally in identical modes is evident in research into identical medical practices in different locations. Gawande, for example, describes differences among surgical team practices in an experimental setting (2002, pp. 29–30), in hospital-based hernia operations (2002, pp. 38–41), and in hospital-based cystic fibrosis treatments (2007a, pp. 205–30).[3] Practice-learning entails choosing a mode of practicing.

Such choice can be a matter of personal proclivities, aesthetics, or other values. Groopman's novice chooses a mode that fits his own criteria for good diagnosing ("clarity," "effectiveness"). Similarly, "rabbi-ing" in the US is not a unitary practice: some privilege study and/or teaching in their rabbinate; others construe it as a counseling practice or a mediation one; still others, as a community relations practice focused on smooth interactions with the surrounding non-Jewish majority. Similar variability characterizes the practice of university-based chaplaincy (Gallos and Yanow, 1976; cf. the discussion of anaesthesiologists below). Aspects of personality (e.g. narcissism, about which Dr. T, introduced below, spoke at some length) may also play a role in leading certain persons to take up certain practices and shape them in particular ways.[4]

A practitioner moving to another practice setting would, then, have to learn the new group's ways of doing things (cf. Cook and Yanow, 2011 [1993], p. 370). Here is the organizational *cultural* dimension of practicing: a practice's ways of knowing and doing enact collective values, beliefs, and feelings. Petroski talks at length about "the *Press*" way of doing things, at times comparing it with other newspapers' delivery practices. He also notes how paperboy practices changed over time, responding to new styles in newspapering and new modes of delivery (automobiles replacing bikes and therefore adults replacing pre-adolescents). It is not only the newspaper's demise that would constrain one's becoming a *Press* delivery person; its organizational culture would have to be learned, which can only be done within the practice itself.

6. *Evaluating a practice*. Evaluative criteria for judging the performance of the practice are grounded in each practicing: "[J]oining and participating in a practice necessarily involves attempting to achieve the standards of excellence operative in the practice at that time" (Yanow and Tsoukas, 2009, p. 17). Neither Groopman's novice surgeon, focusing on clarity and effectiveness, nor Petroski, on neat, uniform folding and on non-exploding flipping, is inventing these standards. Each, in effect, internalizes the criteria for acceptable work displayed by masters in each practice. In Petroski's case, we watch him watching how paperboys' papers stack up while listening to their stories about flipping, collecting, and so on, aiming for a "properly folded" paper.

Evaluative measures are a shared property of the practice, put into play by masters who seek to maintain self- and other-recognition as such, as well as by novices who seek to become recognized as members of that practice.[5] In dispersed organizations, in which practitioners, from forest rangers to "street-level bureaucrats" (Kaufman, 1960; Lipsky, 1980; Prottas, 1979; Weatherly, 1979), toil beyond the purview of supervisors, internalizing the practice's evaluative criteria is crucial, from the perspectives of both personal conduct and managerial oversight.

7. *Becoming a master.* Mastery is achievable:

> [W]ith every successful day, a veteran paperboy became more convinced of his talents. . . . [He] could count his draw faster, fold his papers faster, pack his bag faster, ride his bike faster, flip his papers faster, finish his route faster. . . . He flipped his 120 papers on days that younger boys doorknobbed their fifty. (pp. 270–271)

This "flow" and its aesthetic dimensions do not always come quickly. It was not until his seventh year of training, writes Gawande, that "a simple slice through skin [had] begun to seem like nothing, the mere start of a case" (2002, p. 22). "Graduating" from focal to subsidiary awareness has an appeal, as he notes with respect to what made him want to become a surgeon: ". . . not to be an amateur handed the knife for a brief moment, but someone with the confidence to proceed as if it were routine" (2002, p. 16). Observing that a resident "begins with none of this air of mastery" (2002, p. 16), Gawande describes the process of developing and internalizing the identity of "Doctor."

Reflecting on his learning, Petroski shows how much of his knowledge has moved to subsidiary awareness:

> Folding and flipping papers had by now become second nature. I could do it in my sleep, I could practically deliver my route with my eyes closed, my legs knowing the distance between the houses and my arms the distance to the stoops. But I always kept my eyes open to see where the papers landed. . . . By the end of my first summer delivering papers, my whole body and mind had become accustomed to beginning at Linden Boulevard and turning at the cemetery. . . . To alter the familiar course was to invite confusion. Whenever I deviated from the routine, instead of delivering my papers by instinct I had to think. . . . (pp. 186–187)

11.1.2 The Problematic of Mastery-Learning: Enter the Life-Cycle

Becoming a competent practitioner is central, then, to practice theorizing: learning, achieved through repeated acts using practice-relevant tools, is expected to lead novices to mastery. Table 11.1 summarizes the theorized relationships between these two stages—novice and master—from the perspectives of learning, tool-awareness, and the surprises that affect the latter.

But what about *being* a master? Introducing transitional stages between novice-ry and mastery, as in the guilds' three-stage or Dreyfus and Dreyfus' (2005) five-stage models, Table 11.2a, while adding other aspects of practice theorizing, underscores what Table 11.1 highlights: novices and advanced

Table 11.1 From novice-ry to mastery

	Novice-ry	Mastery
Learning	repeated practicing	—
In focal awareness	"how" and "what": tools, movements, intended action, . . .	"what" (e.g. content, in teaching) or "nothing" (see below)
In subsidiary awareness	—	"how": tools, movements; the "nothing" of a fugue state ("what must be done *simply is done*," Dreyfus and Dreyfus, 2005, p. 788; emphasis added)
Surprises/ puzzles	"everything" is new and in focal awareness	irregularities, extended "interruptions" (leading from subsidiary to focal awareness)

Table 11.2a Nuancing the move from novice to master: stages of learning

	Novice-ry			Mastery	
Guild	Apprentice		Journeyman		Master
Dreyfus and Dreyfus (2005)	Novice	Advanced beginner	Competence	Proficiency	Expertise
Focal awareness	on tools, movements, intended action, . . .			on content (e.g. in teaching) or on "nothing"	
Subsidiary awareness	—			tools, movements (e.g. a fugue state; "what must be done *simply* is done," Dreyfus and Dreyfus, 2005, p. 788, emphasis added)	
Surprises/ puzzles	"everything" is new			"interruptions," irregularities	

beginners learn, filling in what is missing from practice know-how on the road to mastery; journeymen learn to become competent, proficient, and expert; masters, lacking nothing, need no further learning.[6]

Adding the "conscious competence" model[7] crosses degrees of mastery—competence—with awareness of that competence, producing four stages: unconscious incompetence, where one is not aware of what, specifically, one needs to learn; conscious incompetence, where one becomes aware of specific missing knowledge or ability (and where explicit, "deficit-directed" learning can begin); conscious competence, when one is fully focused on—attending to—what one is intending to do (an intentional-attentional practice); and unconscious competence, in which practice elements that had been in focal awareness have moved to a subsidiary realm of tacit knowledge.

Mapped against the other models (see Table 11.2b), this one's first stage, unconscious incompetence, extrudes to the left, introducing the conceptual

Table 11.2b Practicing across the life-cycle
(New columns and rows in italics; vertical lines are intentionally skewed)

<table>
<tr><th></th><th>Pre-novice</th><th colspan="5">Novice-ry</th><th colspan="5">Mastery</th><th colspan="2">Post-mastery</th></tr>
<tr><td>Guild nomenclature</td><td></td><td colspan="2">Apprentice</td><td colspan="6">Journeyman</td><td colspan="2">Master</td><td colspan="2"></td></tr>
<tr><td>Dreyfus and Dreyfus (2005)</td><td></td><td>Novice</td><td colspan="3">Advanced beginner</td><td colspan="2">Competence</td><td colspan="3">Proficiency</td><td>Expertise</td><td colspan="2"></td></tr>
<tr><td>Conscious competence model</td><td>Unconscious incompetence</td><td colspan="3">Conscious incompetence</td><td colspan="4">Conscious competence</td><td colspan="3">Unconscious competence</td><td colspan="2"></td></tr>
<tr><td>Life-cycle of practicing</td><td>Pre-practice choosing, informing</td><td colspan="2">"Just learning"</td><td colspan="5">Practicing</td><td colspan="3">Maintaining</td><td>Declining due to illness or age</td><td>Retiring</td></tr>
<tr><td>Focal awareness</td><td>Self: traits, inclinations, emotions</td><td colspan="2">tools, movements, intended action, . . .</td><td colspan="8">content (e.g. in teaching) or "nothing" (e.g. a fugue state; "what must be done simply is done")</td><td colspan="2">bodily and/or mental state(s), including movements</td></tr>
<tr><td>Subsidiary awareness</td><td>—</td><td colspan="2">—</td><td colspan="8">tools, movements</td><td colspan="2">?</td></tr>
<tr><td>Surprises/puzzles</td><td>"everything"</td><td colspan="2">"everything," in a more directed way</td><td colspan="8">"interruptions," irregularities</td><td colspan="2">body/mind-generated irregularities</td></tr>
</table>

possibility of an earlier point on the novice-to-mastery progression. Here is Petroski trying on the idea of joining *The Press* and practicing on his own, on the bed, in the driveway, and in the street in front of his house before his first day on the job. Trying to produce a good finished "product," he is not yet aware of all he does not know. Considering a pre-novice phase with its own modes of learning raises the possibility of a counter-phase at the other end of the practitioner-practice life-cycle: post-mastery (retirement; changes spawned by illness or age) and its implications for learning. The idea of such a life-cycle with variegated modes of learning challenges the linear, deficit-remedying view. As Lampert (2010, p. 1) notes about practice language and teaching, ". . . the infinitive form [to teach] can suggest that the [practice] action is to occur in the future, after something is learned, while the [gerund] form teaching allows us to hold out the possibility that *learning also occurs while doing the work*" (original emphasis). The master, in this view, may also be engaged with learning—although not the deficit-filling learning implied by the future orientation.

The concept of novelty sheds further light on the variability of practice-learning across a practice's life-cycle. Learning processes that lead to the formal start of practice-learning—individuals' decisions to educate themselves about practicing, bits of prior knowledge shaping those decisions, and the processes that bring phenomenological priors (personal background, a priori knowledge) to bear on such choices—may all be generated by or generate further novelty for the prospective practitioner. On showing up for his first day of work, Petroski experienced a shocking initiation ritual, itself a form of learning (missing from the practice literature), which made him miss that day's formal instruction (2002, pp. 78–79). From such unexpected novelty, new practitioners move to the "anticipated novelty" that suffuses their early practice phases: all is now potentially surprising, as expectations meet practice realities. Unexpected novelty returns when facing injury, illness, or age-related changes.

Mastery-learning is less self-evident. From a practice-life-cycle perspective, mastery is not just novice-ry's end state, but something needing maintaining, also a form of learning, albeit different from novice-learning. It can also require change-oriented learning in response to new circumstances. Learning of either form is not always easy, as Gawande (2002, p. 29) notes: "With repetition, a lot of mental functioning becomes automatic and effortless . . . Novel situations, however, usually require conscious thought and 'workaround' solutions, which are slower to develop, more difficult to execute, and more prone to error." Indeed, master-practitioners in all manner of fields are known to disregard evidence of practicing that is no longer effective. Both maintenance- and change-learning mean reclaiming for focal awareness some of what has been subsidiary, often for an extended period of time. In submerging focal awareness of materials and processes, has a master's inclination (and perhaps ability) to learn been "unlearned" in ways that might contribute to mastery-practice problems?

11.2 An End to Inquiry? Mastery and Learning

> It would be as foolish to think we have reached
> the limits of human knowledge
> as it is to think we could even know everything.
> There is still room enough to get better,
> to ask questions of even the dead,
> *to learn from knowing when our simple certainties are wrong.*
>
> —Atul Gawande (2002, p. 201; emphasis added)

We expect novices to make mistakes; that, after all, is part of practice-learning. What about when masters err? Misflipping is not the only sort of practice complication, and work-practice stories are rife with examples of masters who assume that they have and know all the answers. At best, such certainty—albeit perhaps manifesting passionate commitment to the practice—can lead to inattention; at worst, to malfeasance of one sort or another. Novelty is, in a sense, defended against (cf. Kuhn, 1970, on scientific practice-communities' normal science resisting innovations from marginal members); and learning cannot take place if masters are not prepared to recognize that they, or their certainties, might be wrong.[8] Such recognition requires the interruption of mastery's regularized practices in ways that return certain aspects to focal awareness. Complete disruptions, occasioned by crises, rare events (as when the roof caves in; Christianson et al., 2009), the unusual (Garud et al., 2011; see also Weick, 1993; Weick and Roberts, 1993), and other acts that startle, are, of course, hard to ignore and may lead to change-focused learning. What about other sorts of acts that should—for the sake of good or better practicing—bring about disruptions in regularized actions, but do not? Might some habits of mind that are crucial to "practice-awareness" be "unlearned" in moving to mastery, thereby explaining an "unwillingness" or "inability" to engage in practice-inquiry when problems arise?

Table 11.3 Types of surprise and attendant response

Type of surprise	Malfunction	Temporary breakdown		Total breakdown
		Mild	Persistent	
Type of response	Coping in a way still absorbed in the task at hand	Attention to the task	Reflective planning	Analytical/theoretical reflection

Adapted from Yanow and Tsoukas (2009, Table 1).

In the subsidiary work-process awareness that characterizes mastery, reflective self-inquiry or self-explanation is no longer at the fore, explaining the tacit-knowledge character of "theories-in-use" (Argyris and Schön, 1974). Practice-related focal-to-subsidiary-awareness shifts also explain discrepancies between theories-in-use and "espoused theories" (Argyris and Schön, 1974): explicit awareness of and articulateness with respect to one's theories of action, formed during novice-ry, become submerged the more, and the longer, one practices. As practicing increasingly responds to "facts on the ground," enactments may well diverge from espousals, the latter having been forged in an earlier moment on the learning path toward mastery and fixed in that time.[9] Will Groopman's surgeon, perhaps facing practice-problems twenty years down the road, remember that he chose "clarity" and "effectiveness," or why?

It is clear that in mastery, the focal awareness necessary to novice-ry cannot be sustained; "performing" requires moving things to subsidiary awareness. Otherwise, the practitioner is like the centipede cellist Mstislav Rostropovich invoked in his master class with Yo Yo Ma (Sanders Theater, Harvard, 1976): asked what its 59th leg is doing when #36 is up, it freezes mid-stride, incapacitated of motion by the need to make tacit knowledge explicit;[10] or like Petroski's paperboys who were "not able to think about what they were doing *lest their hands lose their own train of thought*" (2002, p. 90; emphasis added). Still, that lack of focal awareness may lead to problems in mastery-level practice. Four "end of inquiry"-related issues frame possible avenues for exploration: surprises, human "tools," shortcutting, and reflective practice.

1. *Surprises.* Kinds of surprise, disturbance or interruption in regularized mastery-practicing have been usefully taxonomized, ranging from "malfunction" through "temporary breakdown" to "total breakdown" (Heidegger, 1962; Dreyfus, 1991; Knorr Cetina, 2001; see Table 11.3 and discussion in Yanow and Tsoukas, 2009).[11] Each of these calls into play a

different kind of improvisational response, ranging from spontaneous re-adjustments that do not require a shift in focus ("absent-mindedly" reaching for my glasses on top of my head) to the more mind-ful, requiring the practitioner to return practice minutiae from subsidiary to focal awareness. The literature treats such interruptions as intrusions on the master's focus, their impact to be overcome with the quick return of practice elements to subsidiary awareness. Bringing practitioner life-cycle, practice-learning, and interruptions together, Table 11.4 highlights the practice-theoretical assumption that mastery is a matter of regularized practice unless (and until) surprised. Ongoing learning to sustain mastery, which may include an orientation to novelty, is absent.

What if, instead, such interruptions are part of the master's process of *learning to sustain mastery*, including when surprises challenge? Novelty, in this view, can enter only with persistent and total breakdowns—precipitated by surprises, now seen as generative—which capture the practitioner's attention; without surprises, regularized practice continues, as if practice-learning were absent. Moreover, such novelty might enter either individuals' practicing or the collective practice.

As surprises do not arrive labeled as such, however, responding to them requires a practitioner who is open to recognizing them, and practice theorizing predicated on encountering surprises needs to account for why some masters are more open to them than others. Among the anaesthesiologists they studied, for instance, Klemola and Norros (2001) identified two distinct practice modes, each associated with a different epistemic orientation, suggestive of different proclivities toward recognizing surprises and mastery-learning in response to them. Those acting out of an "underlying quest for certainty and detachment" characteristic of medical thinking's dominant technical-rational view followed a *reactive* habit of action, in which "observation [in practicing] is identified with passive reception of sensory images yielding a secure basis for knowledge" (by contrast with Groopman's surgeon-novice actively learning how to observe): "*Without recognition* of the inherent uncertainty of the process, the situation was experienced as predictable . . . ." Others, open to the idea of an unpredictable world, developed an interpretive practicing *with "reflective and critical capacities"* (Klemola and Norros, 2001, p. 462; emphases added). In addition to showing contrasting modes of practicing anaesthesiology (section 11.1.1, point 5), this suggests a link among predisposition, surprise-receptability, and knowing-learning. Might practitioner openness to novelty and inquiry require such a reflective-critical habit of mind?

Table 11.4 A practitioner-practice life-cycle: learning and surprises

	Prior to beginning	Novice/ Apprentice	Journeyman	Master		Late-life/inactive mastery
Life-cycle of practicing	pre-practice choosing	"just learning"	practicing	practicing-maintaining	practicing-changing	declining retiring
Practice-learning	informing; talking, thinking; testing out; trying it on	book; lab/clinic; imitation of physical movements (kinesthetic learning)	regularizing	none (according to practice theory); satisfaction derived from competent mastery	ongoing inquiry; openness, willingness to register surprise; reflectiveness; passionate humility	adjusting to bodily, cognitive, emotional, financial, health, and other status changes
Kind, source of: • **novelty/change;** • **surprises/puzzles/ interruptions/ disturbances;** • **intervention**	"everything"	"everything," but directed, focused; learning situational variations	none (according to practice theory); exceptions are brought to Master. Kuhn: potential sources = not-yet fully socialized members	does not see surprises unless/until they overwhelm; see Table 11.6	from margins, feedback, backtalk; see Table 11.6	body, mind, "human materials," "the practice," society

2. *Errors and human "tools."* Part of sustaining mastery entails dealing with errors or "misbehaviors," which also surprise, shock, and puzzle—colleagues, if not practitioners themselves. As noted above, we expect novices to make mistakes or to act in ways not fully in keeping with a practice's evaluative criteria; not so masters. But we know that master-induced errors occur: the surgeon, for instance, operating on the wrong leg; the senior manager misjudging a key meeting. In medicine, various work-arounds have been developed to forestall such errors (e.g. marking the leg requiring surgery with an X, or the use of lists, discussed below). But even then, "accidents" occur.

One explanation is that repetitive action—beyond the master's focal awareness—induces boredom and inattention. Petroski describes it this way:

> A paperboy on a bicycle spent a lot of time looking backwards, watching the fate of the last paper flipped even as he was reaching into his bag to grasp the next paper to flip. . . . [W]hat most caused us to miss was our ennui. The routineness of the task led us to dream of the perfect route. . . . Just as routinely, our dreams were shattered. . . . And it was just as well. The dream route would be a sure route to total and permanent boredom. . . . [T]edium and weariness lead to a lack of attention and carelessness, and these to errors and mistakes. . . . Seeing a pretty girl in every window would cause a paperboy to misflip his papers, not because their watching made him nervous, but because their being in every window made him care less. His weariness and dissatisfaction at the perfection of his route . . . would lead him into error and failure. (2002, pp. 269–70)

Presumably, re-flecting on the tossed paper—the semi-automatic turning to look backwards—and seeing it miss would return the paperboy's awareness to the matter at hand.

Practice theorizing, by and large, sources surprises in inanimate objects such as misplaced eyeglasses, malfunctioning automobiles, problematic fence-construction (Heidegger, 1962; Knorr Cetina, 2001, p. 178; Schön, 1987, p. 26, respectively); theoretical language references tools, materials (Schön, 1987), and equipment (Dreyfus, 1991). Schön's reflective-practice theorizing (1987, pp. 26–29) includes the surprise of the practitioner's materials "talking back" as she or he has a "conversation" with them. It is not clear that this engagement with objects malfunctioning or misplaced is helpful in theorizing masters' errors and other work-practice surprises in which it is humans who "talk back": doctoring, judging, lawyering, managing, ministering, nursing, teaching, therapizing—any arena that brings practitioners together with patients, clients, students, employees, and persons in other roles, even if these interactions are mediated by tests, files, stories, events, maps, plans, and the like. There are worse practice complications than misplacing eyeglasses. How do I handle this employee's problems, this client's demands, this patient's attraction for me (or mine for her), this student's excuses?

Because of their seriousness, "disturbances" to work practices involving human "materials" also need theorizing. Do the specifics of interacting with clients, patients, employees, customers, and so on submerge in awareness in the same way that material objects do? Gawande's observations on the relative ease of slipping the knife into skin after seven years of practice-learning suggests that something has shifted—and it is not, he infers, only the feel of the knife itself. In another example, four decades of developments in US medical practices have driven out the once-characteristic interpersonal "laying on of hands," leading current medical education to re-emphasize the centrality of the physician's human "materials." Groopman's (2007, pp. 168–169) observation concerning surgeons is tantalizing in its suggestion of theorizing possibilities: "[T]he conventional wisdom states that surgeons must have 'great hands'. . . . Most surgeons learn dexterity through repeated practice. Where they differ most . . . is in how they conceptualize a patient's problem. . . ." The kinesthetic dimensions having moved to subsidiary awareness, practitioners' attention can shift to the human dimensions.

Human-initiated disruptions might include surprises generated by solicited feedback (e.g. from peers, friends, or a consultant) or aspects of the practice itself (e.g. an annual performance evaluation). Surprises might also come unsolicited, as in backtalk from a "conversation" with one's human "materials," such as psychology professor Dr. T experienced with his students, leading him to change his customary practicing (Yanow and Tsoukas, 2009; further discussion follows in point 4 below).[12]

3. *Shortcutting*. Several human-focused practices seem to involve ways of delimiting a practitioner's engagement, shortcuts being a remedy for "too many 'human materials,' too little time." Groopman's narrated exchange during medical rounds (2007, pp. 236–238 *passim*, reformatted as dialogue) between a hematology fellow presenting a new case and the hematologist, a Dr. Stephen Nimer, presents one form:

> *Hematology fellow* (Hf): "I calculated all of his parameters, including his marrow findings. His calculated score puts him at intermediate-II risk on the IPSS. Based on his score, I would just transfuse him and not do anything beyond such supportive measures."

Dr. Stephen Nimer (SN): "I'm not interested in where he scores on the International Prognostic Scoring System . . ."
Hf: "Well, we could use a different scoring system, based on the [WHO] classification—"
SN: "You are missing the point."
Hf: "But he has IPSS intermediate-risk-II disease."
SN: "Wait a minute. . . . What's wrong with that? Did you really mean to say that?"
Hf: "Well, why not?"
SN: "Do you agree that the patient has MDS due to prior chemotherapy?" . . . beginning to lead the fellow down a different path [of reasoning].
Hf: "Yes."
SN: "Then you should know that the IPSS classification excludes patients who [names condition] . . . . [D]o you need to know the IPSS classification in order to take care of any patient?"
Hf: "Well, we calculate the IPSS all the time."
SN: "Yes, that's true. But last week this man's white blood cell count was 3,200, and in 7 days it fell to 1,900. . . . So I don't really care about the IPSS at this point. I know this is a man who is headed for big trouble, a man who's rapidly deteriorating and needs treatment right away. Not simply supportive measures like transfusion. Treatment right away."

"As Nimer later explained to me," Groopman adds (2007, p. 238),

> he routinely encounters young physicians who relinquish their own thinking and instead look to classification schemes and algorithms to think for them. . . . [Viewing the case] this way was . . . an artifact of the schema. . . . [Mr. X] was just one of dozens of patients the fellow would see in the course of a week. Algorithms and grids gave him shortcuts around the onerous process of assessing each of these dozens of complex cases.

Limited resources arising from organizational constraints is one reason for "algorithms and grids," and not just in medical practices. In the form of a "rush to diagnosis" via rules of thumb, shortcutting can also be a way to cope with ambiguity. Street-level bureaucracy theorists (Lipsky, 1980; Prottas, 1979; Weatherly, 1979) identified this in the work of practitioners in such settings—police officers, social workers, teachers, and other "front-line" workers whose practicing is characterized by perennial shortages of time and other resources along with a structurally-embedded lack of oversight and ambiguities in measures of success.[13] (For newer practitioners, such as Nimer's hematology fellow, such shortcutting might also be a manifestation of "premature mastery"—mimicking the aspect of a knowing master, analogous to Petroski's finished product, as a visible indicator of "achievement" in practices not easily assessable.) The various shortcuts—algorithms, grids, rules of thumb, standard operating procedures—developed en route to mastery commonly elevate inanimate over human "materials," backgrounding a focal awareness of the human "material" of one's practicing, thereby often shortchanging clients' human attributes in some way, similar in outcome to Petroski's ennui.

Shortcutting also appears in the form of "diagnosis momentum":

> Once a particular diagnosis becomes fixed in a physician's mind, despite incomplete evidence . . . the first doctor passes on his diagnosis to his peers or subordinates. . . . Diagnosis momentum . . . gains enough force to crush anything in its way. . . . When all the pieces of the clinical puzzle did not fit tightly together, I moved some of those that didn't to the side. I made faulty assumptions, seeking to make an undefined condition conform to a well-defined prototype, in order to offer a familiar treatment. (Groopman 2007, pp. 128–129)

Here, too, certainty shuts down openness to surprises or further inquiry, whether coping with resource limitations or with ambiguities: what does not fit is ignored. Analogous to Argyris and Schön's (1974) "self-sealing" managerial behaviors, such closing down leads to what Hawkesworth (2006, p. 10), in the context of research methods, called "evidence blindness," the inability "to accept evidence that impugns [one's] beliefs," despite the compelling character of that evidence.[14] Might reflective practice be a solution to this problematic?

4. *Reflective practice.* "Kevin and I have a history. Mine is right. His is wrong" (Hazle, 1992). Kevin had owned a nightclub in the city center for some time; "I" was the head of the city's redevelopment agency, charged with issuing and renewing licenses for such clubs. This newspaper report subtitle succinctly captures the kind of unreflective practice Schön sought to alter (1983, 1985, 1987, 1991; see also Lanzara, 1991; Ronco and Peattie, 1983).[15]

"I" s unmitigated sense of rightness and certainty echoes Nimer's hematology fellow, as do this minister's reflections on his practicing:

> Over the years . . . I have staked my ministry upon the church going in a particular direction—the direction I deemed proper and right. . . . I have advocated power to the people, but worked like hell to see to it that the people moved in the direction that I thought right and proper. And if I could convince myself that God was on my side, then I would be doubly rewarded—not only winning but being virtuous too. . . . I must learn some new behavior. . . . [Quoting from his course paper:] "I am persuaded that my behavior

> generates a closed system, with nontestable, self-fulfilling results. It is not a self-conscious design, but a result of my doing what comes naturally. . . . [I]t means that my spontaneous behavior produces a system that perpetuates mistrust and diplomacy—and that does not match my self-image . . ." (Argyris and Schön, 1974, pp. 46–47)

Schön's reflective-practice theory holds out the promise of reflection, prompted by surprise, to interrupt such certainty, (re-)opening inquiry and the possibility of change, as diagrammed in Figure 11.1.

regularized action → encounter of surprise → reflection → new action

Figure 11.1 The process of reflection in action[16]

Schön's theorizing was framed as a counter to the ills inculcated by a professional education that privileges rational-technical expertise over non-experimental, clinical, human realities. But comparing "I" and the minister shows that some master-practitioners are more primed than others to remaining open to inquiry: the latter put himself in a situation—a graduate course—in which the external intervention of readings and class discussions, plus explicit feedback from classmates' and instructors' comments, led him to see the problematic character of his practicing for others and the mismatch between its effect and his own self-image. The strength of that surprise (in the quote's last phrase) leads him to want to change his practicing.

By contrast, consider Dr. T, who was willing to appear "publicly not-knowing" in the midst of his lecture in response to backtalk from his students, saying, out loud, "I don't usually do this, but . . ." and improvising an immediate change in his practice (Yanow and Tsoukas, 2009). Arraying these three "masters"—"I," the minister, and Dr. T—on a continuum of reflection, in terms of the sources of their surprises and their contrasting responses, illustrates a range of potentially practice-disrupting disturbances or disconfirming feedback, as well as the presence or absence of an orientation toward learning (see Table 11.5).

Reflective-practice theorizing does not explain how to make masters more inclined to reflect on their practicing or, more crucially, how to induce an openness to inquiry, intellectual or emotional, when the discourses of mastery and expertise convey that not-knowing is tantamount to failure. Gawande (2002, p. 61), for instance, describes surgeons who "see faults everywhere except in themselves. They have no questions and no fears about their abilities. As a result, they learn nothing from their

Table 11.5 Interruptions: sources and responses

	Three "Masters"		
	"I" [agency head]	Minister	Dr. T [psychotherapist, professor]
Orientation toward self (attitude)	self-certain	(now) self-aware; questioning	self-confident, self-aware
Source of practice-disrupting or disconfirming interruption (surprise)	potentially, in clash with Kevin or reporter's questioning	graduate course: puts self in the way of external interventions from instructors, classmates	"backtalk" from his human "materials" (students)
Recognized?	no feedback invited or recognized (seemingly)	confrontation of self-image with new self-awareness and -perception; newly reflective-*on*-action	open to recognizing it; changes course; reflective-*in*-action
Orientation toward change/ Openness to novelty and learning	none visible; unreflective	cognitive; hypothetical potential for action (but see case)	willing to appear publicly not-knowing

mistakes and know nothing of their limitations." Karl Weick (personal communication, December 12, 2011) notes that police officers "are most likely to be killed their fifth year on the job," firefighters in their second to tenth year, "because they think they've seen it all and are not open to continued learning." Managers who enlist assistance in becoming reflective are seemingly unable to recreate such reflection in the consultant's absence (Giovan Francesco Lanzara, personal communication, July 11, 2008, reporting on his own and Schön's experiences). And Klemola and Noros' anaesthesiologists (2001, discussed above) show that differences in reflective capacity are likely rooted in a phenomenological existentialism.

"Reflective practicing," in other words, is not a universal trait, and we do not know what predisposes one master to reflect, rather than another. Groopman's surgeon-novice who began to imitate others "who worked with 'clarity and effectiveness'. . . also observed surgeons who did not seem especially clear in their judgments or effective in the OR. He tried to figure out what made the difference . . ." (Groopman, 2007, pp. 168–169). How did this particular surgeon learn to maintain a questioning attitude? What led the minister to enroll in a course that would challenge his way of being in his practice-world? How did Dr. T learn to be comfortable being publicly not-knowing? How did they break out of what the subsidiary awareness characteristic of mastery suggests should entail an unreflective practice, to a point where each could (re-)engage learning? And what kept "I" from doing so? Groopman again:

> If you do an experiment two times and you don't get results, then it doesn't make sense to do it the same way a third time. You have to ask yourself: What am I missing? How should I do it differently the next time? (2007, p. 239)

But what appears self-evident to Groopman is not so for all. If professional education fosters such blinkered certainty, foreclosing mastery-learning inquiry, might changes in graduate curricula or continuing education programs (commonly required to maintain a license to practice) help?

11.3 Returning Focal Awareness to Mastery: Reopening Inquiry

Learning may be just as much required *in* mastery as it is in *becoming* a master, especially where mastery-errors are concerned, albeit what mastery-learning entails is not entirely clear. What is clear is that reopening inquiry in mastery requires addressing both practices' structural characteristics (in particular, the return from subsidiary to focal awareness) and practitioners' individual characteristics, and the intertwinings of the two. Although heightened defensiveness may be a personality trait of some masters (perhaps situationally explained, in some cases), practice theorizing suggests that more is in play in mastery's response to "errors" than personal characteristics alone: the very mastery of a practice, in which tools-instruments-materials, persons, and bodily, mental, and perhaps emotional orientations toward them move from the practitioner's focal awareness to subsidiary awareness as the practice becomes ever more mastered, may foreclose an orientation toward and framework for anticipating other than ordinary action. If what characterizes mastery is the subordination of explicit learning as practice elements are relegated to subsidiary awareness, the challenge for master-level practice-learning is to resurface an orientation toward learning—in short, for masters once again to become learners. But if learning is associated with novice-ry, reopening inquiry potentially challenges masters' identity and status, calling on them to reclaim a form of focal awareness without inducing the feeling that they are returning to a novice state.

The particular character of mastery-learning is perhaps more readily evident when, for example, perceptual or kinesthetic learning of new ways to perform the same tasks is required to accommodate mental or physical changes due to injury, illness, or advancing years. This is more maintenance-learning than change-directed learning (even if it entails changing physical motions): one is, in a sense, learning to stay "the same." Depending on the extent of the "disturbance," this maintenance-learning can remain submerged or be brought back into focal awareness.[17]

These sorts of learning are difficult enough. Coming to recognize that one's mode of practicing, formed during novice-ry, is counter-productive (to wit, the minister) is, it seems, even more so, not only in emotional-psychological terms, but due to institutionalized aspects of mastery and of professional education. Intervening in a mastery that admits of no need to change hinges on reopening the knowing processes that led to mastery and which characterize its maintenance. Educating *toward* asking oneself questions, as Groopman (2007, p. 239) put it, means educating *away* from the equation of mastery with omniscience, often reflected in an accompanying egotism. Groopman captures the point this way: the mantra "it's a bad disease"

> acted as a buffer against the fear of failure, *a fear that even an accomplished physician . . . carries within himself.* It is healthy and beneficial to invest your ego in healing your patient's disease. But when your ego overshadows that goal, there lies danger. (2007, p. 240; emphasis added)

Working against that fear requires self-trust. Dr. T observed, echoing Klemola and Norros' (2001) anaesthesiologists, that if students generate no backtalk during the class session,

> you can't reflect. . . . It takes time to be reflective. I give myself permission to take time. . . . I trust myself to improvise: if I trust myself as a teacher, then *I can allow the unpredictable* [in the form of student backtalk] *to happen.* (Yanow and Tsoukas, 2009, p. 17, emphasis added)

The challenge is to educate for such self-trust without that turning into unbridled certainty. This could mean educating journeyman-novices (e.g. students in the final term of a professional degree program) to the drawbacks of subsidiary awareness and the need for lifelong learning in the form of reflective questioning, in a way that would enable them not only not to mimic omniscience (as the hematology fellow seems to do), but also to remain open to inquiry in mastery.

Altruism (Monroe, 1996), a desire to combat complicity (Ghorashi and Wels, 2009), or "passionate humility" (Yanow, 2009) might be character traits requisite for producing such openness; observing Dr. T suggests two others. First, remaining open to inquiry—making the self "more permeable," in his words—may entail making that inquiry accessible to others involved in the practicing. For this, theorizing human "materials" is essential. And inviting joint inquiry into practicing appears itself to rest on a willingness to be visibly "not-knowing"—an operational definition, in some sense, of being "taken by surprise." When Dr. T says, out loud, "I don't usually do this, but . . .," he makes his inquiry "public" (within the practice setting), rendering his thought processes and actions—his decision-making—more observable (permeable), his inquiry more accessible, and his rationale more transparent. Gawande makes a similar point, quoting Dr. Richard Bohmer: " 'The surgeon needs to be willing to allow himself *to become a partner* [with the rest of his team] *so he can accept input*' " (2002, pp. 29–30, emphasis added; cf. van Woerkum and Aarts, 2011, p. 180, on "projective hearing," which "presupposes a willingness to listen").[18] This seems to entail a certain emotional self-knowledge, being self-questioning but not defensive, embarrassed, or ashamed. It counters the saying about surgeons which Gawande (2002, p. 15) quotes: " 'Sometimes wrong; never in doubt.' "

This willed openness contradicts the hidden curriculum (Snyder, 1973) of a professional education that educates to expertise operationalized as omniscience—or even to "expert audacity," which Gawande (2007b) defines as courage, wits, and improvisation. The willingness to be publicly open to inquiry—to (appear to) be "non-expert"—requires the readiness to relinquish the sense of control of the situation and/or of others (although not necessarily of oneself). It means living with possible anxieties aroused by not-knowing or by being perceived, publicly, as not-knowing (Yanow and Tsoukas, 2009). This willingness seems to require an other-regardingness—a Buberian "I–Thou"—that is part of setting ego aside and allowing others to share the inquiry stage: humility.[19]

D. K. Cohen and Moffitt (2002, pp. 5–6[20]) illustrate what this stage-sharing might look like—a publicly not-knowing, permeable self willing to relinquish omniscience in favor of reflective inquiry (and perhaps change) in the midst of mastery—in classroom teaching practices:

> The capability to improve in this case would include knowing enough [about the topic] to build on. . . . It would include knowing how to learn—i.e., how to use the examples with a few students, to see how they do and then revise. To do such things teachers also would have to know how to step outside their practice, to observe and revise performance as they go, and be willing to abandon practices that work poorly. . . . [W]hen teachers learn to help students

> write better compositions, they acquire professional knowledge as they realize a central professional value: helping others by virtue of specialized knowledge. They advance their most crucial professional interest, succeeding as teachers, by helping students to succeed. This mutually reinforcing system of improving knowledge, realizing values, and advancing interests is [as] crucial to capability as the potential to improve.

Such openness to inquiry involves according legitimacy to others' local knowledge,[21] whether of situations or of themselves, and perhaps even caring. Two architectural practice-learning sessions (crits) described by Schön (1987, chs. 3–5, pp. 142–152), each involving an instructor and his student, illustrate the differences in approach. Dani, master architect and professor, challenges Michal to discover what it is that she, herself, wants to do in the design exercise. That is his main intervention, along with sketching out some ways she might think about (or inquire into) the situation. He communicates, in not so many words, that he cares about Michal's own sense of architectural practice; she returns with a design that expresses *her* vision, not one that tries to second-guess *his*. It is powerful feedback on the effectiveness of his teaching practice, one of joint inquiry much more reciprocal than what architect-professor Quist establishes with Petra (cf. Katz and Shotter, 1996; also Clark and Mishler, 1992, p. 346 on the "voice of medicine" vs. the "voice of the lifeworld").[22] By not embodying the role of the omniscient expert creating an atmosphere in which questioning is not welcomed, Dani makes himself, and his practice, more permeable, allowing the unpredictable to happen.

As noted above, Schön (1987) located the closure-to-inquiry problem in the design and content of university-based professional education: learning the rules (classroom-based education) and then applying these, in rational-technical fashion, to practice (versus deducing or inferring rules via practicum-based education, such as case-based or clinical teaching; cf. Hummel, 2001; Yanow, 2004). Such programs might be considered obvious places for introducing practice novelties. Yet science was born out of not only a desire to know, but also a desire to control (initially, the natural-physical world it engaged; later, the social world); and work-practices—with their credentialing, licensing, and other institutional aspects—draw on many of those same characteristics of systematic and testable controls. To the extent that their increasing professionalization over the last several decades joins ideas about what it means to be scientific, work-practices may be inextricably tied to visions of omniscient expertise and the capacity for control, driving out the think-ability of master-level inquiry. Countering this closure-to-inquiry problematic requires working with those institutions—the programs, departments, faculties, and associations—charged with maintaining various practices, including teaching, evaluating, and analyzing them.

Table 11.6 suggests some of the differences between traditional ideas about mastery and a more learning-focused mastery, and it frames additional areas in need of theorizing, including what maintenance-learning looks like. Is it "merely" the continuation of the status quo, ignoring situations that do not fit (à la cognitive dissonance), or is it a more (pro)active learning that sustains standard operating procedures? Does it deal with novelty, surprises or interventions? Kuhn's (1970) notion, for instance, that new ideas come from the margins of an epistemic community—from those not yet fully socialized into its mores, habits of thought, ways of experimenting and explaining—suggests a role for novices. Observational research, however, suggests that master-practitioners whose ways of seeing, knowing, and doing face within-practice challenges from the marginal ranks of the novitiate will hold on fiercely to their habituated acts (cf. Christianson et al., 2009). Here is another area needing additional theorizing.

Table 11.6 Inquiry/learning in mastery

	Mastery	
	Traditional view	**Learning-focused**
Orientation of mastery-learning	None, or oriented toward retaining license or credential	Proactive practice-maintaining or -changing
Mastery-learning	No focal awareness of tools, other elements of practicing, until surprised; focal awareness then varies (see Table 11.3)	Permeable self, open to being surprised, willing to register surprise, to be publicly not-knowing; reflective inquiry and learning; passionate humility
Intervention character	Unexpected surprise, external to the individual or to the practice	Self-initiated (self-inquiring), in addition to surprise-generated
Intervention type/source (examples)	Workplace evaluation Client feedback (e.g., complaints) Challenges from the margins (à la Kuhn) "Rare events" (e.g. RR museum roof falling in, Christianson et al. 2009)	Course; teacher; classmate ("Minister") Invited consultant Solicited feedback Backtalk ("Dr. T") Surprise Traditional types/sources (box to left)

11.4 Toward Comparative Practice Studies: Concluding Thoughts

> How many papers a paperboy had to draw was math;
> how he delivered them was engineering.
> How many papers could fit in the bag was math;
> how many more could be fit in was engineering.
> How the bicycle moved with its load was science;
> how he managed to pedal it up a hill was engineering.
> How the papers were supposed to be flipped was science;
> how the papers were flipped was engineering.
> How the papers landed where they did was science;
> how the papers got there was engineering.
> How the newsprint soiled his hands was science;
> how he washed it off was engineering.
> How much a paper boy had to collect was math;
> when he collected it was engineering.
> How many raindrops danced on the head of a paperboy was
>   math and science;
> how he avoided half of them on his speeding bike was engineering.
> And simple as the theory might be, it was never that easy in practice.
>
> —Petroski (2002, pp. 354–355; arranged strophically)

Theorizing "practicing" brings practitioner bodies, minds, and emotions together with the "tools" or "materials" entailed; in organizational settings of various sorts (the newspaper room, the hospital, the classroom); in the context of systems or networks of other practitioners and the institutions that enable, support, and discipline the practice in structured and more informal ways (e.g. professional associations, licensing boards, the state, interpersonal relations); with the evaluative criteria held by a community of practitioners (from a practice's "accepted modes of practicing" to explicit Codes of Ethics at the institutional level). Practices and practitioners are intertwined: practice-learning is social, material, and kinesthetic in ways that reflect practitioners' practice-related traits. That is, work and worker, collective and individual, are mutually influencing, with practices "enrolling" future practitioners who have and/or develop particular, practice-related traits. This fit between practicing and practitioner comes into focus especially in conceptualizing the learning characteristic of a pre-novice phase and what leads certain individuals to choose certain practices.

Given the conserving character of practicing, novelty has hitherto not had a central place in its theorizing. Comparative practice studies—whether comparing different modes of the same practice or looking across different practices—could be useful in conceptualizing the circumstances in which novel aspects might be introduced, such as interventions for improving practicing and practice-learning, including exploring the utility of one arena's practices for others. For instance, City et al. (2009; see also Hough, 2009) have brought medical rounds to classroom practices.[23] Checklists, long used in aviation and other practices, have been adopted in hospitals worldwide (cf. Gawande, 2009).[24] Comparative practice studies, especially of those entailing human "materials," might make novel forms of practice-learning more visible, including those perhaps particular to the "helping professions" (cf. D. K. Cohen, 2011, ch. 3) along with a fuller range of nonformal education: buddying, preceptoring, and mentoring (Hunter et al., 2008); learning "unintentionally" while focusing on something else (e.g. having lunch with one's co-practitioners; see Orr, 1996); learning through "rejecting fragments [of a practice] that repel us" (D. K. Cohen, 2011, p. 25; cf. Groopman, 2007, p. 168). Replacing "engineering" in the section epigraph with "practicing" suggests the kind of learning that comparative studies might theorize in looking across the life-cycles of practicings and practitioners.

In addition to such sources as surprises, disruptions, and reflexivity, novel solutions to longstanding practice problems might emerge from taxonomies of errors tied to a practice's life-cycle, assessing what is related to the practice, what to the practitioner, what to institutional or some other factors, and what to the intersections among these. Does practice-learning vary across types of practicing, and do different practicings handle errors differently? Greater attention to taxonomies of surprises has emerged, in medicine, from "erratic behavior" or "transgression of proper professional boundaries" (Gawande, 2002, p. 100) and the refusal of both practitioners and their co-workers to acknowledge and engage these explicitly, resulting in operating room errors affecting patients' bodies or lives. Or consider the "functional addict" with drug or alcohol problems, or early stage Alzheimer's, which may prompt co-worker cover-ups. Error-focused inquiry intended to generate novel solutions might be institutionalized in a kind of organizational learning process, in particular in a "no-fault" organizational culture (such as Ron, Lipshitz, and Popper's, 2006, airforce *tahkir* processes; cf. Gawande, 2002, pp. 57–64 ff., on hospital M & M—Morbidity and Mortality—conferences, a possible equivalent to the *tahkir*). Within-practice disagreements as to purpose and procedure, noted by D. K. Cohen (2011, pp. 5–6), might also be sources of practice innovations. These, too, need further exploration, as does reconstituting practicing in the face of change.

As suggested here, it might make sense to think of the life-cycle of a practice itself, its phases, from pre-novice to post-mastery, entailing their own forms of practice-learning—from learning as one informs oneself about a practice and makes a decision about whether or not to pursue it, to decline- and retirement-learning. One might envision a structural approach, such as Greiner's (1972), identifying stages and their evolution over a practice's life-cycle of innovation and stability, or an "adult development" approach (Erikson, 1982; Levinson, 1978, 1996), identifying the "infancy," "adolescence," "mature adulthood," and other life phases of a practice. One might also theorize the intersection of practice and practitioner life-cycles, the latter's orientation toward a particular form of work or ways of learning–knowing–doing leading not only to the decision to pursue one practice over another, but also to choices informing the shape of the chosen practice. What might lead a social scientist, for instance, to the practice of ethnographic methods rather than survey research, and even to a particular form of ethnographic practice?

We are accustomed to thinking of organizations as containers for practices, the practicing—managing, doctoring, nursing, teaching—taking place within them. Might it be useful to treat an organization itself as a practice? If, for instance, we conceived of the B&O Railroad Museum (Christianson et al., 2009) as a practice rather than as an organization, what might we see differently in its unfolding acts in response to the roof disaster? Similarly, it might be useful to explore the differences and overlaps between practice theory and organizational theory in the notions of routine, surprise, breakdown, etc. Christianson et al. (2009), again, argue for considering organizational learning as emerging from sudden, and profound, ruptures in routines, calling on organizations to "enhance their response repertoire for dealing with interruptions" (Christianson et al., 2009, p. 13)—an idea central to the practice literature. Conceptualizing human-focused practices as *always* entailing surprises and a set of available responses to these is a potentially generative notion for conceiving of mastery-learning.

Appendix: A Note on Method

The narratives analyzed here are informed by an ethnographic sense of observing, interviewing, and inquiry. Attending to what happens when specific practitioners do what they do in specific practice contexts, they are thickly detailed descriptions of practicing and of what "the" problem is. Evocative en masse, yet ordinary to their core, these narratives' observed and recorded details are likely to escape attention not trained on the everydayness to which ethnographic observation routinely attends. Furthermore, such detail makes comparative analysis possible.

Although other approaches, such as actor-network theory, also look at practices with particular attention to the place and role of non-human objects in them, my own orientation toward this ethnographic form of studying practices was forged by my professional education and experiences as a community organizer and my consequent engagement with participant-observer ethnography. The mode of inquiry that informs this chapter was worked out in a Spring 2005 graduate seminar on reflective practice (although its seeds were likely planted in Don Schön's Fall 1976 MIT seminar on professional education). The 2005 course engaged the question, "Can we recognize reflective practice when we see it?" As my students were themselves experienced, mid-career practitioners, I asked them to identify a manager they knew through work, whether paid or volunteer, whom they and/or others considered to be an excellent practitioner, or a good one. Students were to study that person from the perspective of whether she or he manifested the characteristics of a reflective practitioner as described by Schön (1987; see also Schön, 1991; Ronco and Peattie, 1983). They were to try to arrange to observe that person in the midst of an event or setting in which those characteristics might be visible and video- or audio-tape the session or, failing that, make observational (ethnographic) fieldnotes. In a follow-up interview, they were to discuss what they had seen with the practitioner. In the second half of the course, we studied the tapes or notes together, discussing our analyses. This is how I initially met Dr. T, described here and in Yanow and Tsoukas (2009).

Waldo (1968) and Czarniawska-Joerges and Guillet de Monthoux (1994) also argued for the use of material written for other than academic purposes—in their cases, novels and plays—to derive lessons for management and organizational studies. (For a taxonomy of the uses of literature in organizational studies, see De Cock and Land, 2005, pp. 519–22.) Although I find that kind of analysis useful, it is done for rather different purposes than what I have in mind here: the use of practitioners' reflective observations on their own or others' practices. This is my methodological understanding of Maclean's narrative and how Weick could put it to use as he did.

Acknowledgments

I am indebted to David Cohen and Maggie Lampert for the intellectual nudge that pushed me to re-engage these matters, set aside in the move from Hayward to Amsterdam; to David and Jerry Davis for the invitation to present the first version of this chapter at the University of Michigan's ICOS seminar; to Cees van Woerkum for conversations linking this theorizing to musical practices; to Karl Weick for his enthusiastic response to a previous draft, harking to theorizing high reliability organizations and firefighting and his own paperboy days; to Hari Tsoukas for ongoing support and challenging and careful editing; and to Katharina Dittrich, Alain Guiette, Merlijn van Hulst, and Davide Nicolini for comments on earlier versions. Revisions of the ICOS paper were presented as the Virginia Tech Center for Public Administration and Policy's 2013 High Table lecture, as a keynote address at the 2012 Organizational Learning, Knowledge, and Capabilities conference, the 3rd International Symposium on Process Organization, and Vienna's Institute for Advanced Studies, Wageningen, Tilburg, and Paris-Dauphine universities, and Rishon L'tsion's College of Management Academic Studies. My thanks to the organizers of and participants in these sessions for the opportunities and the discussions.

Notes

1. Lifelong learning is an extensive field of inquiry. See, e.g., Jarvis (2010) for discussion of its many components, including those relevant to practice theory.
2. I make this point in light of a doctoral student's recent comment that his advisors insisted he could only do a practice-focused dissertation on a "professional" practice. The old sociology of work demarcation between professions—ministering, doctoring, lawyering—and other occupations, and their further classification into major and minor ones (Glazer, 1974), have, by and large, lost their theoretical purchase. Theorists' uses of misplaced eyeglasses and stuck gear-shifts also belie that argument. Relatedly, MacIntyre (1985) distinguished bricklaying and planting turnips as non-practices from architecture and farming, which he considered practices, and Dreyfus and Dreyfus (2005) demarcate "crude" skills (e.g. walking, driving) from "subtle" ones (e.g. music, sports, surgery). I find these distinctions untenable: theorized attributes of practicing appear to hold equally for planting and farming; and walking can be a subtle skill for someone recovering from a stroke.
3. Similarly, a survey of thoracic surgeons shows variability, from 50% to less than 5%, in certain procedures (e.g. posterolateral thoracotomy, lobectomy; Israel Waismel-Manor, March 24, 2011 listserv post citing a 2008 article by Rocco,

Internullo, Cassivi, Van Raemdonck, and Ferguson). Cf. Traweek (1988), on the different ways Japanese and US high energy physicists do physics.

4. This relates to the identity dimensions of some practicing—e.g. "Dad" who enacts his workplace Army Captain identity at home, or statements equating the individual with the practice ("I am a doctor"; see point 7 below). It is one place where emotions enter the picture; being judged a "good" practitioner, or a failure, is another. On the absence of emotions in practice theorizing, see 11.1.1, point 2.
5. Which may explain why "newbies" are often more hidebound than masters, who see where "rules" may be interpreted more flexibly.
6. In Dreyfus and Dreyfus' fifth stage, expertise, the expert, unlike the proficient performer, not only sees *what* needs to be done, but sees immediately *how* to do it: as they remark with reference to driving, "what must be done, simply is done" (Dreyfus and Dreyfus, 2005, p. 788)—as if thought were unnecessary. To be fair, they do see some place for thinking: "while most expert performance is ongoing and unreflective, the best of experts, when time permits, *think before they act*" (emphasis added). It is, in their view, a special kind of thinking—not "calculative," but "deliberative"—happening only "when time permits." This deliberative thinking does not involve considering the rules underlying the practice or the reasons for choosing possible actions, but instead reflects "upon the goal or perspective that seems evident to [the practitioner] and upon the action that seems appropriate to achieving that goal" (Dreyfus and Dreyfus, 2005, p. 789). Deliberative thinking does not replace intuition, but improves upon it; cf. Forester (1999).
7. The source of this model is unknown. I learned about it from a then-student, Dr. Jamal Granick (ca. 2003), a practicing psychotherapist who encountered it in his professional studies. Karl Weick (personal communication, December 12, 2011) confirms Granick's and my inability to locate a source. For one genealogy, see Chapman (2003). Some posit a fifth stage, reflective consciousness, in which practitioners are able to hold the unconscious, tacitly known, mastered elements of the practice in conscious (or perhaps semi-conscious) awareness while reflecting on what is happening as they engage those materials.
8. To the extent that, in organizational and management theory, leadership is equated with mastery, the closing down of inquiry is potentially damaging to the organization (see discussion in Collinson, 2012).
9. Which is not to say that discrepancies between word and deed are not meaningful. But I think this practice-oriented account of their origins might add useful theoretical dimensions to our understanding of the phenomenon. Lewin's (1951) notion that change requires "unfreezing," "moving," and "refreezing" seems yet another theorization of this point, where unfreezing entails moving know-how from subsidiary to focal awareness in order to re-engage it (see note 16). Still other literatures touch on "recurring action patterns" (M. D. Cohen, 2009) and the place of knowledge, including novel ideas and responses to

practice surprises, within them: organizational culture, identity, and learning (of a meaning-focused sort; Ybema and Yanow, 2011); reflective practice, discussed below; routines (e.g., Feldman and Pentland 2003); and the transfer or translation of local knowledge across boundaries (Bechky 2003, Yanow 2004). Including "collective mind" in the mix, Michael Cohen (2009, p. 445) added "habit." Although regularized action is one aspect of practicing, "practice" and "routine" are neither synonymous nor coterminous. Practice theorizing itself focuses elsewhere, seeking to explain less the repetitiveness of action than the constellation of acts, discourses, objects (materiality), and body (corporeality) that make "a practice" what it is (see, e.g., Littig, 2013 on high heels in tango dancing): the dynamic interactions among these component elements and how their relationships change during learning processes as focal awareness shifts.

10. Which is why reflection in the midst of practice is so difficult!
11. Surprise can also pose an emotional challenge or elicit an emotional response, as Louis (1980) also noted. Its relation to practicing needs theorizing, see M. D. Cohen (2009).
12. "Backtalk" and feedback are not synonymous: feedback can be solicited; "one does not ask one's materials to talk back—they just do, without being asked, when they resist going where the practitioner is trying to move them. . . . Feedback can come during ex post reflection; backtalk is more immediate . . . and unmediated . . ." (Yanow and Tsoukas, 2009, p. 10).
13. But see Maynard-Moody and Musheno (2003) and van Hulst, de Graaf, and van den Brink (2012, p. 444) for contrasting analyses showing street-level bureaucrats working to help clients.
14. The family resemblance across various formulations of this problematic suggest its extent and significance: "confirmation bias" in psychology, "theory-preserving perspectives" in scientific reasoning (Andrew Falk, personal communication, November 13, 2009), and "garden path problems"—"the potential to fixate on one point of view or hypothesis in problem solving" (Woods, 2000; thanks to Karl Weick for this reference).
15. Taking no position here concerning Cunliffe and Jun's (2005) argument that only "reflexivity," not "reflectivity," leads to change, I use the "ct" spelling in keeping with Schön's reflective practitioner, reflexivity's methodological centrality, and, as Joe Raelin (personal communication, December 27, 2006) notes, the differences in meaning suggested by their respective roots.
16. Both examples raise other questions. The reported account of educational rounds hopes for a day when all educators adhere to a coherent, national (US) model of effective teaching, missing the understanding that a single practicing may have different modes, reflecting local situatedness (see section 11.1.1, point 5), rendering a unified, national model an impossibility. Although hospital checklists essay to identify practice elements when practitioners are not under duress, as a compendium of items that are

capable of being explicitly named, their utility for practice aspects beyond focal awareness may be limited.

17. This orientation toward inquiry echoes in Schön's collaboration with Rein on reframing and "intractable policy controversies" (e.g. Rein and Schön, 1977; Schön and Rein, 1994), his solo work on metaphor (1979), a parallel Merlijn van Hulst drew to my attention, and his work with Argyris. Argyris and Schön (1974, chs. 8, 10) promoted "Model II behavior"—calling on managers or executives not to make unilateral attributions concerning what other individuals or groups think or need—as the solution to problems created by a closed, self-sealing, attributive, self-certain mode of management ("Model I") whose source is defensiveness and which blocks self-inquiry. Its adoption could lead to a more group-based form of inquiry, inviting a kind of co-management rather than individual, authority-based management (see, e.g., Raelin, 2006; Raelin and Raelin, 2006). To what extent this is applicable across practices is not clear, although Ronco and Peattie (1983) does extend beyond managers.

    Lewin's ideas (see note 9) map onto the end of Figure 11.1:

    ... → reflection → unfreezing → moving [new action] → refreezing

    Fiol (2012), however, cautions against assuming that moving and refreezing mean that "old" knowledge has been "deleted," understanding "unlearning," instead, as *dis*placing prior knowledge while not necessarily wholly *re*placing it.

18. Technological innovations in one work arena can also be imported into others where they facilitate "normal" action and, even unintentionally, mastery-level maintenance. Consider the handles, pedals, and automatic "eyes" developed for wheelchaired and other persons to operate bathroom sinks and toilets, now in use for non-impaired action, including medical personnel's hygiene-related practices.

19. Remarking on the parallel between remaining open in mastery and "continued updating" in sensemaking, Karl Weick (personal communication, December 12, 2011) observed, "Master fire captains keep their edge by treating each fire as 'something I've never seen before.' They do have a routine structure . . . but they make only partial use of remembered fires as guides" to action in new cases.

20. Schulman (1993) has written about the way that managerial hubris—"people who have a belief they are infallible"—can derail an organization (cf. Collinson, 2012, p. 94). Similarly opposed to humility is Ron Westrum's "fallacy of centrality": the assumption made by those in "central" positions that if something serious were happening, they would know about it; and since they have heard nothing, nothing is happening (cited in Weick and Sutcliffe, 2007; Westrum's case is pediatricians who ignored evidence of child abuse until the early 1960s). I appreciate Karl Weick's pointing me to both of these.

21. The 2002 ms. has since been published as D. K. Cohen and Moffitt (2009). As I cannot locate this passage there, I cite the earlier version.

22. This phenomenological orientation, which underlies interpretive methodologies (see Schwartz-Shea and Yanow, 2012), is also related to Paolo Freire's (1970) pedagogical principle of beginning with what a student already knows and proceeding from there.
23. Schön himself appeared not to see the contrasts between Dani's and Quist's practices, nor did he theorize the scenarios' power or gender dimensions, or their intersections. On this point see also Schmidt (2000).
24. Their educational rounds bring principals, superintendents, union leaders, and teachers together as peers, thereby including the institutions regulating the practice (through their representatives) with the teacher-practitioners and treating teaching as a collective, context-specific undertaking, learned in the practicing itself and continuing on into mastery. Also combatting the rush to diagnosis and keeping their "hands dirty with the data" (in Schön's phrase, ca. 1976–1979), they report requiring the educational practitioners under study and themselves in their own consulting to dwell in the descriptive phase of research for 75% of their two-year contract time.

References

Argyris, C. and Schön, D. A. (1974). *Theory in Practice*. San Francisco, CA: Jossey-Bass.

Bateson, G. (1972). *Steps to an Ecology of Mind*. New York: Ballantine Books.

Bechky, B. A. (2003). Sharing meaning across occupational communities. *Organization Science*,14(3): 312–330.

Chapman, A. (2003). Conscious competence learning model. <http:// www.businessballs.com/consciouscompetencelearningmodel.htm#origins%20of%20conscious%20competence%20learning%20model>, accessed February 27, 2014.

Christianson, M. K., Farkas, M. T., Sutcliffe, K. M., and Weick, K. E. (2009). Learning through rare events: Significant interruptions at the Baltimore & Ohio Railroad Museum. *Organization Science*, 20(5): 846–860.

City, E. A., Elmore, R. F., Fiarman, S. E., and Teitel, L. (2009). *Instructional Rounds in Education*. Cambridge, MA: Harvard Education Press.

Clark, J. A. and Mishler, E. G. (1992). Attending to patients' stories. *Sociology of Health & Illness*, 14(3): 344–371.

Cohen, D. K. (2011). *Teaching and Its Predicaments*. Cambridge, MA: Harvard University Press.

Cohen, D. K. and Moffitt, S. L. (2002). The dilemma of implementation. In *Politics, Poverty, and Pedagogy*. Ms. (May), ch. 2.

Cohen, D. K. and Moffitt, S. L. (2009). *The Ordeal of Equality: Did Federal Regulation Fix the Schools?* Cambridge, MA: Harvard University Press.

Cohen, M. D. (2009). Reading Dewey: Some implications for the study of routine. In P. S. Adler (ed.), *The Oxford Handbook of Sociology and Organization Studies* (pp. 444–463). Oxford: Oxford University Press.

Collinson, D. (2012). Prozac leadership and the limits of positive thinking. *Leadership*, 8(2): 87–107.

Cook, S. D. N. and Yanow, D. (2011 [1993]). Culture and organizational learning. *Journal of Management Inquiry*, 20(4): 362–379.

Cunliffe, A. L. and Jun, J. S. (2005). The need for reflexivity in public administration. *Administration & Society*, 37(2): 225–242.

Czarniawska-Joerges, B. and Guillet de Monthoux, P. (eds.) (1994). *Good Novels, Better Management*. Chur, CH: Harwood.

Czikszentmihalyi, M. (1990). *Flow*. New York: Harper & Row.

De Cock, C. and Land, C. (2005). Organization/literature. *Organization Studies*, 27(4): 517–535.

Dreyfus, H. (1991). *Being-in-the-World*. Cambridge, MA: MIT Press.

Dreyfus, H. and Dreyfus, S. (2005). Expertise in real world contexts. *Organization Studies*, 26(5): 779–792.

Erikson, E. H. (1982). *The Life Cycle Completed*. New York: Norton.

Feldman, M. S. and Pentland, B. T. (2003). Reconceptualizing organizational routines as a source of flexibility and change. *Administrative Science Quarterly*, 48(1): 94–118.

Fiol, M. (2012). Organizational unlearning. Keynote address, International Conference on Organizational Learning, Knowledge, and Capabilities, Valencia, April 25–28.

Forester, J. F. (1999). *The Deliberative Practitioner*. Cambridge, MA: MIT Press.

Fox Keller, E. (1983). *A Feeling for the Organism: The Life and Work of Barbara McClintock*. San Francisco, CA: W. H. Freeman.

Freire, P. (1970). *Pedagogy of the Oppressed*. New York: Continuum.

Gallos, J. V. and Yanow, D. (1976). "Man cannot live by bread alone": A theory of chaplaincy. Seminar paper, "Professional Education" graduate seminar, Division for Study and Research on Education (SRE 202), MIT (Fall).

Garud, R., Dunbar, R. L. M., and Bartel, C. A. (2011). Dealing with unusual experiences. *Organization Science*, 22(3): 587–601.

Gawande, A. (2002). *Complications: A Surgeon's Notes on an Imperfect Science*. New York: Metropolitan Books.

Gawande, A. (2007a). *Better: A Surgeon's Notes on Performance*. New York: Metropolitan Books.

Gawande, A. (2007b). The checklist. *The New Yorker* (December 10).

Gawande, A. (2009). *The Checklist Manifesto: How to Get Things Right*. New York: Metropolitan Books.

Gherardi, S. (2009). Practice? It's a matter of taste! *Management Learning*, 40(5): 535–550.

Ghorashi, H. and Wels, H. (2009). Beyond complicity. In S. Ybema, D. Yanow, H. Wels, and F. Kamsteeg (eds.), *Organizational Ethnography* (pp. 231–253). London: Sage.

Glazer, N. (1974). The schools of the minor professions. *Minerva*, 12(3): 346–364.

Greiner, L. E. (1972). Evolution and revolution as organizations grow. *Harvard Business Review*, 50(4): 37–46.

Groopman, J. (2007). *How Doctors Think*. New York: Houghton Mifflin.

Hawkesworth, M. E. (2006). *Feminist Inquiry*. Philadelphia: Temple University Press.

Hazle, M. (1992). S. J. nightclub closes its doors, blames city. *San Jose Mercury News*, May 14, 1B.

Heidegger, M. (1962). *Being and Time*. New York: Harper & Row.

Hough, L. (2009). Round & round. *Ed.*, 53(1): 23–27.

Hummel, R. (2001). Kant's contributions to organizational knowledge: Do workers know something managers don't? Public Administration Theory Network Annual Conference, Leiden, June 21–23.

Hunter, C. L., Spence, K., McKenna, K., and Iedema, R. (2008). Learning how we learn: An ethnographic study in a neonatal intensive care unit. *Journal of Advanced Nursing*, 62(6): 657–664.

Jarvis, P. (2010). *Adult Education and Lifelong Learning* (4th edition). New York: Routledge.

Katz, A. M. and Shotter, J. (1996). Hearing the patient's "voice." *Social Science & Medicine*, 43(6): 919–931.

Kaufman, H. (1960). *The Forest Ranger: A Study in Administrative Behavior*. Baltimore, MD: Johns Hopkins University Press, for Resources for the Future.

Klemola, U.-M. and Norros, L. (2001). Practice-based criteria for assessing anaesthetists' habits of action: Outline for a reflexive turn in practice. *Medical Education*, 35(5): 455–464.

Knorr Cetina, K. (2001). Objectual practice. In T. R. Schatzki, K. Knorr Cetina, and E. von Savigny (eds.), *The Practice Turn in Contemporary Theory* (pp. 175–188). London: Routledge.

Kuhn, T. S. (1970). *The Structure of Scientific Revolutions* (2nd edition). Chicago, IL: University of Chicago Press.

Lampert, M. (2010). Learning teaching in, from, and for practice. *Journal of Teacher Education*, 61 (1-2): 21-34.

Lanzara, G. F. (1991). Shifting stories: Learning from a reflective experiment in a design process. In Donald A. Schön (ed.), *The Reflective Turn* (pp. 285–320). New York: Teachers College Press.

Lave, J. and Wenger, E. (1991). *Situated Learning*. New York: Cambridge University Press.

Levinson, D. J. (1978). *The Seasons of a Man's Life*. New York: Random House.

Levinson, D. J. (1996). *The Seasons of a Woman's Life*. New York: Ballantine.

Lewin, K. (1951). *Field Theory in Social Science*. New York: Harper.

Lipsky, M. (1980). *Street-Level Bureaucracy*. New York: Russell Sage Foundation.

Littig, B. (2013). On high heels: A praxiography of doing Argentine tango. *European Journal of Women's Studies*, 20(4): 455–467.

Louis, M. R. (1980). Surprise and sense making: What newcomers experience in entering unfamiliar organizational settings. *Administrative Science Quarterly*, 25(2): 226–251.

MacIntyre, A. (1985). *After Virtue* (2nd edition). London: Duckworth.

Maynard-Moody, S. and Musheno, M. (2003). *Cops, Teachers, Counselors: Stories from the Front Lines of Public Service*. Ann Arbor: University of Michigan Press.

Mincey, J. (2009). Re: Article on Sacred Harp singing at Brown. Post to fasola discussion list (Thursday, September 24).

Monroe, K. R. (1996). *The Heart of Altruism*. Princeton, NJ: Princeton University Press.

Nicolini, D. (2012). *Practice Theory, Work, and Organization*. Oxford: Oxford University Press.

Nicolini, D., Gherardi, S., and Yanow, D. (2003). Toward a practice-based view of knowing and learning in organizations. In D. Nicolini, S. Gherardi, and D. Yanow (eds.), *Knowing in Organizations: A Practice-Based Approach* (pp. 3–31). Armonk, NY: M. E. Sharpe.

Orr, J. (1996). *Thinking about Machines*. Ithaca, NY: Cornell University Press.

Petroski, H. (2002). *Paperboy: Confessions of a Future Engineer*. New York: Alfred A. Knopf.

Polanyi, M. (1962). *Personal Knowledge*. Chicago, IL: University of Chicago Press.

Polanyi, M. (1966). *The Tacit Dimension*. New York: Doubleday.

Prottas, J. M. (1979). *People-Processing*. Lexington, MA: D. C. Heath.

Raelin, J. (2006). Does action learning promote collaborative leadership? *Academy of Management Learning & Education*, 5(2): 152–168.

Raelin, J. A. and Raelin, J. D. (2006). Developmental action learning. *Action Learning*, 3(1): 45–67.

Rein, M. and Schön, D. A. (1977). Problem setting in policy research. In C. H. Weiss (ed.), *Using Social Research in Public Policy Making* (pp. 235–51). Lexington, MA: Lexington Books.

Ron, N., Lipshitz, R., and Popper, M. (2006). How organizations learn: Post-flight reviews in an F-16 fighter squadron. *Organization Studies*, 27(8): 1069–1090.

Ronco, W. and Peattie, L. (1983). *Making Work*. New York: Plenum.

Schatzki, T. R. (2005). The sites of organizations. *Organization Studies*, 26(3): 465–484.

Schatzki, T. R., Knorr Cetina, K., and von Savigny, E. (eds.) (2001). *The Practice Turn in Contemporary Theory*. New York: Routledge.

Schmidt, M. R. (2000). You know more than you can say: In memory of Donald A. Schön (1930–1997). *Public Administration Review*, 60(3): 266–275.

Schön, D. A. (1979). Generative metaphor. In A. Ortony (ed.), *Metaphor and Thought* (pp. 254–283). Cambridge: Cambridge University Press.

Schön, D. A. (1983). *The Reflective Practitioner*. New York: Basic Books.

Schön, D. A. (1985). *The Design Studio*. London: RIBA Publications for RIBA Building Industry Trust.

Schön, D. A. (1987). *Educating the Reflective Practitioner.* San Francisco, CA: Jossey-Bass.

Schön, D. A. (ed.) (1991). *The Reflective Turn: Case Studies in and on Educational Practice.* New York: Teachers College Press.

Schön, D. A. and Rein, M. (1994). *Frame Reflection: Toward the Resolution of Intractable Policy Controversies.* New York: Basic Books.

Schulman, P. R. (1993). The negotiated order of organizational reliability. *Administration & Society,* 25(3): 353–372.

Schwartz-Shea, P. and Yanow, D. (2012). *Interpretive Research Design: Concepts and Processes.* New York: Routledge.

Snyder, B. (1973). *The Hidden Curriculum.* Cambridge, MA: MIT Press.

Sudnow, D. (1978). *Ways of the Hand: The Organization of Improvised Conduct.* Cambridge, MA: Harvard University Press.

Tommasini, A. (2009). Streisand's fine instrument and classic instinct. *New York Times,* September 24.

Traweek, S. (1988). *Beamtimes and Lifetimes: The World of High Energy Physicists.* Cambridge, MA: Harvard University Press.

Tsoukas, H. (2011). How should we understand tacit knowledge? A phenomenological view. In M. Easterby-Smith and M. A. Lyles (eds.), *Handbook of Organizational Learning and Knowledge Management* (pp. 453–476). Oxford: Blackwell.

van Hulst, M., de Graaf, L., and van den Brink, G. (2012). The work of exemplary practitioners in neighborhood governance. *Critical Policy Studies,* 6(4): 434–451.

van Woerkum, C. and Aarts, N. (2011). Organizing by projective hearing: The active use of a passive sense. *International Journal of Strategic Communication,* 5(3): 171–182.

Waldo, D. (1968). *The Novelist on Organization and Administration.* Berkeley: University of California, Institute of Governmental Studies.

Weatherley, R. (1979). *Reforming Special Education.* Cambridge, MA: MIT Press.

Weick, K. E. (1979). *The Social Psychology of Organizing* (2nd edition). New York: McGraw-Hill.

Weick, K. E. (1993). The collapse of sensemaking in organizations: The Mann Gulch disaster. *Administrative Science Quarterly,* 38(4): 628–652.

Weick, K. E. and Roberts, K. H. (1993). Collective mind in organizations: Heedful interrelating on flight decks. *Administrative Science Quarterly,* 38(3): 357–381.

Weick, K. E. and Sutcliffe, K. M. (eds.) (2007). *Managing the Unexpected.* San Francisco, CA: Jossey-Bass.

Woods, D. D. (2000). Behind human error: Human factors research to improve patient safety. In Quality Interagency Coordination Task Force and Agency for Healthcare Research and Quality, "National summit on medical errors and patient safety research," September 11. <http://csel.eng.ohio-state.edu/woods/medicine/patientsafety/HFESinput_full_summit.pdf> (accessed May 1, 2012).

Yanow, D. (2004). Translating local knowledge at organizational peripheries. *British Journal of Management,* 15(S1): S9–S25.

Yanow, D. (2009). Ways of knowing: Passionate humility and reflective practice in research and management. *American Review of Public Administration*, 39(6): 579–601.

Yanow, D. (2014). Interpretive analysis and comparative research. In I. Engeli and C. R. Allison (eds.), *Comparative Policy Studies* (pp. 131–159). Basingstoke: Palgrave Macmillan.

Yanow, D. and Tsoukas, H. (2009). What is reflection-in-action? A phenomenological account. *Journal of Management Studies*, 46(8): 1339–1364.

Ybema, S. and Yanow, D. (2011). Studying culture and symbolism in organizations. In S. Ybema, D. Yanow, and I. Sabelis (eds.), *Organizational Culture* (pp. xi–xxxii). Cheltenham: Edward Elgar.

12

Conceptions of Process in Organization and Management

The Case of Identity Studies

Jörgen Sandberg, Bernadette Loacker, and Mats Alvesson

Abstract: Despite the increased use of process perspectives in management and organization studies, what "process" stands for remains highly ambiguous. This chapter develops a typology of the different meanings of the term process using the area of identity studies as the empirical context. In contrast to the "weak" and "strong" views of process within management and organization studies, the typology shows that there exists a continuum of process perspectives in between the "weak"/"strong" views, namely from process as (1) a transition state, (2) sliding, (3) narrative co-production, and (4) an ongoing accomplishment, to regarding process as (5) all-there-is. Several constitutive features of process that have not been previously illuminated are identified, including: ontology, time, space, and agency. Finally, the chapter discusses how the identified process views and their constitutive features can advance not only process research within the area of identity studies but also within management and organization studies more broadly.

12.1 Introduction

While process perspectives have been commonly used in management and organization studies (hereafter MOS) (e.g. March, 1994; Pettigrew, 1990;

Weick, 1979), they have recently gained renewed popularity in areas such as organizational identity (Alvesson, 2010; Ybema et al., 2009), organizational change (Tsoukas and Chia, 2002), strategy (Chia and MacKay, 2007; Whittington, 2006), organizational learning (Clegg, Kornberger, and Rhodes, 2005; Gherardi, 2006), and design (Youngjin, Boland, and Lyytinen, 2006). Some even claim that a "process turn" is taking place in organization studies (e.g. Hernes, 2008).

A core idea underpinning most process perspectives is that organizational and management phenomena such as strategy, identity, decision-making, and knowledge are better understood by conceptualizing them as processes of becoming rather than as stable entities with specific properties (Hernes, 2008; Langley and Tsoukas, 2010; Nayak and Chia, 2011). However, despite the increased use of process perspectives and a more deliberate explication of them (Langley and Tsoukas, 2010; Nayak and Chia, 2011), what "process" stands for appears as highly ambiguous in the literature. As Hernes (2008, p. 23) notes in his extensive review of process studies, although there exist "a number of works that debate the nature of process views [. . .] there is seldom a clear cut line between the understandings of process. With some exceptions (e.g. Bakken and Hernes, 2006; Tsoukas and Chia, 2002; Van de Ven and Poole, 2005) the word process is used merely to emphasize that movement and flux are taken into consideration."

In this chapter we try to provide a clearer articulation of what process stands for within MOS by investigating the different ways in which the term is applied in the area of identity studies. Specifically, the overall aim of the chapter is to identify and develop a *typology* of the different meanings and conceptualizations of the term process within MOS, using the area of identity studies as the specific empirical context. Such a typology is likely to provide a sharper lens for how organizational phenomena can be understood and studied from a process perspective. It may also facilitate communication and clarify analytical options as well as epistemological, ontological, and methodological stances and choices. In particular, typological theorizing potentially enables the development of theoretically meaningful categories of process, facilitates distinctions between different conceptualizations of process, and avoids simple correlational process thinking (Delbridge and Fiss, 2013, p. 329).

The chapter is structured in the following way. First, we provide a brief review of how the term process has been defined within process organization studies. Thereafter, we investigate how the term process has been used within the area of identity studies through a review of eight leading

MOS journals between 2006 and 2012 together with a more targeted review of identity studies within MOS. Based on that review we identify and elaborate a typology of different process views and their key features. Finally, we discuss how such a typology can advance not only process research within the area of identity studies but also within MOS more broadly.

12.2 Process Studies

12.2.1 The "Process Turn" in Management and Organization Studies

Although the term process has been used frequently in MOS, its popularity has increased significantly during the last two decades. Simply running a search in Google Scholar on the term process in the title field of four leading MOS journals (*Academy of Management Journal, Journal of Management Studies, Organization Science,* and *Organization Studies*) resulted in more than 400 hits. The search revealed that the term process has been applied to almost every area of MOS, such as strategy process, communication process, sense-making process, organizational change process, systems development process, production process, work process, and identity process. This interest in process research has generated several special issues (*Academy of Management Journal*, 2013; *Organization*, 2002-1; *Organization Studies*, 2011-9; *Strategic Management Journal*, 1992), a specific standing conference (International Symposium on Process Organization Studies, <http://www.process-symposium.com>), a process website organized by AoM (http://www.processresearchmethods.org/index.html), special interest groups in EGOS and AoM, special book series (Perspectives on Process Organization Studies, Langley and Tsoukas, 2010), and several extensive reviews (e.g. Hernes, 2008; Nayak and Chia, 2011).

A central question for all process research is what "process" stands for. This is because how we understand "process" informs what to investigate, the design of our research, what empirical material to collect, and how to analyze and theorize organizational phenomena. However, the notion of process is far from clear within MOS. Nayak and Chia (2011, p. 292), point in their review to "the indetermination of process" and Langley (2008, p. 2) observes that "process research addresses dynamic questions about temporally evolving phenomena. Beyond this elementary idea, the definition of precisely what process research is or is not can however sometimes seem rather muddy." Moreover, as Cooren et al. (2011) aptly note in relation to process perspectives in communication studies, "a problem in making these [process] views amenable to the broader organization studies field is that, because of their sophisticated conceptions of communicative processes, they often become mired in complexity, immersed in abstract language and unable to articulate similarities and differences among perspectives."

There are several possible reasons for the high degree of ambiguity revolving around the term process. One is that the term has a long and complex philosophical pedigree, ranging from early process philosophers like Heraclitus, James, Whitehead, and Bergson to leading contemporary philosophers and social scientists, such as Deleuze and Guattari (1987), Giddens (1979), Ingold (2000), and Weick (1979) which, taken together, have created a melting pot of different and highly complex views of process (Rescher, 1996; Schatzki, 2010). Another likely reason is that the increased use of process perspectives may have resulted in less reflective applications of the term process. For example, many researchers replace nouns such as "design" and "strategy" with "designing" and "strategizing." But, as Hernes (2008, p. 23) notes, "adding 'ing' to a noun, however much it turns the noun into a verb in linguistic terms, does not much influence either how we conceptualize process or how we formulate all the important questions that come with that conceptualization." A third and related reason is that the process term is not only used by advocates of distinct process perspectives but also by many scholars within MOS that do not necessarily see themselves as process scholars.

A confused and muddled conceptualization of process can be seen as problematic, as it may provide an unfocused and perhaps even sometimes misguided framework for studying organizational phenomena. It is of course important not to exaggerate the need for clarity because, as Langley (2008, p. 2) notes, too much clarity may "misrepresent the richness, eclecticism and variety of [process] research practice." However, given the current ambiguity of the term process it seems important to further articulate its meanings and uses in order to advance organizational process studies.

12.2.2 Attempts to Define Process

The confusion over what process stands for does not mean that no attempts have been made to clarify its meaning. An often-cited clarification is Mohr's (1982) distinction between variance and process theories. As Langley (1999, p. 692) eloquently describes it, "whereas variance theories provide explanations for phenomena in terms of relationships among dependent and independent *variables* (e.g., more of X and more of Y produce more of Z), process theories provide explanations in terms of the sequence of *events* leading to an outcome (e.g., do A and then B to get C)." To take a concrete example, variance theory tries to explain organizational change by investigating the extent to which a set of independent variables such as the environment, leadership, and technology *causes* organizational change. In contrast, process theory tries to explain organizational change by investigating what Mohr (1982, p. 45) calls "probabilistic rearrangement," that is, the processes in which specific events, activities, decisions, etc. coalesce into particular constellations that are likely to create organizational change. Although this distinction is useful in that it highlights the key differences between the prevalent variance theory and process theory, it does not say much about the different meanings and uses of the term process within MOS.

A common way to further clarify its uses is to distinguish between a "weak" and a "strong" process view. This distinction was first made by Chia and Langley (2004) in the call for the First Organization Studies Summer Workshop, focused on process organization studies:

> The "weak" view treats processes as important but ultimately reducible to the action of things, while the "strong" view deems actions and things to be instantiations of process-complexes. The first perspective appears dominant in much of organizational and social scientific research, and tends to be pragmatic, empirically grounded, and analytical in orientation. The latter perspective has been primarily conceptual, strongly informed by strands of process philosophy, theology and the humanities at large, following especially the lead of philosophers such as James, Whitehead, Bergson, and Deleuze.

As a way to further clarify the difference between the "weak" and "strong" conceptions of process, process scholars often try to articulate their ontological assumptions (Langley et al., 2013). The "weak" process view is seen as underpinned by a *substance* ontology, which stipulates that entities (individuals, organizations, etc.) are supreme, and process secondary. An organization is ultimately seen as a more or less stable entity with particular properties. However, at certain times, such as when the external environment changes significantly (e.g. driven by new technologies, regulations, or competitors), the organization may move from one stage to another and, thus, transforms its properties somewhat, as a way to adapt to the changes in the external environment.

The "strong" process perspective is underpinned by a *becoming* ontology and proposes that process, rather than substance, is the basic ontological category. According to the well-known process philosopher Whitehead, a becoming ontology postulates that "the actual world is a process, and that process is the becoming of actual entities [. . .] *how* an actual entity becomes constitutes *what* that actual entity *is*" (in Nayak and Chia, 2011, p. 289). This means that advocates of a "strong" process view conceptualize organization as something emergent and always in the making. As Hernes (2008, pp. xvii–xviii) expressed it, organizations "are ongoing in the sense that they are always in a state of creation, of emergence, of becoming. They are also accomplishments in the sense that they are forged with historical processes that could have turned out quite differently." Therefore, as Nayak and Chia (2011, p. 284) argue, "to understand individuals and organizations processually is to regard them as temporarily assemblages of organizing that are abstracted from an underlying sea of ceaseless change."

Implicit in the distinction between a "weak" and a "strong" process perspective, at least for most advocates of the "strong" one, is that a "strong" process view is superior in that it "is truer to the essential meaning of change (and process) than the 'weak' view" (Van de Ven and Poole, 2005, p. 7). This is for example evident in Nayak and Chia (2011, p. 292) who describe "weak" process views as quasi-processual in that their focus on "how things and events unfold over time is [. . .] not radical enough when it comes to process perspective. A genuine process perspective insists that reality *is* change" (see also Hernes, 2008, pp. 23–24, for a similar argument). However, other process-oriented theorists more closely associated with a "weak" process view, such as Van de Ven and Poole (2005) and Langley (2007) tend to regard the "weak" and "strong" views as different but do not necessarily assume that one view is superior to the other.

12.2.3 A Critique of the "Weak"/"Strong" Conceptualization of Process

While the "weak"/"strong" distinction further clarifies what process may signify, it is also problematic in many ways. A major problem with such a bipolar conceptualization is that it overlooks the possibility of a greater variation of process views. Such negligence prevents the development of a more nuanced and richer understanding of what process means and how it is used within MOS. This becomes particularly salient in that several potential key features, which in various ways make up process, such as "time," "space," and "agency," are even less thematized and articulated within existing dichotomic conceptualizations of process.

One of the central features that make up process is *time*. Process is constantly described as something dynamic, ongoing, and evolving. As Langley et al. (2013, p. 1) say, "process studies address questions about how and why things emerge, develop, grow, or terminate over time." However, it is far from clear what time means in both the "weak" and the "strong" process view. In most instances, process seems to be portrayed as a temporal sequence. For example, in her review of process research, Langley (2007, p. 10) portrayed the temporal orientation of process studies as "process researchers may study their phenomenon by tracing it backward into the past (historical and retrospective studies) by following it forward into the future (ethnography and longitudinal case studies), by examining how it is constituted, or possibly by doing all of these at the same time" (see also Langley and Tsoukas, 2010, p. 11; Langley et al., 2013, pp. 1–4).

Drawing on Bergson's philosophy, Nayak and Chia (2011, p. 295) try to provide an alternative description of how "time" defines process. They claim that "the challenge of the processual approach is to think in time, where time is not the counterfeit movement from point A to B . . . represented by *t0, t1, t2* and so on . . . [instead] to think processually is to recover the continuities and to view the process of transformation as a whole indivisible movement." Yet, it is not clear to what extent the assumption of process as a temporal sequence changes if we regard time as an indivisible movement (as duration in Bergson's terminology) rather than a stream of infinite points.

Space, which is intimately related to time in that "every movement describes a space [and] that at every point of this space the moving body *might* stop" (Bergson, 1911, p. 251, in Nayak and Chia, 2011, p. 294). The quote from Bergson suggests that space is a central feature of process, something also supported by Schatzki (2010, p. 10), who notes "process is at once temporal and spatial." However, as space has been rarely discussed and thematized within process studies, especially not on its own, it is not clear how space defines process in either the "weak" or "strong" view. For example, does process occur in space in a similar way as it is assumed to occur in time? Or is process seen as constitutive of space or perhaps vice versa?

Agency is another central feature of process that is rarely thematized in current conceptualizations of process within MOS. In the "weak" process view, agency is typically highly salient in that individuals and organizations are seen as discrete entities, endowed with autonomy and freedom to make deliberate choices (Nayak and Chia, 2011, p. 285). Yet, as population ecologists have argued for a long time, process may also be strongly determined by external events or constraints rather than human agency. However, what agency implicates in the "strong" view is considerably harder to see. This is because in the "strong" process view individuals and organizations are no longer conceptualized as discrete entities but "as temporarily stabilized event clusters abstracted from a sea of constant flux and change" (Nayak and Chia, 2011, p. 281). In a similar vein, Hernes (2008, p. xv) argues that from a process point of view, organization is "a unique product of circumstances and a unique producer of circumstances." Drawing from the above quotes, agency in a "strong" process view seems at best to be portrayed as "specific circumstances" rather than as human intentions and purposes. Are processes perhaps seen as self-going perpetual, universal motion machines? More recently, however, MacKay and Chia (2013) elaborated a moderated view of human agency, which seems to fall somewhere between the above views by introducing the notion of "unowned" agency. According to them, unowned agency "give[s] primacy to either managerial choice or environmental determinism by elevating the interactive role of choice, chance, change, and unintended consequences in shaping strategic outcomes" (MacKay and Chia, 2013, p. 210).

In conclusion, even though the "weak"/"strong" distinction provides some clarification of what process stands for within MOS, its meaning is still ambiguous in that (a) the "weak"/"strong" distinction overlooks the possibility of a greater variation of process views, and (b) several potential key features of process such as time, space, and agency are rarely thematized and articulated, which exacerbates the problem of understanding what process signifies and how it can be used within MOS.

12.3 The Case of Identity Studies

The aim of the remaining discussion is to provide a clearer articulation of what "process" may signify by investigating how it has been conceptualized and used within the area of identity studies. Studying how process has been applied across several MOS areas would undoubtedly lead to greater breadth and, thus, increased generalization but at a potentially high cost, namely, reduced depth and sharpness in the descriptions of the various meanings of process. We contend that identity studies offers a suitable empirical context for articulating the various meanings of process. First, it is one of the larger areas within MOS, which provides the necessary breadth for capturing the meanings and uses of process in a rich and nuanced way. Second, comparable to many other areas, it is increasingly common to emphasize the processual nature of identity within identity studies (Ybema et al., 2009). Third, similar to most other topics within MOS, it is not easy to grasp what "process" stands for within identity studies, judging from the ongoing debates as to whether identities are primarily fixed, coherent, and unified or changeable, fragmented, multiple, and diverse (Alvesson, 2010; Clarke, Brown, and Hailey, 2009; Collinson, 2003).

12.4 Methodology

In order to investigate what process means and the different ways in which the term is applied in identity studies, we conducted a database search (in the databases Ebsco and Sage) of eight leading journals in organization and management studies between 2006 and 2012 (*Academy of Management Journal, Administrative Science Quarterly, Human Relations, Journal of Management, Journal of Management Studies, Organization, Organization Science, Organization Studies*). The main reasons for choosing those journals are that they (a) provide a good representation of both leading European and US journals, and (b) publish a wide range of different identity studies. Taken together, they are likely to offer both the breadth and depth needed to identify the potential range of process views within identity studies as well as being able to articulate these process views with high precision and clarity.

In order to identify articles to be included in the review we searched for the term "process" in the title, abstract, or as a keyword in the entire database for each journal. Through the database search we identified 87 identity studies. Apart from a handful of conceptual papers (e.g. Bardon and Josserand, 2010; Brown, 2006), the review consisted of mainly empirical identity studies. In addition to the article review, we carried out a more targeted review of identity studies outside the time frame of 2006–2012 as well as outside the eight journals included in the database search. Here, we also considered a few books and book chapters that explored identity questions from a process perspective (e.g. Munro, 2011; Pullen and Linstead, 2006). The purpose of the more targeted review was to find identity studies that enabled greater depth and precision of the different process views initially identified through the main database search (e.g. Sims, 2003; Sveningsson and Alvesson, 2003). Taken together, we reviewed in total about 100 research texts within the area of identity studies.

In the review we focused on how authors conceptualized process but, more importantly, how these conceptualizations were used throughout the paper and/or study. As Wittgenstein and ethnomethodologists have pointed out, what a term means is inextricably linked to the way it is applied in a specific context (Braver, 2012). Although we investigated each paper in full, we mainly focused on the theoretical and, where present, methodological part of the paper as well as on its discussion section, as those parts most clearly highlighted how the authors used the notion of process in identity studies.

Interestingly, of the identity studies we analyzed, only a few explicitly emphasized that they took a "process perspective" on identity. The large majority did not use the term process deliberately but applied it in a rather non-thematic way. Moreover, different process identity notions were frequently composed and applied within one and the same study or analysis. This is for example evident in Brown and Lewis' (2011, pp. 871–874) study of the identity work of professional lawyers. On the one hand, they consider identity to be "multiple," "in flux," "improvisational," and "in-progress." However, as they claim identity work to be an expression of both agency and power, they also emphasize the constraining, normalizing, and disciplining effects of work- and profession-related discourses, striving to define and fix identity in a very particular way.

Nevertheless, even if most papers reviewed follow, as alluded to, a rather variegated understanding of process, we tried to identify the central or dominant process meaning from each of the identity studies articles by closely investigating how the term process was applied throughout the paper. On that basis, we finally identified five, more or less explicitly articulated perspectives on process outlined in the typology below. However, given the constructed, not to say artificial, nature of typologies and the arbitrariness of the labels put on whatever position one wants to represent, propose, or invent, there are good reasons to remind oneself and the reader that the proposed typology is not the only possibility of making sense of the ways in which the term process is used in the identity field. As Locke and Golden-Biddle (1997) point out, how we integrate and differentiate earlier research in literature reviews is as much a matter of rhetorical moves as of objective mappings. Therefore, rather than being too worried about whether everything important about "process" in the reviewed texts is exactly mirrored in the typology, it is perhaps more important to consider the productive-functional aspects of the typology and its vocabulary.

12.5 A Typology of Process Perspectives in Identity Studies

We identified a continuum of process perspectives within identity studies, ranging from process as (1) a transition state, (2) sliding, (3) narrative co-production, and (4) an ongoing accomplishment, to regarding process as (5) all-there-is. Furthermore, the typology proposes that each process perspective is constituted by a specific ontology, time, space, and agency. The continuum of process perspectives and their constitutive features are summarized in Table 12.1 and elaborated below.

12.5.1 Process as Transition State

When process is seen as transition state, it tends to be subordinated to substance in that identity is mainly seen as something relatively fixed and accomplished and only "in process" during a specific period of time

Table 12.1 Summary of process views within identity studies

Constitutive features	Ontology	Time	Space	Agency
Process perspective	The ontological status of process	How time defines process	Where process takes place	What has agency and how it drives processes
Transition state	Becoming subordinate to substance	Linear and episodic	In transitions between specific life stages or unexpected changes	Mainly individual and passive
Sliding	Becoming more prominent but still subordinate to substance	Often episodic but less linear	In between sites	Mainly individual and active
Narrative co-production	Becoming and substance equal status	Continuous and discontinuous (backward and forward)	In narrative co-production	Social–personal interaction
Ongoing accomplishment	Becoming more emphasized than substance	Continuous	In everyday practice	Social–material interaction
All-there-is	Becoming	Continuous and discontinuous (backward and forward)	Everywhere, boundary-less	Process is self-driving, perpetual motion

(e.g. Goodrick and Reay, 2010; Pratt, Rockmann, and Kaufmann, 2006). Process as transition state is thus mainly seen as a temporary in-between state that connects instability and stability of organizational or individual identity (Ibarra and Barbulescu, 2010).

In this type of process perspective, identity studies typically refer to more or less well-known development stages, such as when people are going through specific life stages or passing through important steps in their working life (Pratt et al., 2006, pp. 258–259). In these situations people often transform their sense of themselves. For example, a common situation in which people change their self-identity is in (job) transition phases (Ibarra and Barbulescu, 2010). Similar to individuals, "organizations undergo transitions in their life cycles" (Clark et al., 2010, p. 430) and are, therefore, occasionally asked to recreate and adapt their identity to modulated institutional environments. Identity transformations are also seen as taking place during unexpected changes, which call into question "who, what I am, and what is distinct about me." For example, in their study of a merger of two health care organizations, Clark et al. (2010) show that organizations adapt their identities to changed institutional or organizational conditions in order to resolve conflict and cognitive dissonance.

Within these temporary in-between processes identities are debated and negotiated until a new organizational and/or individual identity is formulated and restabilized. However, in between and at the end of these transformational stages, whether they are expected or not, people and organizations are seen as fairly steady in their self-identities, calling for little interest in transition. It is also important to note that in process as transition, individuals or organizations are seen as primarily passive as their agency is mainly activated by external circumstances, such as changes in the environment or what follows from the transition of time, e.g. going from subordinate to manager or retiring.

12.5.2 Process as Sliding

When regarding process as sliding, neither identities nor identification targets are considered as particularly stable or fixed (Staber, 2010, p. 154). It is rather assumed that individuals are part of different sites and contexts, which promote and constitute various identities and identification targets. Individuals can move amongst these multiple identity sites, but also have to move and switch, such as when former identification sources dissolve (Ashforth, Harrison, and Corley, 2008;

Bowles, 1990; Dutton, Dukerich, and Harquail, 1994; Haslam, 2004). Individuals are therefore endowed with more active agency, as they are often the ones who initiate, or at least regulate, the moves between various identity sites.

The processes of sliding from one identity to another are particularly evident in environments where multiple sources generating and shaping identifications are presumed (e.g. Knights and McCabe, 2003, p. 1589; Kosmala and Herrbach, 2006), such as in team-, project-, and short-term oriented work. Such forms of work do not simply define individuals, they also enable them to draw on, interpret, and identify with particular identity sources in a rather flexible way. Identification resources are thus not considered as being essentially universal or durable (Staber, 2010); depending on the particular social and discursive context, certain sources or scripts might "fit" better or be considered as more appropriate than others (Musson and Duberley, 2007, pp. 160–161). Yet, on balance, the view of process as sliding is somewhat limited as it is organized according to the possible set of identification targets and identity resources available at a given moment and site. Process comes into play mainly as a link between organizational and individual identification resources (Sveningsson and Alvesson, 2003, p. 1164).

12.5.3 Process as Narrative Co-Production

When regarding process as narrative co-production, identity is seen as a relational, multi-voiced, linguistic construct that is recreated and positioned through narrating and negotiating the self across time, different sites, and discourses (Brown, 2006; Down and Reveley, 2009; Ybema et al., 2009). Ontologically speaking, therefore, becoming and substance are more on an equal footing in this perspective than in the previous two. This is because identity is seen as less stable in that its formation is regularly taking place in a narrative co-production between others and ourselves. Moreover, in contrast to the two previous process perspectives, identity is here seen as more strongly socially achieved, that is, as something generated in interaction with others. It is when we are asked or feel encouraged to tell stories about ourselves and when others question our stories about ourselves that identity as process enters into the picture (Sims, 2003). Identity construction is thus understood as a "continuous process of narration where both the narrator and the audience formulate, edit, applaud, and refuse various elements of the ever-produced narrative" (Czarniawska-Joerges, 1994, p. 198).

However, within process as narrative co-production there is a continuum of scholars: from those who regard identity narration processes as more coherent and linear to those who regard them as more multi-faceted and fragmented. The former often see self-identity as assembled out of cultural raw material: language, symbols, sets of meanings, values, etc. derived from countless numbers of interactions with others leading to "a coherent and vivifying life story [which] provides the modern adult with that quality of selfhood that goes by the name of identity" (McAdams, 1996, p. 299). However, for those who regard identity narration as more multi-faceted and fragmented, life stories are not seen as fixed and necessarily coherent products (Boje, 1991), but as something accomplished between actors over time (see also Ybema et al., 2009, p. 303). In this view, identity work can thus be seen as "complexes of in-progress stories and story-fragments, which are in a perpetual state of becoming" (Brown, 2006, p. 732) and also "suffused with power."

12.5.4 Process as Ongoing Accomplishment

In process as ongoing accomplishment, becomingness has overtaken substance as the supreme ontological category in the sense that identity is never given but continually produced and reproduced through our everyday practices. Process as ongoing accomplishment refers to the concrete transitions of individuals, information, or material objects in and across time and—physical or virtual—space, giving rise to a largely decentered agency (cf. ANT), generated through the social–material interaction between ourselves and other people.

West and Zimmerman's (1987) classic work *Doing Gender* can be seen as a paradigmatic example of the process as ongoing accomplishment perspective on gender identity.[1] According to Butler (1999), doing gender identity involves a wide set of social interactions and meaning recreations producing gender effects and gendered identities. Without these ongoing activities gender identities would, in principle, not exist anymore as gendered distinctions and would thus lack social significance and be marginalized and crumble.

Identity work in this process perspective calls, therefore, for constant engagement in forming, repairing, strengthening, or revising the identity constructions that are "enacted and played out through interactions" (Clegg, Rhodes, and Kornberger, 2007, p. 497). To put this idea in Sturdy et al.'s (2006, p. 846) words: identities and identity performances are "built on shifting sands." It is "in the context of the *negotiation, presentation* and *structuring* of identity through knowledge and discourse" (Sturdy et al., 2006, p. 846) that different aspects and versions of identity are affirmed, denied and redefined in everyday performances and interactions as well as in the context of "larger struggles for identity and power" (Munro, 2011, p. 142; see also Beech, 2008).

Hence, within process as ongoing accomplishment, the modes of doing and performing identity can hardly be understood as being self-identical, stable, and linear in different scenes and contexts, as there seems to be no "I" that can stand apart from the particular conditions of its emergence (Butler, 2005). Yet, even if the process as ongoing accomplishment perspective puts a strong emphasis on the ongoing and fluid nature of identity, it does not necessarily assume that identity is exclusively in motion. To argue that "the appearance of stability in any given 'identity' is [. . .] a transient accomplishment" (Ybema et al., 2009, p. 301), also suggests that temporary identity stabilization, as an effect of certain ordering processes, is in part acknowledged.

12.5.5 Process as All-There-Is

In the process as all-there-is perspective, all forms of temporary identity stabilization are gone and identity is seen as entirely fluid. Process shapes all other categories—such as social/material world, discourses, organizations, individuals, or identities. In this perspective, process can therefore not be reduced to a particular space, agency, level, or plane (such as discursive, cognitive, or emotional), as it is ongoing and everywhere. On the whole, the notion of process in this perspective is best understood as an ontological category deeply shaping the multiple visions and orders of knowledge, truth, social realms, and relations (Bardon and Josserand, 2011, p. 502). As a particular "Weltanschauung," process as all-there-is becomes a fundamental principle of the organization of life, and identity.

Hence, "rather than being ontologically secure" (Clegg et al., 2007, p. 497), it is here assumed that identity emerges from multiple relations and processes of organizing. As a consequence, identities in this perspective are not seen as sovereign, a complete substance, or a core element of personality that is to be discovered. For instance, in her study of multiple, ongoing identity (de)constructions in interview situations, Harding (2007, p. 1771), notes that "the sense of a unitary 'I', is never fully present, never fully achievable, but is always engaged in a complex interactional process of becoming-ness." Similarly, in their study of the identity constructions of middle managers, Thomas and Linstead (2002, p. 75) argue that identity is in a permanent state of flux "as various social and linguistic constructs (or discourses) vie with one another for supremacy."

12.6 Discussion: Towards a Typological Theory of Process

The typology developed and elaborated above provides a description of the different process perspectives and their main constitutive features within identity studies. In that regard, the typology can be seen as a contribution to identity studies in that it offers a range of different ways in which identity can be understood and studied from a process perspective. However, the typology does not only advance process understandings within identity studies, but also the process perspective within MOS more generally. It does that in two main ways. First, it extends the "weak"/"strong" definition of process in that it identifies a whole range of other process perspectives in between the "weak" and "strong" perspectives. Second, it goes beyond the "weak"/"strong" definition of process in that it reveals several constitutive features of process that have not been previously illuminated. These contributions are further elaborated below.

12.6.1 Extending the Range of Possible Process Perspectives within MOS

Although the typology suggests a continuum of different process views within identity studies, a central question is to what extent the identified process views are also evident in other areas of MOS. Two questions are important to ask here: (1) how well are the process views within identity studies reflected in, and can be applied to, other areas of MOS, and (2) to what extent do they relate to existing "process theories" within MOS? As both questions concern the more general relevance of the process views articulated in the typology, we consider them simultaneously.

Process as a transition state corresponds with the "weak" process perspective within existing process theories. Looking more specifically, process as transition state seems to map quite well onto those process theories that employ or develop particular time-specific process models or life-cycles, including both predictable or unexpected stages of transition, as well as stages of more steadiness. Here process often comes in as a necessary mediator in sequential or recurrent phases of transition and adaptation (Gioia, Schultz, and Corley, 2000). Process is thus generally considered as a temporary, transient and episodic phenomenon that assists in developing and transferring diverse social or organizational phenomena from instability to newly found stability and constancy (e.g. Clark and Geppert, 2011). Process as transition state also seems to have strong affinities with the hugely popular sense-making theory originally developed by Weick (1979, 1995), in that sense-making theory is confined to specific episodes "that occur from the moment some ongoing organizational activities are interrupted until they are satisfactorily restored (or in some cases permanently interrupted)" (Sandberg and Tsoukas, 2014; see also Maitlis and Christianson, 2014).

Although this process view is reflected in many areas within MOS, such as strategy (Mintzberg and McHugh, 1985) and organization design (Glick et al., 1990), it is perhaps most notable in the area of organizational change, where it is common to study change processes in terms of how an organization moves from one phase to another (Langley et al., 2013; Tsoukas and Chia, 2002). As almost every aspect of organization and management (leadership, strategy, motivation, structure, etc.) goes through transitional phases of various kinds or is drawn into unexpected changes, this process view can be (and is frequently) applied within MOS.

Process as sliding acknowledges multiplicity, and the situational precariousness of identification resources (Alvesson, Ashcraft, and Thomas, 2008, p. 13; Collinson, 2003). This process view seems rather specific for social identity theory and, therefore, potentially harder to map onto other areas within MOS. It is, however, likely that process as sliding may also be relevant for understanding movements between institutional orders and practices. Here the organization hypocrisy idea can be exemplarily mentioned—where the organization moves between talk, decision, and action in order to satisfy diverse interests (Brunsson, 2003). The sliding view may also be used in conjunction with various discourse analytical frameworks, which often explore how people and collectives participate in and move amongst multiple discourses (e.g. Thomas and Davies, 2005). One could also imagine that the process as sliding view can be productively combined with institutional theories in the sense that organizations are switching between different institutional logics in the performance of their tasks, e.g. to attain legitimacy and being productive (Meyer and Rowan, 1977; see also Clegg et al., 2007).

Process as narrative co-production belongs to a broad literature in which the exploration of narratives and stories allows understanding a variety of processes and phenomena suffusing contemporary organizational life, social orders, and relations (Boje, 1991; Brown, 2006, p. 732). Generally, both stories and narrations have a tendency to create "facts" as experience rather than representing facts as information. Working mainly on a symbolic plane, they evoke and communicate images, emotions, fantasies, or tales (Gabriel, 1991, pp. 857–858). Storytelling and narrations are discursive devices that generate various kinds of knowledge and meaning and, in this vein, promote temporary truths and realities (Boje, 1991; Brown, 2006). Process as narrative co-production appears to have a fairly broad application range in MOS. As demonstrated by "the narrative turn" in MOS (e.g. Brown, 2006; Czarniawska-Joerges, 1994) it can be connected to all themes within MOS. However, a note of caution is warranted here, as a focus on narratives tends to de-emphasize more substantive aspects of MOS, such as in areas of strategic changes and mergers and acquisitions, which involve massive material changes.

Process as ongoing accomplishment in identity studies relates closely to process theories based on or inspired by Garfinkel's ethnomethodology. From an ethnomethodological point of view, process is seen as productive and immanent in every performance, thereby constituting both "the doer" and "the deed" (Butler, 1999). As process is ongoing, it involves cycles of actions and reactions, which unfold in different stages, scenes, and discursive or social contexts (Ybema et al., 2009). Here process goes beyond indifferent or distanced practice and conduct; it is about constant enactment, formation, and crafting of organizational knowledge, careers, relations, and identities (e.g. Cabantous and Gond, 2011). Even though ethnomethodology has been applied across several MOS areas (e.g. Llewellyn and Hindmarsh, 2010; Samra-Fredericks and Bargiela-Chiappini, 2008), its micro focus makes it somewhat limited in its applications, particularly if it is linked to conversation analysis. Ideas of process as ongoing accomplishment, however, can be employed in other ways to study a range of different areas within MOS, such as managerial work as consistently adaptive and situational, and strategy as a more or less permanent construction and reconstruction of future directions and how to get there.

Finally, *process as all-there-is* relates closely to those process theories that take a "strong" view of the processuality and becomingness of the world, leaving almost no space for anything outside or before process (Harding, 2007; Tsoukas and Chia, 2002). Advocates of process thinking plead for a "primacy of process over fact" (Chia, 1996, p. 34). Focusing on process and relations is here seen as more real and more important than focusing "on the things which they relate" (Chia, 1996, p. 50). Acknowledging a "fallacy of misplaced concreteness" (Whitehead, 1926/1985), it is strongly questioned whether there is a "world out there" (Goodman, 1978), and "that reality pre-exists independently of observation and as static, discrete and identifiable 'things', 'entities', 'events', 'generative mechanisms' etc." (Chia, 1996, p. 33).

Process as all-there-is also largely overlaps with those process theories that regard the social world as being driven by flows, networks, and connections (e.g. Castells, 2001). These scholars, emphasizing process and unsteady practice instead of stable structures, places, fixed subjects, and objects postulate a "world on the move." In this perspective, hardly anything that is stable and non-processual can be imagined; mobilization and movements of people, things, and relations are most prominent and considered as central to contemporary institutional, organizational, and individual life and order (Urry, 2007, p. 6; Elliott and Urry, 2010).

12.6.2 Revealing Constitutive Features of Process

Extending existing process perspectives within MOS is, however, not the only contribution the typology makes. Its second contribution is that it points at several constitutive features of process that only marginally have been highlighted by existing process theories within MOS, namely: ontology, time, space, and agency. These features further sharpen the distinctiveness of each of the identified process views in important ways.

Although *ontology* has been frequently described as a constitutive feature of process in existing literature in the sense that the "weak" process view is defined by a substance ontology and the "strong" process view by a becoming ontology, the identified typology suggests that ontology defines process in a more complex and nuanced way. As shown, substance ontology dominates in the first two process views (transition state and sliding) in that substance is seen as the basic condition and becoming is a deviation from it. The dominance of substance ontology weakens gradually, so in the third process view (narrative co-production) substance and becoming have similar ontological status. Thereafter, in the remaining process views (ongoing accomplishment and all-there-is) the becoming ontology gets gradually more dominant in that becomingness is seen as defining substance rather than the reverse.

The typology suggests that *time* is one of the most defining features of process. In the first two process views (transition state and sliding), time defines process mainly as linear and successive, such as when going from one stage to another. But sometimes, it also defines process in a less linear fashion (process as sliding) in that individuals are part of multiple processes (that are taking place) simultaneously. In the remaining views, particularly in process as ongoing accomplishment and all-there-is, time seems to define process more significantly in that process is seen *as* time rather than something that takes place *in* time.

A highly related constitutive feature of process revealed in the typology is *space*. In the first two process views, space defines process as that which takes place between specific stages (transition state) or between specific sites, such as between different groups of people (sliding). In "narrative co-production" space defines process as that which happens in a symbolic space (e.g. in narration). In "ongoing accomplishment," space delineates process as that which takes place in everyday practices in which we are constantly involved. In "process as all-there-is," space defines process as taking place everywhere.

Agency appears as another important defining feature of process. In the first process view (transition state), agency defines process as something mainly passive and reactive, in that agency is primarily activated by external events that individuals or collectives need to respond to. In the second view (sliding), agency defines process as something more active in that individuals or collectives are seen as those initiating moves between different (identity) sites. In the narrative co-production view, agency defines process as social–personal interaction. However, in the next two views (ongoing accomplishment and all-there-is) human agency is replaced or, more precisely, decentered into a fluid network of people, materiality and events that constantly create and reproduce process. Agency then almost disappears into what may be described as "hyper-process" reductionism in that process seems to be driven by a driverless perpetual motion machine.

12.7 Concluding Remarks

Despite the significant increase in using a process perspective within MOS—some people even claim that a "process turn" is taking place—most authors use the term process without careful consideration of what it means. The prevalent "weak"/"strong" definition offers some clarification of what process stands for, but its meaning remains highly ambiguous and rudimentary. There is therefore a need to move beyond the "weak"/"strong" dichotomy and unpack and clarify the notion of process in a way that encourages more nuanced views and more precise thinking of how organizational subject areas can be studied from a process perspective.

In this chapter we have proposed and elaborated a typology of the different meanings and conceptualizations of the term process. We have focused on the application of the term process in the area of identity studies and pointed at some basic meanings of process in this specific area: (1) transition state, (2) sliding, (3) narrative co-production, (4) ongoing accomplishment, and (5) all-there-is. We have also argued for their relevance for understanding process views within MOS more broadly.

Taken together, the different process views and their constitutive features advance the existing "weak"/"strong" definition of process within MOS significantly. First, the typology offers a broader range of process views, which can be used to study organizational phenomena. Second, the constitutive features of the different process views sharpen the boundary conditions for the different process views identified. They work as boundary conditions in the sense that they form the boundaries of what each process view stands for and, thus, both enable and constrain the application of the different process views. The constitutive features of each view are therefore important for understanding how the different process perspectives can be applied and used within MOS. Furthermore, the features offer a platform for both further clarifying existing process perspectives and for developing new process views that potentially open up a range of new areas for inquiry into process perspectives in MOS. A typology such as the one presented can therefore be seen as critical for being able to further advance organization process studies, not only in the area of identity studies but also in MOS more broadly.

Note

1. Note, however, that gender identity is constructed in social interaction. The philosophical/theoretical root to this view is Garfinkel's ethnomethodology.

References

Alvesson, M. (2010). Self-doubters, strugglers, storytellers, surfers and others: Images of self-identities in organization studies. *Human Relations*, 63(2): 193–217.

Alvesson, M., Ashcraft K., and Thomas, R. (2008). Identity matters: Reflections on the construction of identity scholarship in Organization Studies. *Organization*, 15(1): 5–28.

Ashforth, B., Harrison, S. H., and Corley, K. G. (2008). Identification in organizations: An examination of four fundamental questions. *Journal of Management*, 34(3): 325–374.

Bakken, T. and Hernes, T. (2006). Organizing is both a noun and a verb: Weick meets Whitehead. *Organization Studies*, 27(11): 1599–1616.

Bardon, T. and Josserand, E. (2010). A Nietzschean reading of Foucauldian thinking: Constructing a project of the self within an ontology of becoming. *Organization* 18(4): 497–515.

Beech, N. (2008). On the nature of dialogic identity work. *Organization*, 15(1): 51–74.

Bergson, H. (1911). *Matter and Memory*. London: George Allen & Unwin.

Boje, D. M. (1991). The storytelling organization: A study of story performance in an office-supply firm. *Administrative Science Quarterly*, 36(1): 106–126.

Bowles, M. L. (1990). Recognizing deep structures in organizations. *Organization Studies*, 11(3): 395–412.

Braver, L. (2012). *Groundless Grounds: A Study of Wittgenstein and Heidegger*. Cambridge, MA: MIT Press.

Brown, A. (2006). A narrative approach to collective identities. *Journal of Management Studies*, 43(4): 731–753.

Brown, A. and Lewis, M. A. (2011). Identities, discipline and routines. *Organization Studies*, 32(7): 871–895.

Brunsson, N. (2003). Organized hypocrisy. In B. Czarniawska and G. Sevón (eds.), *Northern Lights* (pp. 201–222). Oslo: Abstrakt Liber Copenhagen Business Press.

Butler, J. (1999). *Gender Trouble*. New York and London: Routledge.

Butler, J. (2005). *Giving an Account of Oneself*. New York: Fordham University Press.

Cabantous, L. and Gond, J. P. (2011). Rational decision making as a performative practice: Explaining rationality's éternel retour. *Organization Science*, 22(3): 573–586.

Castells, M. (2001). *The Rise of the Network Society*. Malden, MA: Blackwell.

Chia, R. (1996). The problem of reflexivity in organizational research: Towards a postmodern science of organization. *Organization*, 3(1): 31–60.

Chia, R. and Langley, A. (2004). The first Organization Studies summer workshop: Theorizing process in organizational research (call for papers). *Organization Studies*, 25(8): 1486.

Chia, R. and MacKay, B. (2007). Post-processual challenges for the emerging strategy-as-practice perspective: Discovering strategy in the logic of practice. *Human Relations*, 60(1): 217–242.

Clark, E. and Geppert, M. (2011). Subsidiary integration as identity construction and institution building: A political sensemaking approach. *Journal of Management Studies*, 48(2): 395–416.

Clark, S. M., Gioia, D. A., Ketchen, D. J., and Thomas, J. B. (2010). Transitional identity as a facilitator of organizational identity change during a merger. *Administrative Science Quarterly*, 55(3): 397–438.

Clarke, C. A., Brown, A. D., and Hailey, V. H. (2009). Working identities? Antagonistic discursive resources and managerial identity. *Human Relations*, 62(3): 323–352.

Clegg, S. R., Kornberger, M., and Rhodes, C. (2005). Learning/becoming/organizing. *Organization*, 12(2): 147–167.

Clegg, S. R., Rhodes, C., and Kornberger, M. (2007). Desperately seeking legitimacy: Organizational identity and emerging industries. *Organization Studies*, 28(4): 495–513.

Collinson, D. L. (2003). Identities and insecurities: Selves at work. *Organization*, 10(3): 527–547.

Cooren, F., Kuhn, T., Cornelissen, J. P., and Clark, T. (2011). Communication, organizing and organization: An overview and introduction to the special issue. *Organization Studies*, 32(9): 1149–1170.

Czarniawska-Joerges, B. (1994). Narratives of individual and organizational identities. In S. Deetz (ed.), *Communication Yearbook 17* (pp. 193–221). Thousand Oaks, CA: Sage.

Delbridge, R. and Fiss, P. S. (2013). Styles of theorizing and the social organization of knowledge. *Academy of Management Review*, 38(3): 325–331.

Deleuze, G. and Guattari, F. (1987). *A Thousand Plateaus: Capitalism and Schizophrenia*. Minneapolis and London: University of Minnesota Press.

Down, S. and Reveley, J. (2009). Between narration and interaction: Situating first-line supervisor identity work. *Human Relations*, 62(3): 379–401.

Dutton, J., Dukerich, J., and Harquail, C. (1994). Organizational images and member identification. *Administrative Science Quarterly*, 39(2): 293–237.

Elliott, A. and Urry, J. (2010). *Mobile Lives*. London: Routledge.

Gabriel, Y. (1991). Turning facts into stories and stories into fact: A hermeneutic exploration of organizational folklore. *Human Relations*, 44(8): 857–875.

Gherardi, S. (2006). *Organizational Knowledge: The Texture of Workplace Learning*. Oxford: Blackwell.

Giddens, A. (1979). *Central Problems in Social Theory: Action, Structure and Contradiction in Social Analysis*. London: Macmillan.

Gioia, D., Schultz, M., and Corley, K. (2000). Organizational identity, image, and adaptive instability. *Academy of Management Review*, 25(1): 63–81.

Glick, W. H., Huber, G. P., Miller, C. C., Doty, D. H., and Sutcliffe, K. M. (1990). Studying changes in organizational design and effectiveness: Retrospective event histories and periodic assessments. *Organization Science*, 1(3): 293–312.

Goodman, N. (1978). *Ways of Worldmaking*. Hassocks: Harvester Press.

Goodrick, E. and Reay, T. (2010). Florence Nightingale endures: Legitimizing a new professional role identity. *Journal of Management Studies*, 47(1): 55–84.

Harding, N. (2007). On Lacan and the "becoming-ness" of organization/selves. *Organization Studies*, 28(11): 1761–1773.

Haslam, S. A. (2004). *Psychology in Organizations: The Social Identity Approach* (2nd edition). Thousand Oaks, CA: Sage.

Hernes, T. (2008). *Understanding Organization as Process: Theory for a Tangled World*. London: Routledge.

Ibarra, H. and Barbulescu, R. (2010). Identity as narrative: Prevalence, effectiveness and consequences of narrative identity work in macro work role transitions. *Academy of Management Review*, 35(1): 135–154.

Ingold, T. (2000). *The Perception of the Environment*. London and New York: Routledge.

Knights, D. and McCabe, D. (2003). Governing through teamwork: Reconstituting subjectivity in a call centre. *Journal of Management Studies*, 40(7): 1587–1619.

Kosmala, K. and Herrbach, O. (2006). The ambivalence of professional identity: On cynicism and jouissance in audit firms. *Human Relations*, 59(10): 1393–1428.

Langley, A. (2007). Process thinking in strategic organization. *Strategic Organization*, 5(3): 271–282.

Langley, A. (2008). Studying processes in and around organizations. In D. Buchanan and A. Bryman (eds.), *Sage Handbook of Organizational Research Methods* (pp. 409–429). London: Sage.

Langley, A., Smallman, C., Tsoukas, H., and Van de Ven, A. (2013). Process studies of change in organization and management: Unveiling temporality, activity, and flow. *Academy of Management Journal*, 56(1): 1–13.

Langley. A. and Tsoukas, H. (2010). Introducing "Perspectives on process organization studies." In T. Hernes and S. Maitlis (eds.), *Process, Sensemaking, & Organizing* (pp. 1–27). Oxford: Oxford University Press.

Llewellyn, N. and Hindmarsh, J. (eds.) (2010). *Organization, Interpretation and Practice: Studies in Ethnomethodology and Conversation Analysis*. Cambridge: Cambridge University Press.

Locke, K. and Golden-Biddle, K. (1997). Constructing opportunities for contribution: Structuring intertextual coherence and "problematizing" in organizational studies. *Academy of Management Journal*, 40(5): 1023–1062.

McAdams, D. P. (1996). Personality, modernity, and the storied self: A contemporary framework for studying persons. *Psychological Inquiry*, 7(4): 295–321.

MacKay, B. and Chia, R. (2013). Choice, chance and unintended consequences in strategic change: A process understanding of the rise and fall of Northco Automotive. *Academy of Management Journal*, 56(1): 208–230.

Maitlis, S. and Christianson, M. (2014). Sensemaking in organizations: Taking stock and moving forward. *Academy of Management Annals*, 8(1): 57–125.

March, J. G. (1994). *A Primer on Decision Making*. New York: Free Press.

Meyer, J. and Rowan, B. (1977). Institutional organizations: Formal structure as myth and ceremony. *American Journal of Sociology*, 83(2): 340–363.

Mintzberg, H. and McHugh, A. (1985). Strategy formation in an adhocracy. *Administrative Science Quarterly*, 30(2): 160–197.

Mohr, L. B. (1982). *Explaining Organizational Behavior*. San Francisco, CA: Jossey-Bass.

Munro, R. (2011). Identity. In M. Tadajewski, P. Maclaran, E. Parsons, and M. Parker (eds.), *Key Concepts in Critical Management Studies* (pp. 138–142). London: Sage.

Musson, G. and Duberley, J. (2007). Change, change or be exchanged: The discourse of participation and the manufacture of identity. *Journal of Management Studies*, 44(1): 143–164.

Nayak, A. and Chia, R. (2011). Thinking becoming and emergence: Process philosophy and organization theory. In H. Tsoukas and R. Chia (eds.), *Philosophy and Organization Theory* (pp. 281–309). Bingley, UK: Emerald.

Pettigrew, A. M. (1990). Longitudinal field research on change: Theory and practice. *Organization Science*, 1(3): 262–292.

Pratt, M. G., Rockmann, K. W., and Kaufmann, J. B. (2006). Constructing professional identity: The role of work and identity learning cycles in the customization of identity among medical residents. *Academy of Management Journal*, 49(2): 235–262.

Pullen, A. and Linstead, S. (2006). *Organization and Identity*. London and New York: Routledge.

Putnam, L. L., Nicotera, A. M., and McPhee, R. D. (2009). Introduction: Communication constitutes organization. In L. L. Putnam and A. M. Nicotera (eds.), *Building Theories of Organization: The Constitutive Role of Communication* (pp. 1–19). New York: Routledge.

Rescher, N. (1996). *Process Metaphysics*. Albany, NY: SUNY Press.

Samra-Fredericks, D. and Bargiela-Chiappini, F. (2008). Introduction to the symposium on the foundations of organizing: The contribution from Garfinkel, Goffman and Sacks. *Organization Studies*, 29(5): 653–675.

Sandberg, J. and Tsoukas, H. (2014). Making sense of the sensemaking perspective: Its constituents, limitations, and further development. *Journal of Organizational Behavior*. Published online.

Schatzki, T. (2010). *The Timespace of Human Activity: On Performance, Society, and History as Indeterminate Teleological Events*. Lanham, MD: Lexington Books.

Sims, D. (2003). Between the millstones: A narrative account of the vulnerability of middle managers' storying. *Human Relations*, 56(10): 1195–1211.

Staber, U. (2010). Imitation without interaction: How firms identify with clusters. *Organization Studies*, 31(2): 153–174.

Sturdy, A., Brocklehurst, M., Winstanley, D., and Littlejohns, M. (2006). Management as a (self)confidence trick: Management ideas, education and identity work. *Organization*, 13(6): 841–860.

Sveningsson, S. and Alvesson, M. (2003). Managing managerial identities: Organizational fragmentation, discourse and identity struggle. *Human Relations*, 56(10): 1163–1193.

Thomas, R. and Davies, A. (2005). Theorizing the micro-politics of resistance: New public management and managerial identities in the UK public services. *Organization Studies*, 26(5): 683–706.

Thomas, R. and Linstead, A. (2002). Losing the plot? Middle managers and identity. *Organization*, 9(1): 71–93.

Tsoukas, H. and Chia, R. (2002). On organizational becoming: Rethinking organizational change. *Organization Science*, 13(5): 567–582.

Urry, J. (2007). *Mobilities*. Cambridge: Polity Press.

Van de Ven, A. H. and Poole, M. S. (2005). Alternative approaches for studying organizational change. *Organization Studies*, 26(9): 1377–1404.

Weick, K. E. (1979). *The Social Psychology of Organizing* (2nd edition). Reading, MA: Addison-Wesley.

Weick, K. E. (1995). *Sensemaking in Organizations*. Thousand Oaks, CA: Sage.

West, C. and Zimmerman, D. (1987). Doing Gender. *Gender and Society*, 1(2): 121–151.

Whitehead, A. N. (1926/1985). *Science and the Modern World*. New York: Macmillan.

Whittington, R. (2006). Completing the practice turn in strategy research. *Organization Studies*, 27(5): 613–634.

Ybema, S, Keenoy, T., Oswick, C., Beverungen, A., Ellis, N., and Sabelis, I. (2009). Articulating identities. *Human Relations*, 62(3): 299–322.

Youngjin, Y., Boland, R. J., and Lyytinen, K. (2006). From organization design to organization designing. *Organization Science*, 17(2): 215–229.

Index of Names

Index of Subjects

Note: Page numbers in **bold** type refer to Figures; numbers in ***bold italic*** indicate related text on the page.

Printed and bound by CPI Group (UK) Ltd, Croydon, CR0 4YY